D1738944

ARCHITECT OF PROSPERITY

ARCHITECT OF PROSPERITY

SIR JOHN COWPERTHWAITE AND THE MAKING OF HONG KONG

NEIL MONNERY

Published by London Publishing Partnership
www.londonpublishingpartnership.co.uk

ISBN: 978-1-907994-69-2 (hardback)

A catalogue record for this book is available from the
British Library

This book has been composed in Adobe Garamond Pro

Copy-edited and typeset by T&T Productions Ltd, London
www.tandtproductions.com

Cover design by James Shannon
www.jshannon.com

First printing: June 2017
Second printing: November 2017

CONTENTS

INTRODUCTION

THIS IS A BOOK ABOUT a now largely forgotten Scotsman, Sir John Cowperthwaite, who Milton Friedman identified as playing the central role in Hong Kong's remarkable post-war economic success. When this shy, intellectual civil servant arrived in Hong Kong in 1945 it truly lived up to its description as 'the barren island', with an income per capita of only 30 per cent of its mother country, Britain. After World War II, Britain and other countries turned to industrial planning, deficit financing, activist economic policies and high levels of government spending and taxation to engender growth. How much did Cowperthwaite and his colleagues adopt from this emerging global consensus? Virtually nothing. Now Hong Kong's income per capita is 40 per cent higher than Britain's. How did that happen, and who was John Cowperthwaite?

Hong Kong's prosperity is evident the moment you land at its vast, modern airport. Built on reclaimed land around the island of Chek Lap Kok, it serves 60 million passengers each year, making it the eleventh busiest airport in the world. Operating 24 hours a day, its scale, sophistication and efficiency suggest it serves a country much larger than one that is in fact only the world's 102nd most populous.

Anyone who leaves a few years between visits will see how Hong Kong is constantly developing. Since the airport opened in 1998 at a cost of $20 billion, new terminals and concourses have regularly been added, and current debate surrounds whether to add a third runway. Leaving the airport, you may well join a queue of expensive cars crossing Tsing Ma Bridge, opened by Margaret Thatcher in 1997. You will pass the vast container port, with its bowing cranes, and look up at the forest of high-rise housing that stretches in every direction. Soon the famous crowded, illuminated downtown skyline will emerge, stretching further from east to west than you remember. As your eyes scan the ever-changing shiny office blocks and their neon corporate logos, the towering apartment blocks and the crowded shopping malls, you will be left in little doubt that mankind is capable of creating great wealth.

But that capability was not always evident on this small collection of islands. For centuries Hong Kong supported no more than a few thousand people, engaged in marginal activities such as fishing and charcoal burning. The population would rise for a few generations and then fall back. As recently as a hundred years ago, the population was only around half a million, with the majority living at subsistence levels.

The most dramatic period of Hong Kong's economic miracle started as World War II drew to a close. Having been occupied by the Japanese through the war, Hong Kong returned to British rule a broken economy. The population, which had reached over 1.5 million just before the war, had collapsed to around 600,000 people. But the bounce back was rapid, and despite many challenges Hong Kong started to claw its way back to its pre-war levels of activity. And it did not stop there: it carried on growing at pace for the next few decades to become the success story that we see today.

The foundations for this post-war economic miracle were built in the years immediately after the war by the economic policies pursued by the governments of the 1950s, 60s and 70s. Society, business and government combined to create great prosperity for the people of Hong Kong.

Throughout this period Hong Kong had an unusual form of government, being a British colony until 1997. Its governor had very wide powers to create laws, and to enforce them. The Legislative Council advised the governor and formally passed legislation, but a majority of the members of the council were civil servants, appointed by and responsible to the governor. Even the external members were selected rather than elected. It was a system that in the wrong hands could have led to corruption, dissent and disaster, but used well could lead to extremely long-term, rational government. It is thought provoking to see the direction that these British civil servants decided to pursue when free to choose the path they thought would best serve the people of Hong Kong.

The success or failure of the model relied heavily on the colony's professional cadre of civil servants, and Hong Kong was fortunate in recruiting and retaining a group of mostly capable, honest, hard-working, dedicated and thoughtful individuals. They worked effectively as a team, harnessing their talents around shared goals. Perhaps the most important of those goals was a desire to make Hong Kong economically successful. As well as sharing this goal, they shared a broad philosophy about how to do this, driven in part by situation and necessity and in part by beliefs about what would create progress and prosperity.

The man at the centre of this philosophy was John James Cowperthwaite. Cowperthwaite was himself something of a paradox. He was an old-fashioned colonial administrative officer, brought up in Scotland before serving as finance minister of one of the most modern, successful economies of the post-war era, halfway around the world. He was not elected but his approach had widespread support. Although he never had to run for office, that did not prevent him from devising and articulating a set of economic policies that he then implemented, affecting millions of people, who had little say in their creation.

Cowperthwaite would serve in the Hong Kong administration from 1945 until his retirement in 1971. As financial secretary in Hong Kong between 1961 and 1971, Cowperthwaite fashioned a set of economic policies that were at odds with those pursued by most governments of that time. Indeed, they still look very unusual compared with the approach selected by most governments today. Their nature lies far from our own experience, and this lack of familiarity makes one almost prejudge them and reject them as peculiar. And yet Hong Kong's demonstrated success over decades pulls one back to seek the causes behind their spectacular results.

Cowperthwaite was not alone in crafting this approach. He spent a decade as deputy to his predecessor, Arthur Clarke, who was financial secretary between 1952 and 1961. Clarke had pursued a broadly similar policy stance based on similar beliefs, in part influenced by Cowperthwaite. And Clarke's predecessor, Geoffrey Follows, set the foundations in the immediate post-war period. Cowperthwaite's successor, Philip Haddon-Cave, drew heavily on the same set of principles during his tenure between 1971 and 1981. They all enjoyed the support of their governors for such an approach.

So, Hong Kong's economic miracle was guided by several different architects, but Cowperthwaite is perhaps a little more prominent than the others in the group. His twenty-year tenure, first as deputy and then as financial secretary, was exceptional, as was the level of thought and intellect he brought to the fundamental economic issues of the day. That intellectual underpinning and his impressive ability to articulate his thinking made him the leading proponent of a distinct economic philosophy. It was the ideas that Cowperthwaite fashioned and then explained that provided a bulwark against the pressures to change course in a world where compromise so often prevailed. Furthermore, one can argue that his predecessors had fewer alternative paths to follow. When Cowperthwaite took charge many thought that his economic approach had run out of road and were proposing greater government management of industry, centralized economic planning, larger government (financed by higher taxes), loose fiscal policy, and a shift away from free trade. It took great commitment and energy simply to maintain direction in the face of such apparently compelling panaceas.

The policies that these financial secretaries implemented built on Hong Kong's history as an open port where goods and funds could flow freely. They looked primarily to the private sector to generate the wealth of their society. In doing so they were slow to add regulations, and equally slow to offer support to any specific industry or company. Theirs was a philosophy of laissez-faire in the Adam Smith tradition. They hoped that capital and labour would move efficiently to areas where they could earn higher returns, and they were rewarded in seeing precisely that happen each time Hong Kong ran into difficulties.

They believed in low levels of taxation, and in any case found it hard to obtain support to raise taxes materially. Their belief was that with low taxation, funds would flow into investments, which would in turn turbocharge economic growth. They were not against public spending on critical areas such as education, housing and the like, but their constant struggle was to grow these areas within the constraints of modest levels of tax. They fully understood that this often meant saying no to new spending initiatives, or, perhaps more accurately, saying 'not yet'.

Perhaps most surprising to us today is the fiscal conservatism that they pursued, in part because of necessity, in part because they saw it as self-evidently sensible. They achieved government surpluses in all but two years (one of which was the year immediately after the Japanese occupation in World War II), and in fact they aimed to keep a year's worth of spending as a cash reserve. How different that is from the debate in most countries today about how large the annual government deficit can be, and what multiple of GDP is manageable as national debt. Hong Kong enjoyed decade after decade of growth without creating any national debt.

Now, with the benefit of hindsight, we can look back and see how well these policies worked. Milton Friedman, the Nobel-winning economist, visited Hong Kong in 1955 and again in 1963, when he met Cowperthwaite, finding him hugely impressive. Later, in 1997, he gave a speech about the success of Hong Kong, noting its extraordinary growth:

> From 1960 to 1996, per capita income in Hong Kong rose from about one-quarter of that in Britain to a third larger. It's easy to state those figures. It is more difficult to realize their significance. Compare Britain, the source of the industrial revolution, the economic superpower in the nineteenth century, with Hong Kong, a spit of land, overpopulated, overcrowded, no resources except for a great harbour. Yet this spit of overcrowded land is able within four decades to provide its people with a level of income one-third higher than the income enjoyed by the residents of its mother country.[1]

Friedman was certain that there was a very clear reason for the difference in the performance of Britain and Hong Kong:

> The big difference is in economic policy. Hong Kong followed a very different economic policy than Britain. The difference was a pure accident that the Colonial Office in Britain happened to send John Cowperthwaite, now Sir John Cowperthwaite, to Hong Kong to serve as its Financial Secretary.

Sir John Cowperthwaite

Despite there being some articles about him and some effusive obituaries, there have been no published biographies of John Cowperthwaite. He is mentioned in many of the books about Hong Kong, and often cited as central to Hong Kong's remarkable post-war transformation, and yet his story is very much left in the background. One possible reason for this is that Cowperthwaite was a shy, strangely apolitical, intellectual civil servant. He would be proud of what he facilitated but would not have wanted himself to be the story. Indeed, he 'always resisted requests to write an autobiography, believing that his duty was to serve, not to reveal the minutiae of government business'.[2] But to allow him to remain in the shadows deprives us of a well of insight and wisdom.

A possible second reason is that it is what he did not do, rather than what he did do, that in many ways makes Cowperthwaite so special. His approach became known as 'positive non-interventionism'. He himself believed in limiting government's role because:

> In the long run, the aggregate of decisions of individual businessmen, exercising individual judgment in a free economy, even if often mistaken, is less likely to do harm than the centralized decisions of a government; and certainly the harm is likely to be counteracted faster.[3]

His successor, Sir Philip Haddon-Cave, who coined the phrase positive non-interventionism, described it as follows:

> Positive non-interventionism involves taking the view that it is normally futile and damaging to the growth rate of an economy, particularly an open economy, for the government to attempt to plan the allocation of resources available to the private sector and to frustrate the operation of market forces, no matter how uncomfortable may be their short term consequences.[4]

The philosophy was not one of non-intervention, or complete laissez-faire, but rather a belief that any intervention must be carefully analysed and approached with a sceptical mind. Where others might have a bias towards government action, Cowperthwaite's bias was the opposite. Unsurprisingly, he was out of step with his times, as governments around the world grew ever larger and more pervasive. Because of his guiding beliefs, the unique form of government in Hong Kong, and his willingness to rely on rigorous thought, he was very comfortable standing apart from the crowd.

Acknowledging Mark Twain's observation that 'history doesn't repeat itself, but it often rhymes', are there lines that speak to us today from this remarkable period in Hong Kong? Many of the issues faced by Cowperthwaite and his colleagues seem quite familiar. He suffered banking crises, underestimating the need to regulate the banking sector and possibly not fully understanding the complicated structures of financial institutions, and specifically their use of leverage. He was heavily involved in defending free trade in an increasingly protectionist world, where the United States and the United Kingdom were trying to defend local jobs and limit low-cost imports. He worried about how large numbers of immigrants would find jobs and housing. He negotiated for Hong Kong as Britain tried to join the European Economic Community, and as de Gaulle's veto created an early Brexit from the accession negotiations. His economic policies were affected by the breakdown in Sino-American relations, causing Hong Kong's entrepôt role to decline. He worried about where to set tax levels and how best to raise funds. He would not be surprised by the ebbs and flows of economic issues that we face today, as we too search for economic growth after the Great Crash of 2007.

But he would be unconvinced by the policy recipe adopted by most developed countries. He would be shocked by the relaxed fiscal policy of the last few decades. Its resultant level of accumulated debt would cause him deep concern. The equally loose monetary stance of more recent years would look very alien to him, and he would worry about its effects on the integrity of money itself. The widespread government involvement in micro-managing businesses, and attempts to create top-down industrial strategies, would create a fair degree of scepticism. Perhaps most fundamentally, the size of the state in proportion to the economy would shock him, and he would be astounded at how easily governments accepted long-term funding commitments as if access to resources was assured. Given his views on the link between state taxation and spending and growth, he would wonder how one could expect to achieve a high growth rate with so great a level of resources being expended by the state.

The ideas that Cowperthwaite and his colleagues created did not come from trying to occupy the middle ground. They came instead from first principles and experience. Some were individually unpopular, although as a whole they enjoyed wide support. They may be close to impossible to implement in today's world, and of course there is no guarantee that they would work in all situations, but the approach was original, coherent and challenging. Perhaps looking at them through the eyes of their prime architect can help us consider our options today.

This book builds on existing works about Hong Kong, its administration and its economy. I have been fortunate in being able to consult the very good public records that exist in Britain and Hong Kong. Economic statistics, for reasons that will be discussed later, are somewhat harder to find, at least in the earlier years, and a variety of sources have been used.

A key source has been the transcripts of the budget debates at the Legislative Council. In many ways, the budget cycle creates the underlying rhythm for the book. The budgets were an opportunity for the administration to reflect on what had been achieved in the year that had passed, and to assemble in one place the priorities and plans for the year or years to come. The debates were the longest and most engaged of all the Legislative Council's deliberations. The official government members defended their plans; the appointed members ('Unofficials') probed and argued their points. Cowperthwaite in particular used these speeches as an opportunity to explain his thinking, so they are a very valuable addition to the more administrative archival materials. Because he was extremely articulate and deliberate, I have chosen to quote parts of these speeches at length, rather than précis them. In so doing my objective is to give a sense of the way in which Cowperthwaite articulated his thinking, and through that to better understand the man.

In the book, unless qualified, dollar refers to the Hong Kong dollar, with the US dollar being indicated by US$. Amounts are stated in contemporary values. When amounts have been adjusted for inflation this is noted. Hansard refers to the minutes of the Hong Kong Legislative Council.

The first chapter provides some context as to the history of Hong Kong, summarizing the background to post-war Hong Kong, which some readers may not need. Chapter 2 covers Cowperthwaite's life before he joined the civil service, and discusses the economists that he studied and that would so influence him in later life. Chapter 3 starts with his application to join the Hong Kong Cadets, and his diversion to Sierra Leone while Hong Kong was occupied.

His arrival in Hong Kong, his work on reconstruction and his role in the Department of Supplies, Trade & Industry is covered in Chapter 4. With Cowperthwaite focused on industry, Chapters 5 and 6 look at the work of Geoffrey Follows, who was financial secretary in the immediate post-war period. Cowperthwaite's decade as deputy financial secretary, working for Arthur Clarke, is discussed in Chapters 7 and 8. Further challenges would arise in that period, with the Chinese civil war, the US trade embargo with China during the Korean War, and the pressures of protectionism. Through this period Hong Kong would rebound from each challenge and build an increasingly prosperous society. It did this without any aid from the developed world and no financial support from the mother country. Not only did the economy boom, but significant progress was achieved on many measures of development, including education, health and social care.

Cowperthwaite became financial secretary in 1961 and would remain in post until 1971. His first year required him to firefight on several fronts, all of which challenged the laissez-faire model. He had to battle against proposed tariffs on Hong Kong's exports, he had to mitigate the risk of Britain joining the European Economic Community, and he had to deal with a banking crisis due to lax regulation. These issues are covered in Chapters 9, 10 and 11, respectively.

His first budget is reviewed in Chapter 12. There then followed a few benign years in which Cowperthwaite's philosophy was in the ascendency and the economy grew steadily. As shown in Chapter 13, this helped Cowperthwaite create the political and intellectual capital that he would need as the environment turned.

Several challenges arose in the mid 1960s that, once again, tested Cowperthwaite's resolve and his belief in his approach. A wave of immigration put enormous strain on Hong Kong's housing and the government was remarkably active in the housing sector. This, and the government's role more broadly, are described in Chapter 14. Chapter 15 examines the difficulties that emerged from the banking crisis of 1965. In the budgets of 1966 and 1967, described in Chapter 16, there were many voices that pushed for a shift towards much greater planning and intervention and higher taxes as the economy slowed. These calls came at a difficult time for Cowperthwaite but showed his determination to stick with his approach. Shortly thereafter, Cowperthwaite's competence was challenged by the sterling devaluation of 1967, as discussed in Chapter 17. Political arrangements in Hong Kong were tested as Mao's Cultural Revolution spilt over into Hong Kong, as related in Chapter 18. Cowperthwaite addressed each of these challenges and remained broadly true to his principles and, importantly, ensured that economic policy continued to reflect these.

Cowperthwaite's last few years in office, and his later budgets, saw him in the ascendancy, with the economy performing strongly and his reputation secure. Chapter 19 covers this finale. Cowperthwaite retired in 1971, and Chapter 20 looks at Hong Kong after he left government. Cowperthwaite spent much of the year in Hong Kong for a decade after leaving office, before fully retiring to Scotland in 1981. He visited Hong Kong in retirement and would have seen the continuing progress that lasted even through the handover of the territory to China in 1997.

The book's final chapter attempts to draw some lessons from this remarkable story, which seems simultaneously both historical and very contemporary. By the time of his death in 2006, Cowperthwaite could draw on half a century of personal experience to reflect on how Hong Kong had progressed from a barren island to one of the most successful stories of economic development ever. His role in that story is the subject of this book.

CHAPTER 1

AN UNLIKELY START

AN APPRECIATION OF THE ACCOMPLISHMENTS of the Hong Kong people is impossible without reflecting on the weak hand they were originally dealt. While their territory has some locational benefits, these are not unique in the region. Indeed, other early traders from Portugal chose to create a settlement in Macau. And in almost all other respects – natural resources, water supplies, fertile land, topography, and the like – Hong Kong had, and has, little to offer. Nor has Hong Kong enjoyed a history of stability and peace. Instead it has weathered a series of political and human challenges. To have created any economic success in this context was impressive; to have created the level of prosperity that they have is a phenomenal achievement.

A BARREN ISLAND

Hong Kong lies on the southeast coast of China, around 1,200 miles south of Beijing, just inside the Tropic of Cancer. Hong Kong Island itself, at less than thirty square miles in size, comprises less than a tenth of the land area of Hong Kong. The bulk of Hong Kong's 403 square miles lies onshore, in the New Territories.

Most of the island's land is agriculturally unproductive, due to its rockiness and hilly topography. Fresh water is limited, and only adequate to support a small population. Minerals and natural resources exist in negligible amounts. The climate is humid, subtropical and prone to monsoons.

Small numbers of people have fished, hunted and traded in the region for more than 30,000 years. There is evidence that salt production became established around 2,000 years ago, and the area was formally incorporated into China during the Qin dynasty (221 BCE–206 BCE). Perhaps 1,000 years ago pearl hunting became an important activity, and in 1276, during the Mongol invasion, the Southern Song dynasty moved to the area, settling on Lantau Island.

If it was not for its location at the mouth of the Pearl River, and its proximity to Canton, which lies seventy-five miles upstream to the northwest, it is hard to think that more than a few thousand people would be living there, even today. Beyond this slender geographic advantage the real engine of progress has been the people and the society that they created.

TEA AND OPIUM

The Portuguese were the first Europeans to start trading in the area in the sixteenth century, but relations with the Chinese emperors were at best patchy. The Portuguese combined trading with military activities, and in return the Chinese placed increasing restrictions on their trading activities for many years. In 1662 in a bid to cement his position, the regent for the new child emperor, Kangxi, took the dramatic step of evacuating the coastal areas and driving the erstwhile residents inland. Trade evaporated and the area became deserted. Given he would reign for more than sixty years, it was fortunate for traders that in 1669, when Kangxi came of age, he rescinded the ban on living along the coast, and in 1685 he allowed limited trade to restart.

Britain's involvement with Hong Kong began just after that – now over three centuries ago – in 1699, when the East India Company started to trade with China. Trade strengthened in 1711 when Kangxi allowed the British to establish a trading post in Canton. But a problem soon emerged. China's exports to Britain grew strongly, particularly exports of tea. Kangxi and his successors, however, would not open the Chinese market to British goods, and they insisted that all exports be paid for in silver. The result was a constant drain of silver from Britain to China. This was not what the mercantilist British had intended. By the late 1700s the British had created a cunning plan: they would sell opium from British-controlled India to the Chinese in order to pay for the tea they wanted without having to dip into their silver reserves. Whatever its effects on the people of China, the strategy worked perfectly in stemming the flow of silver. In fact, before long opium sales more than covered the cost of tea purchases, and trade on both sides rocketed (Endacott 1964a).

At first the Chinese emperors went along with this for the traditional reason that they were getting a cut of the increased trade via their control of tea exports. By the 1830s the opium trade had grown to around 40,000 chests of the drug per year, worth about £1 million annually* to the Indian government, and mostly illegally imported by British merchants. At this level, opium imports were viewed as being out of control, and the Daoguang Emperor sent an official, Lin Tse-hsu, to suppress the opium trade. He did rather too good a job of it. Tse-hsu put the traders under a form of house arrest and required them to surrender their opium supplies (Endacott 1964a).

Captain Charles Elliot,** the British Superintendent of Trade, recognized he was outgunned and decided to beat a tactical retreat, ordering the opium be handed over, resulting in around 1,000 tons of opium being destroyed. He ordered the merchants to leave Canton while he planned with Lord Palmerston, the Foreign Secretary, how to deal with China.

THE FIRST OPIUM WAR

A few years earlier some British officials and merchants had thought that occupying Hong Kong would provide a safe platform for developing trade, given its location. The proponents of Britain flexing its muscles dusted off this plan.

Gunboats, blockades and military expeditions followed, during which Elliot seized Hong Kong in 1841. It would take another year of fighting, and much indecision in both governments as to what to do, before the Nanking Treaty finally made the British position in Hong Kong clear. The treaty ceded Hong Kong to Britain, opened five Chinese ports to trade, and allowed foreign residents in the trading ports to be tried by British rather than Chinese courts, effectively placing them outside the remit of Chinese law.

Even as Hong Kong became a British possession in 1842, many in the British government would need some time to become reconciled with the implications of

---

* To put this number in perspective, total British government spending at the time was around £50 million, and total defence spending around £12 million.

** Sir Charles Elliot, born in Dresden in 1801, joined the Royal Navy in 1815, and later retired to join the Foreign Office. In 1833 he became Master Attendant to Lord Napier, the Chief Superintendent of British Trade in China, and in 1836 he became Plenipotentiary and Chief Superintendent of British Trade. After founding Hong Kong, he would be Consul General to the Republic of Texas, governor of Bermuda, governor of Trinidad and finally governor of St Helena.

taking control of a 'barren island with hardly a house upon it',[1] and so it was only in June 1843 that the treaty was ratified. Even after becoming a colony, some were not impressed with its usefulness, as illustrated by an 1847 book on China that included a chapter called 'Hong Kong – its position, prospects, character and utter worthlessness from every point of view to England'.

Figure 1.1. Sir Charles Elliot (HKSAR Government).

With a population of around 7,000, mostly engaged in fishing and charcoal burning, Hong Kong Island did not look much like an embryonic global trading hub. As trade grew slowly in the early years, it was soon apparent that there were limitations to having control of only the island, and in enjoying only restricted access to China.

THE SECOND OPIUM WAR

The Taiping rebellion provided an unlikely solution. Between 1850 and 1864 Hong Xiuquan, who claimed to be the younger brother of Jesus, challenged the Qing dynasty, and in the ensuing conflicts more than 20 million people died. Many refugees fled to Hong Kong, boosting the population.

Seeing an opportunity to gain advantage, the British demanded that the Treaty of Nanking be amended to open all of China to British traders, that the opium trade be legalized and that duties on British imports be reduced. To rub salt into the wounds, they also demanded that the English version of treaties take precedence over the Chinese versions. Unsurprisingly these demands were rejected. Britain organized a coalition with France, and with support from the United States and Russia, it attacked the Chinese and occupied Guangzhou in late 1857. The Chinese sued for peace, and under the Treaty of Tientsin in 1858, China opened eleven more ports, allowed foreigners to travel and trade within China, and paid reparations to Britain and France.

Under internal pressure the emperor belatedly decided to make a stand and he reinforced the Dagu Forts, with the intention of limiting the ability of foreign military forces to move up-river towards Peking. The British challenged this position in 1859 but the Chinese succeeded in holding out against the British forces. So, in the summer of 1860, Lord Elgin headed a combined Anglo-French army of 18,000 men that attacked China from Hong Kong. In quick succession they captured the ports of Yantai and Dalian, then the Dagu Forts, then Tianjin. From there they started their march on Peking. The emperor started peace negotiations but then also tortured and killed many members of the British diplomatic mission, so the Western forces continued. In the autumn they destroyed the Chinese army and entered Peking.

The emperor fled and his brother negotiated the Convention of Peking, which was signed in October 1860. This ceded Kowloon to Britain, legalized the opium trade and further opened China up to the Western powers. The relative weakness of the Qing dynasty had been revealed to all. A small European force had comprehensively defeated the Chinese army and had occupied Peking. For now, China had little choice but to comply.

The opium wars were controversial at the time, and even more so now. Gladstone conceded that 'we, the enlightened and civilized Christians, are pursuing objects at variance both with justice and religion'. The debate continues today, with some historians arguing the wars were primarily to open China to trade, others that it was to provide income for the British and Indian governments, the East India Company, and the trading firms of Hong Kong, led by Jardine Matheson (Lovell 2012). Niall Ferguson (2003) notes:

> The only real benefit of acquiring Hong Kong as a result of the war of 1841 was that it provided firms like Jardine Matheson with a base for their opium-smuggling operation. It is indeed one of the richer ironies of the Victorian value-system that the same navy that was deployed to abolish the slave trade was also active in expanding the narcotics trade.

AN EMERGING ENTREPÔT*

The Taiping rebellion and the Western invasion led to a further influx of settlers, and by 1865 Hong Kong's population had risen to over 125,000, of which some 2,000 were Americans and Europeans. Trade flourished as the free port of Hong Kong became a major trading hub for exports flowing from China, and for the growing imports to the increasingly accessible Chinese hinterland.

Figure 1.2. Early Hong Kong (HKSAR Government).

The last piece of the colony, the New Territories, was leased to Britain under the Second Convention of Peking in June 1898 for a period of 99 years. China had just been defeated by Japan in the first Sino-Japanese war, which was fought in 1894 and 1895 primarily over who controlled Korea. Britain once again used China's weakened position to extract concessions. The British negotiator picked the 99-year period in the belief that that was 'as good as forever' – something that British politicians in the 1980s and 1990s would later view as something of an inexactitude. However, in 1898 the acquisition saw the colony expand sevenfold, by about 360 square miles. This predominately rural area would be home to the reservoirs, port facilities and the like that would support Hong Kong's growth.

* An entrepôt is defined as a port or city where goods are imported and then stored and traded, usually to be exported again.

Hong Kong continued to grow and develop in the early twentieth century. The population reached half a million in the mid 1910s, then three-quarters of a million in the 1920s, going above a million in the 1930s. The vast majority of the people were of Chinese descent and a great many were refugees or immigrants, a trend that intensified when Japan invaded China in the 1930s. Business continued to revolve around trade and all its associated support activities. The port grew, as did companies involved in shipping, trading and financing trade.

Society remained very stratified, with the small minority of British residents at the top of the social tree. Chinese residents, however wealthy, occupied a rung below. They were not, for example, permitted to live in the most exclusive areas. Chinese came to Hong Kong to be free to pursue their business activities, but that did not give them any rights in the governance of the colony, or in society. It was a trade-off that would continue for many decades, albeit in an increasingly less unpleasant manner.

A SHIFT IN THE BALANCE OF REGIONAL POWER

Before World War I the British Empire cast its net of influence firmly around the Far East. Queen Victoria had become empress of India in 1877, cementing the absorption of British possessions in India into the Empire. To the south, Australia and New Zealand were loyal and vital members of the Empire. In between, Malaya, Burma, Singapore and a host of islands were linked with trading relationships, defended by the Royal Navy's control of the seas.

The two regional powers, China and Japan, were relatively weak. Russia, France and Germany had limited regional interests. The United States was focused internally on consolidating its position on the American continent. It would be some years before it became a Pacific power. For many years Britain was the dominant power shaping the development of the Far East.

However, after World War I the balance of power began to change. Germany lost its role in the region; America remained isolationist, as did Russia after the Revolution; and France continued to play a minor role. Japan, on the other hand, began to flex its muscles, making demands on China. Before 1914 Britain could have intervened, but by the 1920s this power had waned.

The Washington Naval Conference led to the Five Power Treaty in 1922, changing the balance of sea power. The treaty limited the tonnage of British, American, Japanese, French and Italian capital ships (battleships and battle cruisers) to a ratio of 5:5:3:1.75:1.75. While Britain's capital fleet was two-thirds larger than Japan's, it had to cover the world. This gave Japan prime position in terms of sea power in the Pacific and in the South China Sea. A subsequent treaty limiting the ability to fortify land positions further enhanced Japan's relative regional military position. It became increasingly clear to many in London that British interests in the Far East would be under threat if Japan were to act while Britain was fighting on another front. However, no easy answers were available and the issue was therefore largely ignored, especially with the more proximate threat of Hitler's rise in Germany.

China too was changing. As the Imperial structure broke down in 1911, China fractured both politically and geographically. It was only in October 1928 that the National Government of the Republic of China was established, and it was this government that started to reunify the various provinces (Endacott 1964a). But Japan was unwilling to allow China to free itself from Japan's orbit of control, and it moved ruthlessly to contain China. In 1931 Japan invaded and took control of Manchuria, under a puppet government. In 1932 they attacked Shanghai and exacerbated splits between Chinese factions, so that China was in almost perpetual civil war. Given this, little stood between a lightly defended Hong Kong and an increasingly aggressive Japan. All it needed was for someone to light the fuse.

World War II started with Britain and France battling first Germany and later Italy, when they entered the conflict in June 1940. With the Axis powers having little presence in Asia, the war centred on Europe and North Africa throughout 1940 and 1941. Asia – including the Empire in India, the Commonwealth countries of Australia and New Zealand, and the many possessions and colonies – remained relatively quiet for the Allies.

That was not because Asia had escaped conflict. Japan's expansion continued after it had annexed Korea and invaded Manchuria. In 1937 it captured several strongholds along the Chinese coast. China was already immersed in a civil war between nationalists and communists, but this was suspended to fight Japan. The Chinese soon gained support from the Soviet Union in the form of supplies, and in 1939 this led to Japan attacking Soviet forces along the Soviet–Manchuria border. This went badly for Japan, who quickly agreed an armistice. These conflicts were, however, unconnected to the struggle in Europe.

The jostling between Japan, China and the Soviet Union always threatened to spill over into the wider European war, and this became more likely when, on 27 September 1940, the Tripartite Pact was signed by Germany, Japan and Italy. This treaty was predominantly to align the Axis powers against the Soviet Union, but it also recognized that Germany and Italy would develop a 'new order' in Europe while Japan would do the same in Greater East Asia. They also agreed to ally against any new attacker who was not already in the conflict. It would be this bargain that would globalize the war.

THE BATTLE OF HONG KONG

On 7 December 1941 Japan attacked Pearl Harbour. On the same day Japan also attacked Hong Kong, the Philippines, Thailand and Malaya, and rather belatedly declared war on the United States and the British Empire. President Franklin D. Roosevelt addressed Congress the following day at 12.30 p.m., describing 7 December 1941 as 'a date which will live in infamy', and by 1.10 p.m. the Senate and the House had passed a declaration of war on Japan. At 4.10 p.m. Roosevelt signed the declaration. Britain had declared war on Japan a few hours before, after the Japanese attacks on Hong Kong and Malaya and on hearing of the attack on Pearl Harbour.

It is surprising, with hindsight, to note that the United States did not declare war on Germany at that point. In fact, it would be Hitler who chose to declare war on America on 11 December, when the American Secretary of State received the German declaration. A few hours later Congress declared war on Germany. It is troubling to imagine how different the world might have been if Hitler had not adopted this strategy. Instead of a world war, with a united Britain and America, Churchill's fear of there being two parallel but separate regional conflicts could have come to pass (Gilbert 1991).

Bringing America into the conflict ensured that an Allied victory was inevitable in the long run. But in the short run, for Hong Kong, there was no silver lining. The British government had long understood that Hong Kong was not defensible. Equally, it had been politically impossible to withdraw all forces from the territory. Churchill had acknowledged the problem a year before in a letter to General Hastings Ismay:

> If Japan goes to war with us there is not the slightest chance of holding Hong Kong or relieving it. It is most unwise to increase the loss we shall suffer there. Instead of increasing the garrison it ought to be reduced to a symbolic scale. Any trouble arising there must be dealt with at the Peace Conference after the War. We must avoid frittering away our resources on untenable positions. I wish we had fewer troops there, but to move any would be noticeable and dangerous.[2]

Britain's ability to slow the invading forces relied on maintaining sea power, and this vanished with the sinking of the battleships HMS *Repulse* and HMS *Prince of Wales* off Malaya on 10 December. Without control of the seas, and with air strength comprising five obsolete planes, the approach to Hong Kong lay undefended. The stage was set for a brave but doomed defence.

The Commonwealth forces drew their first line of defence along the so-called Gin Drinkers Line in the New Territories. This series of connected defensive positions proved no match for the Japanese forces and it fell on 10 December. The Commonwealth forces fell back to Hong Kong Island and awaited the Japanese invasion that occurred on 18 December. The Japanese steadily advanced in fierce fighting, engaging in several massacres of Commonwealth forces and wounding hospital patients and medical staff. The knowledge that defeat was inevitable, and a desire to limit the casualties from combat and Japanese war crimes, led the governor, Sir Mark Young,* to surrender, which he did in person at the Japanese headquarters at the Peninsula Hotel on the afternoon of 25 December 1941.

THE JAPANESE OCCUPATION

Japanese forces were to occupy Hong Kong until the end of the war. During their rule, Hong Kong's population dropped dramatically as they stripped the island. The local population was subject to torture and oppression, and thousands of rapes occurred. There would be widespread food shortages, and many of the Chinese population were forcibly repatriated to the mainland. After the war senior Japanese commanders would be tried as war criminals and executed.

The Commonwealth forces, Hong Kong's civil servants and any expatriates who had not left, totaling around 11,000 people, were interned in several prisoner of war camps. Understanding the risk of the Japanese invasion, and the inability to defend Hong Kong, had led the British government to evacuate British family members and children to the Philippines in August 1941. Most of the British prisoners of war were held at Stanley Camp, at the southern end of Hong Kong Island. This makeshift camp would be home to 1,400 men, 850 women and 280 children for three and a half years.

The most senior official at the camp was Franklin Gimson,** who had been appointed colonial secretary and had very unfortunately taken up that post the day

---

* Sir Mark Aitchison Young, born 1886 and educated at Eton and King's College, Cambridge, joined the Ceylon civil service in 1909. He served in the Rifle Brigade in World War I and then returned to colonial administration in Ceylon, Sierra Leone and Palestine. He was governor of Barbados, then Trinidad and then the Tanganyika territory before becoming governor of Hong Kong in September 1941.

** Sir Franklin Gimson, born 1890, graduated from Balliol College, Oxford, and joined the Ceylon civil service as a Cadet in 1914, where he held a wide range of posts. He became governor of Singapore in 1946, before retiring in 1952.

before the Japanese invasion. The governor, Sir Mark Young, had been held for a short period in Hong Kong, but was then shuffled between a series of POW camps in Shanghai, Taiwan, Japan, China and Manchuria. It would be Gimson who would be on the ground to form the very initial post-war administration when Japan surrendered in 1945.

A BLEAK LANDSCAPE

This was the Hong Kong that John Cowperthwaite would first experience as part of the Military Administration in the autumn of 1945. The economy had been ruined by four years of occupation. The Japanese had seized all factories and all trading activities. The Hong Kong dollar had been banned and replaced with the Japanese military yen, which was subject to hyperinflation and was soon worthless. The infrastructure of the colony had deteriorated such that the port, public transport and the like were no longer functioning.

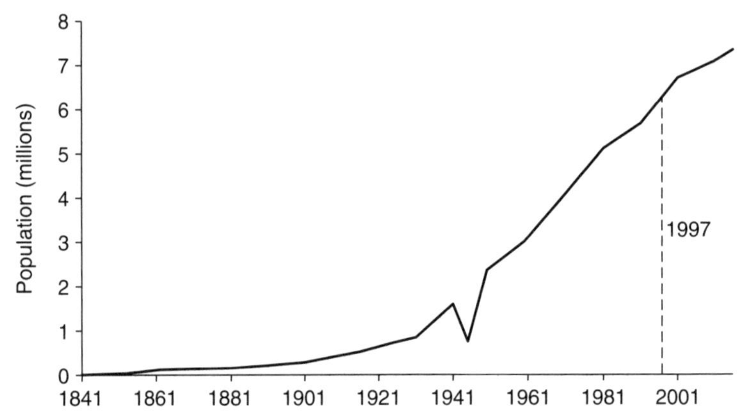

Figure 1.3. Hong Kong's population growth, 1841–2016.
(*Source*: HK Census & Statistics Department.)

The population, which had risen rapidly to around 1.5 million before Japan invaded China, collapsed to around 600,000 by the end of the war (Hambro 1955). It would have been a brave person who would have forecast that this barren, broken, resource-free, indefensible territory would see a remarkable transformation. It can hardly have been evident to the small band of administrators in 1945 that Hong Kong would be the site of an economic miracle. And yet, despite all these disadvantages, it would be. The shrunken population would soon bounce back to its pre-war level. And after that it would keep rising to new record levels through a growing resident population and because of very large numbers of immigrants heading to Hong Kong to enjoy its opportunities and prosperity.

This growing population would experience growing economic health. Hong Kong has a GDP per capita today that is around the same level as that in the United States, in purchasing power parity adjusted dollars, and over 40 per cent higher than that in the United Kingdom.[3] How this happened, and the role of John Cowperthwaite in the story, will be the subject of the chapters ahead.

CHAPTER 2

A CLASSICAL EDUCATION

John James Cowperthwaite was born in the early hours of 25 April 1915 at 33 Thirlestane Road in the Bruntsfield area of Edinburgh, about a mile south of Edinburgh Castle.[1] The house, a four-floor stone building, was typical of the street, where the family probably took a floor. As the first-born child he was named after his father, also John James Cowperthwaite, who was in turn named after his father before him.

AN INTERNATIONAL SCOTTISH FAMILY

Cowperthwaite's parents had married eighteen months earlier on 8 November 1913 at Wemyss Cottage, Ferry-Port-on-Craig, where the 31-year-old John James (father) married the 26-year-old Jessie Wemyss Barron Jarvis.[2] Ferry-Port-on-Craig, now more usually known as Tayport, lies at the mouth of the River Tay, opposite Dundee and fifty miles to the north of Edinburgh.

Cowperthwaite's father was a government surveyor of taxes, and had himself been born in Ferry-Port-on-Craig in 1882.[3] His father, Cowperthwaite's grandfather, had been a boat surveyor in Calcutta and had married his wife in that city in 1877, before returning to become an estuary pilot in Ferry-Port-on-Craig. He died before his son married Jessie, so although Cowperthwaite never met his paternal grandfather, there was already a connection with Asia within the family.

Jessie, Cowperthwaite's mother, had been born in 1887, again in Ferry-Port-on-Craig. Her father had been a master mariner, and it may have been the sea that connected the two families in this small town of around 3,000 people. Jessie's family had relations on the US East Coast, and this gave Cowperthwaite a lifelong link with the United States.

Cowperthwaite's parents had two further children: Janet was born on 16 March 1917 after the family had moved to an attractive two-floor house a bit further south at 55 Ladysmith Road, Edinburgh; and David Jarvis was born on 14 September 1921.[4] By this time Cowperthwaite's father had moved from being a surveyor of taxes to become a land valuations assessor. The family had moved again, to 76 Polworth Terrace, still in Edinburgh but a couple of miles further to the west. This was a more substantial house, and importantly it was near Merchiston Castle School. It was a solidly middle class area, with most of the residents owning their own homes. Within a few doors either side lived an ironmonger, a clothier, a manager and a baker.[5] Two doors down, at number 72, Douglas Gordon Shields lived and worked in his studio, on his way to becoming a famous artist.

Janet went to St Bride's School in Edinburgh and then graduated from Edinburgh University in 1939. She then made what must have been an unexpected marriage when she wed Herbert Morrison in October 1939.[6] He was a black-Jamaican divorced doctor who, at 36, was quite a bit older than her 22 years of age. In January 1940 she travelled to Jamaica[7] via New York to start her new married life.[8] Interracial marriages were unusual, and Janet was drawn into a controversy that played out in letters to the local papers.[9] But the marriage did not last and the couple separated, before getting divorced in 1952.[10] Despite this, their lives remained intertwined through Janet's career as a teacher at Montego Bay High School, starting in 1944. This was the first government-owned high school for girls on the island.[11] In May 1947 she became headmistress, a post she held for many years apart from a stint in Sierra Leone as an education officer between 1953 and 1955, after which she would return as head. Janet would later visit Cowperthwaite in Hong Kong, and he would visit her in Jamaica when he had leave.

Herbert Morrison, Cowperthwaite's brother-in-law, had a remarkable career. His father, a school teacher, had encouraged Herbert to get an education, and to move to New York to try and become a doctor (Goulding 1997). He was the resident medical officer at Kingston Public Hospital between 1930 and 1935, and then senior medical officer at St James Hospital between 1936 and 1958.[12] He was very active in the community, becoming a member of the Legislative Council in 1959, Mayor of Montego

Bay in 1960, and a justice of the peace. Herbert was a great supporter of education, and he supported Montego Bay High School until his death in October 1991.[13] He would offer free medical care and also pay to sponsor needy students. He was also a driving force at the Herbert Morrison Technical High School that opened in 1976.

Cowperthwaite's brother, David, attended Edinburgh Academy and then went on to read Classics at Exeter College, Oxford, in 1939. He was appointed as a 2nd Lieutenant in the Royal Regiment of Artillery in the summer of 1942.[14] Like his brother, he applied to the Colonial Office to become a Cadet, and asked to serve in the Far East. Given the loss of so many of the Far Eastern colonies, he was asked instead to serve with the Nigerian Administrative Service and received his letter of appointment in July 1942.[15] He would work there from 1942 to 1948.[16] Later he became a senior administrator in the Scottish Home and Health Department, rising to become undersecretary. He married Patricia Stockdale in 1944 in Wales. They had a daughter, Sheila Mary, in 1948 when he was working in the secretariat in Lagos,[17] and a second daughter, Ann Elizabeth, in January 1952.[18] David would spend most of his life living in Edinburgh at 1 Abinger Gardens, very near the Murrayfield rugby stadium, before moving to Northumberland Street in the centre of town. Patricia died in 1993. David outlived his older brother by just a few months, dying in October 2006.[19]

Cowperthwaite's parents would live to see their son become Hong Kong's financial secretary, with his father dying in 1967 in Edinburgh and his mother dying a few years later in 1972, also in Edinburgh. The first twenty-five years of Cowperthwaite's life were grounded in the fifty-mile east coast strip of Scotland stretching between Edinburgh, St Andrews and Ferry-Port-on-Craig. And it would also be to here that he would eventually retire. But for the forty years in between, Cowperthwaite would engage with the world.

A CLASSICAL EDUCATION

Cowperthwaite went to one of the most prestigious schools in Scotland: Merchiston Castle School in Edinburgh, founded in 1828 by Charles Chalmers as a boys' boarding school[20] and, until 1930, located at Merchiston Castle, in Colinton, Edinburgh. In 1550 the castle had been the birthplace of John Napier, the inventor of logarithms. The school had a reputation for being a fairly traditional, somewhat formal institution, and its motto 'Ready ay Ready' was perhaps more practical than inspiring. The school produced several successful alumni, and several of Cowperthwaite's peer group also ended up in public service.

After Merchiston, Cowperthwaite won a Spence Bursary[21] to read Classics at St Andrews University between 1933 and 1937, and he graduated with a first class degree.[22] He further consolidated his classical education taking a double first in classics at Christ's College, Cambridge, in two years, between 1937 and 1939.[23] He would in later life occasionally sprinkle some Latin, or a bon mot about the Roman Empire, into his speeches.

Having spent six years studying Classics at university it would have been no surprise if Cowperthwaite had decided on an academic career, either at a leading private school or at a university, but, perhaps because of the war, he turned instead to a different discipline to make his mark. He had little knowledge of economics, but his training in classics gave him a structured mind, a grasp of logic and argument, a sense of history, and an understanding of the human condition. Given that, he would not find it too hard to add the frameworks of classical economics to his toolkit.

THE ECONOMICS OF PROFESSOR NISBET

At the outbreak of World War II, Cowperthwaite went back to St Andrews and took an accelerated degree in economics,[24] gaining a first class honours degree in economics and political science in 1940.[23] He studied under a young economist called James Wilkie Nisbet, who had recently arrived at St Andrews. It would prove to be a formative experience for the intellectual Cowperthwaite.

Nisbet (1903–74) had gained a double first in economic science and philosophy and an LLB with distinction at the University of Glasgow.[25] Between 1926 and 1931 he served as assistant to W. R. Scott, the Adam Smith Professor of Political Economy at Glasgow, and was appointed a lecturer in political economy. In 1935 he moved to St Andrews as a lecturer, and in only three years became a reader in political economy. He would later be appointed as professor of political economy in 1947, a post he held until his retirement in 1970.

Nisbet was a classical economist, and in 1929 he wrote his first book, *A Case for Laissez-Faire*. The book is an unusual mix of classical economics, utilitarian philosophy and the new work of Freud and Jung in understanding human behaviour. It was an attempt to create an economic, philosophical and behavioural case for laissez-faire. He wrote about banking and finance in 1934, and when he first met Cowperthwaite he had just published his third book,[24] *Post-war Britain and Standard of Life*. Nisbet was seen as 'a noted intellectual figure at the university, and a resolute free trader'.

Nisbet was not a dry, conservative economist. Alongside his academic interests he was active in the Officer Training Corp, eventually as commanding officer. He was very focused on student welfare, and he was progressive. He founded scholarships for women studying economics, funded by him. Cowperthwaite and Nisbet were to become lifelong friends.

Alan Peacock, who would later become professor of economics at the University of York, studied political economy under Nisbet in 1940–42 and wrote that Nisbet was a wide-ranging thinker[26]:

> The broad course in Political Economy devised by Professor Nisbet with its strong emphasis on the historical and political background to economic policy has not only offered a useful general education to generations of non-specialists but has taught the would-be professional economist that he must take some responsibility for devising realistic policy measures.

As the subject of economics became more theoretical, more mathematical and more compartmentalized, Nisbet remained firmly grounded in the classical approach. Peacock also remembered that Nisbet was a political economist in the footsteps of Adam Smith:

> When I was one of his students, the Keynesian revolution had hardly taken hold and the consequential developments in technique which required all economists to be fair mathematicians and good applied statisticians were far in the future. In parallel with these changes, Western economists, following the influence of logical positivism, have tried to remove the judgments of value from their economic analysis, and economic policy is regarded in the fashionable and incomprehensible jargon as a problem of 'maximising society's objective function, subject to constraints'. Today, economists work in the shadow of Theil* and Pontryagin** rather than that of Adam Smith and Ricardo. Professor Nisbet has stoutly resisted these changes,

* Henri Theil, a Dutch mathematician and economist, helped develop the field of econometrics. Born in 1924, he studied mathematics and physics at Utrecht University before studying economics. In 1953 he developed the two-stage least-squares methodology to simplify the estimation of simultaneous equation based models of the economy. Later he was professor of econometrics at the Netherlands School of Economics and then at the University of Chicago.

** Lev Pontryagin was a Russian mathematician, born in 1908 in Moscow. He was blinded by an exploding stove at the age of 14 but still made major contributions to the field of topology. He also developed the maximization principle that is widely used in optimization theory. Economists use this to describe how economies move from one state to another.

firmly adhering to Mill's principle that to be a good economist one must be something more than a technocrat.

It is clear how well such an approach suited the young Cowperthwaite, in giving him a framework with which to approach public policy. And one can see how this would be of great value to him in later life when he was be at the forefront of devising policy measures for Hong Kong.

THE INFLUENCE OF ADAM SMITH

Under Nisbet, Cowperthwaite studied Adam Smith and his monumental work *The Wealth of Nations: An Inquiry into the Nature and Causes of the Wealth of Nations.* It would be Cowperthwaite's task in later life to cause an increase in the wealth of Hong Kong, and many of his ideas as to how to do that emerge from the pages of *The Wealth of Nations.* Smith is seen as the founder of modern economics, but he was as much a philosopher as an economist, and his approach to economics was a mix of moral philosophy combined with a rational examination of what drives the practical world. It is clear from Cowperthwaite's speeches and writings that he was enormously influenced by his study of Smith.

For Cowperthwaite, Smith must have seemed like a local kid made good. Adam Smith was born in 1723 on the east coast of Scotland at Kircaldy, which lies half way between the cities of Edinburgh and St Andrews. The ancient town of Kircaldy had grown rapidly as a trading port in the sixteenth and seventeenth centuries. The following century would see the town develop a manufacturing base, further enhancing its prosperity, with important shipbuilding and textile businesses leading the way. Its economic development had a number of similarities to the post-war growth of Hong Kong. And we will see that the town's most famous son would provide a similarly valuable template to Cowperthwaite as he grew into being Hong Kong's principal economic architect.

Smith himself had been greatly influenced when he lived in Paris by François Quesnay, a French economist, who had taken a very empirical approach to understanding how the economy worked. He constructed a 'tableau économique' that described the linkages between different parts of the economy, and he thought that increasing wealth was an appropriate goal to have and to study. The economists around Quesnay became known as the physiocrats, and they tried to explore what created national wealth, rather than, say, the wealth of the ruler or the church. Their political views led them to postulate that true wealth came from agriculture, rather than from trading or industry, which they saw as supporting the unproductive state.

Smith would take a different tack, but he took on board Quesnay's view of laissez-faire: the belief that it is best to leave individuals to choose what to produce and what to consume.*

Intriguingly, Quesnay shared another area of interest with Cowperthwaite: a fascination with China and Confucianism. His book *Le Despotisme de la Chine,* published in 1767, described the Chinese imperial system and highlighted the role given to wise scholars in the administration of the Chinese empire, contrasting that with the role of the church and the aristocracy in France. Confucianism had evolved over the two millennia between the writing of the *Five Classics* by Confucius and Quesnay's book, becoming central to the method of governing China, nowhere more so than in the selection of civil servants.

The use of examinations to select administrators had started under the Han dynasty, with tests first administered in 134 BCE, but it was under the Tang dynasty that the examination system became fully developed and provided a way to reduce the influence of patronage and increase the calibre of the administration (Elman 2000). The syllabus changed over time. In the early centuries it often tested literary or poetry skills, alongside knowledge of the classic texts. In 681 CE a written examination testing knowledge of the Confucian classic texts was introduced, and in 693 CE the exam was opened to a broader set of applicants and started to revolve around the 'five studies': military strategy, civil law, government revenue, agriculture and Confucianism. Over the centuries the number of applicants would vastly exceed the number who would pass, so the exams were hugely competitive. They provided a means of considerable social mobility and they created an administrative elite.

In due course, when in Hong Kong, Cowperthwaite would become part of a very similar administrative elite: the Hong Kong Cadets. Many of his colleagues would study the ideas of Confucius, including the concept of officials acting as *fumuguan,* meaning parents of the people, with its tone of both benevolence and paternalism (Chen 2006). But for now Cowperthwaite was focused on his study of economics and Adam Smith.

The Wealth of Nations was a sweeping exploration of economic ideas, ranging from the benefits of the specialization of labour in a pin factory to the implications of establishing colonies. His framework builds on Quesnay in declaring the importance

* The physiocrats attributed the use of the phrase laissez-faire to Vincent de Gournay, another French economist. As a civil servant he opposed government regulation of commerce, calling it 'bureaucratie': government by desks. His motto is said to have been 'Laissez faire et laissez passer, le monde va de lui même!' ('Let it be and let it pass, the world goes on by itself!').

of free markets and free trade. If individuals, and indeed countries, are to specialize, then they will need to meet their additional needs by trading with others, and in turn for this to be efficient there must be as few impediments as possible. The easier it is to exchange and trade, the more specialization is possible, to the benefit of all.

Figure 2.1. Adam Smith.

As a philosopher, Smith (1776, Book 1) noted how a system based on self-interest could be to the benefit of all with his now-famous moral deduction:

> It is not from the benevolence of the butcher, the brewer, or the baker that we expect our dinner, but from their regard to their own self-interest. We address ourselves not to their humanity but to their self-love, and never talk to them of our own necessities, but of their advantages.

Smith (1776, Book 4) argued that the state should be there to facilitate this natural process, not to dominate it. He argued that a small, focused government would best enhance the wealth of a nation:

> According to the system of natural liberty, the sovereign has only three duties to attend to; three duties of great importance, indeed, but plain and intelligible to common

> understandings: first, the duty of protecting the society from violence and invasion of other independent societies; secondly, the duty of protecting, as far as possible, every member of the society from the injustice or oppression of every other member of it, or the duty of establishing an exact administration of justice; and, thirdly, the duty of erecting and maintaining certain public works and certain public institutions which it can never be for the interest of any individual, or small number of individuals, to erect and maintain; because the profit could never repay the expense to any individual or small number of individuals, though it may frequently do much more than repay it to a great society.

Smith was not naive about the dangers of unbridled self-interest, and was alive to the issue of crony capitalism, noting that 'people of the same trade seldom meet together, even for merriment and diversion, but the conversation ends in a conspiracy against the public, or in some contrivance to raise prices'. But his solution was competition and trade, and a government that created a supportive environment for those mechanisms.

Smith did not see it as government's role to pick winners or be biased towards particular industries or firms. This would be an issue with which Cowperthwaite would engage throughout his professional life, and he would in due course echo the words of Adam Smith (1776, Book 4):

> Every system which endeavours, either, by extraordinary encouragements to draw towards a particular species of industry a greater share of the capital of the society than would naturally go to it, or, by extraordinary restraints, to force from a particular species of industry some share of the capital which would otherwise be employed in it, is, in reality, subversive of the society towards real wealth and greatness; and diminishes, instead of increasing, the real value of the annual produce of its land and labour.

THE CLASSICAL ECONOMISTS

Beyond the central figure of Smith, Cowperthwaite studied the works of Ricardo, Malthus, Mill, Hume and Marx. While Keynes's *The General Theory of Employment, Interest and Money* was published in 1936, even many of Keynes's followers took some years to refine its message and to flesh out its foundations. At the time, the work was seen as arguing that an economy might be stuck at a level of economic activity that did not deliver full employment, and it proposed that government spending, indeed deficit spending, could increase output and employment. Nisbet took the view that

Keynes was mistaken in his approach and argued against it. Cowperthwaite would frequently address these issues later in his life.

For now, Cowperthwaite focused on the classical economists. David Ricardo had built on Adam Smith's thinking and introduced the idea of comparative advantage to promote free trade. This explored how everyone would be better off if countries focused on industries in which they have the greatest level of relative advantage, while then importing goods and services where they were less advantaged (Ricardo 1817). This theory was very much at odds with a traditional mercantilist view that it was best to make as much as possible oneself and try to limit imports. Instead it promoted specialization and trade, and suggested that governments should be relaxed about industries growing and declining as the nature of an economy's advantage shifted. This idea would also echo frequently in Cowperthwaite's later pronouncements and policies.

John Stuart Mill's *Principles of Political Economy: With Some of Their Applications to Social Philosophy* (1848) championed free trade and economic liberty. Mill's views on the role of government in commercial enterprise were ones that Cowperthwaite would draw on in the years ahead:

> In all the more advanced communities the great majority of things are worse done by the intervention of government, than the individuals most interested in the matter would do them, or cause them to be done, if left to themselves.

Thomas Malthus is famous for his view that food production will only grow arithmetically while population will grow exponentially, making it inevitable that famines will occur as a check on population growth (Malthus 1798). At various points when Hong Kong's population soared, as refugees and immigrant numbers surged, Cowperthwaite must have reflected on the idea of a Malthusian catastrophe. He would have been aware of the controversy around Malthus's ideas but, perhaps more importantly, he developed a set of beliefs that the best way to accommodate a fast-growing population was to facilitate rapid economic growth.

We can obtain a good idea of where Cowperthwaite's study of economics would have settled by turning to Walter Eltis,* who has extensively interpreted the classical economists and in particular their theories about economic growth. Eltis (1984) argues that classical economists believed in the essential role of property rights and individual choice:

---

* Walter Eltis is an emeritus fellow of Exeter College, Oxford, where he taught economics between 1963 and 1986. He served as Director-General of the National Economic Development Office, and as chief economic advisor to Michael Heseltine at the Department of Trade and Industry. He has held numerous visiting professorships.

> Economies will function most efficiently where all markets are competitive, and where those who own property determine investment and production decisions. For these to be efficient, entrepreneurs must be confident that they will obtain legal title to the wealth they create.

The role of markets and choice was designed to optimize the allocation of resources, and classical economists argued that:

> Some economic activities are productive and have the potential to generate a net surplus. Others, and especially those organized by the state, are unproductive and can only be sustained from the surpluses of productive activities.

Given the differences in the performance of different sectors, a key determinant of growth is therefore the extent to which surplus profit is generated and is available for investment, and then the extent to which these funds are directed to the opportunities with the highest returns:

> The growth of economies will depend on the re-investment of surpluses from productive activities. If these are absorbed or more than absorbed by the unproductive, nothing will remain for investment, and a nation's output will stagnate or decline.

Cowperthwaite's later speeches, writings and policies would make clear how he had embraced his study of the classical economists, and developed in his own mind a framework for how economies and societies worked. Importantly, his studies had posed the fundamental question of what government could do to increase a society's wealth. As he supplemented his academic studies with real-world experiences, this would be the central question to which he devoted his professional life.

BEYOND THE CLASSROOM

Alongside his academic development, Cowperthwaite found time to play cricket and rugby. Being tall, large and strong, he was an imposing figure on the rugby field, and he played in the first XV at school, and for St Andrews and Christ's College, Cambridge.

While back at St Andrews University, he met Sheila Thompson, who was studying medicine. She was born on 8 July 1918 in Aberdeen and was the daughter of a manager in the Co-operative Society. Her studies were interrupted by the war and she never returned to complete her degree. Instead, by 1941 she was working for the Ministry of Food as a temporary assistant at the Food Office in Cardiff.[22] On 13 September 1941 they married[27] at St Leonard's-in-the-Fields church in Perth.[28]

In April 1941 Cowperthwaite was called up and served until September 1941 in the Cameronians (Scottish Rifles).[23] He did not see action in the Rifles, but one memorable assignment was to guard Rudolph Hess, the deputy führer, who had remarkably flown single handedly to Scotland to try and meet the Duke of Hamilton to broker peace between Germany and Britain.[29] After a long flight in a Messerschmitt Bf 110, and after darkness had already fallen, he parachuted into Scotland, about twelve miles from his intended destination, the home of the duke, whose power Hess had significantly overestimated.

Hess was captured by the Home Guard and was taken by the 11th Battalion of the Cameronians to Maryhill Barracks, where he spent an uncomfortable night in the guardroom cell.[30] He eventually met Hamilton, who reported back to Churchill, who organized Hess's interrogation and confinement. For a while Hess was held at Buchanan Castle, near Loch Lomond, before being transferred to the Tower of London and then to various prisons until he died in 1987.

AN EDINBURGH BASE

Cowperthwaite had moved from his father's house in Polworth Terrace in Edinburgh to a flat in Ravelston Gardens, three miles to the west of Edinburgh Castle. He and Sheila would have only a few short weeks together here in 1941[31] but it would remain their UK home for many years. Ravelston Gardens comprises three art deco blocks with 48 flats in the Ravelston area of Edinburgh. They had been built in the mid 1930s, 'proving that Edinburgh was in touch with the very latest architectural ideas in the 1930s, these flats ... were among the first buildings to bring the International Style to the city' (MacDonald and MacDonald 1989). Even today the buildings are protected as architecturally important.

Having started his military service in the very early part of World War II, he must have concluded that he would be better placed to contribute to the war effort as a civil servant. Educated, married and now in his mid twenties, Cowperthwaite had decided to apply to become a Hong Kong Cadet.

CHAPTER 3

CADET COWPERTHWAITE

THE HONG KONG CADETS

IN 1941 COWPERTHWAITE APPLIED TO join the British Colonial Administration Service in Hong Kong and was selected as a Hong Kong Cadet in November 1941.[1] It is unclear why Cowperthwaite chose Hong Kong rather than applying for, say, a post in the more prestigious Indian civil service, or at the Treasury. He certainly had the intellect to do so. Maybe he recognized that he would be more successful in a smaller pond, with less politics and more opportunity for an individual to shine. At that time Hong Kong was a relatively small colony.

Maybe Cowperthwaite was attracted by the very special position held by the Hong Kong Cadets. Despite the rather unimpressive sounding title, the Cadets were a powerful force throughout the colony, and held many of the key posts. To become one was to become part of a high-flying elite. And the Hong Kong Cadets rose to positions of power more rapidly that in any other part of the Colonial Service,* although this did not stop them complaining if a non-Cadet was promoted over them.[2]

---

* Hong Kong Cadets could head a department, or even become colonial secretary in eleven to fourteen years, whereas in Ceylon or Malaya it typically took more than twenty years

The founder of the Cadet scheme, Sir Hercules Robinson,* had become governor in 1859. He was unimpressed with the quality of the administration and put this down in part to the low quality of recruits and in part to their inability to speak Chinese and therefore to interact with the majority population. He decided to kill two birds with one stone by recruiting well-educated and talented individuals in the United Kingdom and then have them spend two years learning Chinese in Hong Kong.[3] They would then be available to be deployed for 'higher' appointments that became vacant.

Figure 3.1. Sir Hercules Robinson.

* Sir Hercules Robinson, born 1824, served in the army and then in colonial administration. He became lieutenant governor of St Kitts in 1855. When he became governor of Hong Kong in 1859 he was only 35 years old. From 1880 until 1889 he was High Commissioner of South Africa.

The scheme was very much in tune with the times. The Northcote–Trevelyan Commission had issued its 'Report on the Organisation of the Permanent Civil Service' in 1853, calling for entry to the civil service to be via competitive examination rather than patronage. The Colonial Office had been thinking along similar lines, as had the Indian civil service. It was therefore quickly approved by the Secretary of State, the Duke of Newcastle, who noted that the proposal was 'of such vast importance to the good government of the Colony that no time should be lost in putting effect to the scheme proposed'.[4]

Three candidates were selected by the civil service commissioners and sent out to Hong Kong (Collins 1952). All were successful. Cecil Clementi Smith rose quickly through the ranks in Hong Kong, became governor of the Straits Settlements, and ended his career as High Commissioner for Borneo. Walter Deane ran the police force for over twenty years. Malcolm Tonnochy ended up running the prison before dying at the early age of 42. Despite these successes, the next three Cadets were only recruited in 1865, with a further Cadet joining in 1867. A global depression meant that it was not until 1879 that the next Cadet joined (Tsang 2007).

The Cadets formed a powerful elite in the administration of Hong Kong. Steve Tsang, an expert in Hong Kong's history and governance, points out that only 85 Cadets were recruited between 1861 and 1941, and that all those who stayed to retirement at some point ran a department. Three became governors of Hong Kong and six became governors or High Commissioners elsewhere in the Empire. Six served as colonial secretaries (Tsang 2007). So although Hong Kong was smaller than India or even Malay, a Cadet could be fairly sure that they would have the chance to serve at a high level.

Cadets were selected by a competitive exam that was shared with the other Eastern colonies, with candidates being able to express a preference for where they might serve. The Hong Kong Cadets shared a similar background – 'a solid, though not rich, upper middle class family, went to a public school ... and then went up to one of the older universities' – and were not brought up with expensive tastes or habits. They were 'not too brilliant' but rather 'a leader who could safely be sent to wherever and could be relied upon to function with the minimum of supervision, and to act sensibly and calmly in the face of the most difficult circumstances'.[5] In general, they were academically solid, but there were a few Cadets who were quite scholarly in their study of the Chinese language, or of Confucianism. And there were a few who were academically brilliant, such as Cowperthwaite.

Cadets were expected to be able to turn their hands to most tasks. They were generalists, thrown at key tasks or posts, and expected to learn quickly. They enjoyed considerable status within the colony and developed a powerful *esprit de corps*. This community could therefore defend its values that, at their best, included objectivity, integrity, willingness to show initiative, standing above departmental interests, putting Hong Kong's broad interests first, and the ideas of *fumuguan*.

However, not everyone was enthusiastic about the abilities of the Cadets. Sir William Peel, who was governor between 1930 and 1935, wanted to have the Hong Kong and Malay Cadets serve in each other's territories, commenting that:

> Hong Kong is very circumscribed and, apart from the posts of District Officer and Assistant District Officer in the New Territories, all members of the cadet service are stationed in this city. The result is that, not only do they live for years in one another's pockets, but they never get a change from their environment. It has impressed itself on me very strongly that this state of affairs leads to considerable 'nerves' among a large number of the service; a few are robust enough to withstand it, but some of them become perhaps rather too 'die-hard'.[6]

And while many Cadets were themselves progressive, it was not until 1946 that an ethnic Chinese Cadet, Paul Tsui, was appointed, and only in 1959 was a female Cadet, Bridget O'Rorke, selected.

The cohesion of the Hong Kong Cadets survived the introduction of a unified Colonial Administration Service in 1932, as had been recommended in the Warren Fisher Report in 1930 (Kirk-Greene 1999). In theory, Cadets would be able to serve anywhere across the Empire, but the reality was that Hong Kong Cadets continued to be appointed by the governor of Hong Kong and deployed at his discretion.

By 1937 there were thirty-seven Cadets. Norman Smith, the Hong Kong colonial secretary, wrote to William Ormsby-Gore, the colonial secretary in London, pointing out that 'during the past ten years this relatively small service has lost eleven administrative officers through causes other than retirement' and that there was an urgent need to increase recruitment.[7] He followed this with a request that two Cadets be recruited for each of the following two years.[8] In the end, one, Ronald Holmes, was appointed in 1938. The next appointment would be that of John Cowperthwaite in November 1941.

Cowperthwaite was remarkably fortunate in the timing of his appointment. A few months earlier and he would have spent the war interned by the Japanese. Instead he was diverted to serve in Sierra Leone on the west coast of Africa. Coincidentally, his brother, David, who had also wanted to go to the Far East, would serve in the administrative service in Nigeria, 2,000 miles further along the African coast, between 1942 and 1948.

SIERRA LEONE

Cowperthwaite was appointed as a Cadet in the Colonial Administration Service in Sierra Leone with effect from the date he had become a Hong Kong Cadet, 17 November 1941, and he arrived in Freetown around 12 February 1942.[9]

Freetown had been a key trading centre for the transatlantic slave trade, but in 1787 it became a territory for freed slaves. This role accelerated with the formation of the Sierra Leone Company, which settled those who had escaped slavery during the American Revolution by seeking the protection of the British army. With the abolition of the slave trade in 1807, a further wave of settlement occurred as slaves were liberated in Freetown. In 1808 Freetown itself became a British colony, and later the interior of the country became a British Protectorate, Sierra Leone.

In most respects Freetown was very far away from the struggles of war. Its position meant that there were no Axis forces within thousands of miles. However, the colony did play a role in the war by providing some recruits to the armed forces, and, more importantly, Freetown is a natural harbour, of strategic value in protecting the routes around the west coast of Africa. This was critical as the Mediterranean (and therefore the route through the Suez Canal) became too dangerous for most Allied shipping, and so the link between the United Kingdom and the Eighth Army in North Africa, and the forces in India and beyond, went past Freetown and on round the Cape of Good Hope.

Even during the war holidays were taken, and the *Sierra Leone Gazette* recorded that Cowperthwaite took twelve weeks' leave in 1943, departing on 21 September. It noted that his leave period should only start from the date of arrival at the first port in the United Kingdom.[10] He left England to return on a Blue Funnel ship, the Nestor, departing Liverpool on 25 February 1944, heading to Freetown before travelling on to South Africa and Australia.[11] On this return trip his wife, Sheila, accompanied him. They would arrive in Freetown on 16 March 1944. Later in the year their only child, John James (Hamish) Cowperthwaite, would be born in Sierra Leone.

After an absence of around six months he resumed his work in the provincial administration department[12] as a district officer. The district officers were the lynchpins of the British administration in the field. They coordinated the work of the various technical departments, such as education, health and public works, to better meet the needs of their district. They were the first line of administration, and also the first line of the judicial system, often acting as magistrates, or arbitrators, in local issues. While they were further from the corridors of power than those in the more powerful but bureaucratic world of the secretariat, they enjoyed considerable autonomy, and many preferred to be out amongst the local population.

A glimpse of the work that Cowperthwaite and the other administrative members of the colony's government undertook can be seen in the steady flow of the published *Royal Gazettes*. Every couple of weeks the governor would approve the release of the latest gazette, highlighting the activities of a well-organized small colony. For example, the gazette published in April 1944, just after Cowperthwaite's return, records a fairly typical mix of activities, ranging from the mundane to the significant. Various government appointments and staff moves are announced, alongside the passage of bills on their way to becoming law. The verdicts and sentences of the courts are recorded, as are notices about goods that have been abandoned or seized and then put up for sale. Some exam results are mentioned, as are the awards of some scholarships. A notice reminds government personnel that they cannot travel without proof of a smallpox vaccination. A 'roll of honour' listed locals killed in action while serving elsewhere.

Occasionally there was a major supplement: when the prices of goods needed to be set under the Defence (Prices of Goods) Regulations 1940, for example. There must have been considerable work involved, since many brands got their own specific price, and those prices could vary across five zones within the colony. Four ounces of Lyons tea cost one shilling and six pence (£3.05 today, adjusted for inflation[13]), cabbages were eight pence a pound (£1.34), cigarettes around one shilling and three pence for twenty (£2.56), and a bottle of Johnnie Walker a princely sixteen shillings and three pence (£33.06). This experience of seeing how the administration set prices would be of use to Cowperthwaite when he eventually got to Hong Kong.

Cowperthwaite left the Sierra Leone Service on 5 April 1945, at which time he was working in the secretariat.[14] This was the key executive body of the administration, dealing with major issues of policy and finance. Other departments would handle the work of policing, education, health and the like, but the secretariat was where key choices about priorities and resource allocation were made. It was the ideal place for Cowperthwaite, and he would spend most of the rest of his career playing increasingly important roles in the secretariat in Hong Kong.

THE HONG KONG PLANNING UNIT

After the fall of Hong Kong in 1941 there had been little thought about what to do if the colony was recovered at the end of the war, since all efforts were focused on survival and then on organizing the fight back against Germany and Japan. With America dragged into the war, the odds of victory swung towards the Allies, but it was very unclear whether the United States and China would allow Hong Kong to return to its status as a British colony. As the war progressed, the British started to reflect on the desirability of recovering Hong Kong, so they started to consider what would need to be done to achieve that end.

The Hong Kong Planning Unit, which was set up in August 1943, had the objective of preparing for the return of the territory, so that the United Kingdom could seize the initiative and re-establish control if at all possible. Norman Smith, who had been colonial secretary in Hong Kong, came out of retirement to head the unit. He started to build its capabilities and personnel, and by February 1944 there were nine officials at work. In September 1944 David MacDougall took over and expanded it to over twenty posts. The group started to prepare a series of policy directives (Donnison 1956), covering administration, Chinese policy, police, prisons, immigration control, labour policy, social welfare, medical and health policy, dangerous drugs, opium, postal and telecommunications services, financial policy, and a monetary and fiscal guide. The assumption was that Hong Kong would be recovered following an opposed landing, and the Planning Unit staff would be attached to the troops coming ashore.

By the spring the unit's activities were accelerating, and Cowperthwaite was ordered to join the unit in early 1945. He was penciled in to work in the supply division,[15] which is where he would indeed focus when he arrived in Hong Kong. He ended up joining the unit on 5 April 1945[16] and started work at the civil affairs headquarters at 2 Park Street in Mayfair, London.[17]

As it became clear that Hong Kong would go through a period of military administration, the Planning Unit staff itself was militarized in May 1945 and the thirty-eight staff were given military ranks, with Cowperthwaite taking the rank of 2nd Lieutenant within Civil Affairs, Eastern Command. The organizational structure now moved from one centred on writing papers to one structured to become the new administration. MacDougall was the Chief Civil Affairs Officer, with a deputy, and a secretariat department. Seven other departments were established: works, supply, legal, finance, welfare, police, and trade and industry (Donnison 1956).

Planning work continued on the basis that the Allies would slowly work their way up towards Japan, taking one island or territory at a time.[18] However, events would accelerate this timetable, leaving many elements of the plan incomplete.

THE RACE TO ACCEPT THE JAPANESE SURRENDER

Early on the morning of 6 August 1945 the *Enola Gay* dropped 'Little Boy' on Hiroshima. Around 80,000 people died that day, and tens of thousands would die over the following months from radiation. On 8 August, the Soviet Union opportunistically abandoned the Soviet–Japanese Neutrality Pact and declared war on Japan. The following day, 9 August, saw the Soviet Union invade Japanese-controlled Manchuria, and later that day a second B-29 Superfortress, Bockscar, headed for Kokura. Already behind schedule, they encountered heavy cloud cover over the city and so diverted to their secondary target, the city of Nagasaki. Running low on fuel, the crew had decided that if the cloud cover were equally bad there, they would have to drop the atomic bomb in the ocean. However, a break in the cloud just after 11 a.m. meant that 'Fat Man' was delivered as planned, killing a further 40,000–70,000 people immediately. Such is the happenstance of war that small changes in the weather decided who lived or died on such a mass scale.

The Pacific War suddenly went from a war of attrition that could be expected to last for many months to a rapid finale. The Emperor of Japan announced the surrender of his forces on 15 August, and the Japanese forces in Hong Kong accepted defeat.

In the early days of August the British had become very worried that a combination of the proximity of Chinese forces and the US opposition to maintaining the British Empire could hinder the re-establishment of Hong Kong's status as a colony. At Yalta, Roosevelt had even proposed that Hong Kong be returned to China despite an emotional outburst from Churchill. Britain needed to move quickly and take control in the hope that possession was nine-tenths of the law.

On 10 August the cabinet discussed the issue of how to ensure that it would be Britain that took control of Hong Kong should Japan surrender more quickly than had been expected.[19] Hong Kong was clearly in the operational area of Chinese general Chiang Kai-shek, and it would have been normal for the Japanese forces in Hong Kong to surrender to him. To thwart this, London formed a naval task force under Admiral Sir Cecil Harcourt and ordered it to proceed at pace to Hong Kong.[20] But Harcourt was two weeks away. Churchill lobbied President Truman to allow Britain to take the surrender, and on 18 August 1945 Truman gave his support to Churchill's plan, so long as he could coordinate that with the Chinese forces.[21]

Franklin Gimson, the interned colonial secretary, acting on his own initiative, declared himself acting governor on 16 August and started negotiating with the Japanese for their surrender. The Japanese forces protested that it was not yet clear to whom they would surrender, but Gimson insisted that they comply with his instructions or be held to account later. The Japanese commander backed down. A week later Gimson received explicit orders, which had been smuggled into Hong Kong via the ambassador at Chung-king, to take control,[22] but he had already started to take over the administration of the colony, at least in theory. He commissioned those internees able to help to assist him in taking control, but for a few days he had no choice but to rely on Japanese troops to maintain order.

Figure 3.2. Gimson meets Harcourt (IWM ABS781).

On 30 August 1945 Harcourt's fleet arrived in Hong Kong. It must have been a huge relief to Gimson to see the impressive force comprising two aircraft carriers, a battleship and a number of cruisers and destroyers sail into harbour (Tsang 2004). The following day Harcourt established the military administration that he would head and he appointed Gimson as his deputy. A week later, on 7 September, MacDougall arrived with his team from the Hong Kong Planning Unit to run the civil administration in what was now the Civil Affairs Unit, reporting to Harcourt as commander-in-chief.

Gimson accepted his replacement by MacDougall with good grace and was warmly thanked by Churchill by telegram on 8 September:

> My admiration has been aroused by the vigour and courage with which you, in spite of the ordeal of internment, yourself took the first steps, and later gave your assistance to Admiral Harcourt, in re-establishing British rule in Hong Kong. I want you and those who worked with you to realize how highly I appreciate your unyielding spirit and fine work.

Having now established a clear presence on the ground, Harcourt formally accepted the Japanese surrender on 16 September 1945.

Figure 3.3. Harcourt (third from right, sitting) accepts the Japanese surrender as MacDougall (second from right, standing) looks on.

MACDOUGALL'S ORDERS

En route to Hong Kong, MacDougall received his orders defining his key goals as chief civil affairs officer for Hong Kong[23]:

> Your objectives are the maintenance of law and order and the prevention of disease and unrest. This will involve, amongst other things:-
> (i) The establishment of a police force
> (ii) The establishment of military courts
> (iii) The control, as far as possible, of the influx of civilians by land and sea
> (iv) The establishment of relief camps and the provision of relief for distressed persons
> (v) The provision of medical treatment in those camps, in hospitals or elsewhere
> (vi) The taking of adequate measures of public health and sanitation
> (vii) The restoration and maintenance of essential public services
> (viii) The control and distribution of supplies
> (ix) Responsibility for enemy state property and the property of absent owners

(x) The setting up of such wartime control (e.g. exchange control, censorship) as may be deemed necessary
(xi) Treatment of renegades and quislings in accordance with the terms of the special directive issued to you
(xii) The establishment of currency, banking and fiscal arrangements
(xiii) The control of prices and wages
(xiv) The greatest possible use of local resources

To achieve these objectives MacDougall was to be provided with 'around 314 officers with the appropriate subordinate staff and equipment'. In addition, he could draw on military personnel, which would prove vital in the weeks and months ahead. The War Office was explicit that he should carry out his orders with an eye to the long-term objectives of colonial policy. These put considerable emphasis on economic recovery, and were described as follows.

(i) The reconstruction of the Colony's financial and fiscal resources
(ii) The re-organisation of civil courts, police and prisons
(iii) The rehabilitation of commerce and industry, including agriculture and fisheries
(iv) The reconstruction and development of public and private utilities, and in particular of the port and air services
(v) The re-organisation of hospitals and other public health and sanitary organisations
(vi) The re-organisation of the educational system of the Colony
(vii) The implementation of all other aspects of policy of His Majesty's Government for colonial administration and development
(viii) Preparation for the transfer of the administration to a civil government

While Hong Kong formally remained under military administration, Admiral Harcourt was keen that the civil affairs unit took responsibility for the recovery plan as quickly as possible. When MacDougall landed in Hong Kong, Harcourt met him at the airport and was clear that he saw his role as running his cruisers and that he looked to MacDougall to run the colony. In order to give MacDougall room to manoeuvre, Harcourt agreed to send a signal to the War Office: 'Please inform Secretary of State for Colonies, (signals) congestion so great that I can send civil signals only once a month.'[24] MacDougall believed that Harcourt's agreement to limit the flow of information to London would enable the local administration to get on with the reconstruction task. Later he would argue that:[24]

> We had a whole month, every month, free and then reported what we had done retrospectively. This is why we got so far ahead; everything we did was just click, click,

click, and before they knew it things were done, fait accompli. We did things they would never have thought of, things they would never have authorized. We overprinted Japanese notes; I put minimum wages up in half an hour from fifty cents to two dollars; in a week we paid fifteen thousand people on the streets $2 a day. These things would have taken months to do.

A RARE LEADER

David MacDougall had been a Hong Kong Cadet before the war. While certainly part of the establishment he was also very much his own man, and unlike many of the Cadets he had been sceptical about the quality of administration in the immediate pre-war period.

Figure 3.4. MacDougall (second from left) and the party that escaped from Hong Kong (IWM HU464565).

MacDougall had made a daring escape from Hong Kong on the day of the surrender, alongside a Secret Intelligence Service agent and a Chinese admiral.[24] They made it to Repulse Bay and headed for a torpedo boat, with the Japanese forces only a couple of hundred metres away. As they escaped they came under machine gun fire. MacDougall was hit in the heel and the shoulder and Admiral Chan's hand was shattered. A number of men were killed, but the survivors made it to the Chinese coast and met up with the resistance.[25]

MacDougall made it back to Britain and worked in the ministry of information under (Gerard) Edward Gent, who would later become High Commissioner of Malaya in 1946.[26] Gent asked MacDougall to head up the Hong Kong Planning Unit. He was dynamic and threw himself into the tasks in hand, showing initiative and energy. Both before and after arriving in Hong Kong, he was not afraid to use his judgment, and to take independent action.

After the military administration, MacDougall would become colonial secretary. His independence and progressive attitudes would cause him to fall out with Governor Grantham, and when the married MacDougall, whose family was in Britain, had an affair in Hong Kong, Grantham considered this unacceptable. Aged 45, MacDougall took early retirement in 1949 and became a farmer in Suffolk.

BRITISH RULE RE-ESTABLISHED

Britain had succeeded in its goal to re-establish a British administration. The logic behind this plan was to maintain the prestige of the British Empire in the Far East. Little thought had been given to how a broken Britain would finance its far-flung Empire, or benefit from it. Over the next two decades much of the Empire would fall away, often without rosy economic prospects. Hong Kong would be an exception. Rather than independence, over fifty years of colonial administration lay ahead, and from the rubble of the occupation an economic wonder would emerge. But first there was an urgent need to find food, water and fuel, and to begin the reconstruction of this broken colony.

CHAPTER 4

A FOCUS ON INDUSTRY

INITIAL RECONSTRUCTION TASKS

When MacDougall arrived in Hong Kong he dived straight into the reconstruction. He was greatly helped by the officers and men of the Royal Navy as well as army and RAF personnel. Many of the interned civil servants offered their assistance, even when it meant that their repatriation was delayed (Collins 1952). Given the administration was very short staffed, and with new staff arriving slowly as they managed to get from London to Hong Kong, everyone needed to turn their hands to a wide variety of tasks.

The military administration overall proved a great success.[1] The rule of law was quickly reintroduced. By 1 September all Japanese had been interned in Kowloon and British rule had been reinstated. No major epidemics took hold and sanitation was quickly brought back to acceptable standards. By early October those who needed to be repatriated to the UK had been, with the exception of some difficult cases.

One of the most urgent issues was to re-establish a functioning currency. The Japanese yen had been used during the war, and Gimson's administration had just overprinted these yen notes. When MacDougall arrived he decided to rapidly switch to the Hong Kong dollar, despite there being a shortage of currency. The switch took place on 14 September, leaving most people with no usable cash. To pump cash into circulation, the government paid more than 30,000 unskilled labourers to clean up the city, distributed $150,000 to the destitute, and provided a rehabilitation allowance of $1 a day to essential workers (Donnison 1956).

Figure 4.1. Issuing of new currency (IWM detail of A31079).

Infrastructure work that had been started under Gimson accelerated under the military administration. The electricity generating companies needed funds and technical support, but power was soon available. The telephone company, the gas company and the dockyard were all able to operate commercially almost immediately. Banks reopened for domestic business on 17 October. In reviewing the period of military administration, Harcourt argued that 'there is little doubt that Hong Kong established and maintained a commercial lead over other ports on the China coast'.[1] This he ascribed to the fact that:

> The native qualities of the Chinese population were, perhaps, from the beginning, the Administration's most notable asset. At no time during the whole period did the public mind waver from its initial confidence in a golden future for the Colony and its people.

COWPERTHWAITE PITCHES IN

On the same day that Japan surrendered, 15 August 1945, the War Office had confirmed Cowperthwaite as a staff captain within the proposed Hong Kong secretariat.[2]

It would take weeks for the various members of the Planning Unit to make their way out to Asia. With the need to reposition millions of people, transportation was far from straightforward and the team would end up using available flights and ships to crisscross the globe. It was not until 19 October 1945 that Cowperthwaite left the United Kingdom and he only arrived in Hong Kong on 6 November 1945,[3] ready to work for Brigadier David MacDougall.[4]

Cowperthwaite was appointed as a senior officer grade III with the rank of captain[5] to work in the secretariat. Their work mostly involved coordinating the recovery plan that MacDougall and the Hong Kong Planning Unit had developed in London, and introducing all the regulations that they had prepared.[6] MacDougall was relieved to see some additional support, and wrote on 7 November 1945 to Gent at the Colonial Office, saying:

> Here is a brief report. I should have written it long ago, but there are only 24 hours in the day. Danby, Cowperthwaite and Jean Bond arrived last night, and I am putting them all into this central office to relieve the strain. It is clear from what they say that the London end is nearly as hard-pressed as here.[7]

Beyond re-establishing British control and the rule of law, much of the secretariat's work was on finding supplies and helping commerce to restart. The Planning Unit had assumed that the government would monopolize the import and export trade for the first six months after reoccupation. But the entrepreneurial spirits recovered faster than expected, and in October there was a powerful demand to reopen the colony to private trade. Exchange within the sterling area was allowed on the 12 November, and on 23 November private trade was permitted under a licence system (Donnison 1956). On 4 December, full exchange dealings were sanctioned within an exchange control framework. With the physical repair of the port underway, and with the main Chinese trading cities taking much longer to recover, Hong Kong was in prime position to recover its role as a trading entrepôt.

A NEW DEPARTMENT FOR SUPPLIES, TRANSPORT & INDUSTRY

The post-war military administration realized the importance of re-establishing supplies of food and basic commodities, such as fuel. Alongside these essentials, there was a desire to get trade and industry restarted as soon as was feasible, in part to generate jobs and incomes for the returning workforce. To coordinate the government's efforts, MacDougall established a new, temporary department – the Department for

Supplies, Transport & Industry – in September 1945. Colonel Alexander Burgess was appointed as its first head.[8]

Burgess arrived in Hong Kong on 11 September 1945 and discovered that the ex-internees had created an organization to control various commodities.[9] Burgess took charge of this and set about locating and taking control of what supplies there were.

> Stocks were found in tunnels in the hillsides, in godowns, banks, garages, basements, private houses and other buildings, and at the time these were being looted by Chinese and others.

The primary focus in the early days was on obtaining basic foodstuffs and energy supplies in a disorganized world. The department needed to locate supplies, negotiate their acquisition and move them to Hong Kong. On the issue of reviving industry, Burgess started by conducting a survey of the situation:[9]

> Local manufacturing has largely ceased. The dockyards, sugar refinery, cement works and engineering works will require extensive repair. In the cotton industry, however, the looms and knitting machines were found to be in good condition. The rubber canvas shoe factories are in a position to produce 20% of their former output, whilst the safety match, felt hat, peanut oil, electric-torch and leather shoe industries are ready to commence work as soon as raw materials in reasonable quantities are available.

At the end of November Burgess summarized the first three months of the department:[10]

> The period has been beset by lack of staff, lack of supplies and a long series of problems arising from the chaos left behind by the Japanese. In the circumstances much has been accomplished. Very much more remains to be done.

Food had come from three sources: supplies left by the Japanese, foods bought or smuggled from the mainland, and three shipments of rice amounting to just over 16,000 tons. There were very limited supplies of condensed milk, salt and dehydrated vegetables. Some further supplies of canned meats, flour and frozen foodstuffs were expected shortly. The next priority was coal and firewood, both of which were difficult to obtain.

Remarkably, a number of factories had begun to operate again, including printers, rice mills, soap manufacturers, bakeries and the like. Bread distribution was a success, and bread was now available at 50c per pound, where it had been selling at $6 per pound. Prices fell as supplies enabled entrepreneurs to restart and then to compete against each other. Burgess hoped that he could get this to occur in more areas.

Figure 4.2. Queuing for rice rations (IWM detail of A31085).

In October 1945 the administration considered and agreed a proposal to extend the remit of the department to support the rehabilitation of trade and industry in the colony.[11] For some months the focus would remain on obtaining basic supplies, but the department would then play an increased role in facilitating economic revival.

COWPERTHWAITE JOINS THE DEPARTMENT OF SUPPLIES, TRANSPORT & INDUSTRY

Alongside his work in the secretariat, in January 1946 Cowperthwaite was promoted to senior officer grade II and major and was appointed to manage price controls in the Supplies, Transport & Industry branch,[12] working for Burgess. Cowperthwaite will no doubt have been a diligent administrator, and he will have been familiar with the responsibilities from his time in Sierra Leone. Although he would prepare hundreds of price control notices, e.g. that the price of a 14-ounce tin of condensed milk should move from $0.70 to $0.67, he had a wider perspective. Price control was applied to a narrow range of goods during the military administration and it was clear that the objective was to manage constrained supply and to set prices to encourage increased supply.

The early opening of Hong Kong to trade was helpful in Cowperthwaite's attempts. Controlling prices for essential items purely by edict was unrealistic, as people needed to buy food and the like. The government also imported key staples such as rice, and distributed these at below cost in an attempt to hold inflation down. It was estimated, for example, that the subsidy on rice cost the Hong Kong administration around $150,000 a day. However, the reality of the situation was that the government struggled to find adequate supplies. The reoccupation had happened much more quickly than expected, and the key supply lines had therefore not been fully established as intended. Given that (Donnison 1956)

> the colony had largely to fend for itself, making use of abandoned Japanese stocks, or of supplies imported from the mainland of China by every sort of contrivance and improvisation.

But over these early months supplies for many essentials were obtained. For example, four shipments of coal totalling more than 25,000 tons were received in February, and about the same amount was used by the power stations.[13] Nearly 10,000 tons of food, mostly rice and flour, arrived. There was even space for 6,271 cases of cigarettes and 1,064 cases of rum. By March coal imports were over 30,000 tons, and food imports nearly doubled in tonnage.[14]

By February 1946, 280 of the colony's 800 electric cotton looms were operating. 28 rubber factories had reopened, as had a number of canvas shoe manufacturers. Seven confectionery factories started to manufacture sweets in March, and four rubber factories started to produce bicycle tyres. The lack of consistency of supplies meant that production stopped and started as shipments arrived, but at least a number of industries had started to produce once more.

RETURN TO CIVILIAN RULE

On 1 May 1946 Sir Mark Young returned to Hong Kong after his recuperation in Britain. It had been widely felt that it was important that he return as governor to symbolize that while Hong Kong may have been occupied, it had remained a British colony under his 'uninterrupted governorship' (Endacott 1964a).

The new post-war civilian administration had three main priorities: to get the economy working again, to achieve financial self-sufficiency, and to implement a new political settlement. The administration would succeed on the first two, but not in the way that they expected or planned, and they would make no progress at all on the third.

The government assumed that getting the economy working again would take many years and require much support. In fact the recovery was fast, and required simply that the government create the conditions for economic activity to occur. The administration did this and private companies quickly restarted their pre-war activities, then adapted and grew as the situation developed. In getting the environment right, Hong Kong was ahead of many of its neighbours, and much of Europe. For Cowperthwaite and the other members of the government it would provide ample evidence of where the government could act usefully, and where it could not.

Figure 4.3. Sir Mark Young.

Cowperthwaite would play an important supporting role in Hong Kong's recovery. He maintained his link with the secretariat and his main role in the Department of Supplies, Transport & Industry. He was involved in the work to get the port back to its pre-war capacity, being appointed to the Port Executive Committee in June 1946,[15] a post he held until March 1947. On 21 August 1946 Cowperthwaite was appointed a Justice of the Peace.[16]

In the best traditions of the Cadets, Cowperthwaite was now operating over a wide range, and in the DST&I he would test the normal procedures and regulations of government. Appropriately, therefore, if rather belatedly, on 8 October 1946 Cowperthwaite was officially appointed as a Cadet Officer with effect from 5 April 1945, the date he had started work at the Hong Kong Planning Unit.[17] Later this would be backdated to the date he would have started as a Hong Kong Cadet: 17 November 1941.[3]

STRUCTURE OF GOVERNMENT

Throughout Cowperthwaite's career Hong Kong was governed as a colony, with little by way of democratic processes or institutions. Government was vested in the governor of the colony, who was responsible to the Privy Council and to the Secretary of State in London. The governor was appointed by the UK government and was ultimately responsible for the administration of the colony and for its government (Endacott 1964b).

An executive council advised the governor. It comprised five ex-officio members (the Senior Military Commander, the colonial secretary, the Attorney General, the Secretary for Chinese Affairs and the financial secretary), plus one other official appointed by the governor. The governor also chose six non-officials, called Unofficials, typically past or present members of the Legislative Council.* The executive council had few powers of its own but did have influence through its role as the governor's advisory board.

The Legislative Council had the responsibility of making new laws. The governor presided and in 1946 the council comprised nine official and eight unofficial members. The five ex-officio official members of the executive council also sat on the Legislative Council, with the remainder appointed by the governor. One Unofficial was chosen by the General Chamber of Commerce, and one by the Justices of the Peace. The remainder were chosen by the governor.

With the significant power they had over who sat on the councils, and the ability to rely on officials' votes, the governor and the government were always able to have a majority. Nonetheless, the government would usually not railroad legislation through the council, particularly on sensitive issues. Unofficials could and did play an important role in debating, improving and legitimizing legislation.

The Legislative Council had three subcommittees, two of which would be of great importance to Cowperthwaite. The Finance Committee comprised the colonial secretary, the financial secretary, the Director of Public Works and all the Unofficials. The Public Works Committee consisted of the Director of Public Works, the financial secretary and all the Unofficials. In addition, the Attorney General chaired the Law Committee.

Administration was undertaken by a civil service organized into departments. Above the departments sat the secretariat, which coordinated government activities,

* Between 1946 and 1948 the executive council had seven official and four unofficial members. The Legislative Council composition moved to eight official and seven unofficial members in 1947, then nine and eight in 1951, and twelve and thirteen in 1964.

set priorities and developed policy. Within the secretariat there were four divisions: general administration, controlled by the deputy colonial secretary; finance, under the financial secretary; defence, run by the Defence Secretary; and establishment, reporting to a Public Services Commission (Endacott 1964b). Importantly, the financial secretary could not be overruled by the colonial secretary and had the right to deal directly with the governor on issues within their remit.

TOMMY THOMSON TAKES OVER AT THE DST&I

When the military administration handed over to its civilian counterparts on 1 May 1946, Burgess was demobilized and Walter 'Tommy' Thomson,* another Hong Kong Cadet, took over as director of the Department of Supplies, Trade & Industry. On 6 June 1946 Cowperthwaite was appointed to continue to work in the department[3] under the civilian administration.

Shortly after his arrival, on 21 June 1946, Thomson wrote a letter to the financial secretary, Geoffrey Follows, outlining his assessment of the department and describing its role in some detail.[18]

Given the procurement section would continue to be responsible for procuring raw materials for industry, supervising the food programme, and identifying and tracking all government cargoes, Thomson was frustrated at the lack of senior staff, pointing out that 'at the present moment all the Executive officers from this department – there were three – have left for home on demobilization'. He went on: 'this is a very unfortunate state of affairs, particularly since I am far from happy about the comprehensiveness of the records of incoming War Office cargo compiled during the Military Period'. The issue of staffing the procurement section would cause issues in the future.

Turning to the price control section, Thomson argued that 'too little, in my opinion, has been done about moulding this important section into a small but cohesive striking force against the rising cost of living in the Colony'. He observed that there had been a very clear focus on controlling the prices of the most important commodities, mostly those imported by the government itself, such as rice. For the 'great mass of other commodities imported by commercial firms', the department had conducted

* Walter 'Tommy' Thomson, born in 1905, was appointed a Hong Kong Cadet in 1929. He worked for the Supply Mission in Washington, DC, during the war and then the Hong Kong Planning Unit. After running the DST&I he was Deputy Director of Commerce and Industry in Nigeria, before returning to Hong Kong as Defence Secretary in 1950. He died aged 47 in 1952.

a 'sniping campaign' that Thomson viewed as 'valueless', instead proposing that price control be limited to a narrower agreed list of essentials. Once again he expresses his concern about resources with the price control section consisting of only 'two Europeans and two Chinese inspectors, one of whom doubles as a clerk'.

The rice section was, fortunately, better staffed, but here Thomson expressed his desire to raise some senior salaries to retain staff, which again would lead to later problems.

The trade and industry section was also tasked with assisting industry. Thomson was very supportive of this having seen such support be very valuable to companies in America and Canada. Despite also being understaffed, he credited the section with

> reviving the rubber and the rubber shoe industry, the textile industry (on a limited basis), the biscuit industry, the chocolate and sweet industry, the aluminium industry and the most recent agreement assuring the supply of newsprint and paper to the Colony at reasonable prices.

Thomson's greatest concern about recruiting and retaining the people he needed lay within the more commercial fuel, marketing and accounts sections. Here his staff were leaving for the commercial sector, and were vocal about the inadequacy of the salary levels:

> All of the employees in these sections – Chinese and European alike -- are commercial men who each have their own special knowledge and niche, and oftentimes their responsibility is very large. Last month, for instance, our sales through these three sections were $16 million, or probably 33% of the Colony's whole business. Since we take a percentage of all business done, inevitably, if we administer properly, we must make a tidy profit for Government. To continue to administer properly, however, is the problem for at present the commercial world rates the services of employees more highly than we do and each week brings its crop of resignations on grounds of insufficient pay.

Thomson's plan was to run the department as if it was a commercial organization, and pay accordingly. He put forward his views forcefully and directly, in the best traditions of the Cadets, arguing that since the department could afford to pay commercial salaries, 'it seems a pity to spoil the ship for a ha'porth of tar'. He was also well aware that his ideas were not consistent with normal government rules:

> I know this means breaking all the rules and regulations governing the engagement of Government personnel, but I must insist that in my opinion it is necessary.

In an interesting attempt to sugar the pill, Thomson argued that the department was already operating well outside normal governmental procedures anyway, with its constant trading, intergovernmental swaps and bartering.

Thomson concludes his note with his recommendations. Uncontroversially he asks for a few more people and to extend price control and trade and industry activities. But he ends with two recommendations that would create issues in the future, asking for:

> S. T. & I. to be put on a commercial basis provided that it will meet all its purchasing, administrative and running expenses and still show a profit to the Government. In order to achieve some continuity of staff and to stop the stream of resignations in Rice, Fuel and Marketing Sections, all replacements or new recruitments to be on commercial rates. Recruitment and salary to be at the discretion of the Director.

Thomson got agreement to manage the department as he wanted but the conflicts of running a commercial organization within a government department would reappear later when Cowperthwaite was in charge. For now, however, Thomson and Cowperthwaite concentrated on delivering the commodities needed and on managing prices and supporting industry.

THE FIRST YEAR OF THE DST&I

The year 1946/47 was very busy and successful for the department. The period of military administration had seen a replenishment of key supplies, with the establishment of reasonable stock levels of rice, flour, sugar and peanut oil; adequate stocks of coal; and poor supplies of textiles and luxury items.[19]

Rationing of rice, flour, peas and peanut oil continued through the year, and at times supplies were hard to obtain. Rice was rationed at 6.4 taels* per day but difficulties in maintaining supply meant that the ration was cut to 5.6 taels a day on 3 May 1946 and to 4 taels on 23 May. Even at this reduced level there were weeks when the rationed amount was unavailable. It was only after the crop that supplies would increase in the autumn. On the other hand, in various months extra sugar supplies reached Hong Kong, resulting in the ration being more than doubled in the summer months. Unsurprisingly, the price of key commodities in short supply rose, causing difficulties among the population.

---

* A tael is a Chinese measure of weight, equivalent to around 38 grams. There are 10 mace in a tael and 16 tael in a catty.

The DST&I was at the centre of a very substantial trading hub, finding supplies where it could, arranging for their shipping to Hong Kong, and then distributing them. When a shortage developed, the department tried to intervene. For example, when a black market developed in knitting wool, the administration made government supplies available and distributed one pound of wool per ration card. The public was still free to purchase other supplies from shops but the intervention provided supplies to all, helping to depress prices. Barter was frequent, with the department swapping peas and surplus army biscuits for Japanese coal.

Outside of the core rationed items, the department was rarely the sole supplier of a product, and it was content to allow free importation of goods and their sale in the colony. Private enterprise found supplies alongside the DST&I, and they were encouraged to do so. However, the administration had a number of resources that were not available to private enterprise, e.g. military supplies, and it was able to finance purchases more credibly. The government supplies helped keep prices close to their controlled level and limited the extent of black market activities, and they often created useful profits too.

The DST&I was responsible for controlling trade but this was not an area that the government chose to regulate heavily. As they reported:

> Controls on trade have proved one of the most difficult problems in view of Hong Kong's peculiar position as an entrepôt. While the merchant's belief in laisser-faire* could not be fully accepted, it was recognised that the fullest freedom compatible with the welfare of the people and international obligations must be accorded.[19]

The second main area of activity for the DST&I was price control. The military administration had done relatively little in this area because supplies were so scarce that control was not really practical. By May 1946, only thirty-one items were subject to price controls. The DST&I broadened this to around 700 products by March 1947. However, the control was still conducted with a light touch, working with suppliers, importers and distributors. Price control was intended

> to permit margins which, while being high enough in relation to the normal practice of the trade to offer some inducement to co-operate, were low enough to afford some real relief to the public.

The fact that food, fish and fresh vegetables were not generally subject to price controls showed an understanding of how private enterprise worked. Price controls

* The original draft of the report read 'merchant's academic belief in laisser-faire' but Cowperthwaite crossed out the word 'academic'.

were used sparingly in these sectors because such controls could easily reduce supply and cause any available commodities to be diverted to nearby territories.

The third area that the department covered was trade with Japan. Japan was occupied by the United States, and the US Occupation Authorities managed all trade and required that all business be conducted on a government-to-government basis, and in US dollars. Hong Kong was keen to import Japanese coal, textiles and yarn, and the DST&I managed this, even setting up a supply office in Tokyo. Hong Kong businesses could then commission the DST&I to trade for them, and the cash that they deposited with the department would turn out to be a vital source of liquidity for the government.

The industry section provided advice to businesses, and also helped to procure raw materials. Over its first year it advised more than 5,000 businesses and played an important role in helping facilitate the purchase of yarn for the textile industry. Sometimes the need for assistance would fade, as for example it did with obtaining rubber. After the war the department controlled imports directly, but by October 1946 a regular supply was obtained from Malaya and the trade returned to a normal commercial basis.

From September 1946 Cowperthwaite wrote the department's monthly reports that were sent to the colonial secretary and the governor. He could survey activities across the whole department, and while he stuck to the sparse, tested format of earlier reports for a while, they gradually contained his more expansive style.

There was a ban on exporting glass and several bottle dealers had tried to get around this by exporting glass bottles to be recycled abroad. Exporting bottles was therefore banned. The September report notes that to circumvent this, bottle dealers were discovered to be breaking bottles because no ban existed on exporting broken bottles. The report dryly notes that 'the re-export of broken bottles has now been prohibited'.[20] However, the following month it notes that 'bottle dealers have now adopted the expedient of exporting bottles filled with coloured water which is labelled "dye"'.[21] The November report reveals that exports of 'beer bottles filled with other than beer'[22] had been added to the prohibited export list. By March 1947 the report noted that a new 'ingenious smuggling device has been detected': very large framed pictures were being exported with five or six sheets of glass in the frame.[23] Glass would eventually be freed from control in June 1947 when world supplies had recovered.[24] Cowperthwaite's coverage of this skirmish between entrepreneurs and regulators would teach him not only how the private sector could respond and adapt at speed, and the complexity of any government body replicating that, but also the importance of thinking about the second-order effects of any proposed regulation.

The reports discussed at length the department work with specific industries where government-to-government discussions were needed. For example, the department had conversations with the UK Ministry of Food over the winter of 1946/47 to facilitate the importation of preserved ginger.[25] At first the price proposed by the United Kingdom was too low to enable the Hong Kong manufacturers to cover their costs. Eventually, though, a price was agreed that allowed Hong Kong to export 300 tons to the United Kingdom at a price that gave manufacturers a 7 per cent profit.

A bigger prize came when the department sent a representative to Japan to agree a trade deal under which Hong Kong could import Japanese yarn. After several false starts all the issues were resolved, and 2.2 million pounds of cotton yarn arrived in Hong Kong on 1 January 1947. In the monthly report, Cowperthwaite underlined the significance of this:[26]

> The weaving and knitting factories, after their long period of idleness, should be back in production in the first week of the new year. Their production of badly needed consumer goods should do much to stimulate agricultural production in the rice-producing areas of South-East-Asia.

Obtaining sufficient quantities of yarn would be an ongoing problem for some months, with the department looking to Japan and other countries for supply. The sporadic nature of the arrival of raw materials made it difficult for manufacturers to manage their costs and be competitive in the world market. Despite this, at least the industry had resumed its pre-war activities, if not reached the levels of pre-war output.

In the eleven months to April 1947 the department had a turnover of more than $178 million. Due to a lack of resources, the difficulties of always knowing the full costs of purchases and the very significant delays in the presentation of some invoices, it was unclear how much profit had been made. It would turn out to be quite satisfactory, as would the ability to use the float provided by receiving funds in advance for purchases. However, the rather chaotic accounting practices, and the explicitly commercial nature of some of the department's activities, would cause problems in due course.

In the monthly report for May 1947 Cowperthwaite mentions for the first time that discussions were underway with a number of firms, mostly operating in Shanghai, to move their plant to Hong Kong.[27] The companies operated in a number of industries, including the production of yarn, fountain pens, telephones and enamelware. As conditions deteriorated in China over the next few years, this trend would grow in importance and provide significant growth for the colony.

COWPERTHWAITE BECOMES DIRECTOR

In June 1947 Thomson left Hong Kong to assist with supply issues in Tokyo and Washington. There had been complaints about the way the department had been too restrictive in allowing private enterprise to operate. Some also complained that prices were too high. Thomson had made some enemies and it was politic for him to be promoted. The *South China Morning Post* came to his defence:

> The Department has played a major role in restoring the colony's economy. It is primarily responsible for the frequent tributes paid to the Colony by visitors – that Hong Kong is the most comfortable, stable and cheerful place in the whole of the world's war devastated areas.[28]

In these mixed circumstances, the thirty-two-year-old Cowperthwaite was appointed to act as Director of Supplies, Trade & Industry on 13 June 1947.[29] He was now running a major department. On 16 June 1947 he signed the first of what would be many notices to appear in the Hong Kong Government Gazette, adding the words 'raw rubber' to a regulation on export controls. Two days later, 'in exercise of the powers conferred upon [him] as a competent authority under Defence Regulation 50 of the Defence Regulations, 1940', he set the maximum price of Cowlac Malted Milk at $1.55 per 14-ounce tin. These were the early foothills of Cowperthwaite's deployment of executive power. On the same day, and more in keeping with the man he would become, he revoked the Motor Vehicle (Allocation and Control) Order (1946) with immediate effect.[30]

By 1947/48 government activities had narrowed to importing rice, flour, sugar, butter, fresh meat, coal and coke, cotton and rayon yarn, with other commodities now being handled by normal commercial channels.[31] Obtaining supplies could be rather haphazard. Rice, for example, was allocated by the International Emergency Food Committee, based in Singapore, and Hong Kong's quota had been increased from 48,000 tons in the second half of 1946 to 80,000 tons in the first half of 1947. In theory this would have allowed the rice ration to rise from its very reduced level of 4 taels a day. However, in the first three months of 1947 only 12,000 tons actually arrived. Then, in April, 11,000 tons arrived in a single month, but at the same time Hong Kong's allocation was reduced to 100,000 tons for the whole of 1947. Given the uncertainties, the ration level was modestly increased on 18 May from 4 taels per day to 4.8 taels, and then to 5.6 taels on 6 August.

Rice was sourced from Siam (Thailand), Burma and Egypt, and its flow was subject to seasonality, shipping capacity and levels of spoilage. In Hong Kong a distributor, Wing Wo Hing, would supply the allocated rice to around 150 shops, where the million people covered by rations could buy it. The price of rice depended on the import price and the changing mix of supplies. Between early 1947 and March 1948 the cost of Siamese rice rose from £29 per ton to £41 per ton. Burmese rice was around £5 per ton more expensive and Egyptian rice around £8 more expensive. This led to consumer prices increasing from 33c to 44c per catty in March 1947, then to 48c that November, and to 54c in March 1948. These very steep increases were of considerable concern to the government but there was little that could be done to avoid them, other than to keep improving sourcing.

Flour came mostly from Australia, and it was again subject to irregular supply, exacerbated by it being shipped in full shiploads of around 8,000 tons. The department smoothed the flow by moving to shipment quantities of around 2,500 tons. Sugar was sourced from Mauritius, with around 20,000 tons being imported by the government. Butter and fresh meat posed a challenge because of the need to obtain refrigerated shipping space, which was in short supply. The government imported about 3,000 tons of meat and around 400 tons of butter. Tinned butter was returned to the private sector in early 1948.

Sourcing and shipping fuel, and in particular coal, was the other main supplies challenge. In total, 358,635 tons of coal, gas and coke were imported over 1947/48. A third of this came from Japan, which the department managed, on a government-to-government basis. The rest was sourced mainly from India, South Africa and the United States on behalf of the department by the main pre-war importers. Fuel prices remained broadly stable over the year and supply levels were adequate.

The slight increase in the availability of goods around the world somewhat eased the task of the trade section. Import controls were limited. Export controls prohibited the re-export of rationed goods, and of essential goods such as building materials. Price control policy remained 'by a mix of persuasion, threat and cajolery to bring a continuous downward pressure to bear on all price margins, without going so far as to force prices so low as to drive goods underground into a black market'.[31] There was an attempt to formalize exchange controls but this became complicated and reverted to being managed on an ad hoc basis.

When Japan was opened to private trade in August 1947 on a quota basis, the department helped Hong Kong firms obtain eighteen of the twenty British colonial spaces and even four of the UK places. This would create a solid base for further trade expansion with Japan, all of which required involvement from the department, particularly around conducting US dollar transactions. Through this activity the department would build further significant cash balances.

Once more the department helped the textile industry obtain cotton yarn. As supplies became more available, and the price of yarn fell, there was a boom in the weaving and knitting industries. Capacity utilization jumped from 50 per cent to 60 per cent, and there was an increased need for new equipment. The success of the industry would not go unnoticed further along the coast in Canton and, as the civil war in China intensified, many Cantonese textile firms took another look at relocating to Hong Kong.

In early 1948, Cowperthwaite's parents – his father now 65 and his mother 60 – visited him in Hong Kong, arriving on board the P&O liner 'Canton'.[32] They would see their son running a large and complex department, but questions were beginning to be asked about the future of the DST&I. Despite paying commercial salaries, personnel numbers had dropped from 225 to 173 heads, and it was proving especially difficult to recruit executive officers and accountants. This in turn had meant that the accounts were not up to date, and in particular the profit and loss accounts for 1946/47 and 1947/48 had not been produced, despite Cowperthwaite's belief that 'it is certain that costs have been amply covered'.

In summarizing his report for 1947/48, Cowperthwaite reflected on the future of the department:

> The commercial functions of the Department are obviously of a temporary nature, but, while policy is to return trade back to commercial channels as soon as this can be done without prejudicing supplies of the commodity in question, it appears likely that these functions will in some instances have to be continued much longer than originally anticipated, but their exact duration cannot be forecast.[31]

He concluded with a rather ambivalent perspective about the role the department might have in future economic planning. In the thick of the department's activities, he had not yet clarified the role of the government and commercial sectors:

> Some of the Department's other functions are also temporary and will disappear with the return of normality but for others there appears to be a continuing need in the post-war world of ever multiplying economic control and planning. In some directions work is, if anything, increasing.

THE WORK OF THE DST&I 1948/49

The work of obtaining supplies continued into the new financial year.[33] The rice quota for 1948 was raised to 115,000 tons. By September 1948 flour availability was adequate for it to be de-rationed, with other products following suit over time. Coal supply improved further. Importation and distribution remained in the government's hands, but purchasing and shipping was managed by the main commercial importers on behalf of the department. The one exception to this was trade with Japan, which remained on a completely government-to-government basis. The price of coal fell over 1947 and 1948, in large part because shipping costs fell as merchant ship capacity rose. In total across all categories in 1948/49, the department imported over 500,000 tons of product in more than 400 vessels.

Price control continued, but as supplies became more abundant prices fell naturally to their controlled level, or in many cases below it. The department's use of controls to encourage free market supply had worked.

The total staff of the department fell to around 150 by 1949. One area where staff continued to be scarce was within the accounting function, with only around nineteen accountants and bookkeepers tracking a turnover that had increased to more than $275 million by 1948/49.* Indeed, the chief accountant left for the accounting firm of Lowe, Bingham & Matthews and, unable to find a replacement, the responsibility for the accounts was passed to that firm. In May 1948 the assistant accountant resigned, leaving 'no one left capable of conducting the routine work of the department under the guidance of Lowe, Bingham & Matthews'.[34] With limited resources, the department's accounts were behind schedule, and this, combined with its unusual remit, would cause Cowperthwaite a significant headache.

CONTROVERSY ABOUT THE DST&I'S TRADING ACTIVITIES

The unusual arrangements at the DST&I caused significant disquiet among government auditors, who were unhappy about the department acting outside normal regulations and because of the difficulties in keeping accurate records in the post-war period. The Director of Audit, Percival Jennings, identified several practices in the department that were at odds with normal colonial regulations. Rather unhelpfully, he decided to send a report directly to the Director-General of Colonial Audit, without giving the governor, Sir Alexander Grantham, any prior warning. The governor was left managing a damage-limitation exercise. He laid the audit report before the Legislative Council on 9 February 1949.

* For 1948/49 the cash turnover of the department was split $138 million Japanese trade, $78 million rice trade, $29 million fuel, $20 million cotton and yarn, $4 million meat and $2 million butter.

Realizing that he also needed to contain the issue in London, Grantham wrote to the colonial secretary on 19 March 1949.[35] He referred back to the memo that Thomson had written in June 1946, summarizing the recommendations:

> The Department should continue to be operated on a commercial basis. This involved two major departures from normal practice –
>
> (a) that staffing arrangements, including salaries, should so far as possible be left to the discretion of the Director of the Department, and
> (b) that the trading activities of the Department should not be subject to the normal principles of Government finance laid down in Colonial Regulations.

Grantham explained why his predecessor had agreed to this, and argued that he viewed managing the department commercially as 'inevitable'. However, the Hong Kong government had not asked London for approval to run suspense accounts for funds pending transactions, which were off the government's books, and so he was left on the back foot. He felt the need to explain a US dollar account that operated directly between the Allied Commander in Japan and the colony, rather than via the Treasury in London. Relationships between the governor and the Director of Audit were clearly strained, as Grantham notes that 'the Director of Audit has forwarded a report of the four Japan Trade Accounts to the Director-General of Colonial Audit, but he does not appear to have supplied me with a copy'.

Grantham emphasized some improvements: the accounts were now operated in Hong Kong dollars, reducing exposure to US dollar risk; an accounting firm, Lowe, Bingham & Matthews, was producing a set of accounts; and government had not given any guarantees over the accounts. But he was left apologizing for not getting approval to operate in this way. He promised that the various suspense accounts would be reorganized as suggested by the financial secretary. On the broader issue of whether to operate commercially, Grantham notes:

> It is without enthusiasm that I view the continued carrying on of commercial dealing in a department of Government. Nevertheless, for as long as world controls continue, and for so long as certain branches of trade must necessarily be handled on a Government-to-Government basis, I fear that trading by Government must remain.

On the vexed issue of the department being able to recruit independently, Grantham suggests this issue has largely disappeared:

> The question of the authority of the Director of Supplies, Trade and Industry to recruit staff and to pay salaries at commercial rates is one that is not of such vital

> importance... In actual fact, the Director very soon ceased to act entirely on his own authority, and the position now is that he seeks authority for all appointments and salary changes.

The issue was perhaps not seen as critical in London, because it was only six months later, on 27 September 1949, that Grantham received a reply.[36] The Secretary of State accepted that the irregularities had arisen out of the exceptional circumstances after the war. He gave his retrospective approval for the various departures from colonial regulations. Going forward he agreed that the department be allowed to continue its trading activities and be largely run on commercial lines.

He also acknowledged the need to involve the Legislative Council more fully in supervising the department. While it had been Thomson who had established the unique way that the department worked, with local support, it was Cowperthwaite who had been in charge for some time and operated the department in its quasi-commercial form. And it was Cowperthwaite who had spent a great deal of time dealing with the issues raised by the Director of Audit.

REORGANIZATION

On 1 April 1949, shortly after Grantham's letter to the colonial secretary about the DST&I's activities, the department was reorganized, with the industry section moving to a new department, the Department of Commerce and Industry, headed by Kenneth Keen, another Cadet. This built on the old Department of Imports and Exports. Cowperthwaite was to remain as Director of Supplies and Distribution.

In fact, shortly after this, on 3 June, he went on leave, travelling with his wife and son via the United States before taking the Queen Mary from New York to London, arriving on 2 August 1949.[37] He remained on leave until the end of the autumn, returning to work on 28 October 1949.[3] Dermont Barty ran the department during his absence.[8]

When he returned there was a further reorganization, with Kenneth Barnett taking over as the Director of Supplies and Distribution on 24 October 1949. Cowperthwaite would act as deputy director, being formally appointed to that role with effect from 14 November 1949.[38] Although the department's role had been expanded, it must have been a strange period as he worked as deputy director in a part of a department he had once run. Cowperthwaite will no doubt have reflected deeply on the differences between private enterprise and government activities, and the difficulties of running a successful commercial organization, flexible to market needs, within a government structure.

On 18 March 1950 Arthur Clarke, who was the deputy financial secretary and also the Director of Commerce and Industry, took over from Barnett as Director of Supplies and Distribution.[8] Cowperthwaite remained as deputy within the supplies and distribution department, starting what would become a very long and productive working relationship between Clarke and Cowperthwaite.

The appointment of Clarke in the spring of 1950 facilitated the absorption of the Department of Supplies and Distribution into the Department of Commerce and Industry later that year. On 1 September 1950 Cowperthwaite ceased to be Deputy Director of Supplies and Distribution, and instead became Assistant Director of Commerce and Industry under Arthur Clarke.[39]

Clarke would become Follows's successor as financial secretary in May 1951. He therefore stepped down as the Director of Commerce and Industry in September 1951. He would bring Cowperthwaite across as one of his deputies.

ACCOUNTING FOR THE DST&I

It was only in September 1950 that Lowe, Bingham & Matthews produced the accounts for the DST&I for the period from 1 May 1946 to 31 March 1950.[40] These were subsequently revised following amendments by Clarke, and reissued in January 1951.[41] The accountants noted that:

> The records generally were in an unsatisfactory and incomplete state. It was explained that this was due to the difficulties arising from the receipt of the large quantities of stores without documents and an inability to employ sufficient and suitable staff.

They observed that the Director of Audit had attempted a partial audit of the books but that this effort was later abandoned. While not wanting to duplicate the points made to the Director-General of Colonial Audit in 1948, Lowe, Bingham & Matthews noted:

> In our opinion the need to provide an adequate accounting system and employ sufficient staff – if need be to meet an emergency – at rates in excess of normal Government salaries, was underestimated. There was also an absence of liaison with the Treasury, as a result of which the reconciliation of the Department's accounts with the Treasury necessitated lengthy investigations.
>
> No clearly recorded policy was laid down for recording the disposal of British Military Administration stocks, collection of BMA debtors, or payment of BMA creditors; the details of these items were obtained only after extensive research by our staff.
>
> As a result of these deficiencies and inefficiencies in staff and system, the preparation of these accounts has been unduly arduous and protracted.

However, the department had traded profitably. The estimated surplus for the 1946 to end-March 1950 period was $67 million. Half of this came from the rice section, a quarter from the marketing section, and the rest from the Japan trade and industry sections. In addition, because traders would deposit sums when they ordered items, but the Treasury would only pay out this cash post-invoice, the department had created very large cash surpluses held in suspense accounts. These sums were of great help in financing the recovery programme.

LESSONS FROM THE COALFACE

For Cowperthwaite, running the DST&I was a formative experience. He had seen the contrast between the commercial world and that of government. Much had been achieved in very difficult circumstances but equally, the problems of running a dynamic, market operation within government had led to criticisms. He had seen his previous boss, Tommy Thomson, run into difficulties, and he had too. For a while his career plateaued. Fortunately, in a tight-knit group of senior administrators his actions could be carefully weighed and an informed assessment made. In the end, Cowperthwaite's career and reputation would not be affected by the challenges he encountered at the DST&I. With hindsight we can see how critical that department was to Hong Kong's recovery and to financing the government. And the experiences he gained there would further reinforce his views on the role of government for many years to come.

CHAPTER 5

THE FOLLOWS FOUNDATION

While Cowperthwaite was wrestling with supplies and industry, the new financial secretary, Geoffrey Follows, took overall charge of the government's post-war economic and financial policies.* He had been seconded to the War Office as Chief Financial Advisor to the Civil Affairs Unit in the post-war military administration, arriving in Hong Kong on 8 October 1945.[1]

Throughout the period of military administration he worked closely with MacDougall, who had great respect for him:

> Follows was an exceptionally able chap and he didn't care for the rules. He was quite audacious, he took chances. He had a finger in every pie. I would never, ever formulate a policy without consulting Follows most closely. I was very strongly guided by him always. He was a key figure.[2]

MacDougall and Follows had adjoining offices, with a private door between them, and they would spend many hours together discussing policy. Follows would take the lead on the economic and financial implications of a decision, and MacDougall the Hong Kong and Chinese context. Together they made a powerful team.

* (Charles) Geoffrey Follows was born on 4 July 1896 and educated at Wellington School in Somerset before serving in the King's (Liverpool Regiment) in World War I. He then worked in the Seychelles, the Colonial Office, Gibraltar, and Northern Rhodesia, where he was Chief Secretary. He retired in 1951 and died in 1983.

As the military administration gave way to civilian rule, one of his first tasks was to develop the first post-war budget. Since the civilian government only took charge on 1 May 1946, the normal budget cycle of presenting the budget in late February for the financial year starting 1 April was impossible. The governor, Sir Mark Young, made a holding speech at the Legislative Council on 16 May 1946, pointing out that the financial position was extremely unclear, not least because there was also no agreement yet as to whether Hong Kong or the United Kingdom should pay for the period of military administration. What Young did say was that all the pre-war reserves were gone, the government was broke, and expenditures would outstrip revenues.

FOLLOWS'S STRATEGY OUTLINED IN HIS FIRST BUDGET

Follows laid out his financial approach and budget to the Legislative Council on 25 July 1946. He had decided that his strategy was to engineer a rapid return to normality, which he considered to be vital. Given the wrecked infrastructure and economy this would be costly and would require investing ahead of any ability to raise matching levels of revenue, but he believed that:

> Rehabilitation cannot be a gradual process. To be effective it must be carried out with the greatest possible speed so our repair programme must be the maximum which can be efficiently supervised by the staff available.[3]

The financial implication of this strategy was planned expenditure of $160 million for the eleven months to the end of March 1947, half of which was 'a first instalment of the sums which will be required to repair the ravages of war'. But he estimated that revenues would only be around $50 million, excluding wartime taxes levied under the War Revenue Ordinance. He assumed that he had no choice but to borrow, ideally from the British government.

But Follows had a second strategic objective: to regain financial independence from the United Kingdom, a status that Hong Kong had enjoyed from 1858 until the Japanese invasion. Follows explained to the Council that for as long as they ran deficits, and were dependent on the British government, Britain would retain the 'right to exercise a considerable degree of financial control' over the colony. It was clear that he did not see this as a good thing:

> I think it will be generally agreed that our aim should be to reduce our dependence on His Majesty's Government to a minimum at the earliest possible date and with this

> end in view I feel sure that the Government may count on the support of Honourable Members in any measures which may prove necessary to augment our revenue.[3]

Furthermore, Follows assumed that the colony might not be able to rely on support from war-torn Britain for very long. The United Kingdom had significant reconstruction expenditures itself, and had run up enormous debts through the war. For reasons of both control and security, he knew Hong Kong must free itself of any reliance on the UK exchequer.

The only way Follows could achieve his two objectives was for revenues to rise materially, driven by a strong economic recovery. He raised taxes in a number of areas, such as harbour charges and railway fares. These were all useful but Follows knew he needed both to tax business profits and salaries – taxes that had only been introduced with great resistance under the War Revenue Ordinance – and to get the tax base to grow rapidly.

His first task was to ensure these existing revenues did not disappear. Before the war Hong Kong had had no tax on income or profits, and such taxes had only been reluctantly agreed as a temporary wartime measure. To retain this tax Follows argued that the War Revenue Ordinance had not included a provision for the tax to fall away 'when the war ended' but rather with the 'termination of hostilities'. Since there was as yet no peace treaty or a declaration by the Council to that effect, he announced he intended to continue to collect the tax. Under this pedantic interpretation Follows was able to retain the revenues from the tax, at least for now.

Even with this, Follows could not balance the books. Some consolation could be drawn from the fact that the expected expenditure was in large part special or extraordinary, but that still left a need for much higher revenues. For now, though, he was focused on enabling the recovery to occur.

Even in those early post-war days, Follows could see the green shoots of the recovery, and the remarkable bounce back that would occur, observing:

> When it is considered that this rate of revenue collection has been reached only 10 months after the liberation of the Colony I think Honourable Members will agree that it represents a very remarkable recovery.

Despite this, it was clear in Follows's mind that he needed to tax earnings and profits for the foreseeable future. Furthermore, he saw the wartime approach as muddled and intended to introduce what he called a 'normal form of income tax'. He knew he faced a battle. It was a battle that he, Clarke and Cowperthwaite would all join. But all would end up rekindling the pre-war resistance to such an income tax.

THE CONTENTIOUS PRE-WAR HISTORY OF INCOME TAX

Hong Kong's absence of an income tax before the war was an anomaly that the UK government and many Hong Kong officials had attempted to end. In 1938 a taxation committee, chaired by the then financial secretary Sydney Caine,* had been established to achieve this. Perversely, the committee agreed that if revenue were required, an income tax would provide the best approach. However, they argued that such revenues were not needed and doubted that it would be possible to administer such a tax in Hong Kong. With this unhelpful steer they recommended further review.

With the outbreak of World War II the governor, Geoffrey Northcote,** wanting to support the war effort, turned again to incomes and profits. Caine worked up a plan, based on Ceylon, under which Hong Kong residents' worldwide income would be taxed at between 5 per cent and 10 per cent. This taxation of a person's whole income would become known as a 'normal income tax'.

As soon as he floated the proposal, extremely vocal opposition was made clear. The *South China Morning Post* accused the government of treating Hong Kong like 'an everlasting orange, to be squeezed as required'.[4]

When the government brought the measure for debate to the Legislative Council on 9 November 1939, the proposals came under sustained attack from the unofficial members, in an uncharacteristically heated and aggressive debate. The debate would colour the discussion of income tax for decades to come. Sir Henry Pollock, as the senior unofficial member, was the first to speak, listing all the bodies opposed to the measure and concluding that:

> The imposition of income tax would be a disastrous form of taxation to adopt. Anybody who understands the mentality of the Chinese must realise that such a measure as income tax would be likely to cause the flight of capital from this Colony and that it would probably deter new factories and enterprises from starting here.[5]

---

* Sydney Caine graduated from the London School of Economics in 1922 before joining the Inland Revenue and then the Colonial Office in 1926. He was financial secretary in Hong Kong in 1937, before returning to the Colonial Office in 1940, where he became Deputy Under Secretary of State in 1947. He was knighted in 1947 and moved to the Treasury.

** Geoffrey Northcote was born in 1881 and after attending Balliol College, Oxford, he joined the Colonial Service in 1904. He served in Kenya, Northern Rhodesia and the Gold Coast before becoming governor of British Guiana in 1935. He became governor of Hong Kong in 1937. Poor health forced his retirement in 1941 and he died in 1948.

Mr Chau Tsun-nin had a dire warning:

> This revolutionary method of raising revenue in this Colony is going to place us in a position where not merely the prosperity but the whole financial structure may be imperiled.

He contended that the way that Chinese families ran their finances made an income tax inappropriate:

> Book-keeping for the average Chinese merchant is divided into two very separate compartments. There is the general recording of transactions with the world at large which is dealt with by the employees of what is known as 'the outer counter', but there is an additional set of books which are kept in 'the inner counter' by the proprietor or partners of the business maintained under conditions of extreme privacy.
>
> An official invasion of the 'inner counter' means to a Chinese business man a great deal more than the disclosure of his business secrets. It is the breaking down of a traditional element in business procedure which has been regarded for centuries as a fundamental form of security, and with it would go a degree of confidence which might undermine the whole structure of business life.[5]

Not a single unofficial member gave their support. Even Mr Lo Man-Kam, the sole Chinese member of the Taxation Committee, where he had supported the concept of such a tax, declared that 'income tax is not suitable for Hong Kong, and cannot be equitably administered ... it will do irreparable harm to the Colony'.[5]

Despite Caine's attempts to turn the tide, Northcote beat a tactical retreat and proposed morphing the old Taxation Committee into a War Revenue Committee comprised of four Chinese businessmen, four British expatriate businessmen, two other non-Chinese businessmen, four British civil servants and two British academics (Littlewood 2010). In addition, he felt it necessary to pledge that he would not use the official members' majority to overrule the unofficial members on the matter, setting an important precedent on the issue.

THE 'SCHEDULAR' COMPROMISE

Despite extensive lobbying from Northcote, the new committee rejected Caine's proposal and instead proposed a 'partial' or 'schedular' income tax. This was not a tax on a person's total income at all but rather three taxes on three types of income (Littlewood 2010). There would be a property tax on the rental value of property, a salaries tax on salaries, and a profit tax on businesses. Income outside Hong Kong would be exempt. The committee proposed a maximum tax rate of 10 per cent, with a series of generous allowances so that only a small minority of people would be subject to it.

This compromise was enacted under the War Revenue Ordinance of 1940, and with it the framework for Hong Kong's rather unique tax system was set. After paying a tax on its profits, a business paid no further taxes on them as it distributed that income. The authorities did not keep a comprehensive record of business ownership, so the flow of income to business owners remained opaque and private. The same was true for properties: the tax applied to the property and not to the owner, and so it was quite possible to own many properties and pay no tax. Because there was no need to add up income from different sources, the tax system did not aggregate a person's income or wealth, thereby protecting privacy.

The salary tax started at a low level of 4 per cent, and there were generous allowances for having children and being married (Littlewood 2010). Only a tiny minority of the working population was taxed, and this remained the case when an additional schedule taxing interest payments was added.[6]

Tom Black, the Accountant General, became Commissioner of Tax. With no local experts available, he appointed Arthur Clarke, a Cadet, as one Assistant Commissioner and recruited Cyril Van Langenburg, from Ceylon, as another. To assess tax demands, six younger chartered accountants from the United Kingdom who had some tax experience were appointed as examiners. Two arrived on the last flying boat service in June 1940, three arrived later by ship around the Cape, and one, sadly, was torpedoed and never arrived. These five raised £1 million by the fall of Hong Kong.[7]

Arthur Clarke, who would later be Follows's deputy and successor, was promoted to be Commissioner of War Taxation, and in June 1941 he wrote a review of the system[8] concluding that it had worked well and had 'been accepted by the public'. He argued that a normal income tax 'would have been little short of disastrous', largely because of the very opaque ownership structures of Chinese businesses.

During the war, the Hong Kong Planning Unit had turned its mind to how to raise taxes after Britain regained control. Hong Kong's status as a free port limited the ability to raise indirect taxes, and there were severe doubts as to whether even the War Ordinance system of direct taxation could be maintained, as noted in a memo to MacDougall before the Japanese surrender:

> I should regard it as extremely improbable that property tax, salary tax, profits tax or interest tax are likely to be imposable within the next five years without injurious effect on the recovery of the Colony's prosperity. We should certainly confine ourselves to the expression of the pious hope that the Ordinance may be enforced some years hence.[9]

THE 1946 DEBATE ON A 'NORMAL' INCOME TAX

It is surprising that Clarke, who was now Follows's deputy, and who had concluded in 1941 that a normal income tax would have failed, was unable to dissuade Follows from announcing in his first budget 'the desirability of replacing the taxes now levied under the War Revenue Ordinance by a normal form of Income Tax'.[10] The opposition to such a measure was as strong as it had been before the war. For some reason, it was a lesson each financial secretary needed to learn for themselves.

When the unofficial members of the Legislative Council responded to the budget, much later than usual, on 5 September 1946, it was a rerun of the 1939 debate. Mr Leo d'Almada e Castro, a Portuguese member who had opposed the measure before the war, started the opposition, arguing that the tax would be easily evaded.[11] Chau Tsun-nin reiterated his comments of 1939, that the tax 'would involve inquisitorial enquiries into people's private affairs'.[11]

The unofficial members unanimously lined up against a normal income tax and asked the governor, Sir Mark Young, to take on board the conclusions of the 1939 and 1940 debates. Young agreed to do so but reiterated the need to find new revenue sources, signaling that he did not feel bound by the earlier decisions:

> On the contrary it is a question which it is our duty now most carefully to re-examine. For that purpose and for the purpose of considering every other possibility of increasing our revenue both by exploring new sources and by augmenting existing rates, I am setting up immediately a Taxation Committee on which I shall invite some of the Unofficial Members of this Council to sit.

And he closed the debate reiterating the strategic imperative of regaining financial independence from the United Kingdom.

THE 1946 TAXATION COMMITTEE

Follows chaired the 1946 Taxation Committee, which had a wider membership than its predecessors and included Cowperthwaite's boss Tommy Thomson, the director of the DST&I, and also the bishop of Hong Kong.[12] The committee came to much the same set of conclusions as previous reviews, and in December 1946 it argued that while a normal income tax would 'theoretically result in the most equitable distribution of the burden of taxation', it would take too long to introduce and have a number of issues.[13] Equally, the committee accepted that it was necessary to have some form of tax to cover the deficit. The report proposed sticking with the pre-war system.

Young and Follows felt that they had no real choice but to go along with this proposal.[14] Eric Pudney,[15] the Taxation Committee's secretary, was charged with drafting the bill that would move the pre-war system into peacetime legislation, since it was becoming increasingly hard to maintain the fiction that the War Ordinance still applied (Littlewood 2010).

Pudney introduced the idea of a standard, flat rate of tax across the different schedules – property, profits and interest, and for higher incomes – with lower salaries paying a lower rate of tax. The war rates had been 7 per cent on property and 14 per cent on profits and interest. Pudney thought the standard rate might be set at 25 per cent.[16] Bands below the standard rate would be abolished except for salaries.

Pudney also proposed a voluntary scheme of personal assessment. Taxpayers could choose to be taxed on their total income at the progressive salary rates, which for many taxpayers would be to their advantage. Pudney disclosed his thoughts about his 'normal' tax Trojan Horse in an internal memo:

> If the great majority of such taxpayers elect for personal assessment, it will be clear that the objections to normal income tax are not very widespread and in 1948/49 it should be possible to introduce legislation more on the lines of the Model Ordinance.[17]

THE 1947 BUDGET

Follows's second budget, in March 1947, gave further ammunition to both sides of the income tax debate. The economic data was much stronger than expected and government revenues were 'more buoyant than could reasonably have been foreseen after the dislocation caused by a prolonged period of enemy occupation'.[18]

For 1946/47, rather than $50 million of revenue, Follows anticipated the colony would produce $78 million, a number he would later revise upwards to $82 million. Recurrent expenditure would come in at $86 million, somewhat below forecast. So instead of his predicted recurrent deficit of $40 million for 1946/47, it would actually turn out to be only $4 million. Special expenditure was now expected to be around $40 million, around half of the original estimate.

While the rebound showed that the current tax rates were not stifling growth, it also showed there was no need for higher taxes to balance the books. Follows emphasized the challenging path ahead given the scale of work that still needed to be completed, the lack of any reserves and the doubtfulness of any loans being available. But hc was also able to aim for a small nominal recurrent surplus for 1947/48, many years earlier than he had expected.[18] This was a remarkable step towards achieving the goal of financial autonomy.

In their replies, the Unofficials welcomed the positive trends but they were sceptical that an income tax was needed.[19] They felt that Follows was deliberately underestimating projected revenues in order to create the need for the tax, and many reiterated their objections to it.

Several felt that the information provided did not adequately support the need for it. One problem for the Unofficials was that Follows kept his budget speeches fairly brief, and much of the information about the budget was incomplete when circulated to them. This was no doubt partly a result of the administration still recovering from the war, but it was also blamed on departmental numbers emerging late in the process and on difficulties at the government printers. It was a problem that irritated many unofficial members, who felt they could only partially scrutinize the budget. The process would be significantly improved under Clarke and Cowperthwaite.

INLAND REVENUE BILL (1947)

Follows published a draft of the new income tax bill on 7 March 1947, and a month later he introduced the Inland Revenue (Tax on Earnings and Profits) Bill.[20] It was in essence a continuation of a schedular tax on salaries, profits and property income.

The media had been active in opposing the bill. The *South China Morning Post,* for example, argued, with some justification, that the proposals had 'been adopted on dictat from London', adding: 'If the imperial government thinks it can stifle protests it may be persuaded to revise its ideas.'[21] A Chinese anti-direct tax committee was formed, and local protests organized.

The unofficial members of the Legislative Council were in a more difficult position having all been brought onto the Taxation Committee. Follows described their position as being in favour of direct taxation but wanting to postpone its introduction and cap the rate at 10 per cent. Such a position gave Young a narrow window of opportunity and he took it. Given the combined hostility of the unofficial members of the Legislative Council, the local population and the media, Young decided to make a major concession in reducing the proposed tax rate from 25 per cent to 10 per cent, and he took the unusual step of speaking in the debate in favour of the bill.

Despite this, the unofficial members still argued against the bill at the Legislative Council on 1 May 1947. They objected to the measure being 'rail-roaded' through, expressed doubts as to the need for the revenues, argued that such an approach would not in practice work and that it would be inequitable. But the government did get support, based on keeping the schedular approach, amending the bill as it was reviewed, and by keeping the rate low. The government was always able to pass the bill with its officials' majority, but Young was keen to show at least some broader support existed. He explained his logic in a dispatch to London, after the debate, noting that his tactic had worked:

> I agreed to the inclusion of a 10% rate in the Bill. I felt that the main consideration was to establish the machinery for direct taxation, for once that was accomplished any adjustment in the rate which might become necessary to meet a change in conditions would not present the same difficulty. I hoped too that this decision might result in one or two Unofficial members voting with the Government. In this my hopes were more than realized for four Unofficial members finally supported the measure.[22]

For now, the long and acrimonious debate on direct taxation had been closed. But, despite their public statements, many saw this as an opening move. In London, Treasury and colonial officials exchanged notes welcoming the votes from the unofficial members but observing that they had asked the governor to make the standard rate as high as was considered practical.[23] They saw the proposed 10 per cent rate as merely a first step:

> I should add that we take the view that in Hong Kong's present financial position, the 10% rate is only a beginning and as soon as possible, the rate should be increased towards the original 25% target.

The contrast between a 10 per cent tax rate with generous allowances and UK policy was profound. The standard rate of tax under Attlee was 45 per cent, just slightly below the 50 per cent rate applied during the war. The top rate was 92.5 per cent.[24] Perhaps equally importantly, with the erosion of allowances the number of families paying income tax jumped from around 3.8 million before the war to 14.5 million by 1948/49 and to 17.8 million by 1958/59 (Clark and Dilnot 2002). Where before the war you needed to earn significantly above average earnings to pay tax, under Attlee someone on half of average earnings became a taxpayer.

GOVERNOR GRANTHAM

In May 1947 Young's term as governor ended, and in July Sir Alexander Grantham took office.* Young had provided an important continuity between the pre-war and post-war colony and had successfully overseen the rebirth of the Hong Kong economy.

Figure 5.1. Governor Grantham.

However, he had failed in his aim of creating a new political settlement in Hong Kong. When Young landed at Queen's Pier on 1 May 1946, as the returning governor, he brought a new message for the people of Hong Kong, promising them 'a fuller and more responsible share in the management of their own affairs ... the fullest account being taken of the views and wishes of the inhabitants'.[25] Young proposed the establishment of a more democratically elected Municipal Council. He described this in more detail in a speech in August 1946, outlining what would be known as

* Alexander Grantham, born in 1899, went to Pembroke College, Cambridge. After serving in the 18th Hussars he was appointed a Hong Kong Cadet in 1922. He was colonial secretary of Bermuda (1935–37) and of Jamaica (1938–41), Chief Secretary of Nigeria (1941–44) and governor of Fiji (1945–47). He was governor of Hong Kong between 1947 and 1957. He died in 1978.

the Young Plan. Over the next year it would gain support in both Hong Kong and London.

But the plan did not outlive the retirement of its author by very long. It had limited support among the Hong Kong elite. Grantham, who was an ex-Cadet, claimed in his inaugural address to the Legislative Council that he came 'with no new policy, no new mandate, no new brief',[26] but while he worked on improving the plan for a Municipal Council for a while, he would end up dropping the Young proposals.[27] He would instead work with the old, unelected arms of government.

THE WEAK BANKING BILL OF 1947

In December 1947 Follows introduced a bill requiring any organization conducting banking business to hold a banking licence.[28] This had not previously been required, and many so-called banks were actually engaged in currency speculation and general trading. The requirements were not onerous. There was a fee of $5,000 per annum and a requirement to make available various documents including a balance sheet. But there was little real provision for supervision or detailed regulation.

This light-touch approach was in keeping with the broader view that regulation should be minimized. There was also an argument that the banks should not be too closely regulated for fear that that would create an obligation by the government to support depositors if a bank went bust. This was not an obligation the government wanted, and for now the level of deposits and the number of savers was low. Later, under Cowperthwaite, this lack of regulation would create significant problems.

THE GRANTHAM AND FOLLOWS APPROACH TO FISCAL POLICY

Grantham and Follows would present the next four budgets together. There was a typical pattern: Grantham would describe the situation of the colony more generally, and lay out broad policy, and the less loquacious Follows would then cover the bookkeeping side of business. In many ways Follows would be the one to create the policy, but unlike Clarke and Cowperthwaite he did not invest much time in describing his underlying philosophy.

In the next two budgets, delivered in 1948 and 1949, Follows and Grantham defined some of the key elements of their approach to taxation and government spending. These included the primacy of trade, the imperative to keep taxation low, the need to balance the books and the importance of taking a conservative view. Grantham and Follows shared these beliefs. They were an effective team, with Grantham taking the higher ground and also trumpeting the many areas of government investment. Follows worked away at making it happen.

THE PRIMACY OF TRADE

Grantham introduced each budget with a constant view that trade was the economic bedrock of the colony, which, combined with a nascent industrial sector, provided funding for government works. In his 1948 budget he said:

> It is upon (trade and industry's) prosperity that Hong Kong depends. Given good trading conditions, revenue will flow into the Colony's exchequer, and Government will be able to carry out projects of economic and social development. If business is depressed, Government's revenue falls off, and by consequence the amount of development and other works that can be undertaken.

And in 1949 he again highlighted the role of trade:

> Trade is the life blood of this Colony. If trade is good everyone prospers, the Exchequer is full and we can afford to spend more on social services and other developments than would otherwise be the case. If trade is bad, then everyone suffers, including Government revenue and hence the things that Government can undertake.

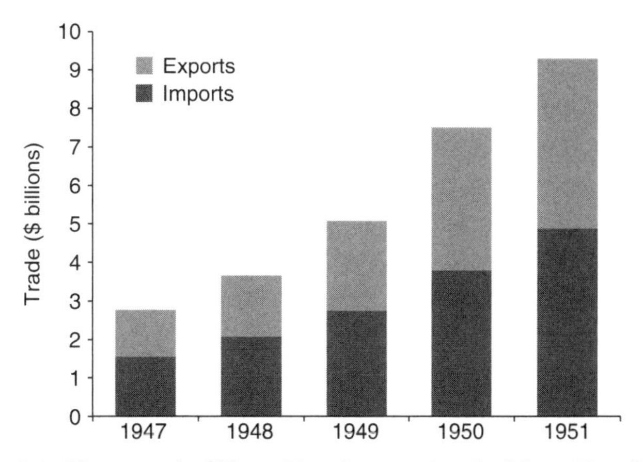

Figure 5.2. The revival of Hong Kong's entrepôt role: Hong Kong's trade levels 1947–1951. (*Source*: Hong Kong Statistics 1947–1951.)

For Grantham during his early years as governor, trade was vital, and he was very relieved that Hong Kong had succeeded in restoring the traditional trading activities. He ascribed this to Hong Kong being 'an oasis of political and financial stability in the Far East'. Grantham and Follows's success in creating the right environment for trade can be seen in the growth of imports and exports (both important in an entrepôt) over the period, despite many challenges.

Trade would more than triple between 1947 and 1951, with Hong Kong regaining its role as the pre-eminent entrepôt in the region.

THE IMPERATIVE TO KEEP TAXATION LOW

Follows believed that government could do many things that would improve the lot of the colony's population but he believed that these efforts should be limited by the need to maintain a competitive level of taxation, thus attracting trade and enterprise. As he noted in his 1949 budget speech:

> It would be a fair question to ask, 'If there are so many necessary things to be done, why not increase taxation substantially, so that you will have enough money to enable you to do them.' The answer to this is Hong Kong's peculiar position as an entrepôt and not, in the main, as a producer. Although we offer better facilities, and greater security than most of our competitors in this part of the world, they are relatively expensive. We don't want to kill the goose that lays the golden eggs by increasing taxation, and so the costs of trading in and through Hong Kong, to the extent that trade will be driven away.

In language that few European politicians would have used at the time, he expressed a moral and pragmatic view of the need to limit taxation, most emphatically during the 1950 budget debates:

> Taxation I regard as an evil. Admittedly an unavoidable evil, but in the case of Hong Kong we have to be especially careful, for we know that if we overdo it we shall drive business away to neighbouring places.

THE REQUIREMENT TO BALANCE THE BOOKS WITH CONSERVATIVE ASSUMPTIONS

Follows and Grantham took the view that the books must be balanced. Furthermore, they refused to be optimistic about revenues, fearing that that would create unaffordable spending commitments, especially in a recession. They also rejected running a deficit or dipping into reserves on a planned basis. And so revenues limited expenditure.

The conservatism looked excessive, especially with hindsight. From the very first post-war budget a pattern emerged: the forecast for the government deficit would look quite worrying in the budget before the start of the year; it would then show significant improvement in the estimates during the year in question; and then further improvement would be seen as the accounts were finalized and reported in the following year's budget. Typically, revenues were stronger than had been expected and spending fell short of original estimates.

In the 1948 budget Follows upgraded estimates for the previous year (1946/47) and the current year (1947/48). The now-anticipated surpluses would later be revised further upwards as revenues overperformed these estimates.[29] Despite these historical surpluses, Follows remained very cautious for the upcoming year. He argued that the expected revenue numbers were inflated due to a catch-up effect of delayed direct tax payments, which would be paid in arrears, and he was nervous about the broader slowdown in the global economy and had therefore assumed some slowdown in trade.

This pattern of outperformance would continue throughout his period in office, with Follows being conservative in his forecasts across all six budgets that he presented.

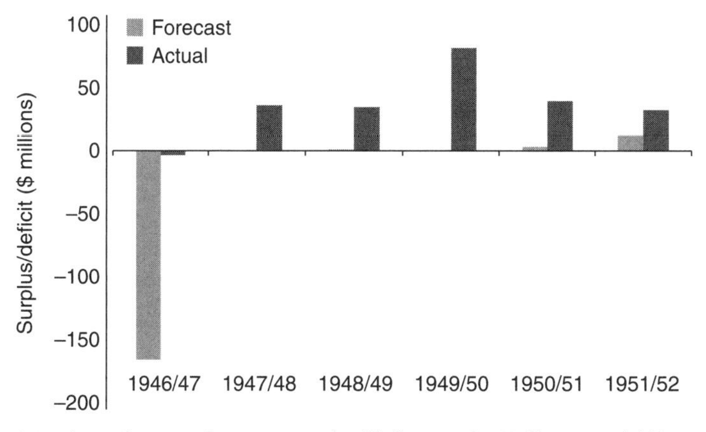

Figure 5.3. Actual versus forecast surplus/deficit under Follows, 1946/47–1951/52.

In 1948, aware that it was beginning to look as if there was spare money to spend, Follows raised the bar on the necessary target surplus by arguing that by 1950/51 it would be necessary to meet both recurrent and special expenditure from annual revenues, rather than using loans to cover reconstruction spending. It would not be the last time he would shift the goalposts.

DST&I FINANCES THE RECOVERY INVESTMENT

In fact, Follows was not really borrowing to any material extent to fund the reconstruction work. He had the authority to raise loans but had actually made little use of this. For the early post-war period the reconstruction work was marked as 'special expenditure' or 'public works extraordinary', and the capital expenditure paid for by government as it was incurred. The ability to do this was because Cowperthwaite's department, the DST&I, had very large cash balances due to receiving payment for supplies before having to pay for them itself. But Follows warned that this source of finance would not be available in the long term:

> It has been possible to utilise the large floating balances available on the Supplies, Trade & Industry Trading Account to finance capital expenditure. Unfortunately, these balances are not as large as they were and they will not always be available.[29]

FINANCIAL AUTONOMY

The financial position of the colony had improved much faster than had been expected. Local revenues covered expenditures, and indeed surpluses were being achieved. In June 1948 Grantham asked that the colony be released from Treasury control over its finances,[30] which initiated a round of discussions in London and Hong Kong. Grantham summarized the proposed new arrangements in a letter to the Colonial Office on 24 September 1948.[31] The Secretary of State would still need to approve the annual estimates, large investments and any new loans, but these were rather theoretical controls, and indeed the Hong Kong government would in practice further weaken the control that London had. At the Legislative Council of 20 October 1948 Grantham was able to report the new framework of financial independence that had been accepted by the UK government.

The administration had achieved one of its key strategic goals: financial autonomy. Despite almost all the senior civil servants being from Britain, Hong Kong would be managed primarily for the benefit of Hong Kong.

Follows took extended leave from the end of May until the end of November 1948. Accumulating several annual holidays into one longer break every few years was quite normal, dating from the times when the long sea passage home would make short breaks impractical. Clarke would act as financial secretary while Follows was away, and he was in Hong Kong at the announcement of Hong Kong's financial autonomy. Follows, while on leave, must have reflected on the success of the first three post-war years.

READY TO BE TESTED

In the midst of Hong Kong's post-war devastation, Follows had laid out a strategy that seemed ridiculously ambitious. And yet Hong Kong had built a new economy from the ashes. Follows had created the framework but he had then stood back and let the businesses and people of Hong Kong do the heavy lifting. He had set the goals of a rapid recovery and financial independence. He had constrained spending to a level that allowed low taxation and allowed the private sector to reinvest their profits. He had rejected borrowing and the running of a deficit. And he maintained an open economy, free to trade broadly without restrictions.

With that structure in place, the businesses of Hong Kong had rebuilt the entrepôt trade to a higher level than had existed before the war. There were other sectors that contributed too – a nascent industrial base and a tourist industry – but the key had been the rebuilding of trade.

It was a great achievement. But just as it seemed that Hong Kong was set to push trade further, external events would test the resilience of the colony's recovery.

CHAPTER 6

THE DECLINE OF THE ENTREPÔT TRADE

For over a century Hong Kong's main source of income had come from its role as an entrepôt between China and the rest of the world (Riedel 1974). It had been this that had pulled living standards above subsistence levels. Many of the economic activities in Hong Kong, such as banking, ship repairs and storage, depended on this flow of goods. Miraculously, the collapse in this trade during the war had been reversed and new levels of trade had been achieved. But external events would put all that progress at risk and require Hong Kong to adapt to changes that undermined its entire economic model.

CHINA AT WAR

The Chinese civil war between Nationalists and Communists had resumed after World War II, and by 1948 the Communists were gaining the upper hand. On the battlefield, the People's Liberation Army won a string of victories through 1948 and 1949, and in the Nationalist-inclined cities, hyperinflation and a devaluation of the currency against gold caused a loss of support among the middle classes.

As Follows presented the 1949 budget, the Communist forces were preparing to cross the Yangtze river before their final push on the Nationalist capital of Nanjing. Follows used that budget to underline the importance of being prudent. He believed it made sense to 'hope for the best, but prepare for the worst'. The upheaval in China created risks to trade and, therefore, to revenues. And expenditures would need to cover increased spending on security: both on policing and on defence.

He was proud that the reserves now stood at around $60 million. Given his concerns about the year ahead, he had taken counsel from the unofficial members as to whether to raise taxes just enough to balance the books or slightly more to help build the surplus further. It must have come as little surprise that they argued for the former. He therefore proposed a balanced budget, with no material surplus or deficit, achieved by some minor increases in duties and the like, with the proviso that if trade deteriorated, an emergency budget would be needed.

But Follows still cautioned that increased capital expenditure and salary costs could also threaten the balancing of the books. He argued that a fundamental assessment of what government departments were doing was needed and that pruning needed to occur.

The 1949 budget debate is perhaps best seen as laying down some markers for the future. For the previous few years, capital spending had been framed as war recovery spending. Now members could see that very large sums would be required on an ongoing basis to build a modern infrastructure. It would be expensive. The Unofficials were keen that such spending was not financed from additional general taxation, as was happening in the United Kingdom, believing that such taxes would damage the prosperity of the colony. But there were only three options available: finance capital spending from general taxes; finance capital spending from loans; or limit capital spending to that which could be raised in a low-tax environment. This was a debate that would run for many years.

CHINA TURNS COMMUNIST

While 1949 had looked very uncertain in advance, trade had in fact increased by nearly 40 per cent, and government revenues had been much stronger than expected, partly due to one-offs.[1] However, the challenges posed by disruption in China had not gone away.

When Canton fell to the Communist forces in October 1949, the civil war ended, with the Communists taking control of the mainland. This in turn created a wave of immigration to Hong Kong, with refugees living in very poor conditions throughout the colony. In May 1950 the flow had become so great that a quota on entry was introduced to try and match the inflow of people to the level of those leaving the colony (Endacott 1964a). By 1951 the population was nearly triple what it had been in 1945, standing at over 2 million, and people continued to come despite the government closing the border in 1951 (Oyen 2007). Uncertainty as to what would happen next was widespread.

In his 1950 budget Follows forecast a small deficit for the coming year, driven by increased spending, and Grantham argued that this had to be addressed by increasing taxation, despite the fact he still viewed tax 'as an evil':

> Government has decided that the gap should be bridged by increased taxation, but not to such an extent ... as will kill the goose that lays the golden eggs.[1]

Follows faced the tricky task of once again raising his forecasts for the previous year while simultaneously arguing that his forecast of a deficit for the next year was robust enough to justify raising taxes. For 1949/50 he predicted that revenues would fall by a quarter, producing a $7 million deficit. For many this seemed unduly conservative, so he argued that the previous year's revenues included $30 million of windfall gains. Follows knew that the credibility of his argument was weak so he decided to address the issue head on:

> It has been alleged in certain quarters, that for some unspecified ulterior motive, I deliberately under-estimate revenue and over-estimate expenditure. Anyone who takes the trouble to look up the figures will see straight away that the latter allegation is quite untrue because from 1947 onwards the final expenditure figure has consistently been slightly above the original estimate, though the variation has been comparatively small. The suggestion that revenue is deliberately underestimated is of course the type of criticism to which the result achieved this year is bound to give rise.

It was not a very strong argument.

The second string to his argument was once again to raise the bar by asserting that Hong Kong now needed not only to be financially independent but also to hold significant reserves, and Follows introduced a new objective of having a reserve equal to a year's revenues:

> It will no doubt be urged that there is no necessity to take such a step, and that the deficit could be met from surplus funds which we have gradually accumulated since the Colony was re-occupied. This, however, would not be sound finance. The Colony cannot be regarded as reasonably secure until it has reserves amounting to at least a year's revenue. Personally I consider that, in these troublous times, a reserve of one year's revenue is not enough.

Given these new objectives, Follows argued for the need to raise direct taxes, and he proposed that the standard rate of tax increase from 10 per cent to 15 per cent. The tax increases were expected to raise $12 million, closing the projected deficit.

The unofficial members reacted negatively. They doubted that the deficit would in fact occur, and argued that if it did there were better ways to meet it. A number argued that the cost of government was too high and several mentioned that an efficiency expert who had been employed the previous year had not yet delivered any real savings. Some raised the concern that the income taxes only affected around 100,000 of the 2 million population and it was therefore inequitable that all the burden should fall on this richer minority.

In his reply Follows argued that there was broad consensus on the expenditure plans, notwithstanding a general desire to find efficiencies. He also believed there was consensus to balance the books. He discussed alternative ways of raising taxes, including a head (or poll) tax that would ensure everyone contributed. He had rejected this because he believed there would always be large numbers unwilling or unable to pay, and it would not make sense to imprison them, making the tax effectively voluntary.

In closing the debate Grantham remarked that he did not view the Unofficials as some form of opposition but rather as partners who provided 'the spur where a spur is needed, or the check-rein where a check-rein is needed'.

At the next Legislative Council on 3 May 1950, Clarke, in his role as acting financial secretary, amended the proposed tax rate to 12.5 per cent instead of 15 per cent, and took up an idea that the Unofficials had raised of a business registration tax. This compromise was accepted and the rate of tax would remain at this level for many years to come.

THE KOREAN WAR CHALLENGES THE ENTREPÔT TRADE

Just as Hong Kong was struggling to adjust to the Communist victory in China, civil war broke out in Korea. At the end of World War II the Soviet Union had occupied Korea north of the 38th parallel, creating two governments: one in the north, supported by Russia and China, and one in the south, supported by the United States. The North, with support from China and the USSR, invaded the South on 25 June 1950. The North Korean forces advanced extremely quickly, rapidly destroying much of the South Korean army. On 27 June the United Nations called on North Korea to withdraw. With China's seat on the Security Council being held by the Taiwanese Republic of China, and with the Soviet Union boycotting the United Nations, the Security Council supported intervention against the North.

A coalition led by the United States quickly deployed a very large force, which by September numbered around 180,000 troops, the bulk of which were American.

These UN forces successfully pushed back the North Korean forces, recapturing Seoul at the end of September. The South, supported by the UN forces, then crossed the 38th parallel in pursuit of the retreating North Korean army. This breach of the 38th parallel caused China to intervene, with 200,000 Chinese troops entering Korea in late October. The scene was now set for a protracted struggle that would continue until July 1953.

In the autumn the United Nations placed an embargo on trade with China covering a wide range of strategic goods. In December the United States went further, effectively placing a complete ban on exporting goods to China or from re-exporting Chinese goods to the United States from the colony. Hong Kong's role as an entrepôt was in mortal danger, and in 1951 a visiting American journalist described Hong Kong as 'this dying city' (Endacott 1964a).

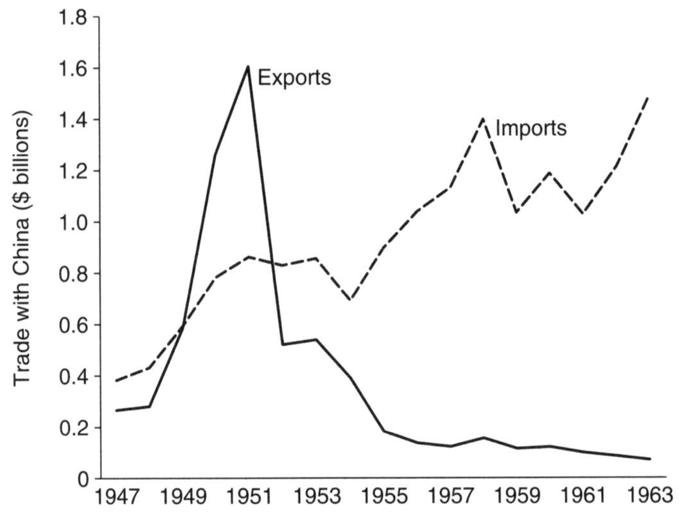

Figure 6.1. The collapse of Hong Kong's entrepôt role for China: Hong Kong's trade with China, 1947–1963. (*Source*: Hong Kong Statistics 1947–1963, Census and Statistic Department.)

Exports to China had grown to $1,604 million by 1951 (Szczepanik 1958). A year later this number had dropped to $520 million and by 1955 exports were only $182 million. Imports from China were steadier, at around $800 million, but this was mostly comprised of foodstuffs and essentials, most of which was consumed in the colony rather than exported. The entrepôt trade would remain subdued for years to come.

THE EMERGENCE OF INDUSTRY

Fortuitously, rather than decline, Hong Kong morphed from relying predominantly on trade to being an industrial powerhouse. The communist success in China had generated mass immigration into Hong Kong, and the immigrants were to prove skilled and hard working. At the same time, entrepreneurial manufacturers moved capital, equipment and themselves from nearby cities, in particular from Shanghai. Driven by the attraction of Hong Kong's property rights and its status as a safe haven, this group of industrialists would lay the foundations of Hong Kong's industrial growth, particularly in textiles. They would absorb the cheap labour that came from the mass migration.

In 1947 there were 972 factories in the colony, employing 51,000 people (Szczepanik 1958). By 1949 this had grown to 1,426 factories and 81,000 workers. By 1954, 2,494 factories would employ 115,000 people. By 1970, 17,000 factories would employ around 600,000 workers (Endacott 1964a). By 1955, textiles would employ around 30 per cent of these workers but would account for 60 per cent of Hong Kong's exports. A new industry that had started just after the war blossomed out of adversity. Capital would flow into the colony, and savings would be reinvested, as the market created a solution to the decline of the entrepôt role.

As early as 1948 Grantham had welcomed the progress made in manufacturing and industry, despite shortages of raw materials and machinery. New industries were starting up, which would in due course provide a critical manufacturing base for the colony:

> There were certain new developments, such as cotton spinning and plastics, and interest was evinced from Shanghai in the possibilities of Hong Kong as an alternative industrial area, in spite of certain comparative disadvantages, such as limited water supply, scarcity of suitable sites, and more stringent labour regulations.[2]

The growth of the industrial base had a significant effect on the role of Chinese businesses in the colony. Much of the entrepôt trade had been managed by, or at least involved, the great British trading houses, called the Hongs. Jardine Matheson, Swire & Sons, Dodwells, Inchcape, Booker and others had been central to the growth of Hong Kong before 1941. But they were badly affected by the Communist victory in China, which 'deprived Jardine Matheson and Swire's of most of their core business' (Jones 2000). The Hongs retreated and diversified their businesses into Australasia and South America and even into Europe, and their role in the industrialization of Hong Kong was minor. The great textile advance, for example, was led by Chinese families, using their own funds and investing their retained profits. They did use loans, but they did not generally look for outside investors, nor did they raise material funds via the stock exchange (Schenk 2001). This shift in the relative power of British and Chinese business enterprises would give the Chinese community and its leading businessmen an increasing influence over the years ahead.

While celebrating the growth of industry, the government did not consider taking a principal role in its development. By contrast, the UK government had been busy nationalizing key industries. Civil aviation was nationalized in 1946. Then coal, railways and road haulage in 1947. Electricity and gas in 1948, and steel in 1951. The UK government asserted that by taking the 'commanding heights' of industry into public ownership, these industries could be managed for efficiency and for the long term. They argued that, under private sector ownership, these businesses were under-invested, sub-scale and inefficient. Attlee's Labour government also believed that by having around 20 per cent of the economy owned by the state, the economy could be better planned and managed. Attlee was a strong believer in a planned economy, and argued that the nationalization programme was

> an essential part of a planned economy that we are introducing into this country. They are designed to help in promoting full employment, economic prosperity and justice for all. They are vital to the efficient working of the industrial and political machine of this country. They are the embodiment of our Socialist principle of placing the welfare of the nation before that of any section and of dealing with every problem in a practical and businesslike way.[3]

Where Hong Kong would look to the private sector and Adam Smith for its salvation, the United Kingdom turned to government planning and Karl Marx.

DST&I

Clarke, as acting financial secretary, gave an update at the Legislative Council of 3 May 1950 on the operations and accounting for the DST&I, now renamed the Department of Supplies and Distribution. He started by confirming the proposed reorganization of the department:

> It is now common knowledge that Government has taken the decision to terminate the existence of the Supplies and Distribution Department as a separate entity, and to amalgamate it with the Department of Commerce and Industry. The first step to this end has been taken by the appointment of one officer to be head of both departments. That officer happens to be myself.

He then promised that the accounts that Lowe, Bingham & Matthews were still compiling would be laid before the council as soon as possible. Clarke also took the opportunity to reinforce the message that the government would be extremely happy to exit the commercial arena:

> On the subject of Government trading generally, I can but repeat the words in Your Excellency's Despatch, that Government views its continuance without enthusiasm.

By December the accounts had still not been presented to the council, prompting Mr P. Cassidy to ask if they had been completed. Follows could only say that they had been, but that they were being revised because of disagreements as to how much was owed to the United Kingdom for military administration supplies.[4]

By the 1951 budget debate Follows had issued the accounts, and could reveal that the surplus held by the Department of Supplies and Distribution was over $67 million. He noted that while this seemed like a very large sum, it had been accumulated over several years.[5] He decided that $30 million of this surplus would be held as a fund to cushion any dramatic price rises in essential commodities such as rice. The rest would be used to create a development fund to pay for capital projects. With some other surpluses from trade with the government of Japan, this fund would start with around $55 million.

Despite this unexpectedly positive surplus, one Unofficial, Cassidy, was extremely critical of the way in which the department's accounts had been handled, and the lack of oversight that had been shown. He claimed that irregularities and negligence had occurred.[6] At the next Legislative Council Follows defended the way the accounts had been addressed. He gave his support to the executive officers involved, providing significant protection and support for Cowperthwaite. He pointed out that the staff had been thrown into a task for which they had neither the experience nor the training, but a task that nonetheless needed to be undertaken. Given that, Follows thought that:

> In the circumstances, I submit that the results reflect much credit on those who were responsible for the control of the department during this difficult period.[7]

FOLLOWS'S LAST BUDGET

By the time Follows delivered his last budget in early 1951 Hong Kong already seemed more stable, despite trade levels falling with the embargo. Government revenues were now predicted to be $70 million higher than forecast. Follows attempted to justify his earlier conservatism, initially by arguing that the forecasts had been appropriate at the time, when the outlook was very uncertain.[5]

As usual, he argued that there were several one-offs in the revenue numbers, and that there had been some unexpected benefits from local factors. In addition, he claimed that expenditure had also risen rapidly, but here he included $50 million that had previously been charged to a loan account for post-war reconstruction and instead treated it as expenditure in 1950/51. He noted that if this accounting change had not been made, then the revised estimate of expenditure would have been $200 million: very slightly below the original forecast.

Having attempted to explain the mis-forecasting that had led him to push for a rise in direct taxes, Follows attempted to play the conservative card again for 1951/52. He alluded to the US trade embargo and forecast that revenues would be $247 million, $27 million below his revised estimate for the current year. With forecast expenditure of $233 million, he saw a surplus of $13 million. He expected to pay some of this to the United Kingdom as a contribution to increased local defence costs.

Follows spent a considerable part of his summing up underlining the need to build up a significant reserve as a safeguard against a downturn:

> I should have been happier if, in relinquishing responsibility for the Colony's finances, I could have pointed to unappropriated reserves equivalent to one year's revenue or say $250 million, instead of the total of just under $180 million which has now been reached. I would therefore again stress the importance of building up our reserves still further.

The response from the Unofficials was predictable.[6] They all praised Follows's stewardship of the government finances since the end of the war and thanked him warmly for his work. With no tax increases proposed they were sanguine about the budget and took the opportunity to raise specific issues where they had expertise or interests. A number pointed to the very high percentage of the budget taken up by security spending, at well over 20 per cent of expenditure. But the most contentious issue surfaced when Chau Tsun-nin, the senior unofficial member, raised the issue of whether the tax increases of the previous year should be reversed given the expected surplus.

Follows replied on 28 March 1951, rejecting the call to change tax rates:

> I am sorry that two Honourable Members should have suggested that, because the financial position is satisfactory at the moment, we should take the opportunity to reduce our standard rate of tax to the former level of 10 per cent. Although the position at the moment may be satisfactory I think that these Honourable Members will agree that the future gives cause for concern.

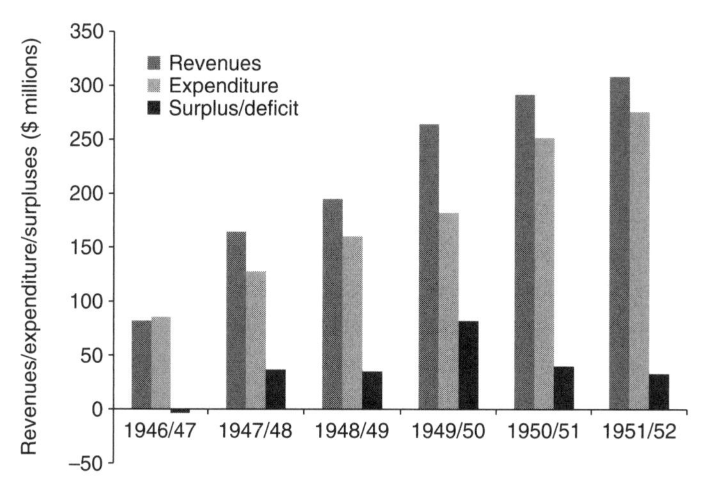

Figure 6.2. Government revenues, expenditures and surpluses under Follows, 1946/47–1951/52. (*Source*: Hong Kong Statistics 1947–67, Hong Kong estimates.)

FOLLOWS'S SELF-ASSESSMENT

Follows ended his budget with a review of his six years' tenure:

> For the first year, or rather eleven months, after the restoration of Civil Government, revenue amounted to only $82 million, and it failed by $3½ million to cover even our limited normal expenditure of those days.
>
> When Hong Kong was re-occupied, the only funds remaining at the disposal of the Colonial Government consisted of some holdings in our own pre-war loans and certain special funds totalling less than $2 million. We have since succeeded in accumulating surplus funds which will probably total something in the region of $178 million by the 31st of March. Moreover, in August 1945, the public debt amounted to $26¼ million. We have spent on the rehabilitation of the Colony in one way and another quite $200 million, but because this has been largely financed from our surpluses and new issues have been kept to a minimum, the public debt today has only risen by $38¾ million to the very low level of $65 million.
>
> These are remarkable figures and they have been rendered possible by the surprising resilience and recuperative powers which Hong Kong has always displayed throughout her history. But the credit for this rapid recovery must go to the commercial community for their resourcefulness and to our leading bankers for their faith in the future, and their readiness to take risks when they were called upon to finance the work of rehabilitation.

CHAPTER 6

THE FOLLOWS FOUNDATIONS

Shortly after the end of the 1951 budget season Follows started his retirement. He attended his last Legislative Council on 2 May 1951, and after that Arthur Clarke would attend as acting financial secretary and then as substantive financial secretary. Follows had indeed achieved a great deal in six years. He had made a number of fundamental choices that would establish the path for Hong Kong's prosperity.

A working administration had quickly been established, capable of raising revenue and spending on government priorities. This had been achieved in a previously occupied territory where little had been left of the pre-war infrastructure. The population had bounced back from its wartime low of around 600,000 and now stood at over 2 million.

Follows had decided to spend heavily on reconstruction. His initial plan forecast capital expenditures that greatly exceeded expected revenues, even though he was unsure how he would have raised the money. Some had proposed a more gradual approach, but his accelerated recovery had clearly worked. He set the goal of financial autonomy from London and achieved this much earlier than expected.

He had supported a limited role for government in commerce through the activities of Cowperthwaite's DST&I, but this was driven by necessity rather than choice. As these needs fell away, so did the government's activities. This was quite different from the increasingly active role played by the state in the United Kingdom and other Western nations. And as challenges from China and Korea, sanctions and immigration emerged, it was the business sector, not the government, that decided how to adapt. Follows took a path that was quite different from almost every other finance minister of that time. His aversion to government involvement in industry would work apart from in the banking sector, where his weak banking regulation would lead to problems in later years.

After the immediate post-war recovery period, Follows had underlined the need to balance the books – indeed, to run a surplus. Where Keynesian deficits prevailed elsewhere, Follows increased the bar as to how big a surplus and reserve he targeted. First he set the objective of meeting recurrent expenditure, then to meeting recurrent and capital expenditure, then to doing that and paying down recovery loans, then to building a reserve, and by the end of his period in office he argued that it was a requirement to hold a year's worth of revenues as a reserve.

He had also set the pattern of being conservative with the budget. Revenue forecasts were pitched at a level that looked fairly certain to be delivered, rather than at the expected level. And expenditure estimates were consistently above the level of actual spend. This conservatism delivered significant budget surpluses and would be adopted by his successors.

Follows's fiscal conservatism and his caution did not mean that he did not welcome a very significant rise in government expenditure. He was extremely pleased to have presided over a rapid and expensive recovery plan, and to have seen expenditures triple under his stewardship. But he was clear that he operated under constraints as to the optimal level of taxation, and he also believed that low taxation now would encourage investment and a higher tax take later.

AN UNSUNG HERO

Follows is in many ways the unsung member of the post-war financial secretaries who facilitated Hong Kong's economic rise. And yet he was central to establishing many of the key policy elements that Clarke and Cowperthwaite would maintain. Maybe his shorter tenure, combined with the need to construct the basic foundations, has caused his role to be underestimated. Perhaps it was also the fact that Clarke and Cowperthwaite were more comfortable discussing their broader philosophy that has caused Follows's role to be somewhat less prominent. But there can be little doubt that if Follows had pursued a different path in those post-war years, the future of Hong Kong would have been very different.

CHAPTER 7

DEPUTY FINANCIAL SECRETARY

COWPERTHWAITE WAS APPOINTED TO BE the acting deputy financial secretary on 4 April 1952, taking over from fellow Cadet Robert Marshall Hetherington DFC.[1] Once more he was working for Arthur Clarke, who had become acting financial secretary in May 1951 and was confirmed as financial secretary in February 1952. Clarke had clearly come to respect Cowperthwaite when they worked together at the Department of Commerce and Industry. Cowperthwaite would now spend the next two decades at the heart of economic and financial policy in Hong Kong.

ARTHUR CLARKE

Born in Athlone, Ireland in 1906, Arthur Grenfell Clarke was educated at Mountjoy School in Dublin and then at Trinity College, Dublin. He too was a Cadet, joining the service in 1929 and arriving in Hong Kong in 1930. During the 1930s he had worked in the Department for Chinese Affairs, the secretariat and the Department for Imports and Exports. He became Assistant Commissioner of War Taxation in July 1940 and then Commissioner of War Taxation in October 1940, just before the Japanese invasion.[2]

Interned during the Japanese occupation, he was on leave for a year after the war. He returned to Hong Kong in September 1946 to act briefly as Estate Duty Commissioner before being appointed as Assistant Financial Director (Exchange Control) in January 1947 and then deputy financial secretary, under Sir Geoffrey Follows, on

1 April 1948. He would hold this post until 1951 (Ure 2012), when he took over as financial secretary. Alongside these roles he was also appointed as Director of Commerce and Industry in February 1950 and as Director of Supplies and Distribution in March 1950, where he worked closely with Cowperthwaite.

In practice, Clarke took over when Follows went on leave on 12 May 1951, but he was designated acting financial secretary because Follows had accumulated 446 days of leave and so was theoretically in post until that had been taken.[3] The governor obtained agreement that Clarke's promotion to substantive financial secretary occur somewhat earlier. Clarke would be paid $2,533 per month, with generous travel, accommodation, pension and holiday provision. Cowperthwaite would be paid $1,650 per month.[*4]

THE PAINLESS BUDGET

Cowperthwaite was appointed just as Clarke presented the 1952 budget. At the Legislative Council of 5 March 1952, Grantham described the deteriorating economic situation,[5] observing that Hong Kong's prosperity now depended both on the entrepôt trade and on the emerging industrial base, both of which faced significant issues. Trade was down as a result of the United Nations embargo on the export of strategic and semi-strategic materials to China, and because the United States had imposed further restrictions against China, Hong Kong and Macau.

To make matters worse, Japanese manufacturers were increasingly competitive. Despite calls for protectionism, or negotiating a quota deal with Japan, Grantham believed this problem could only be addressed by improving efficiency:

> It is no good talking about putting up a tariff barrier round Hong Kong to keep out goods from other countries which can be produced more cheaply than our factories can do, because the real threat is in our export markets. The cure lies largely with our industrialists themselves in improving their efficiency.[5]

Despite these headwinds, Grantham noted that government revenues had exceeded expectations, and although expenditure was ahead of plan, there was still a substantial surplus. He highlighted the investments made in housing, education and welfare, which he believed should continue despite the poor economic environment and the flow of refugees into the colony.

---

* Inflated by the retail prices index this would be equivalent to £53,000 and £35,000 per annum today. Or if adjusted by average earnings, £140,000 and £90,000 per annum.

Clarke then went through the numbers in great detail. As had become routine with Follows, Clarke could report that past estimates and forecasts had been exceeded. For the year just ending, 1951/52, a healthy surplus was now expected. Despite expenditure being $51 million higher than the original forecast, revenues were expected to be $84 million ahead. In fact, all this supposed expenditure overspend was due to a change in the accounting treatment of the loan account, so the conservatism of the Financial Department was alive and well.

For 1952/53 Clarke forecast a deficit of $45,000. Clarke made much of the challenges that lay ahead in achieving the planned level of revenues and also pointed out that the Department of Commerce and Industry's surplus would dry up as it ceased trading. This had contributed $21 million in 1950/51, which had been credited to the development fund. He underlined the very heavy expenditures in the plan, including education, housing, defence and the like. Perhaps to emphasize how much the government was doing, he went through each area of spending in some detail and pointed out many individual projects, ranging from a new abattoir to a new airport.

He argued that spending would need to be met from taxation. For now the growth in the tax base and greater effectiveness at collecting taxes could provide the funds, but he had little doubt that eventually tax rates would need to rise, or new revenue sources would need to be found. However, he was not yet proposing increasing the main tax rates, leading to the budget being described in the press as 'painless'.

Given that, the Unofficials praised Clarke's maiden budget at the next Legislative Council.[6] Chau Tsun-nin, for example, accepted the 'grim reality of our declining trade and the new, intensified competition from Japan' while making clear his opposition to further 'crippling' tax rises.

The third and final Legislative Council discussion on the budget took place on 27 March, having been moved back a day because of a clash with a horse racing event. Budget adjustments meant that Clarke now forecast a small deficit of $4 million and he proposed some minor tax increases.[7] It was a symbolic move to signal his determination not to run a deficit and a continuity of economic philosophy.

Later in the year Clarke proposed that the colony gift $8 million to Britain, in addition to the $16 million budgeted contribution, to defray the cost of having had to strengthen the garrison and the defence of Hong Kong.[8]

THE 1953 BUDGET

Cowperthwaite was more heavily involved in the preparations for the 1953 budget that Clarke presented on 4 March 1953. In his address to the Legislative Council, the governor noted that trade had been badly hit in the first half of 1952 but had then stabilized.[9] Government finances were even stronger than previously estimated, but Grantham downplayed their health. He spoke proudly of the progress that had been made in education, health and housing. In education, for example, there were now more than 1,000 schools with around 9,000 teachers. Pupil numbers stood at 200,000: about double the level in 1948.

Clarke followed and, noting that revenues for 1952/53 had been well ahead of forecast, he predicted a surplus of $65 million. Clarke went on to argue that there were several one-offs and non-repeatable elements in the revenue numbers. But there was no hiding the fact that the numbers looked much better than had been estimated a year earlier, so Clarke moved the goalposts. Instead of needing to run a surplus, he proposed that there was a need to build a significant reserve, as had been suggested by Follows, in a Revenue Equalization Fund, 'for the purpose of meeting any serious shortage of revenue for a particular year, or for meeting any non-recurrent increase in expenditure in any particular year'.[9]

He proposed building up the fund to 'the level of one year's revenue', starting with a $100 million contribution straight away. On this basis the substantial surplus for the year just passed could now be considered as barely adequate. For 1953/54 Clarke forecast that revenues would total $349 million and expenditure $328 million, producing a surplus of $20 million. Clarke viewed this as satisfactory, and was once more able to avoid raising tax rates. However, he made clear that he believed that tax rises would be inevitable if services continued to grow.

The budget was well received and the Unofficials showered compliments on the governor and the financial secretary.[10] The Revenue Equalization Fund was welcomed, to ensure that public services continued to grow at a steady pace. The target of running continuing surpluses was not explicitly drawn out but was implicitly accepted.

In the wrap-up debate on 26 March, Clarke took some time to describe his approach to government budgeting, and how the demand for services and the preference for low tax might be managed in the future.[11]

> Government does not work upon a business basis; it does not produce a profit and loss account. Government acts for the people it governs and Government, if it is to be worthy of the name, must provide the services which are necessary if the life of an organized community is to proceed in an orderly manner. If that is accepted, then it follows that Government has to find sufficient money to provide for these services.
>
> Taxation in this Colony is still comparatively light, and for so long as that happy state of affairs prevails the principle we are adopting in budgeting is that Government will provide the services demanded, as economically as possible, and then will find the money to pay for these services.

> At some stage in the future we shall reach the point where the provision of more services for a section of the community will mean hardship on another section by way of unduly heavy taxation. Then we shall have to change over to the alternative method of adjusting our expenditure to available revenue.

COWPERTHWAITE'S DEBUT LEGISLATIVE COUNCIL

Clarke had accumulated enough holiday entitlement to be away on leave from 24 April 1953 to 25 December 1953,[12] and Cowperthwaite acted as financial secretary during his absence. Cowperthwaite attended his first Legislative Council on 29 April 1953, standing in for Clarke.[13] It was a brief meeting and he did not speak.

When he attended again on 20 May 1953, he was busier, proposing three resolutions.[14] The first was a change to the Revenue Reward Fund, which provided rewards for information leading to the seizure of contraband; the second dealt with who should approve gifts of surplus government stock; and the third dealt with abandoned claims and write-offs. He attended the ceremonial Legislative Council of 2 June 1953 to celebrate the coronation of Queen Elizabeth II, that same day, and to hear the governor mark the occasion with a Loyal Address.

At the meeting of 26 August 1953 he introduced three bills – the first time that he introduced legislation himself.[15] The Fire and Marine Insurance Companies Deposit (Amendment) Bill made changes to the requirements to operate an insurance company in the colony. Insurers could either lodge a deposit as they had historically done or they could avoid doing so if they were licensed as solvent under the UK regulations. Similar changes required a Life Assurance Companies (Amendment) Bill to be tabled. On a separate theme he also tabled the Police Officers (Special Cases) Pensions Bill, which made whole the pensions of police officers who had transferred from the United Kingdom to the colony in the immediate post-war period. All bills were seconded and agreed without debate.

Cowperthwaite introduced a further bill, the Hongkong and Shanghai Banking Corporation (Amendment) Bill, at the 9 September session. At the 23 September session he introduced the Business Regulation (Amendment) Bill and the Official Signatures Fees (Amendment) Bill. At the 7 October meeting Cowperthwaite introduced a resolution to deal with the adjustments to the budget – the Supplementary Provisions for the Quarter ended on 31 March 1953. Again it was agreed without debate. On 21 October he tabled the Telephone Ordinance to agree the rates that could be charged by the telephone company for calls to a new exchange that they planned to open. At the next few meetings he dealt with loan provisioning, supplementary estimates updates and further pension issues.

Clarke returned to attend the Legislative Council of 31 December 1953. Cowperthwaite must have been pleased that he had arrived at the top table, if only on an acting basis. He had attended seventeen Legislative Councils (from 29 April to 16 December), dealt with several resolutions and introduced six bills. All had gone smoothly. He had spoken sparsely, and factually, with little of the emphasis and colour that he would later use. No doubt he was keen to be seen as quietly competent rather than too controversial or too forward. That could wait until later.

THE SHEK KIP MEI DISASTER

The meeting of 31 December was a watershed, preoccupied as it was by the disaster at Shek Kip Mei. A shanty town occupied by immigrants from the mainland had been destroyed by a major fire on Christmas day 1953. More than 50,000 people were left homeless and needed emergency help. More generally, the fire showed the dangerous conditions in which many refugees and residents were living. The governor expressed his sympathy for those involved and described the difficulties involved in rehousing such a large number of people.

Grantham could see that the private sector had not created the housing that was needed for the very large inflow of migrants. At this stage he did not try to analyse whether that was due to a lack of capital, a lack of land, poor skills, shabby construction or one of many other proposed explanations. For now he committed the government itself to rebuild on the existing site, with better utilities and fireproofing, and to drive a programme of constructing multistorey buildings to provide basic housing. He anticipated that it would be costly but decided that it needed to be done. The specifics could come later.

The Shek Kip Mei site itself was cleared and in due course would be used to build the Shek Kip Mei housing estate. The new apartments were functional and extremely small but they had the benefit of modest levels of rent and sound construction.

COWPERTHWAITE TO THE UNITED STATES

For most of 1954 Cowperthwaite would be away from Hong Kong. On 11 February 1954 he went on leave. He travelled first to Singapore and then took the SS Benmacdhui from Singapore to London, arriving on 27 March 1954 with his wife, Sheila, and their nine-year-old son.

Between 29 August and 12 December Cowperthwaite was attached to the British embassy in Washington to ensure that the embassy had a good understanding of Hong Kong's trade position in dealing with America and various trade organizations. In addition, Governor Grantham had agreed to do a series of lectures across the United States. The objective was to increase awareness of Hong Kong in the United States and to improve its reputation. Hong Kong had been seen as providing a route to circumvent America's sanctions on China. Grantham arrived in New York on the Queen Mary and opened his lecture tour with a speech entitled 'Hong Kong; its importance to the free world' at Cornell on 27 September 1954. Speeches followed in New York, Washington, Baltimore, Boston, Detroit, Los Angeles, San Francisco and Kansas City.[16] Grantham later wrote that he wanted to create a favourable impression of the colony and to destroy false impressions. He tried to portray Hong Kong as a 'bastion of freedom', or 'the Berlin of the East' (Grantham 2012).

Grantham was at home in America, in part because he had married an American, Maurine, and in part because he had made many American friends in Hong Kong. The United States kept an important official presence in Hong Kong, with more staff in its consulate there than anywhere else in the world. Rumours abounded that this was due to a very significant intelligence effort focused on China. Officially, many regional offices were in Hong Kong. Either way, the US governmental links with Hong Kong were strong, and in Washington the Granthams were guests at an official dinner at the State Department and had lunch on board the yacht of the Secretary of the Navy.[17] On his return to Hong Kong Grantham gave a report to the Legislative Council of 17 November about his tour, highlighting the successes that he felt had occurred. Cowperthwaite returned to his duties in Hong Kong on 16 December 1954.

THE 1954 BUDGET

While Cowperthwaite was away, the normal budget cycle continued. At the Legislative Council of 3 March 1954, the governor reiterated the government's commitment to free trade, even going so far as to say that 'if it were not for our obligations to the United Nations, the sterling area and the International Monetary Fund we should not have any trade controls at all'. Given stagnant trade it was fortunate that industry had developed to fill the gap:

> We were all at one time too ready to think of Hong Kong only as an entrepôt and to say that industry could never really prosper. That attitude of mind is changing, largely no doubt as a result of the realization that if it were not for the exports of our factories

> we should be even more in the economic doldrums than we already are. The export of Hong Kong products accounts for nearly 30% of all our exports.

Given Shek Kip Mei, Grantham emphasized the government's attempts to provide much better housing for the majority of residents. Work to establish a housing authority that would build, own and rent properties was under way. But the government was very aware of the potentially negative effects of its involvement in the sector:

> One thing we should bear in mind is that low cost housing either by the Housing Authority or by other organizations which receive financial aid from Government, whether by direct grant or by loan, is subsidized housing. This means that it will compete with private low cost housing. We do not want to get to the stage where subsidized housing will kill private housing.

Grantham covered initiatives in many other areas, noting successes and sketching out what more was being done. Financing these improvements was never far from his mind. He was very aware that building a school or a hospital was only part of the equation; after that, funds were needed to run it. This distinction between capital expenditure and recurrent expenditure was an ongoing concern, and not just the first-order issue of capital spending increasing recurrent spending but also the second-order issue that increased recurrent spending limited the ability to embark on future capital spending:

> Wouldn't it be wonderful if a fairy godmother were to wave a wand and give us all the money we needed? But that wouldn't be enough for we should then have to have a considerably increased staff to build the hospitals, and the schools and the houses and everything.

Clarke again upgraded his forecasts for the previous year and had to admit that 'it cannot be argued that the financial position of the Colony at the commencement of this year could be regarded as other than sound'. For the current year, 1953/54, revenues were forecast to be $389 million and expenditure $385 million.[18] There were no major changes in the shape of either expenditures or revenues.

For the first time Clarke had constructed a five-year forecast, and he was concerned that it suggested that revenues might grow more slowly in the future and be outstripped by expenditure. For the five years from 1953/54 he forecast that revenues would total $1,830 million and expenditure $1,963 million: a deficit over the five years of $133 million. Capital works cost a further $301 million, producing an estimated deficit of $434 million. Clarke warned that this must be funded from revenue, and probably from increased taxation. But for now he was happy to leave this as a warning shot, and he once more held tax rates stable.

Clarke knew he could hardly push through tax increases with the background of surpluses coming in each year. If he needed any reminding, the senior Unofficial, Dr Chau Sik-nin, chided him gently at the next Legislative Council:

> I do not, however, share his pessimism for the future, but as this trait appears to be traditional in post-war holders of our purse strings, we accept it with respect in the knowledge that it is infinitely better to be conservative these days than otherwise.[19]

The idea of using loans rather than increased taxes had also been raised, and Clarke was keen to shoot down this idea. He accepted that loans would lead to future generations bearing part of the costs and that there was an argument that this was fair since they would also share the benefits. But he was doubtful about this line of reasoning. What if investments that were made were made redundant by future technologies? Why not use the colony's reserves and leave future generations the task of replenishing them? What about the other needs that future generations were being left to sort out?

SETTING UP THE HOUSING EFFORTS

In April, a few months after the disaster at Shek Kip Mei, the government started to lay out its new housing policy. A Housing Bill was debated at the Legislative Councils of 7 and 28 April 1954, and a housing authority was set up. The authority would be given land sites at an advantageous price and would be required to build low-cost blocks of flats.[20] The government was very keen to ensure that anything other than the most basic units would be provided for by the private sector. They were also keen that the tenants pay a level of rent that would return the government's investment along with a modest interest charge.

Some doubted whether the government was wise to take on the task of dealing with an estimated 600,000 people, plus however many more might come to the colony in the future, and they wondered if the government really had the ability to run such a programme. But in the end the bill was passed. A resettlement bill strengthened the government's ability to move squatters into new developments, and to enforce safety regulations in shanty towns.[21]

Over the years ahead, the government's housing programme would be very substantial; it would go too fast for some and much too slowly for others. But the strategy had been set for the government to make a massive intervention in the housing market, quite at odds with its approach in almost every other sector. The officials convinced themselves that the government alone could orchestrate this huge programme of entry-level housing.

These low-cost housing units were very basic. In the early buildings a family of five would get only 120 square feet and a family of three 86 square feet. The walls were bare concrete. Communal toilets and bathrooms were situated in the centre of each floor (Tu 2003). But the rent was low and the buildings were regulated. Demand was high and soon there were long waiting lists to get into the programme. Even today these waiting lists remain, and the rent for government housing is well below private rent levels.

THE 1955 BUDGET

Shortly after his return from the United States Cowperthwaite resumed the role of acting deputy financial secretary with effect from 14 January 1955, taking over from Christopher Melmoth. He was back working with Clarke for the 1955 budget.

Introducing that budget, Grantham observed that trade had continued to fall, with 1954 trade levels being 11 per cent below the 1953 level,[22] but fortunately industrial development had continued.

The issue of the housing and resettlement of squatters was very much to the fore again, with the Urban Council fleshing out its plan for a substantial programme of constructing low-cost, multistorey housing, built by the government, which would then act as landlord. The investment was designed to be repaid with a 3.5 per cent compound interest over a forty-year period. This paralleled the government's policy in other areas such as water supplies, which was to charge a rate that covered commercial costs and provided a base return on investment without attempting to make a profit from the provision of a vital service.

Clarke started by summarizing the trading operations of the DST&I since the war.[22] He acknowledged the accounting difficulties but was keen to emphasize how valuable the activities had been. He revised upwards the surplus that had been achieved since the war:

> To the 31st March, 1950, it appeared that a total profit of $67.8 millions had accrued from trading in rice, coal, firewood, meat, certain other commodities, and from the financing of trade with Japan. During the year 1950/51 there was a further profit of $21.7 millions; in 1951/52 $15.4 millions; and in 1952/53 $3.5 millions. For the last financial year 1953/54 there was a loss of $12.9 millions. Over the whole period since the war there has therefore been a net profit of over $95 millions.

What he did not mention was how important the cash balances had been to funding Hong Kong's recovery.

As usual Clarke raised the estimated surplus for 1954/55, and he expected that to rise substantially as the numbers were finalized. Given that, he felt he could describe the financial position as 'fairly secure', not least because he declared reserves were 'approximating to, and possibly exceeding, one year's revenue'.

For 1955/56 Clarke forecast a deficit of $32 million, mostly due to non-recurrent public works. However, Clarke emphasized how quickly general spending had been growing, and how expectations for services such as education would continue to grow. Like a broken record he warned again that increased spending might lead to increased taxes in the future. Once again, however, he chose not to fight that battle yet.

Clarke announced that he had abandoned the exercise of producing a five-year plan given the inability to forecast either revenues or the need for additional expenditure, as had occurred after Shek Kip Mei. However, in place of a plan Clarke then spoke, for the first time and at length, about his economic philosophy. He started by arguing that 'the Colony's financial position is I think, governed by the Colony's economic position'.

Given the primacy of the economy, he then discussed how this had evolved since he had first come to Hong Kong twenty-five years earlier, when the key activity was as an entrepôt for Chinese trade. What industry there was then, such as the dockyards, supported trade. The economy ebbed and flowed with world trade, and there was nothing that the government could do to influence that. But that changed:

> The introduction of the principle of Imperial Preference as a result of the Ottawa Agreement* coincided broadly with the commencement of the Sino-Japanese 'Incident', which brought an influx of labour into the Colony. Businessmen with vision and foresight saw what this might mean. They realized that if they established factories here they would have to import all their raw materials; that even the power which they required would have to be imported; but they started industrial development in the faith that with the two advantages of a preferential tariff and abundant labour they could compete, at least in the Commonwealth, with manufacturers elsewhere. In 1954, no less than thirty per cent of our exports, by value, was accounted for by local

* Imperial Preference was a system of reciprocal trade agreements between the parts of the British Empire (and later, as Commonwealth Preference, between members of the Commonwealth). Being a member allowed Hong Kong to export goods to the United Kingdom and to other member countries free of tariffs.

> manufactures, and I think it is probable that this trade is now the largest contributor to our national income.

In that context Clarke turned to the issue of what the government could do to help the economy. He started by looking at what could be done to ensure capital was available:

> We can do little to encourage capital to come here or to remain here, apart from two things; firstly, to place as few restrictions as possible on its movement; and secondly, to allow it to have as good a return as possible by keeping the rate of tax on profits low.

On the issue of growing trade he saw no material role for the government, arguing that growth depended on the skills of Hong Kong's merchants and banks. For industrial development Clarke saw some limited levers available to government, in particular the provision of competitively priced land and support in promoting trade.

Clarke summarized his approach as follows:

> If we look after the Colony's economy, revenue will look after itself, provided our tax collecting methods are efficient. If we can do something constructive to help the Colony's economy, we shall automatically increase our revenue. Any considerable increase, I say deliberately 'considerable increase', in the rate of direct taxation at a time when the economy is strained might well in the end bring about a reduction of revenue rather than an increase. Until we are reasonably sure that our economy is on a sound basis, our proper course seems to be to limit our non-productive expenditure as far as possible, but not to hesitate to draw on our reserves for sound economic projects if we have to do so.

No doubt with support from Cowperthwaite, Clarke had for the first time articulated a very classical view of the limited role for government, and its reliance on the private sector to create wealth. Before its time, and certainly at odds with most Western governments, Clarke believed that his job was to look after the supply side of the economy. He was signing up for a low-tax, high-growth model of development.

SAVED BY INDUSTRY

In July 1955 Governor Grantham wrote to the Secretary of State for the Colonies summarizing the growth of Hong Kong's industrial base.[23] He described the lack of industrial development before World War II and the limited growth post-war because of a scarcity of raw materials. But the collapse in entrepôt trading activities, had fortunately coincided with a surge in industrial development, in particular in textiles, driven by the influx of labour and capital.

Grantham noted that industrial growth had come despite the lack of land and water, costly energy supplies and a tiny internal market. While there were 1,160 factories employing 60,000 people in 1948, by 1955 these numbers had doubled. This growth had led to several countries proposing tariffs against Hong Kong goods, and Grantham tried to quash arguments that the growth was due to trademark infringements, unfairly low wages or the re-exporting of Japanese goods. He was particularly keen to highlight that immigration required economic growth, which in turn necessitated industrialization:

> Industrialization had been Hong Kong's economic salvation in the last four years. It has provided for at least a bare subsistence for the swollen population and now represents a more important part of the Colony's livelihood than does its traditional entrepôt trade. The population is now increasing naturally at about 65,000 a year. There is almost no possibility of emigration, except return to the Chinese mainland. The UN High Commissioner for Refugees concluded that the only practicable solution at the moment lay in integration of the refugees into the economy of the Colony. In such a context 'economy' can only mean industry.

WHAT ABOUT LANCASHIRE?

The Conservative prime minister of the time, Harold Macmillan, was copied on Grantham's report and scrawled on it a note for the Chancellor of the Exchequer and the President of the Board of Trade:

> That is alright for Hong Kong, but what about Lancashire? This problem will have to be tackled some day.[24]

Lancashire was the centre for cotton manufacturing in the United Kingdom and it reacted strongly against the increasing competition from the Far East. In late 1955 the director of the Federation of Master Cotton Spinners' Associations visited the colony and on his return to the United Kingdom argued for restricting imports from Hong Kong, India and Pakistan. Sir Cuthbert Clegg led a mission from the UK Cotton Board in early 1957 proposing that Hong Kong volunteer to suspend shipments of manufactured cotton goods to the United Kingdom. Oddly enough, the Hong Kong Cotton Spinners' Association and the Chinese Manufacturers' Association demurred. Lancashire MPs, the UK press and even the UK government sought to isolate Hong Kong and get them to acquiesce. The stage was set for a bitter struggle.

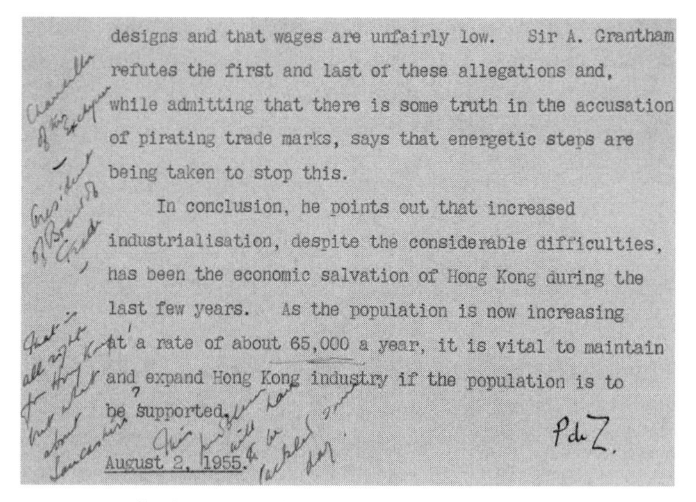
designs and that wages are unfairly low. Sir A. Grantham refutes the first and last of these allegations and, while admitting that there is some truth in the accusation of pirating trade marks, says that energetic steps are being taken to stop this.

In conclusion, he points out that increased industrialisation, despite the considerable difficulties, has been the economic salvation of Hong Kong during the last few years. As the population is now increasing at a rate of about 65,000 a year, it is vital to maintain and expand Hong Kong industry if the population is to be supported.

August 2, 1955.

Figure 7.1. Macmillan's note: 'What about Lancashire?' (The National Archives).

While the United Kingdom argued it was pro-free trade in theory, in practice it wanted to protect jobs in the United Kingdom. With Imperial Preference, and as a member of the General Agreement on Tariffs and Trade, it could not enact protectionist measures without breaking previous agreements. The search for a voluntary brake on Hong Kong's exports was the best option available to maintain the fiction of being pro-free trade while dealing with the very real political issue of managing the decline of the UK textile industry.

Unsurprisingly, the US government was under similar political pressure from its textile industry, and as Hong Kong had more success it would face a more challenging trading environment going forward.

COWPERTHWAITE KEEPS HIS HEAD DOWN

While these trends emerged, Cowperthwaite focused on the task in hand. He spent the rest of the year in part as deputy financial secretary and in part as deputy financial secretary (economics). These were the two deputy jobs that reported to the financial secretary.

In October 1955 Cowperthwaite was acting financial secretary and attended the Legislative Councils of 12 October and 26 October. He introduced an order on company fees[25] and updated government spending budgets through supplementary provisions.[26]

Cowperthwaite was the diligent deputy, working in the background. But he was gaining a very broad understanding of the financial and economic issues that Hong Kong faced. In due course he would draw heavily on this period of apprenticeship.

CHAPTER 8

WINNER'S DOUBTS

STABILITY AND PROSPERITY

HONG KONG HAD SUCCESSFULLY REBUILT its post-war economy, navigated through the decline of the entrepôt trade and grown a significant industrial base. While there were complaints in the developed markets about the impact of Hong Kong's exports on local jobs, these were contained. The population continued to grow, but at a more controlled rate, increasing from around 2.5 million in 1955 to 3.2 million by 1961. Immigration was more manageable, and this gave the government some space to catch up on the provision of housing, education and health care.

Over the next six budgets, between 1956 and 1962, Clarke and Cowperthwaite would preside over this period of greater stability and, in turn, growing levels of government revenue and expenditure. For Clarke this success would make him increasingly concerned about maintaining spending based on the success of the private sector. For Cowperthwaite it would confirm that the government should limit its role and trust the market to allocate resources for the benefit of all.

Between 1952/53 and 1961/62 government revenues nearly tripled from, $384 million to $1,030 million: a growth rate of around 12 per cent per annum. But whereas revenues grew by 7 per cent annually between 1952/53 and 1956/57, they grew by 15 per cent per year between 1957/58 and 1961/62. Having weathered the less plentiful early years, revenues were strong through Clarke's later years. Earnings and profits tax grew at around 7 per cent annually, with revenues from land sales growing much faster.

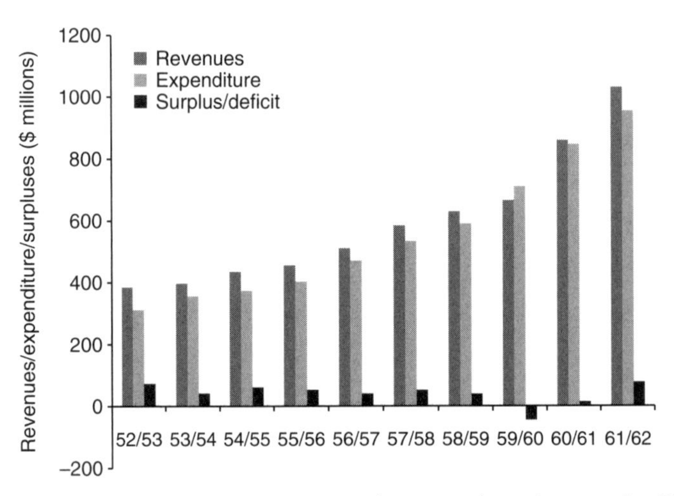

Figure 8.1. Government revenues, expenditures and surpluses under Clarke, 1952/53–1961/62. (*Source*: Hong Kong Statistics 1947–67, Hong Kong estimates.)

The growth in expenditure slightly outstripped the growth in revenues. In 1952/53 spending was $312 million, and this had tripled by 1961/62 to $953 million, an annual growth rate of 13 per cent. Despite this, revenues had exceed expenditure in every year but one, producing a run of surpluses.

CONTINUED FORECASTING CONSERVATISM

Throughout his period in office Clarke's worrying forecast deficits for the year ahead became rosier estimates a year later, with further improvements by the time the final outcome was calculated. He was aware that this pattern was getting predictable. For example, when in 1956/57 he estimated a deficit of $43 million based on a major rise in spending of nearly 18 per cent,[1] he observed that his record of conservative estimating might lead some to doubt this forecast:

> Seeing that this year we budgeted for a deficit of over $35 millions, and now expect a surplus of over $16 millions, I imagine that there will be a distinct tendency to regard the estimated deficit with some degree of complacency, if not scepticism, and I need hardly say that I trust that such scepticism will be justified.

Over his ten budgets, the actual out-turn would always be better than the original forccast.

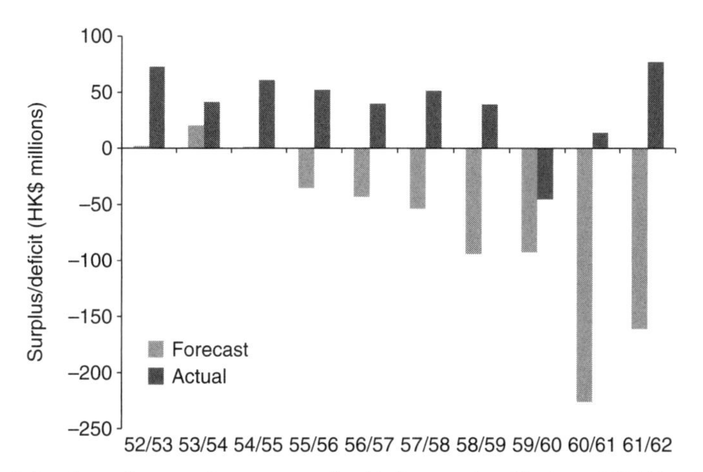

Figure 8.2. Actual versus forecast surplus/deficit under Clarke, 1952/53–1961/62.

The source of this underestimation was a conservative forecasting of revenues and usually an underspending on capital projects. There was almost always some economic black cloud on the horizon and in that context being bullish about the economy and therefore revenues would have been brave. And yet each year the challenges were somehow less severe than expected, and they were met with unpredicted success.

SPLITTING RECURRENT AND CAPITAL SPENDING

Clarke pushed hard to separate capital spending from recurring costs. He saw it as critical that current revenues should cover current costs, and without identifying capital spend this was hard to assess. Clarke could see that some very major items, such as the reservoir and the airport, would be lumpy capital expenditures, and it would be more transparent if capital spending was more clearly identified. This would highlight future choices when capital spending could not be covered by ongoing revenues:

> The position seems to be that, when we have a substantial reserve in hand, and for so long as we are able to meet all our commitments from revenue, we have no real cause for concern. When we find that we cannot pay for all our commitments from revenue, then we must look to financing our capital expenditure from our reserves, or by borrowing, or by increasing taxation, in that order of priority.[1]

In the 1957 budget Clarke started to clearly distinguish between ongoing recurrent expenditure and capital non-recurring public works:

> We are now giving consideration to proposals that for future years we should confine the Budget merely to recurrent revenue and to recurrent expenditure; capital receipts and capital expenditure being dealt with in the form of a Capital Budget.
>
> If this system were to be adopted for the present Budget, then the whole bill for Public Works Non-Recurrent would probably be taken out of the Budget and transferred to Capital Expenditure. Receipts which might also be considered as non-recurrent would similarly be transferred to the Capital Budget, but the net result undoubtedly would be that we should have a substantial surplus on our recurrent Budget.[2]

To emphasize the conceptual line that he was increasingly drawing between recurrent and non-recurrent spending, Clarke included a new schedule in the 1958 budget pack drawing out these numbers:

> The fundamental purpose of capital and recurrent budgets is, I imagine, to make it clear, both to Members of this Council, and to the Secretary of State, how far recurrent revenue is adequate to meet recurrent commitments, present and future, whilst at the same time meeting at least a proportion of capital costs.[3]

COWPERTHWAITE BROADENS HIS ROLE

In the mid 1950s Cowperthwaite had become Clarke's clear deputy and he had an increasingly broad remit. He would often cover both deputy financial secretary roles: the economic brief and the financial brief. Throughout most of 1956 he acted as Director of Commerce and Industry. In recognition of his responsibilities he was promoted from Cadet Officer Class II to Staff Grade in November 1956, putting him in the top dozen or so Cadets in Hong Kong in terms of rank.[4] When, in 1959, the Staff Grade was split into three subgrades (A, B and C) and renamed, he was appointed as an Administrative Officer, Staff Grade A, on a salary of $5,900 per month.*

---

* Approximately £95,000 per annum now if adjusted for inflation, or £210,000 adjusted for average wage growth.

THE SUEZ CRISIS AND ITS LONG-TERM EFFECTS ON HONG KONG

Introducing the 1956 budget Grantham emphasized the 'formidable tasks ahead' for Hong Kong in growing trade and industry.[5] He saw the pressure from immigration as being problematic in terms of providing housing and jobs. In addition, water supplies were tight. But the budget itself introduced few new measures and was a model of continuity.[1] The main developments in 1956 were not economic: they were driven by the crisis over the Suez Canal.

In July 1956 President Nasser of Egypt nationalized the British- and French-owned Suez Canal. It would have reverted to Egypt anyway in 1968 but Nasser was annoyed that Britain and the United States had withdrawn from funding the building of the Aswan Dam. This in turn was in protest at Egypt moving closer to the Soviet Union, and American annoyance at Nasser formally recognizing the People's Republic of China. Nasser hoped that playing Russia off against America would be to his advantage, and he was also keen to diminish British influence in the Arab world.

Britain was trying to consolidate its power in the region, particularly to contain Russian influence, and the Baghdad Pact of 1955 created an alliance between Iraq, Iran, Pakistan, Turkey and the United Kingdom. This 'Northern Tier' of countries was designed to stand between Russia and the Middle East more generally. Britain wanted Jordan to join the pact but Nasser helped foment opposition to this, and also persuaded King Hussein of Jordan to dismiss the British commander of the Arab Legion, Sir John Glubb. Anthony Eden, the British prime minister, saw Nasser as an impediment to Britain's strategic goals in the Middle East.

Meanwhile, Nasser was also supporting the rebellion in Algeria against French rule. This bitter struggle was consuming the French nation, and senior politicians saw Nasser as effectively attacking France itself. France and Israel had also strengthened military ties by working together on nuclear research and through arms deals. Shimon Peres, the Director General of the Ministry of Defence, told the French during a visit to Paris that Israel would need to attack Egypt during 1956 before Nasser received substantial weapons supplies from Russia, which could be used to invade Israel. Britain, France and Israel had increasingly aligned interests of containing Nasser.

On 29 October 1956 Israel invaded the Sinai and the Gaza strip, rapidly advancing towards the Suez Canal. The following day, Britain and France issued an ultimatum to both parties to withdraw from the canal zone, which both sides ignored, and so, on 31 October, Britain and France started Operation Musketeer, first destroying the Egyptian air force and then invading and taking control of the canal zone. Later it would become public that Israel, France and Britain had colluded to create this sequence of events, having jointly planned this action for many months.

The invasion created a very powerful backlash. The British public were deeply divided, and the opposition Labour Party condemned the government. In heated debates in the House of Commons, some Labour MPs even compared Eden to Hitler. The anger was in part driven by the fact that Russia had just invaded Hungary, and the West's outrage seemed rather disingenuous if it felt that some invasions were justifiable but others were not.

Many in the Arab world were horrified at the invasion. Saudi Arabia imposed a total oil embargo on France and Britain, and threatened to escalate this further. America became increasingly worried that the Arab world would turn against the West more generally and limit oil supplies, so it led a call at the United Nations for a withdrawal. While Britain and France could use their vetoes to thwart this for a while, America was able to turn up the economic pressure because the pound was being heavily sold in the foreign exchange markets. In the four days after 30 October, the Bank of England lost US$45 million in reserves and the Chancellor of the Exchequer, Harold Macmillan, asked for assistance from the IMF. The United States ensured this was not forthcoming.

Britain could see no realistic option but to comply and withdraw, and on 6 November Eden announced a ceasefire. For Britain, the Suez invasion was a turning point. The country was bitterly split on the merits of the invasion and embarrassed at how events had revealed Britain's true weakness. Eden, sick and defeated, resigned, to be replaced in January 1957 by Harold Macmillan.

Three strands emerged from the Suez crisis that would affect Hong Kong in the years to come. The first was a further move away from the idea of colonial power, particularly 'east of Suez'. Hong Kong would increasingly be seen to be on its own. The second was Britain's inability to protect sterling. Given the need to turn to the IMF and the United States, this raised questions about sterling's role as a reserve currency. Sterling's weakness would later have a major impact on Hong Kong. And the third was that the discomfort caused by the split with the United States led Macmillan to quickly try to repair the relationship with Eisenhower. In March they met in Bermuda and largely returned relations back to their pre-Suez state. As US–UK relationship warmed, Macmillan embarked on a plan that would draw America into providing protection to the colony.

HONG KONG BECOMES A JOINT UK/US DEFENCE PROBLEM

Macmillan could now contemplate a further strategic goal. Under the McMahon Act of 1946 the American government was forbidden from sharing nuclear technology with Britain, despite the close cooperation that had existed through World War II. Britain had continued its own research, and in April 1957 it tested its first H-bomb. But the costs of conducting this research alone were very high, and Macmillan wanted the repeal of the McMahon Act, thus enabling Britain to benefit from America's research spend. Macmillan was scheduled to meet with Eisenhower in October in Washington and he hoped to start lobbying, albeit without much confidence that he would achieve much.

Just before Macmillan's trip Russia successfully launched Sputnik I, winning the race to be first into space. This shook American confidence deeply. Emerging problems in the Middle East had also led America to question whether it had made the correct call over Suez. Macmillan met a subdued Eisenhower, who was much more amenable to cooperation. On the second day of the visit, the head of the CIA warned the two leaders that Russia's nuclear research would have caught up with that of the United States within three to five years (Horne 1988). At the end of the meeting Eisenhower, to Macmillan's great surprise, proposed setting up two joint Anglo-American committees: one to collaborate on weapons and one to collaborate on nuclear cooperation. It spelled the end of the McMahon Act.

As part of the deal Macmillan agreed that Britain would not support the People's Republic of China taking the Chinese seat on the UN Security Council. In return, the United States agreed that Hong Kong would now be viewed as 'a joint defence problem', effectively providing a guarantee that the United States would support Britain should China threaten the colony. This last part of the agreement was to be kept secret for many years (Horne 1988).

COWPERTHWAITE BECOMES ACTING FINANCIAL SECRETARY AGAIN

Grantham and Clarke delivered the 1957 budget.[2] Grantham again emphasized the impact of the level of immigration, which had led to the population nearly quadrupling over the previous decade. Despite spending over $300 million on housing, the need for more housing capacity was as great as ever. Progress had been more steady in education and health care. Once more the budget brought continuity rather than surprises. Revenues had been a bit stronger than forecast, expenditure a little lower. The surplus for the prior year was ahead of forecast. Despite a fall in the value of UK government securities held by the Hong Kong government, reserves were still valued at around a year's expenditure. The forecast for the year ahead was for a deficit, but everyone expected the actual result to be better than that, and Clarke did not propose raising tax rates. Given that it had so few changes in policy, the budget aroused little interest in the press or beyond.

Clarke took extended leave from 5 April to 26 November 1957.[6] Cowperthwaite was again appointed as acting financial secretary during his absence.[7] He attended the Legislative Councils in April and May but did not speak.

At the meeting on 5 June 1957 he introduced the Hong Kong Tourist Association Bill, having acted as chair of the Working Committee on Tourism the previous year. The committee had recommended setting up a body to represent the diverse tourist sector and to encourage cooperation amongst participants. Rather unusually, the committee recommended that the association be set up by government, in order that its voice carry more weight. In addition, the committee proposed that the governor appoint the board, at least for the first three years, to ensure it had effective representation while it assessed how best to operate.

Cowperthwaite continued to attend Legislative Council until Clarke returned for the meeting on 18 December. He introduced a few minor measures, such as a bill to allow some franking machines to be used to pay stamp duty, but he was largely silent through the late-summer and autumn meetings.

THE END OF THE GRANTHAM ERA

Grantham retired at the end of 1958 and made his farewell speech at the Legislative Council on 18 December. He celebrated the story of Hong Kong since he had become governor in mid 1947. The post-war reconstruction had occurred smoothly, and the fabric of the colony had gone from strength to strength. Additionally, Hong Kong had dealt with being 'flooded out with refugees while simultaneously [its] trade was being penalized as a result of the United Nations and United States embargoes on trade with China'.[8]

Grantham was clear what lay behind this success:

> The answer to that is the people of Hong Kong. What is their particular genius? Is it not their industry, their intelligence and their ingenuity? I think it is and besides this they are realists. They get on with the job, there is an absence of humbug about them

> and they are imbued with the spirit of co-operation. Furthermore it has always been a tradition of Hong Kong to let the genius of its people work to their own advantage and hence to the advantage of the community generally, without their initiative being frustrated by an excess of state planning.

Grantham also tried to deal with that very difficult conundrum of the lack of democracy in Hong Kong – an issue that would reverberate until the end of British rule and beyond, to the current day. Returning to the observation of the realism shown by the people of Hong Kong, he observed that:

> They are not taken in by catchwords such as democracy. Not that democracy is not a very fine thing: it is. But many people use it as a catchword and make a mistake of regarding it as an end in itself, whereas it is only one of the means to an end, that end being individual freedom and liberty. And here in Hong Kong despite the fact that the constitution of this Council and of Executive Council is not democratic, I venture to say that Hong Kong is one of the most live and let live places in the world. Liberty and freedom are actualities.

This contrast between the lack of democracy and yet the high degree of freedom and economic success would trouble many in the decades to come.

As Grantham left the colony on 31 December 1957,[9] Cowperthwaite too was packing his bags. He had accumulated a considerable amount of leave and he took this between 5 January and 8 October 1958.[10] He would miss the arrival of the new governor and his economic news.

NEW GOVERNOR, NEW INDEPENDENCE

Only six weeks after being appointed governor on 23 January 1958, Sir Robert Black* made the annual address to the Legislative Council on 6 March, ahead of the budget.[3] He paid many compliments to the popular outgoing governor and signalled that he wished to continue most policies unchanged.

He highlighted the success with which the economy had dealt with the trade embargoes by growing industrial output, and also more recently services. Equally, he recognized the strains from very large flows of refugees and a rapidly growing

* Sir 'Robin' Robert Brown Black was born in Edinburgh in 1906 and read classics at Edinburgh University before joining the colonial service in 1930, serving in Malaya, Trinidad and North Borneo. As an intelligence officer during the war, he was captured in North Borneo and was a prisoner of war. Later he was colonial secretary in Hong Kong (1952–55) and governor of Singapore (1955–57).

population. He pointed to the boom in private construction, and the works of the housing authority, the control of diseases such as tuberculosis, and the growth of education and health provision.

He identified two concerns: the formation of the European Free Trade Association and the pressure in Britain to limit textile imports from Hong Kong. On both he promised unspecified government action.

He finished his inaugural address with an important announcement as to how the financial relationship between the United Kingdom and Hong Kong would become even looser, with London's ability to direct policy virtually removed:

> I have to report a decision recently taken by the Secretary of State. He has approved a considerable relaxation in the financial control which he exercises over Hong Kong. In 1948 the Colony was released from Treasury control and given a large measure of autonomy over its own finances. The control which the Secretary of State still retained at that time was that his approval was required for the annual Estimates, for supplementary provisions exceeding $1 million in the case of capital expenditure and $¼ million in the case of recurrent expenditure, for the issue of any loan and for any expenditure involving important points of principle. The Secretary of State has now informed me that, in view of the good standing, financial and administrative, of the Colony, he will further relax his control and will no longer require the Estimates to be submitted for his approval; nor will he require supplementary provisions to be authorized by him.

The goal of total financial independence had been achieved. While Hong Kong was nominally a colony, in domestic matters it had complete autonomy. This was a tribute to the economic policies followed by the Hong Kong government, which had been so manifestly successful. But it was also part of a pattern of Britain losing influence and interest in Asia as the Empire shrank and as Britain turned inwards to address her own economic issues.

THE 1958 BUDGET

Clarke followed this address with the 1958 budget. The prior year's forecast deficit was now forecast to be a small surplus and he expected the actual to be a much larger surplus of over $50 million.

For 1958/59 Clarke forecast that revenues would total $554 million and expenditure $641.5 million. This included extensive non-recurrent public works, such as airport improvements and investments in water supplies. These projects were estimated to cost $183 million in the coming year and totaled over $750 million of future commitments. Clarke noted that recurrent expenditures were more than covered by revenue and that he hoped the deficit would be smaller than forecast. In that context, he once more felt that there was no need to raise tax levels.

The budget was widely welcomed and once more was workmanlike rather than radical. It was a simple continuation of the existing policies. But with much to be done by business, and with the government very focused on handling immigration and housing, no one complained about that.

THE 1959 BUDGET

The governor spoke before Clarke and emphasized the free-trade nature of the colony:

> We are, I suspect, the only true free-trade entity left in the world, and I am proud that we have remained so and I am sure that all of you here share that pride. When others impose restrictions on us we have little with which to bargain and few weapons with which to protect ourselves. But world opinion cannot be unconscious of our struggle to withstand the onslaught of political doctrines, to maintain freedom of speech and action, and to care for and help the thousands of refugees in our midst with what resources we have, resources made available by our own ingenuity and courage.

Figure 8.3. Governor Black visits an electronics factory.

Black was clear that to develop industry the government's key role was to create an environment in which industry could succeed:

> Government's most important duty is to create a favourable climate in which both trade and industry can develop. But all of us must beware of complacency. It is true that there are as few restrictions as possible, taxes are low, and we endeavour to keep Government interference to a minimum.

But he could not refrain from suggesting some ways in which government helped. He pointed to education, and the new technical college. He mentioned how the government supported trade marketing. He encouraged industrialists to become more efficient and to diversify. He also mentioned that he had set up a committee, chaired by Cowperthwaite, to look at the pros and cons of establishing an Industrial Development Corporation or Bank that would steer investment by a 'selective loan policy'.

The same workmanlike approach was evident in the budget discussions of 1959, which followed a now-familiar pattern.[11] Surpluses for previous years were revised upwards, with revenues and expenditures at ever higher levels. For 1959/60 revenue was forecast at $605 million and expenditure at $692 million. Of this, $181 million was public works. This produced an estimated deficit of $87 million but few believed that such a deficit would in fact occur. The reserves were strong. The *South China Morning Post* devoted only two columns to the budget, noting that 'in the face of such proud opulence his magnanimous concessions on the subject of duty on toilet paper, tooth-paste, lipstick and the like are regarded as slightly derisory'.[12]

THE INDUSTRIAL BANK COMMITTEE

The Industrial Bank Committee was appointed by the governor in January 1959, with Cowperthwaite as chair. Its objective was to determine if there was a need for an industrial bank to finance industry in Hong Kong. The committee observed that a number of countries had set up such institutions. In the United Kingdom the Industrial and Commercial Finance Corporation and the Finance Corporation for Industry had been established in 1945 to help firms obtain medium-term finance, and longer-term finance through the stock market, respectively. However, the growth of offerings by commercial banks had limited the need for these institutions.

Various developed countries had industrial banks, mostly focused on helping very small enterprises, and some underdeveloped countries had development banks, largely to channel foreign funds. One can see Cowperthwaite's hand in the committee's report, debating whether Hong Kong's experience was closer to the developed or underdeveloped model, concluding that it was:

> perhaps most closely akin to those of Europe in the late nineteenth century – a developing industrial economy that has already passed out of the primitive stage, and reached what it is now fashionable to call 'the stage of self-sustained growth'.[13]

In evidence to the committee, the most predisposed body, the Chinese Manufacturers' Association, argued that such a bank could support industry generally and in particular 'give assistance to industrial undertakings in the form of easier conditions for loans', 'assist manufacturers to stabilize prices of their products' and 'help new branches of industry to grow'.[14]

Some back-of-the-envelope estimates were made as to the scale of industrial investment, assumed to be around $115 million annually, stemming primarily from reinvested profits. Private finance was substantial, with business profits running at about $700 million and industrial profits accounting for around $135 million of that. Equity funding for industrial concerns from the stock market was trivial. The government had played a minor role in providing favourable terms on the renting of land for factories. The committee also observed that banks were evolving, so that while they still mostly lent for the short term, there was an understanding that these facilities would roll-over, providing medium-term funding. The banks told the committee that they estimated industrial lending to be of the order of $205 million.

The committee spent considerable time and effort trying to identify a sound industrial opportunity that had been hampered by lack of finance. Several submissions to the committee claimed these were numerous, but in practice only two could be identified, both occurring some years before. This lack of evidence of 'any concrete case where an industrial development had failed to secure finance in Hong Kong but could properly have secured it from a specialized industrial bank' was a damning piece of evidence for Cowperthwaite and the committee.

Given that, the committee concluded there was no need for an industrial bank, and after considerable internal process issued its report to that effect in June 1960.[13] Cowperthwaite had once again shown his willingness to work hard to master his brief and to be in command of his subject. He was a safe pair of hands and was given many problems to tidy up. While working on the Industrial Bank, on 1 January 1960 Cowperthwaite was awarded an OBE (an Officer of the Order of the British Empire).[15]

THE 1960 BUDGET

The 1960 budget meetings were significant, not because of the budget measures, which were all in line with the previous few budgets, but because of a question that

Clarke would pose about future economic policy. A question that would be left hanging until Cowperthwaite answered it two years later as financial secretary.

In introducing the 1960 budget on 24 February 1960, the governor emphasized the ongoing need to build low-cost housing. A recent survey had significantly raised the estimated number of squatters: to 500,000 on the ground and 70,000 on rooftops. With the planned building of forty blocks each year, to house 100,000 people, there was more than a five-year backlog of demand.

Clarke announced that the final surplus for 1958/59 was ahead of previous estimates. But for the current year, 1959/60, Clarke forecast that the out-turn would be a deficit of $86 million. Revenues had, as usual, outperformed the original forecast, by nearly $30 million, but expenditure was also higher. In particular, the Department for Public Works had actually spent its entire budget, and indeed had spent more because of rainwater damage over the year. More than $178 million of public works had been carried out.

For the coming year revenues were forecast at nearly $669 million and expenditure at $936 million.[16] This included public works of $290 million and produced a deficit of $267 million, which Clarke described as 'a somewhat alarming figure'. Clarke felt that costs would be somewhat lower and revenues somewhat higher, but even layering these assumptions into the equation left an adjusted deficit of $154 million, a figure that Clarke felt was 'still an alarming one'. He did not feel it was right to meet this level of spending from reserves and therefore proposed both slowing spending and increasing revenues.

On spending he argued:

> We shall clearly have to have a re-examination of the Public Works Programme. Up to the present, money has not been denied for essentials, particularly water, resettlement, and schools. I think the time has now come when we shall have to look at schemes, both existing and projected, with a view to considering whether they really are essential or whether they are merely desirable.

On revenues he proposed raising $35 million from higher petrol and tobacco duties, reducing the planned deficit to $118 million under his favourable scenario. For probably the first time the projected deficit worried Clarke and had clearly caused him to think deeply about how to meet Hong Kong's objectives in the years to come.

CLARKE QUESTIONS LAISSEZ-FAIRE

Despite the success that Hong Kong had enjoyed since the war, Clarke posed a fundamental question as to whether Hong Kong should continue with its laissez-faire policy stance or whether it should move to a more planned approach. He could see that public expenditure might well rise over the years ahead, both to finance infrastructure and to cover normal annual running costs. He was concerned about the ability to meet these expenditures, particularly as Hong Kong exports were increasingly subject to trade impediments. Clarke started with a warning:

> We have, I think, come to a turning point in our financial history. [Reserves] will carry us through next year, but what then? Are we to go on running deficits each year and running down our reserves until there is nothing left? Are we to borrow on the best terms we can? Or are we to step up the rates of tax?

Clarke then surveyed the increasing level of tariffs that were being raised against Hong Kong goods around the world. He acknowledged that there was no point trying to retaliate given the size of the economy. So he posed a question:

> There seem to be two courses we can follow.
>
> We can carry on as we are doing. We can continue to allow our industry to expand; to continue to increase our exports to promising markets year by year, with our manufacturers competing against each other, cutting their prices, cutting their profit margins, until those markets are closed, or partially closed, to us, with the disruption to our economy that must follow.
>
> Or we can do something to plan our economy. We can see to it that for the future we do not advance past the point where markets have to be closed to us because we are selling too much, too quickly, too cheaply. This means that we would have to abandon our traditional policy of laissez faire at least as far as exports are concerned. We would have to guide and direct; we would have to regulate and control.
>
> Which course should we adopt?

It was clearly a critical moment, where the economic philosophy of Hong Kong could have swung away from the laissez-faire policies of the post-war period. All of the Officials and Unofficials, and all leading Hong Kong businesses, could see the world moving into trade blocks and could anticipate how vested interests around the world might fight the threat of cheaper imports from the Far East. In most countries, the ideas of planning were being enthusiastically championed, and not just in centrally planned economies. In Europe, in Japan and even in the United States, the prevalent philosophy was that the invisible hand needed help.

Unsurprisingly, the unofficial members of the council were struck by the question that Clarke had posed, and were quick to see its importance. Mr Barton responded:

> There is, of course, no simple solution to this problem. While I am afraid the policy of complete 'laissez-faire' which served us so well in the fifties might well lead us to economic disaster in the 60's, I would be reluctant to advocate a sudden switch to the regulations and controls that are the price to be paid for a highly planned economy.[17]

Barton wondered whether there was

> a middle way ... a path well clear of the dangerous abyss into which the 'laissez-faire' route might lead us, but clear also of the throttling jungle of too many controls – a path of guidance and direction, but which would leave us free, as before to make our own decisions and our own mistakes.
>
> To sum up, this middle path of guidance from both Government and the Banks should lead to the diversification of our industries (and the) Government might assist the situation by adopting Pioneer Industry techniques.

Others such as Mr R Lee welcomed the idea of even greater government guidance to coordinate Hong Kong's exporters, and thus mitigate the backlash against them in overseas markets.

The Legislative Council did not try to reach any resolution and Clarke was happy to leave his question hanging. He knew that he would soon be retiring, and that it was for the next generation to decide what path to take. For now, laissez-faire seemed to have little support and few willing to champion it as a route for economic success. It would be a couple of years before an answer, crafted by Cowperthwaite, would clarify the government's position.

Between 15 April and 4 May 1960 Cowperthwaite again acted as financial secretary in Clarke's place. His position as successor was increasingly clear. When Clarke returned, Cowperthwaite took extended leave between 26 June and 1 November 1960, returning in time to work on Clarke's last budget.

CLARKE'S FINAL BUDGET

On 1 March 1961 Clarke delivered his tenth and last budget. Sir Robert Black introduced the budget as normal. He praised the successes of the colony's industrialists and merchants, noting that exports were strongly up in 1960. He expressed relief that protectionist pressures around the world had been held in check. Hong Kong enjoyed preferential trading terms in the Commonwealth but Black felt that these might be surrendered as the European Economic Community and the European Free Trade Association developed, as a way of meeting Hong Kong's strategic goal of a 'general lowering in world tariffs'.[18]

Talk of active intervention in industry was gone, replaced with vague references to the success of the government in marketing abroad and to sounding out industrialists.

As usual, the governor noted the successes in health, education, housing and resettlement. He highlighted the work that had been done in social welfare by voluntary organizations. The biggest government role was in getting refugees and those in slums into modern housing. In reaction to those that criticized the colony for not doing more, Black commented:

> We are not callous, calculating capitalists who deny the rights of those still living in our slums to better housing. Our calculations we direct, we hope in a realistic and unsentimental way, to discovering how to fulfil our humanitarian role within the boundaries of this small geographical location, and within the limits which its size and lack of natural wealth impose on our capacity. We can only do what we have set out to do if we remain a going concern, and, to ensure this in our peculiar conditions, we depend on our ability to maintain confidence, to attract capital to our midst, to exercise the minimum of interference in legitimate economic enterprise, and to find and keep markets abroad for the goods which we make in the factories which give employment and a livelihood to the people. We hope that our critics will come to understand better what is at stake in Hong Kong.

Clarke then described the financial situation. He had been quite concerned a year before, but for the current year, 1960/61, revenues were $114 million ahead of the previous estimates and expenditures were down. Clarke had placed constraints on spending by departments and had asked for savings in recurrent spending, leading to spending being about $60 million below plan. The deficit was revised to $55 million, and Clarke was again confident that this number was 'unduly pessimistic' and that the final numbers would show a positive variance to this – indeed, a small surplus was likely.

For 1961/62 Clarke forecast that revenue would be $878 million and expenditure $1,072 million, netting a deficit of $194 million. Within this, non-recurrent public works accounted for a record $352 million. He warned that he did not expect the favourable tailwinds of 1960 – which he thought 'were the result of a boom such as has never been experienced before in the history of Hong Kong' – to be repeated. In fact, he sensed that a number of industries had flattened out and might even decline.

Clarke felt there were a number of ways to finance a deficit. A lottery was possible, as was borrowing locally via Treasury Bills. He ruled out longer-term local borrowing because he believed that 'the local investor is not interested in long term fixed interest securities'. As for borrowing abroad, Clarke asserted that 'we cannot hope to raise any money on the London market at present'. That left borrowing from an international bank or asking for loans from the UK Exchequer. While these options were possible, 'we must satisfy any possible lenders that we have done our best by way of increased taxation, and by local borrowing'. To that end he introduced a number of tax increases on betting duty, stamp duty and fuel duty.

But most significantly, Clarke doubled the level of property tax to the standard rate of 12.5 per cent. The lower rate had been agreed in 1941 as a quid pro quo for the existence of rent controls, but these had long since gone. These various tax rises would contribute $35 million, leaving a revised deficit of $160 million. Clarke proposed aiming for that and not raising income taxes for now.

That did not prevent Clarke from revisiting the defects of the colony's approach to income tax, which he considered inequitable and subject to evasion. The Commissioner of Inland Revenue had described the current system as 'a piece of horse and buggy legislation in a jet age' and had lobbied him to address the main problems. But Clarke felt that making changes would only lead to a new set of inequities, leading him to say:

> I have rejected the Commissioner's request for patching up the Ordinance. I have instead recommended to Your Excellency that immediate consideration be given rather to the replacement of our present thoroughly unsatisfactory system of direct taxation by a full income tax.

Having set the ball rolling, he gave his parting shot: 'I leave the suggestion with Honourable Members, and with my successor.'[18]

REFLECTIONS

Clarke ended his last budget with some deliberations on his time in office:

> During my period of office, Hong Kong has grown out of all recognition. This place seems to have a remarkable resilience: a setback seems merely to provide the incentive for, if I may borrow an expression from our great neighbour, a greater leap forward. My belief is that this growth, punctuated as it has been by occasional setbacks, is what is naturally to be expected in a free economy, with a free people.
>
> For the year 1930, when I arrived here first, the figure for Revenue was $27,818,474, and that for Expenditure was $28,119,646, showing a deficit, a most alarming deficit, of over $300,000.
>
> Just before I assumed my present post, in 1949/50, our Revenue was $264 millions. Last year, ten years later, it was $665 millions. Ten years ago, our Expenditure

> was $182 millions: last year it was $710 millions. Ten years ago our expenditure on public works was $17½ millions: last year it was $171 millions. These figures are, I think, pretty good indications of the growth of Hong Kong and of its economy; as our economy expands, so must our revenue and our expenditure increase. Expenditure next year is estimated for the first time to exceed $1,000 millions; I expect that in much less than ten years from now it will exceed $2,000 millions.
>
> I expect that, when that time comes, my successor will have just the same problem that I have always had – where to turn to find the money. And, Sir, I expect, too, that my successor will make exactly the same mistake that I have always made. He will underestimate his revenue, because, like me, like so many of us, he will never be able to comprehend how new and successful industries can be created overnight out of nothing, in the face of every possible handicap; how new trade can suddenly start up in some way that has never been thought of before; he, like me, will never be able to comprehend how on earth our enterprising, ingenious, hardworking people can ever manage to accomplish so much with so little.

In their remarks three weeks later, the Unofficials broadly agreed with the shape of the budget, and with the rise in property tax.[19] They enthusiastically congratulated Clarke on his stewardship of the economy and government finances over the previous decade and looked forward to working with his successor, who was already well known to them.

The governor warmly thanked Clarke for his thirty-one years of service:[20]

> One has to add to his intellectual gifts and skill in financial matters, a sense of humour through which he has often introduced an atmosphere of Hitchcock's suspense into this august Chamber. Throughout all his service he has been a devoted friend to Hong Kong, and in these last years he has become one of its really great public servants.

Clarke had been a very successful steward of the Hong Kong economy for a decade. He had skilfully administered the colony's finances and navigated the early crises created by sanctions, immigration, a vast housing programme and emerging blocks to free trade. But he was unsure of the way forward, and what mix of laissez-faire and intervention would be optimal. That was a question that would be left to Cowperthwaite to answer.

CHAPTER 9

FINANCIAL SECRETARY AND CHIEF TRADE NEGOTIATOR

On 17 April 1961, shortly before his forty-sixth birthday, Cowperthwaite was formally appointed financial secretary. His twenty busy years had provided him with a very wide understanding of how government operated, and he came to the job with a deep reservoir of relevant experience. He had created and implemented policy, he had run what was effectively a commercial trading organization within a government department, he had grasped at close hand how the private sector responded to many dramatic changes, and he had sat alongside the financial secretary for a decade learning the job and reflecting on what he would do if he were in charge. And now he was.

The governor had had no hesitation in asking the Secretary of State for the Colonies, Iain MacLeod, to appoint Cowperthwaite, making much of his economic and financial experience.[1] Cowperthwaite would be paid $6,300 per month* and get subsidized accommodation,[2] free medical care, a generous seventy-eight days of holiday a year, a pension of 60 per cent of his final salary payable from the age of fifty-five, and he would be entitled to first class travel.

Clarke had finished getting the 1961/62 budget through the Legislative Council just before handing over, so Cowperthwaite had nearly a whole year

* Worth £95,000 per annum today adjusted for inflation, or £215,000 per annum if adjusted by the intervening increase in average wages.

before he would be called upon to deliver his first budget. And in that time he could decide how to address the two issues that Clarke had tabled before his departure: whether to maintain the government's laissez-faire stance and whether to try once more to introduce a full income tax. However, rather than a period of peaceful contemplation, his in-tray suddenly filled with a range of new challenges that would make his first year unexpectedly busy. The first of these was a wave of protectionist measures targeted at Hong Kong's most important export industry: cotton textiles.

THE GROWTH OF THE TEXTILE INDUSTRY

The textile industry was one of the great success stories of post-war Hong Kong. Rope making had started in the late 1800s to serve the fishing industry (Szczepanik 1958). Traditional cotton weaving had existed in Hong Kong since the 1920s as a small cottage industry, but the modern textile industry developed when Shanghai industrialists relocated to Hong Kong in the late 1940s, bringing modern machinery and a deep skill base (Riedel 1974). It was a win–win opportunity, with the Chinese industrialists escaping the new Communist regime and with Hong Kong offsetting the collapse in the entrepôt trade.

Figure 9.1. A textile factory.

The sector had grown rapidly through the 1950s, expanding from yarns and fabrics into made-up goods and garments.* Between 1949 and 1959 the output of cotton yarn and cotton cloth had more than quadrupled. The industry had invested heavily over the years, and by 1960 there were nearly 500,000 cotton spindles and an estimated 15,000 looms busy in the colony. In addition, there were associated dyeing and finishing facilities. The higher-value-added modern garment industry had only begun in 1956 but it had grown very rapidly and by 1959 garment exports had risen to $793 million: about the same level as in Japan.[3]

By the early 1960s the textile industry was the biggest trade earner for Hong Kong, with textiles and clothing accounting for over half of all domestic exports. This export industry was essential to Hong Kong's ability to import food, energy and machinery and, with the collapse of the entrepôt trade, to its prosperity.

THE UNITED KINGDOM AND THE UNITED STATES FEEL THE STRAIN

The two biggest markets for Hong Kong textiles, the United States and Great Britain, had large, struggling textile industries, which were badly hit by the rapid rise in Hong Kong's exports. In the United Kingdom it was the Lancashire textile region that bore the brunt, and this had led to a voluntary agreement, called the Lancashire Pact, being established in 1959. Under the pact, Hong Kong manufacturers agreed to some voluntary restraints on exports to the United Kingdom for three years starting in January 1959. With exports to the United Kingdom effectively capped, Hong Kong's manufacturers intensified their efforts to grow in the United States.

The US government had come under increasing pressure from its domestic manufacturers to stem the tide of cheaper imports from Hong Kong and other Asian countries. Henry Keans, a former US Assistant Secretary of Commerce, had visited Hong Kong to discuss the issue twice in 1959. He emphasized that US textile manufacturers were suffering and suggested an 'orderly marketing procedure': effectively an agreed voluntary level of quotas.[4] His argument was that 'America's balance of payments difficulties were arousing protectionist sentiment' and that it would be in Hong Kong's self-interest to head this off by voluntary restraint.[5] Shortly after this, Congress had proposed a US 8¢ per pound penalty fee on cotton imports to offset US subsidies paid to exporters. However, the US Tariff Commission rejected this

* Yarns are continuous lengths of interlocking fibres, e.g. cotton thread or extruded polyester, spun on spindles. Yarns are then weaved into cloth or fabric on looms. The resulting cloth can be cut and dyed, then sewn to make clothes.

proposal in June 1960, and President Eisenhower accepted their recommendation on 30 August 1960.[4]

But the incoming Kennedy administration reopened the issue: on 13 March 1961, just as Cowperthwaite was taking up his new post, Luther Hodges, the new US Secretary of Commerce, announced that it might be necessary to introduce textile import quotas. On 3 May 1961, President Kennedy called for an international conference on the textile trade. His objective was to find a way within existing trade treaties to reduce the impact on the US textile industry. He was probably hoping for voluntary export controls on the part of low-cost countries such as Hong Kong.

There were those in the United States who believed in free trade, as represented by an editorial in the *New York Times* on 4 May 1961:

> President Kennedy's program for assistance to the textile industry implies that he is seriously thinking of imposing quotas on textile imports into this country. If any such quotas are set he will have made a serious error bowing to political pressure which he should have withstood. The imposition of textile import quotas would ... contradict this country's long and ardent advocacy of the freest possible international trade.

But there was no doubt that President Kennedy needed to be seen to have taken up the cause of the US textile industry, which had broad support in Congress.

In the United Kingdom and the United States there was much discussion about how it was that Hong Kong, a new player in the industry, had become so competitive. Several illogical arguments were advanced. Some argued that they were pricing below their costs and therefore losing money. Others that they were somehow receiving subsidies. The reality was much more straightforward but much more unpalatable to the British and American industries: the Hong Kong companies had invested more heavily in modern equipment; they used this equipment more intensively, often running three-shift, 24/7 operations; and they had lower labour costs.

COWPERTHWAITE DRAWN IN

On 1 May 1961 the three leading Hong Kong textile associations announced that they would not renew the Lancashire Pact. Suddenly Cowperthwaite was thrown into a set of trade negotiations concerning Hong Kong's most important export industry. In late May, just a month after becoming financial secretary, Cowperthwaite flew to London with Herbert Angus, his Director of Commerce and Industry, to represent Hong Kong at discussions sponsored by the US government. At these meetings they were asked to limit textile shipments to the United States and Canada, and to withdraw the statement that the Lancashire Pact would not be renewed.

Cowperthwaite and Angus returned to Hong Kong and asked the textile associations to form a committee to discuss their response. The associations declined to do so but did agree to meet with Angus informally. But on 29 June the three associations reiterated their opposition to voluntary restraints, stating that:

> The three associations have not been blind to the crushing impact of the UK quota, as evidenced by the increasing operational cutbacks which are seriously threatening to bring on a first-class crisis in the local cotton industry.[6]

Cowperthwaite was left trying to reconcile the opposing perspectives. He believed in the benefits of free trade but he knew there were severe risks for Hong Kong in antagonizing the United States and Britain. His assumption was that the Hong Kong manufacturers would be driven by self-interest, but their obstinacy made his task of crafting a deal much more difficult.

However, he was sure that there was no value in imposing retaliatory tariffs and quotas. Classical economics suggested such a move would only reduce people's welfare, and on a practical level Hong Kong's small size meant that it was not a useful bargaining chip. He was also aware that Britain had stood alone as an open economy in its century of greatest growth before World War I. Whereas in 1914 Germany had an average tariff level of 13 per cent, France 20 per cent and the United States 30 per cent, Britain's average tariff level was 0 per cent (Hobsbawm 1987).

GENEVA

The debate was renewed at the GATT discussions held in Geneva between 17 July and 21 July.* Cowperthwaite attended as representative for Hong Kong,

* The General Agreement on Tariffs and Trade was a multilateral agreement, first agreed in 1947, which reduced tariffs and trade barriers between signatories. Major progress was made during the Geneva Round (1955–56), the Kennedy Round (1962–67) and later the Tokyo Round (1973–79). The Uruguay Round (1986–94) set up the World Trade Organisation (WTO) on 1 January 1995, which incorporated previous GATT proposals and took the lead.

which despite neither being a nation nor a GATT member did have a clear interest in freer trade.* Notwithstanding this, Hong Kong's textile trade featured heavily. A proposal emerged out of the talks whereby Hong Kong would voluntarily limit volumes sold of certain important textile items and categories. Cowperthwaite described it as a standstill agreement pending a long-term solution under which Hong Kong would give up its rights under GATT for one year from October 1961 in return for importing countries loosening their restrictions on trade. Cowperthwaite noted that it would be difficult for Hong Kong to be successful if it challenged an agreement that had the support of most of the developed world, but he did express some practical reservations about how the scheme would work and what the base period should be for the allowable levels of exports.

These discussions rumbled on through the late summer and autumn of 1961. The Hong Kong textile manufactures came to realize that there was not going to be unfettered free trade for a while, and they had therefore started to cooperate with the government to get the best deal possible. They had put extending the Lancashire Pact back on the table, making a UK–Hong Kong deal a possibility. Cowperthwaite followed up on his discussions with the United States to see if there was a better bilateral deal available.[7] However, the focus remained on the GATT proposals, and on 10 November 1961 Cowperthwaite met with the members of the Hong Kong Cotton Board, who finally accepted the Geneva GATT proposals, limiting exports for one year starting from October 1961.[8]

COWPERTHWAITE STEPS BACK TO WORK ON HIS FIRST BUDGET

In early 1962 the various negotiations were continuing, but with greater cohesion being shown by the various parties in Hong Kong. Cowperthwaite turned to work on his first budget, which was to be presented at the end of February. In late January Herbert Angus, who was now both the head of the Department of Commerce and Industry and the chairman of the Cotton Advisory Board, went to Geneva to take part in the international textile conference. Cowperthwaite felt sufficiently relaxed to miss the meeting to continue working on the budget.

* Average tariffs for GATT participants were 22 per cent in 1947, around 15 per cent by the Kennedy Round and below 5 per cent after the Uruguay Round (Bown and Irwin 2015).

In late February a delegation went to Lancashire to work out how to extend the pact. The United States was again considering a proposed levy, this time for US 8½¢ per pound of cotton products. Hong Kong had a useful ally in Japan, which was also a major exporter of textiles to the United States, but was also a substantial importer of US cotton, which gave them some negotiating power.

As Cowperthwaite approached his first budget the outcome of these various talks were still foggy, but at least they looked as if they would end in a negotiated compromise rather than a more damaging ban on this key export sector.

THE UNITED STATES RAISES THE STAKES

The short-term Geneva GATT proposals required Hong Kong to voluntarily limit some exports, and for the United States, the United Kingdom and others to loosen their blocks on imports. But this was an uneasy compromise given that Hong Kong manufacturers wanted to increase their exports to boost profits and employment and that the developed countries wanted to mitigate the effect trade was having on their inefficient textile industries. All sides wanted to develop a longer-term approach to trade.

In March 1962 the United States asked Hong Kong to exercise 'restraint' on their exports of eight categories of textiles. However, textile exports to the United States accelerated, putting the administration under significant political pressure. It was also very hard to corral the diverse, entrepreneurial Hong Kong producers to work together and to agree to limit their output. On 19 March the United States announced that these textile categories would be subject to an import ban prohibiting their sale in the United States.

With the stakes suitably raised, talks took place in Washington between 26 March and 14 April, and during these the ban was extended to fourteen more categories of textiles. On 24 April a joint statement from Washington and Hong Kong did not show any real meeting of the minds, and Hong Kong's governor, Sir Robert Black, described the outcome as 'very disappointing'.

The level of support for unbridled free trade was not high. In a sign of the prevailing mood, in May 1962 *The Economist* called the Hong Kong textile operators 'buccaneers', arguing that

> whenever some semblance of an orderly trading arrangement for general advantage looms in Hong Kong, it is trampled to bits by rampaging freebooters.[9]

A LONGER-TERM AGREEMENT

Negotiations on a longer-term agreement continued throughout 1962, and on 10 September a nineteen-nation International Textile Conference took place in Geneva. Cowperthwaite represented Hong Kong as part of the UK delegation, supported by Holmes, the director of the Department of Commerce and Industry. Cowperthwaite would only attend this conference briefly because he had to attend the Commonwealth Prime Ministers' Conference in London taking place at the same time.[10]

The deal agreed by Cowperthwaite in Geneva settled the textile issue for the foreseeable future. Under this longer-term agreement there would be quotas for textile exports to the United States and other countries for the five years up to 1967. In theory, imports would be allowed to flow more freely, but importing countries could impose restrictions when there was 'market disruption'. This vague description would lead to much disagreement.

All of Hong Kong's textile exports to the United Kingdom were subject to quotas under the Lancashire Pact. The United States restricted imports in thirty out of sixty-four textile categories, Canada restricted four categories, Norway two and Germany solely the shirts category.

The agreements created some certainty for the textile industry and protected the existing level of exports, but they also demonstrated the problem of relying on textiles to provide export growth for the colony and profits growth for industrialists. The textile industry had provided a great boost to Hong Kong's industrialization but it was now stuck between external limits to trade and rising labour costs, which the industry's success had itself in large part caused.

SHARING THE PIE

The imposition of quotas meant that Hong Kong manufacturers and distributors and the government faced the unwelcome task of agreeing how to divide those allowances up between different firms. Several approaches had been tried in different sectors over the years, including allocating quotas on a first-come, first-served basis; or as a function of production capacity; or according to the previous year's exports; or based on government authorizations; or as a mix of these approaches. In addition, there were disagreements on whether the quota should be awarded to the manufacturer or to the distributor or shipper. The government proposed that the best approach would be to allocate quotas based on performance in past years, so that those who had built up the trade would be the ones to benefit from it in the future.

RESHAPING THE TEXTILE INDUSTRY

The constraints on exporting cotton textiles had several consequences as the industry adjusted to the new environment. The most immediate was the reduction in the purchase of capital equipment for the sector. Since this was mostly imported, it did not cause a major problem for Hong Kong. This was accompanied by the sector consolidating as smaller firms found it hard to adjust to the more difficult market.

As any economist, or observer of Hong Kong business leaders, would have predicted, the industry quickly worked out how to optimize their profits given the fact that quotas were set in terms of weight of natural cotton. Manufacturers moved to higher-value-added textiles, e.g. into finishing and into clothing (Riedel 1974).

In addition, manufacturers moved to grow their synthetic textile output as a way to circumvent the quotas. Investment in synthetic textile machinery boomed, particularly after the mid 1960s, and was estimated to be running at more than $500 million by 1970. This trade would eventually also be constrained by a non-cotton textile agreement with the United States in 1971, but for the 1960s it gave manufacturer's a new avenue for growth.

THE SEARCH FOR NEW OPPORTUNITIES

With the reduced opportunity to invest in the textile sector, industrialists looked for new areas in which to invest their capital. There would be considerable debate in the colony about whether the private sector should be left to decide on its own, unaided, or whether the government needed to play an active role in choosing the areas of focus. In the end it would be the industrialists who would choose to invest in plastics, electronics and wigs.

Plastics was one of the great post-war growth industries, as immortalized by Mr McGuire in the film *The Graduate* made in 1967. In fact, the first Hong Kong plastics factory had been established in 1947, but in 1955 there were still only forty-three plastic factories employing 844 people in the colony. By 1960, though, this had grown to 363 factories with 14,907 employees, and in the following two years employment in the industry doubled.[11]

The industry relied on imported polythene and polystyrene, which was shaped using injection moulding machines. These machines, unlike most textile equipment, were domestically produced, so the plastics industry also supported a domestic machine manufacturing industry (Riedel 1974). In its early years the focus was on making packaging for other industries, and on a specialization in making artificial flowers for export, particularly to the United States.[12] By 1960 plastic flowers were made in over 300 factories and made up 5 per cent of all of Hong Kong's exports, although their share of exports would decline from that level. As the industry developed it shifted to include plastic toys, which would double to make up 8 per cent of domestic exports by the end of the decade.

Whereas there had been a small plastics industry in the 1950s, the electronics industry only started in the 1960s. The industry specialized in the assembly of transistor radios. Components were sourced mostly from Japan, even after Japan tried to hinder the birth of the industry by imposing an embargo on exporting components to Hong Kong in 1962. This attempt both failed to slow the Hong Kong manufacturers and at the same time caused a recession for Japanese component companies, and the embargo was soon lifted (Riedel 1974). The industry grew rapidly, diversifying into televisions in 1964 and into computer components in 1968.

Wig manufacturing was another industry that only emerged after the textile industry had met resistance. Wig exports would grow from virtually nothing to around 8 per cent of domestic exports by 1970. In the mid 1960s the industry specialized in wigs made from human hair, and one of the advantages that Hong Kong manufacturers enjoyed was the easy availability of Chinese hair, which was both cheap and well suited to wig construction. In the late 1960s and early 1970s demand would shift to synthetic fibre wigs and the industry would struggle to maintain its relative position. However, for the second half of the 1960s the industry played an important role in generating export growth.

PROTECTIONIST DEMANDS WIDEN

Expanding into new areas did not fully resolve the protectionist pressures faced by Hong Kong industrialists. For example, the move into transistor radios led the British Radio Equipment Manufacturers Association to lobby the British Board of Trade to intervene.[13] Whereas in 1960 around 2,400 radio sets were exported to the United Kingdom, by 1964 more than 1.1 million were. This was a very large proportion of the total of 2.75 million sets that were manufactured that year in Hong Kong.

These tended to be lower-priced sets, but the British manufacturers argued there was 'no knowing' where this trend would end. And they were very concerned that the Hong Kong manufacturers were engaged in 'that well know Hong Kong technique for expanding business, namely price shaving'.[14] Haddon-Cave, as Director of Commerce & Industry, wrote to Cowperthwaite having analysed the industry, concluding that the ex-factory cost of a set was around $100 (£6.25) and with freight, distributor costs, UK duties and UK purchase taxes of around 45 per cent, total costs were £9 versus British-made sets selling at £13–£16.[14]

In this sector the Board of Trade accepted that the competition was not unfair, but that did not prevent continued political pressure in Hong Kong's largest markets for greater protectionism against cheaper imports.

LESSONS FOR COWPERTHWAITE

The world of trade and trade barriers was not new to Cowperthwaite given his previous roles, but he may have been surprised at how much of his first year as financial secretary was taken up with trade issues. It would be the same for much of his time in office.

Cowperthwaite was intellectually convinced by the benefits of free trade, but he was willing, nonetheless, to get into the detailed workings of international trade diplomacy to do the best deals that were practically possible. He argued that Hong Kong's exports should have the freest possible access to maximize economic growth. And even where others imposed tariffs on Hong Kong, he argued against reciprocating. He did not believe that a small open economy, such as Hong Kong's, could gain by adopting protectionist measures.

Once more Cowperthwaite saw first hand how businesses showed remarkable ingenuity in finding the best way to deal with issues. As he had experienced at the Department of Supplies, Transport & Industry, he saw industry adapt its investment and focus each time a new regulation or tariff was introduced. It confirmed his view that it was naive to imagine that government could plot as successful a path for the deployment of assets as could be done by the private sector itself.

But for many the rise of protectionism abroad reinforced Clarke's question as to whether it might be time to move away from a pure laissez-faire model. Maybe it was time to look for a more planned, more managed approach. This would only be reinforced by the potential threat of 'Brentry'.

A BUSY LIFE BEYOND THE OFFICE

Despite Cowperthwaite's heavy workload he pursued a number of hobbies and socialized widely. He and his wife had developed a broad group of friends in Hong Kong, including many Brits, Chinese and Americans.[15] Sheila was passionate about Chinese art and became an accomplished painter herself.

One of the great benefits of office was the financial secretary's residence on Shouson Hill Road, Deep Water Bay. This beautiful neo-Georgian house was located near Aberdeen, on the south side of Hong Kong Island. It must have been an oasis of calm away from the activity of the Secretariat. Built in 1935 for Sir Shouson Chow, it had been bought by the government in July 1947 for Follows. It was spacious, with a large veranda and a tennis court in the grounds. Even the residence became a way for Cowperthwaite to signal his frugality when at various points he would turn down the chance to have it redecorated at taxpayers' expense; and when he was offered air conditioning, he refused on the basis that such an offer was not available to Hong Kong residents.

Figure 9.2. The financial secretary's residence in Deep Water Bay.

Cowperthwaite would play a round of golf whenever he could on Sundays, and he would play lawn bowls at the Indian Recreation Club.[16] He also became a voting member of the Royal Hong Kong Jockey Club and teamed up with Edward Tyrer to own three horses.* Tyrer had become a close friend in the immediate post-war administration, when Tyrer had been a captain handling policing. In 1952 he had become assistant commissioner, and in 1966 he would briefly serve as commissioner before retiring early over disagreements about how to police the communist protests that year.

* Edward Tyrer, born 1917 in British Guiana, was educated at St Paul's School and at Exeter College, Oxford. He joined the Trinidad police force in 1937. After military service in the army during the war, in September 1945 he joined the Hong Kong military administration and then the Hong Kong Police Force.

Their horses had some success, initially with Justin and even more so with Persian Rose, born in 1958 and suited to wet conditions. Cowperthwaite would often go and see the horse train at 5.30 a.m. before heading to the office. Tyrer and Cowperthwaite sold Persian Rose in 1968, just after Tyrer had retired, for $8,000. The new owners were delighted that the ten-year-old showed good form, and it won more than $6,000 on its first outing with them.[17] But Cowperthwaite would have had few regrets. He was not driven by accumulating wealth for himself, and he clearly greatly enjoyed the mix of activities that made up his varied life.

Founded in 1884 the Jockey Club occupied an important social and economic position in the colony. It had been granted a unique monopoly over pari-mutuel betting at horse races, and this proved to be a goldmine, generating huge profits. Most of these were used to support charitable causes, making the Jockey Club the largest supporter of charitable causes in the colony and a key player in providing welfare services to those in need. For example, in 1969 the Club gave $10 million to charity.

The club had 200 voting members, appointed for life, and selected from the thousands of ordinary members. It was a great privilege, and a source of social cachet, to become one. While there were Chinese voting members (although less than half), there were no women voting members (Wong 2015). Even after his retirement, Cowperthwaite would return to Hong Kong and take his place in the voting members' enclosure.

CHAPTER 10

THE THREAT OF 'BRENTRY'

As Cowperthwaite was addressing protectionist sentiment towards Hong Kong's textile exports, a broader and potentially more extensive problem emerged driven by Britain's decision to apply to join the European Economic Community (EEC). It was clear that such a move could have a profound impact on Hong Kong, which could export tariff free to Britain, its largest market. How would the EEC's common external tariffs affect this? If Hong Kong were viewed as an external territory, its exports to the United Kingdom would be subject to the high tariff walls protecting the EEC. These tariffs would damage not only the textile trade but all other exporting industries as well.

BRITAIN CHANGES ITS MIND ON EUROPE

Britain had decided not to participate in the European Coal and Steel Community that had been created by the Treaty of Paris in 1951. When the Treaty of Rome was signed in 1957 establishing the EEC with its original six members (France, West Germany, Italy, the Netherlands, Belgium and Luxembourg), the United Kingdom again chose not to participate. But in July 1961, Britain's prime minister, Harold MacMillan, announced that the United Kingdom (along with Ireland and Denmark) would apply to join the EEC. Most existing EEC members were very positive about the potential inclusion of Britain, and in November 1961 negotiations started (Ludlow 1997).

As early as October 1961 Britain's negotiator, Sir William Gorell Barnes,* sought Cowperthwaite's views, while he was in London, as to how Britain's entry might affect Hong Kong.[1] Cowperthwaite welcomed the chance to comment and noted that there were strong feelings in Hong Kong about the need to be actively involved in the negotiation process. They agreed that they would try to achieve Associated Overseas Territory (AOT) status for Hong Kong, as was enjoyed by France's overseas *departments*. Failing that, Cowperthwaite thought that Hong Kong would find tariff-free quotas acceptable, in part because they could be policed fairly easily. If pushed, Cowperthwaite thought Hong Kong could also accept some rules against disruptive trading.

On his return to Hong Kong Cowperthwaite took soundings from colleagues and then wrote to Trafford Smith confirming the preference for AOT status and inviting Gorell Barnes to visit Hong Kong to better understand the situation.[2] Gorell Barnes took up that invitation and visited the colony in mid December 1961. After his trip, Gorell Barnes sent Cowperthwaite a copy of his report and a background briefing report prepared for the negotiating delegation:

> I doubt whether I am behaving very properly in communicating to you… I must, therefore, ask you to treat as strictly confidential not only the contents of the report itself but also the fact that I have sent you a copy.[3]

The report summarized Hong Kong's objectives: to maintain unrestricted entry for her products into Britain; to limit any quota restrictions against her in Europe; and to avoid any 'reverse' preference against her goods in Britain (e.g. not to favour Italian goods over Hong Kong goods).[4] The data in the report explained why these were the priorities. In 1960 Hong Kong exported $585 million of goods to the United Kingdom and only $150 million to the six EEC members, $107 million of which was to West Germany. This low level of trade was due to Hong Kong goods being subject to strict quotas. A third of Hong Kong's exports to Britain were textiles and another third clothing. It was these industries' trade with Britain that exercised the Hong Kong government, not least because it was in these industries that the large inflows of refugees found employment

It described the various solutions that might exist, should full AOT status not be forthcoming. These included a so-called Morocco protocol, where Hong Kong goods

---

* Sir William Gorell Barnes, born in 1909, attended Pembroke College, Cambridge. Between 1932 and 1939 he was in the diplomatic service serving in Baghdad, Lisbon and London. During World War II he was Clement Attlee's personal assistant, a role he also played when Attlee became prime minister. In 1948 he returned to the Foreign Office as Assistant (then Deputy) Under Secretary of State.

would have free entry to Britain but pay duties if they were then re-exported within the EEC. Or there could be duty-free quotas, either into the United Kingdom or into the EEC. Or Hong Kong could pay the normal EEC tariffs, of around 20 per cent, and not be subject to quotas. This would means imports to the United Kingdom would now be subject to tariffs where they had not been before, and this could significantly reduce Hong Kong's exports to Britain.

By February 1962 it was becoming clear that the AOT option was unlikely to be available and that the outcome would therefore be some mix of the less attractive options.[5] James Vernon* kept Cowperthwaite informed of how things were developing and he in turn passed his views back, including the rather odd thought that Hong Kong needed the profitable UK market in order to price more keenly elsewhere when competing with Japan.[6]

As Cowperthwaite came to draft his first budget in the early part of 1962, he faced major uncertainties about the future of free trade and about whether Hong Kong's favourable access to its largest market, the United Kingdom, might change structurally forever. With the United Kingdom and the United States looking as though they were moving away from a liberal free-trade approach, he will have considered how that affected the issue that Clarke posed in his last budget: was it time for Hong Kong to de-emphasize its laissez-faire approach?

BACK TO EUROPE

Cowperthwaite's involvement in shaping the UK position on Hong Kong in the EEC negotiations increased substantially in the summer of 1962. He met the British negotiating team in London on 4 June 1962 and discussed the fact that the EEC appeared to be inflexible regarding Hong Kong imports.[7] Cowperthwaite noted that the existing members appeared to have a general fear of Hong Kong. He then went on to Brussels on 6–7 June to have informal discussions with officials in the EEC. These talks went well and the UK delegation let Sir Robert Black, Hong Kong's governor, know that Cowperthwaite had

> impressed the Germans in particular with his readiness to envisage a guarantee by Hong Kong against disruption in sectors other than textiles if this was the necessary price for reasonable treatment of Hong Kong's exports of these items. He also

* J. W. Vernon, born 1915, educated Wallasey Grammar School and Emmanuel College, Cambridge, worked in the Ministry of Food before joining the Colonial Office in 1948, becoming assistant secretary in 1954.

> impressed Harkort (the German delegate) with the argument that Hong Kong exports would only be able to surmount the tariff if wages were decreased; and that, as Hong Kong had to export to live, the result would be not a failure to export but a reduction in the standard of living.[8]

HOIST BY HIS OWN PETARD

As discussions stretched into the autumn, Cowperthwaite kept in close touch with the negotiating team. But it appears that he kept much of the information to himself – a trait that several colleagues noticed over the years. In October 1962 Cowperthwaite became alarmed that specifics of the negotiations, and the fact that there had been detailed dialogue with him, would be made public. He wrote an irritated telegram to Vernon, arguing that there had been an 'almost complete silence' in Hong Kong about the impact of the EEC negotiations based on the pretext that negotiations about Hong Kong had not seriously begun.[9] He went on:

> A statement now outlining the extent of the ground already surrendered by Her Majesty's Government would certainly provoke questions which I would be hard put to answer and probably bring a substantial loss of confidence. I would not normally suggest a continued course of public unenlightment but the position we now find ourselves in makes it the better choice between two evils.

Cowperthwaite then raised a curious constitutional issue. He objected to any statement that the 'Hong Kong government' had been consulted on the basis that while he himself had been asked his views on the British government's position, he had not been permitted to consult the executive council.

Unsurprisingly he received a rather cold reply on 8 November from Trafford Smith, who said the British team were rather 'puzzled' by Cowperthwaite's claim that the Hong Kong government had not been consulted.[10] He noted dryly:

> This is quite contrary to our understanding of the position, and we are at a loss to know how this misapprehension can have arisen between us.

Trafford Smith went on to describe in detail how he had expected Cowperthwaite to have kept the governor informed, and how the governor would have made decisions on whom to consult. Indeed, he quoted telegrams from the governor saying that he had kept the executive council and even some business leaders reasonably well informed. In their file notes it is clear that the British negotiators thought

Cowperthwaite was being somewhat abstruse about the situation but they had decided to accommodate him.

When Cowperthwaite was next in London later that month, he, Vernon and Trafford Smith had a discussion and agreed that there had been misunderstanding on both sides.[11] Trafford Smith let Gorell Barnes know that they were now in agreement that the two governments should aim to be outwardly in harmony about wherever the talks ended up but that the Hong Kong government was merely informed at key points rather than having been consulted and given their agreement. This reflected the reality both that the Hong Kong officials were not directly involved in the negotiations and that in many ways none of the potential outcomes were attractive to them. However, Cowperthwaite had perhaps played his cards slightly closer to his chest than a more seasoned politician would have done. In Hong Kong he could manage information and rely on his superior intellect to keep control. On this bigger stage, with others who did not know him or his reputation and for whom he was not a central figure, he had nearly come unstuck.

With the air cleared, Cowperthwaite flew to Brussels to lunch with Gorell Barnes and with Mr Reimer, the chairman of the Hong Kong Working Party, representing the EEC members, on 28 November 1962. Reimer explained that the current members were under pressure from their own textile manufacturers and that there was also a need for safeguards to ensure that any concessions applied only to products made in Hong Kong itself, and not merely exported via Hong Kong. Gorell Barnes and Cowperthwaite sensed that Reimer was trying to be as helpful as he could be but that there were significant issues still to be resolved and that any solutions might take some considerable time to emerge.[12]

NON, NON, NON

In December Gorell Barnes could see that the French delegation were being difficult about finding a solution for Hong Kong.[13] He speculated that this was very much under orders from Paris. It would soon be clear that this was just part of a broader opposition on the part of France to British membership. In January de Gaulle effectively vetoed the British application, despite dire warnings from the other members and from America, arguing (Lacouture 1991):

> Britain is insular, maritime, bound up by its trade, its markets, its food supplies, with the most varied and often the most distant countries. Her activity is essentially industrial and commercial, not agricultural. She has, in all her work, very special, very

> original habits and traditions. How can Britain, in the way that she lives, produces, trades, be incorporated in the Common Market as it has been conceived and as it functions?

The final meeting of the negotiating teams took place on 28–29 January 1963, drawing the process to a close (Ludlow 1997). From a purely parochial view of preparing his second budget this was fortuitous timing for Cowperthwaite. From the broader perspective of Hong Kong's manufacturers and traders the collapse of the talks came as a great relief. Uncertainty remained, but at least one potentially material risk had been averted.

This all enhanced Cowperthwaite's reputation in Hong Kong. In the 1963 budget cycle Cowperthwaite was publicly thanked by the members of the Legislative Council for his work in managing Hong Kong's interests in the United Kingdom's negotiations with the EEC. Mr Ruttonjee, for example, praised his work:

> His is now a familiar face in the conference halls of Geneva, Brussels, and London and my honourable Friend can claim without fear of contradiction that he is on bowing if not on speaking terms with more international personalities than any other Financial Secretary before him. As our ambassador, he has earned the gratitude of the Colony. The countries of the Six are now much more aware of the very real need for Hong Kong to export, of our problem of people, of our shortages and deficiencies, of the political importance of Hong Kong and of our achievements in the face of unbelievable odds. No one could have done a better job for us; no one would have put more heart and soul into doing it.[14]

Cowperthwaite could file away the issue of Britain joining the EEC for now but it would emerge again in the years ahead. For Hong Kong the general global effort to reduce tariffs and trade barriers was very welcome. The moves by smaller blocks, such as the EEC, to create external tariff walls was a threat, as were the forces of protectionism. Cowperthwaite knew what side of the debate he was on and he would argue that corner regularly over the years ahead.

For now, some used the risk to Hong Kong's trade of a putative British entry to the EEC to further question the wisdom of pursuing a laissez-faire, free-trade agenda. Once more there were arguments as to whether Hong Kong should change course, or at least water down its historical stance.

CHAPTER 11

A BANKING CRISIS

TO ADD TO HIS WORRIES, a banking crisis created further uncertainty in Cowperthwaite's first year as financial secretary. It would be a foretaste of a bigger crisis that would hit him and the government hard in 1965. Cowperthwaite would be slow to learn the lesson that banking is not a typical industry.

HONG KONG'S UNUSUAL BANKING SECTOR

In the best traditions of laissez-faire, the banking sector in Hong Kong was lightly regulated. Unusually, the colony did not have a central bank. The traditional role of issuing notes was performed by certain private banks, which kept reserves against the notes issued. Regulation was performed by the financial secretary's department, rather than by a specialist group. The role of lender of last resort was hazy, but the responsibility for financial stability rested with the financial secretary. Cowperthwaite, like previous financial secretaries, was explicit about being willing to let banks go bust and to let depositors lose their funds. Their logic was to ensure that the risk of bank failure was not implicitly adopted by the state, and they had the classical view that depositors were taking risk in 'investing' their money at a particular institution. This might work when there were a small number of more sophisticated, wealthier depositors, but the approach would be tested to destruction in the 1960s.

The banking sector was split into four parts: Hongkong and Shanghai Banking Corporation (HSBC), which itself controlled around a third of the market; local Chinese-owned banks, which had a similar share; foreign-owned banks, with a bit less than a quarter of the market; and banks owned by the Chinese state, with about a tenth of the market. The local Chinese banks were often run as extensions of their owners' broader economic activities and tended to be more focused on gold trading and property speculation than the foreign-owned banks, which had more traditional banking models. The links of shared ownership between local Chinese-owned banks and their associated group operating companies meant that deposits in those banks were often used as cheap equity finance in the booming property development sector.

CREDIT GROWTH STARTS TO OVERHEAT THE REAL ESTATE MARKET

The banks had enjoyed significant growth in the 1950s and in 1960. New banks opened and most banks expanded their branch network further in order to grow their deposit base. With extensive advertising and high interest rates, deposits grew rapidly. These deposits were then lent out, and in the 1950s this had provided useful capital for the growing manufacturing sector. However, by 1960 the real estate industry was booming and much of the lending headed there. The costs of winning new contracts rose, and land prices were up to eleven times their 1954 levels (Jao 1974). To maintain returns, more leverage was used, financed in many cases by associated banks.

Alongside the real estate boom, the stock market soared in early 1961. In the first half of the year many stocks rose by 20–50 per cent, particularly those with land or property interests. New stock issues were snapped up, with stocks being bought on unofficial margin in order to boost returns (Jao 1974).

Depositors had very little protection from a bank defaulting, and with no state-backed deposit guarantee scheme, they were wary about leaving their money in any bank that looked at risk. With banks lending on increasingly risky property projects, and against dodgy collateral, and where bank owners could use depositors' funds to extend credit to their associated property companies, it was only a matter of time before a bank run started.

THE LIU CHONG HING BANK

In June 1961 exactly that happened with the Liu Chong Hing Bank. The bank had been set up by Liu Po Shan in 1948 to collect small deposits in the Chinese community. It incorporated in 1955 and expanded rapidly. They had a very extensive depositor base, generally of poorer families attracted by the bank's high interest rates, and to support these rates the bank lent to higher-yield sectors such as property development. It was estimated that by 1961 over three-quarters of its loans were in real estate.

In the midst of a bubble mentality on the stock market, reports started circulating that some of the Chinese banks were in difficulty, and on 14 June 1961 a crowd gathered outside one branch to withdraw their deposits. Over the next two days long queues formed outside all of their branches, with an estimated 20,000 customers trying to withdraw their savings (Jao 1974).

The bank's problems were publicly blamed on 'malicious rumours', but it was well known to the government that the bank was poorly managed. Cowperthwaite organized a rescue for the bank to prevent a broader problem, asking the Hongkong Bank and the Chartered Bank to provide support (Schenk 2001). The bank continued to trade, perhaps surprisingly with four members of the Liu family as directors.

DIFFERENT VIEWS ON THE BENEFITS OF REGULATION

The Liu Chong Hing failure was not a real surprise. The year before, when he was financial secretary, Clarke had said that (Schenk 2001) 'control over banks was quite ineffective and there was a need to enjoin stricter standards if the risk of a serious failure by some of the Chinese banks was to be avoided'.

Clarke had considered establishing a central bank (Schenk 2001). Cowperthwaite instead favoured light regulation and inspection. But both routes revealed some of the conflicts at the heart of financial regulation in Hong Kong. New regulations would need to be enforced and it was not clear that the government had the skills or the capacity to do that. And if the sector was regulated, the government might be seen as having a responsibility to depositors should a bank fail.

Cowperthwaite would find that banking crises would unsettle the economy, and his personal position, more than once. In his time as deputy financial secretary and during his first few years as financial secretary, his views on the benefits of free competition and a laissez-faire approach seemed to apply just as much to banking as to other sectors. He would be slow to understand the second-order effects that a bank failure created. It also appears that Cowperthwaite, like many economists, had a poor grasp of how banking worked, and in particular how they were able to create credit. Leo Goodstadt (2007)[1] describes how, in 1960, Cowperthwaite's response to a Belgian banker's explanation that his bank's loans far exceeded their deposits 'was one of incredulity'. At first he was convinced that creating such credit must rely on accounting irregularities, and was surprisingly slow to grasp how fractional banking worked.

Eventually, Cowperthwaite realized that the antiquated approach to banking regulation needed to be updated. In this he initially had the support of the more professional banking concerns in the colony, although they would later try and water down the restrictions that tighter banking regulation would demand. In December 1961 he therefore asked H. J. Tomkins, an advisor to the Bank of England, to propose legislation for regulating banking operations in the colony.

The run on Liu Chong Hing Bank gave Cowperthwaite a crash course in how banking failure might occur, and an early indication about how a failure might turn into a broader crisis. He would take steps, somewhat slowly, to improve banking regulation. However, his understanding about how a crisis in the banking sector might hit the broader economy was still unformed. Whereas he could translate the lessons of classical economics into clear policy proposals for the manufacturing, trading and service sectors, it had less to say about the implications for banking and finance. This omission would come back to bite him in 1965.

BANKING REFORM

The rescue of the Liu Chong Hing Bank in June 1961 had underlined the risks being taken by banks that used deposits to participate in property development and speculation. While subsequent investigation had shown that Liu Chong Hing Bank was poorly managed, and had blurred the line between depositors' funds and owners' capital, the primary issue had been one of liquidity. The bank had significant deposits that were in theory available for depositors to withdraw, but they had lent these out in long-term loans, predominantly to property speculators. With negligible liquid assets, any run on the bank rapidly threatened its survival. And with no depositor protection, customers were quick to withdraw funds from any institution that concerned them.

Banking regulation was known to be weak, and even before the war the government recognized the need to strengthen it, particularly for banks dealing with personal savings. But no action was taken and then the war intervened. In response to a flood of banks opening after the war, and a concern that some of these were involved in smuggling or destabilizing speculation, a Banking Ordinance was introduced in 1948 (Schenk 2001). However, this did little more than require banks to hold a licence. Catherine Schenk (2001) has summarized the paucity of regulation:

> There were no reserve requirements, nor statutory liquidity ratios, and no requirement to publish or even to prepare complete balance sheets. So long as the $5,000 licence fee could be raised, individuals or groups were free to attract deposits and operate as banks.

The excuse for not doing more was that local Chinese banks had largely grown out of currency exchange shops, and that the growth in deposits had been fairly recent. There was, of course, some truth in this. In the immediate post-war period deposits were small, generally belonging to the wealthy, with the smaller banks focused on foreign exchange. Credit was advanced carefully, and generally to manufacturing projects. But deposits started to rise quite rapidly in the late 1950s, increasingly from a wide base of depositors, for whom the deposits represented a very large part of their savings. And credit was being used for more speculative activities, particularly in the property sector. The combination of a broad unprotected depositor base, a lack of regulation and increasingly aggressive lending practices meant the 1948 ordinance was no longer fit for purpose.

Even the limited banking regulations that did exist were applied with a light touch, and basic data on the financial sector was not collected or used. The belief in markets sorting themselves out was strong. Some believe that even high-level data would have helped policy makers identify increasing risk taking; for example, Goodstadt (2007) notes that the overall loan/deposit ratio was estimated at 48 per cent in 1954, 67 per cent in 1959 and 70 per cent in 1964. This increasing leverage combined with a view as to the security of the loan book could have informed policy makers, but in practice it did not.

Whatever the historical reasoning, it had become apparent that the regulations needed to catch up, and by 1963 Cowperthwaite would argue that 'the [1948] ordinance is of little practical use for the protection either of depositors or of the general financial security of the Colony'.[2] This assessment was somewhat late in coming. Clarke had told a Bank of England official of his concerns in 1960.[3]

HELP FROM THE BANK OF ENGLAND

After some persuasion the Bank of England agreed to help draft a new set of banking regulations, and the bank's H. J. Tomkins was commissioned in December 1961 to do so. He arrived in February 1962 and set to work, using a combination of the North Borneo Banking Ordinance and a draft produced by Reginald Oliphant, the head of Hongkong Bank (Schenk 2001).

He fairly quickly produced a draft that he sent to the Banking Advisory Committee in March 1962. It included a requirement to hold higher levels of liquid assets, proper auditing of banks' books, reporting of activities to the financial secretary's department, and regulation and supervision of licensed banks. Banks would be required to maintain a satisfactory liquidity ratio. Banks would also have to have capital of at least $5 million, and 25 per cent of their liabilities needed to be in cash, gold or deposits with other banks.[4] Importantly, it included some protections for depositors.

As expected, there was debate about some of the measures. Oliphant lobbied for his own proposals, which would have strengthened Hongkong Bank's position and reduced the effect of regulations on its business (Goodstadt 2005). The smaller, local banks wanted an exemption from many of the measures, and more time to implement them. In general, Tomkins did allow them significant exemptions, subject to them accepting no more than $2 million in deposits and not calling themselves banks. However, the government largely went ahead with Tomkins's proposals.

Tomkins and Cowperthwaite discussed the proposals, and possible variants. They were agreed that the financial secretary should not have the power to set interest rates, or the terms of lending, since that would give him control he did not want. There was debate as to whether a central bank should be created, but in the end Cowperthwaite and the Hong Kong government succeeded in their rejection of this idea. For different reasons, Tomkins and Cowperthwaite agreed that there should be limited ability for the financial secretary to intervene in detailed policy and practice. Cowperthwaite because he did not want to interfere with the market, Tomkins because he 'was reluctant to leave a lot of taps and levers lying around for inexperienced hands to twiddle'.[5]

After much discussion about the role of the various regulatory bodies, it was agreed that banks would have to submit quarterly returns on business performed, and to be subject to supervision and regulation, which would be conducted by a Commissioner of Banking and a Banking Supervisory Committee.

SLOWLY MOVING TO TIGHTER REGULATION

The draft Banking Ordinance was published in April 1962, just after Cowperthwaite's first budget. It had been a comprehensive piece of work, completed in a short period of time. Now it would be batted around the Hong Kong establishment for over a year before coming to the Legislative Council, largely unchanged. On 19 June 1963 Cowperthwaite presented his proposed Banking Bill to the Legislative Council.

Cowperthwaite summarized the purpose of the bill:

> It is designed to provide a minimum paid up capital and published reserves, to ensure adequate liquidity, to prevent speculation with depositors' funds and, by a system of bank inspection, to ensure the maintenance of sound banking practices.[6]

Cowperthwaite accepted that the banking sector was an integral part of the economy of the colony. It had moved from a focus on exchange to taking deposits and funding investments. While this brought advantages, it also brought risks:

> The whole banking system on which our economy now depends so largely has become more vulnerable to any loss of confidence in banks on the part of the general public; and protection of the savings of the individual, who relies on the fiduciary status implied by the title 'bank', has become a matter of greater public concern.

He had begun to realize how the sector created particular danger where bankers pursued risky speculation with other people's money:

> Most of our bankers are indeed conservative men, in the good sense; and I must pay a tribute here to the imagination and foresight with which they have nurtured the growth of our commerce and industry and of all the other elements in our economic and social development. But there are a number of bankers who have conducted and are still conducting their affairs in a manner completely foreign to the traditions of sound banking. The truth is that they are not really bankers, either by experience or in practice. They regard their banks as convenient channels for securing control of the public's funds for their own speculations in land, in shares and in similar ventures, without regard to banking principles. It is against this kind of abuse of banking and of the name 'bank' that this Bill is aimed. Sound banks will hardly be affected by it as it embodies the principles they already follow.

Through the process, Cowperthwaite had learnt a great deal about banking economics, behaviour and regulation. But it is not clear that he saw this as an urgent area for action. His slow pace at bringing the Banking Ordinance to the Legislative Council was matched by it taking another year for it to become law. And when the new regulations came into force in December 1964 banks were given a further twelve-month period to comply. When, in early 1965, a major banking crisis occurred, Cowperthwaite might well have wished he had pushed a little harder, and a little faster, on regulating the banks.

Alongside the demands that Hong Kong manage its exports, and with Britain's potential entry to the EEC threatening the low tariffs that Hong Kong enjoyed within the Commonwealth, this banking crisis added further political weight to those who questioned whether the laissez-faire stance of the government had run its course and whether the colony needed to find a new, more regulated approach to banking and to other industries.

CHAPTER 12

COWPERTHWAITE'S FIRST BUDGET

A PARTIAL ANSWER REGARDING LAISSEZ-FAIRE

As the forces of protectionism grew, as the access to Hong Kong's biggest market narrowed, and as the banking sector showed the dangers of light regulation, there was great interest in the business community and the press as to where Cowperthwaite would stand on Clarke's challenge to laissez-faire. Given his preoccupation with trade matters it is perhaps not surprising that Cowperthwaite spoke very infrequently during his first year in office about the broader economic issues. In fact, he was largely silent during the Legislative Councils of 1961.

But he did make some remarks at the first Legislative Council in January 1962, in response to a question from Ruttonjee about whether rising rents would have a negative effect on inflation and living standards. His answer suggested a preference to let the market be left to work, but at the same time highlighted the very substantial government activity involved in increasing housing supply:

> Rent is basically a matter of supply and demand and Government must consider what it can effectively do to improve the position by influencing either factor. There is little that can be done or should be done on the demand side. So far as supply is concerned

> let me say straight away that any attempt to bring rents generally under control would almost certainly make the housing situation worse, not better. The private builder will not build if his investment in housing, unlike other investments, is subjected to statutory restrictions. The result would be, assuming effective control, that existing tenants would be accommodated at rents below market price and others would have no accommodation at all.

He argued that the private sector was very active in constructing new homes, investing nearly $200 million in capital to house around 70,000 people. Having championed the role of the entrepreneur and the market, Cowperthwaite then performed the tricky task of explaining how active the government was in the housing market, with programmes that aimed to resettle 100,000 people annually and house a further 20,000 in low-cost housing. The Housing Authority, the Housing Society and the Settlers Housing Corporation would use more than $50 million of government loans, plus some of their own funds, to provide accommodation for another 40,000 persons. And the Civil Servants' Co-operative Housing Schemes would spend $25 million of loan funds this year to produce housing, other than resettlement, for about 70,000 persons next year.[1]

Those wanting to understand exactly where Cowperthwaite stood would have to wait for his first budget speech. While remaining reticent about his overall approach, Cowperthwaite made no attempt to move towards a planned economy. As the *Far Eastern Economic Review Yearbook* of 1961 put it:

> Despite the urgings from the academics, the Government continued its policy of supervising economic progress without any overall plan. Left to the fortunes of opportunity and indiscipline, the economy prospered.[2]

Cowperthwaite's only other intervention at a Legislative Council prior to his first budget was when he introduced the Government Lotteries Bill on 14 February 1962. The idea of a lottery had been introduced by Clarke. It would be run by the government and would pay 60 per cent of its revenues out in prizes, with profits being allocated to social welfare projects in the colony. Cowperthwaite expected the proceeds to be relatively modest: around $2 million per annum for the first few years. But this would be a significant addition to the sum of around $4 million that the government had given to private welfare organizations in the last year. The sums raised would in fact be much greater than predicted. It was another example of where the line between the private and public sectors was somewhat blurred.

COWPERTHWAITE'S FIRST BUDGET

When he was appointed financial secretary in April 1961 it had appeared as if Cowperthwaite had nearly a year to prepare for his first budget: a speech that would set the tone for his time in office. At the beginning of the year this must have seemed like plenty of time, but the year had been consumed with overseeing the trade negotiations with the United States and Lancashire, representing Hong Kong's interests in the United Kingdom's discussions with the EEC, and putting in place an examination of the colony's banking regulations. It was fortunate that Cowperthwaite had a reserve of experience that enabled him to juggle these demands on his time. In early 1962 Cowperthwaite prepared to deliver his first budget to the Legislative Council for their approval.

The governor, Sir Robert Black, set the context at the Legislative Council on 28 February 1962. He described the economy as broadly trading in line with expectations, with re-exports slightly down and exports of domestically manufactured products slightly up.[3] He expressed concern about increasing competition, especially in textiles, and he pointed out that the recent census indicated that there would be a significant increase in the labour force due to young Hong Kong-born workers coming of age, and that to maintain employment this would require exports to grow at around 10 per cent per year. He saw a need for increasing productivity, and also a need to develop new industries. Black thought that there had been good progress in education, housing and public health, and he highlighted the steps that had recently been taken to provide the beginnings of a social welfare programme. Cowperthwaite would have approved as the governor emphasized that these investments were dependent on economic growth, as were much-needed investments in critical infrastructure, particularly in water supply and roads.

Having set the scene, Black gave the floor to Cowperthwaite to introduce his first budget. Cowperthwaite struck a modest tone:

> Sir, I face the task of introducing the Colony's budget for the first time with some diffidence as I realize that I can aspire neither to the lucidity nor to the wit of my predecessor. I am also very much aware that during his ten-year tenure of office he saw the Colony's annual expenditure rise from $170 million to his last estimate of $1,075 million and that he wound up his last budget speech with the prophecy that in much less than ten years more it would reach $2,000 million. I fear that to-day we will be taking a first by no means inconsiderable step along this road.

When Cowperthwaite stepped down after a decade in office, annual expenditure would not be $2,000 million though: it would be around $3,000 million.

THE TRADITION OF CONSERVATISM IS RETAINED

As was customary, Cowperthwaite started by updating the Council on the out-turn for previous years. And as was now almost expected, both years would show government finances to be much stronger than had been originally forecast. 1960/61 was now expected to show a surplus of $14 million versus the $55 million deficit Clarke had estimated a year before, and against an original forecast of an 'alarming' $154 million deficit.

A similar improvement was now expected for 1961/62, where the original forecast of a deficit of $161 million had:

> once again, melted away to give place to the revised estimate that there will be a surplus of $21 million. And I suspect once again that the final figure will be higher, perhaps $50 million or even more. My predecessor has given me permission to put the blame for this error of forecasting on him, if blame it be, but has told me that he will accept no further responsibility in the matter.

Cowperthwaite then turned to the estimates for 1962/63. Revenues were forecast to be $1,058 million. The tax on salaries and profits was expected to raise $205 million, Post Office revenues were estimated at over $60 million and land sales were expected to raise a record $106 million. Expenditures were forecast to reach $1,226 million, including $438 million of non-recurrent public works. These numbers produced a forecast deficit of $168 million. Cowperthwaite teased his audience about the ways in which he had considered raising taxes to cover the deficit, and raised the issue once again of moving to a 'normal' full income tax. Acknowledging that it would take some time to move to a new taxation system, he explained that he had considered raising the tax rates under the existing system but concluded that the projected deficit was not large enough to warrant this move.

THE LINK BETWEEN TAXATION AND CAPITAL INVESTMENT

Cowperthwaite reflected further on advice that he had received to raise earnings and profit taxes while profits were buoyant, an argument that he had rejected because of his belief that capital was efficiently allocated by the private sector in Hong Kong:

> Enterprise in Hong Kong has a good record of productive re-investment and I have a keen realization of the importance of not withdrawing capital from the private sector of the economy, particularly when it is responsible for an important part of the public services. I am confident, however old-fashioned this may sound, that funds left in the hands of the public will come into the Exchequer with interest at the time in the future when we need them.

He had clearly thought carefully about how to allocate resources between the private and public sectors. He could see the benefits that came from public spending, but he also recognized the benefits of private investment. And in making the trade-off as to where to direct the marginal resources, he was aware of how productive investments generated compound returns over time.

PECUNIA NON OLET

In good budget tradition of having some giveaways, Cowperthwaite announced that he would abolish the conservancy fee charged for the removal of 'nightsoil' from multistorey buildings that did not have water-borne sanitation. Drawing on his classical education he emphasized that this was because the tax fell on the poorest, and was expensive to collect, rather than because he objected to taxing unpleasant acts, noting:

> The Roman Emperor, Vespasian, imposed a tax on public conveniences. When his friends remonstrated with him, saying that he should not levy so degrading a tax, he held up a coin, sniffed it and said 'This coin does not smell'.

A LIMIT ON BORROWING

Cowperthwaite then turned to the medium term, having resurrected the idea of completing a five-year forecast. It showed that between 1962/63 and 1966/67 capital expenditure for existing programmes would be around $2,570 million: around double the amount for the previous five years. Recurrent revenues would fall from 127 per cent of recurrent expenditures to 115 per cent. To Cowperthwaite this left a gap that needed to be filled. He described the conundrum he felt:

> Now how do we plan to fill the gap? Here I am in something of a dilemma. I am told by the taxpayer that taxes, in particular income tax, should not be increased until we have borrowed, preferably from abroad. Foreign lenders on the other hand,

> particularly non-commercial ones, feel that they should not be asked to lend to us, when there are so many other needy clients in the world, until we have increased our taxes, not perhaps as high as some of our neighbours, but at least to a significantly higher level than at present.

He felt that local borrowing would be difficult and expensive, and he was concerned about the burden it would place on future generations:

> The fact that previous generations have handed down to us a substantial public heritage by way of roads, port, etc., almost completely free of debt, seems to me to impose some limitation on the validity of the theory that by borrowing we should, or could, pass on the burden of development to the next generation.

Cowperthwaite hoped that a 'middle road' might be found, with half the deficit being covered by tax rises and half by borrowings. He promised to keep the issue under review and to maintain the practice of compiling a five-year forecast despite the additional administrative burden that this entailed – a burden that met some resistance from the department heads.

A PARADIGM FOR PUBLIC SERVICES

Cowperthwaite used his first budget to describe his views on public services in more detail. He was aware that public services would grow substantially over the years ahead, both in the breadth of services offered and in terms of the usage rates of each service. Given this expected growth, his main concerns were that the services be set up in a way that enabled a smooth and affordable extension of these services. He saw several issues, the first of which was whether the true economic costs of provision were being recognized:

> In one sense some public services are too cheap at present. I have always been a little unhappy that the price of some services, such as housing and water, should be based, as they are, on interest rates and redemption periods which are so very far out of line with those applying in the private sector of the economy. This has, perhaps, not had any very serious consequences so long as services have been financed almost wholly from taxation. At the latest when we begin to finance these services with borrowed money, but preferably rather earlier, it will be necessary to reflect more realistic interest rates and redemption periods in the prices we charge; to continue present practices would produce a severe financial burden on general revenue and a gross degree of inequity.

His second concern – and one that he would reiterate in the years ahead – was whether public services were a safety net for those who would not otherwise be able to afford these services or a broader entitlement for citizens who could in fact pay for them themselves. For Cowperthwaite universal provision only made sense with a progressive tax policy, which the colony did not have:

> In a full welfare state, where welfare services go hand in hand with steeply progressive personal taxation, the administrative convenience of providing free or nominally priced services to rich and poor alike is not seriously prejudiced by considerations of equity. We do not have a steeply progressive taxation system and I often wonder whether the substantial subsidies we give, for example, in education, to all, irrespective of ability to pay, are really justified.

He used the subsidy directed at education to illustrate his point:

> I am told, although I have not checked the figures myself, that every single pupil in a Government secondary school receives a subsidy of at least $1,150 a year out of a recurrent cost of $1,470. In Government primary schools the subsidy is $352 out of $402. In subsidized schools the subsidy is rather smaller but nevertheless very substantial. There are, of course, a considerable number of free places in addition. It would seem to me that there is a strong case for higher standard fees with subsidized places only for those who need them.

THE INTRACTABLE LINK BETWEEN PUBLIC SERVICES, TAX AND GROWTH

But it was not just the equity issue that concerned him so much as the ability to make affordable public services available to a broader part of the community in the years ahead without having to halt the investment in infrastructure:

> The worrying thing is that we are still very short of giving an adequate public service to the whole community. The main reason for the comparative ease with which we have so far financed our expansion is that we have been providing services for only part of the population, while taxing the whole of it.

He then tried to provide a framework for officials and members of the Legislative Council as to the balance of service provision, growth and taxation. He explicitly linked these issues together. Because he saw that there was a natural growth of expenditure as public service provision widened, he was keen that new services and the level of provision be very carefully considered:

> The question is, will our wealth grow rapidly enough to make it possible to provide, at reasonable rates of taxation, public services at their present standards, and at the cost these standards involve, to meet the reasonable needs of the whole community? Sometimes I have wondered if our standards and the consequential cost were not too high for this to be possible. Recently a head of department, whom I will not name, said in a press interview that the service he was providing cost only half as much per head of the population as the same service costs in Britain. I am not sure what he meant to show by that, but, as Britain has about four times the income per head we have, his service in fact costs, in relative terms, twice as much as the British one does – and, this is the frightening thing – he says he must expand further.
>
> I myself believe that, if we are not careful, at the rate at which we are going we will reach a point in the not very distant future where we cannot afford to expand the public service any further, although we are still not providing a full and adequate service. To put the matter in over-simplified terms, we have a choice between quantity and quality. I have hopes that increasing wealth will allow us to have a full public service of reasonable quality but I fear that in a number of spheres our standards are at present set at a level which will make it necessary to call a halt before that stage is reached.

In this, his first budget, Cowperthwaite had neatly provided enough continuity and a little change. The *Far Eastern Economic Review* called it a 'standstill budget' offering taxpayers a reprieve.[4] He had begun to outline his philosophy on how public services might develop, and how they would be constrained by the need for a low level of taxation. This in turn made economic growth essential. A faster level of growth would allow greater public provision, and a slowdown in economic growth could lead to basic needs being unmet. It would not be until the wrapping-up debate on the budget that Cowperthwaite would clarify the question as to what policies could best deliver this essential growth.

LEGISLATIVE COUNCIL'S RESPONSE TO THE BUDGET

The response from the Unofficials to Cowperthwaite's first budget was very positive. No doubt this was in large part because while he had raised issues and questions, he had not raised tax rates. When the Unofficials replied on 19 March, each had their own particular points that they wanted to make – mostly about keeping taxes low, but also about pursuing their pet areas for intervention. Each member congratulated

Cowperthwaite on his maiden budget speech as they replied in turn. Most also emphasized the importance of keeping tax rates low, following the lead of Barton, who was the first to speak:

> The big question which Government has to face is how much additional direct taxation can this Colony face up to without serious damage to our economy. I shall stick my neck out by suggesting that the ceiling for direct taxation in this Colony should be 20% – that is to say about half what it is in neighbouring countries – in the belief that any increase, or even the fear of any increase, over this figure would do irreparable damage to the Colony's economy.
>
> If we are to continue to attract new industries – and we are all agreed that we must do so – we must remember that we are in competition with our neighbours for these industries.[5]

The Unofficials were clear on their desire to keep tax rates low, and indeed to continue to reject the idea of a 'normal' income tax. But several members thought there was a need for greater intervention in the economy and in housing. Barton and others felt that the colony could get some outside experts to help create a plan for economic development over the next five years. Barton referred back to the dilemma that Arthur Clarke posed two years before as to whether to continue with laissez-faire or to use greater planning and controls, making clear his preference that government help manage capacity in the textile industry:

> The decision at that time Sir, was that laissez faire must continue, and our largest industry the textile industry is now paying the penalty for having expanded 'too fast and having sold too much too quickly and too cheaply'.
>
> As you are aware, Sir, this particular industry has now changed its tune, and the Government has received many representations, not only for controlling the imports of cloth from Japan which are used by our garment industry for exports, principally to the USA, but also for controlling the rate of the industry's further expansion.
>
> The reason why I raise this controversial issue in this debate is that I believe it will help Hong Kong's cause in all our most important markets if it can be stated in this Council Chamber that the industry is prepared to accept some form of Government control to regulate its expansion, and has indeed been advocating it for some months past.

Ruttonjee returned to the issue of rent controls, which he had raised earlier in the year, arguing for intervention in the housing markets. Believing that the market could not fix itself, Ruttonjee agreed with Cowperthwaite that the solution was to encourage private investment in construction, but with the addition of a cap on its return on capital of 12.5 per cent: a rate that he believed would not discourage investment. In addition, he proposed government controls over rents:

> What is needed is a Fair Rents Tribunal – a strong impartial body to which tenants can bring, free of charge, their complaints against rent increases, for assessment and decision, much in the same way as tribunals assess compensation for those obliged to move out of protected premises.

While these measures might well improve affordability, he left unsaid why he thought these measures would encourage greater supply. As usual, the unofficial members set a tone rather than a plausible alternative strategy, and as usual their comments represented their own specific interests and a general commentary on the government's programme.

COWPERTHWAITE ACKNOWLEDGES THE OPPOSITION TO TAX REFORM

Cowperthwaite listened carefully to these points being made and then replied at the next meeting on 30 March 1962.[6] First he addressed the issue of the best form of income tax, revealing again that successive financial secretaries found it very difficult to reconcile themselves to the somewhat illogical, but pragmatic, solution that was already in place:

> I have been left under no illusion about the opposition to full income tax. I should explain first that I do not mean by this necessarily the complex British system; it means simply that tax would be payable on an individual's total taxable income, on a sliding scale with personal allowances, instead of on various sources of income at a flat rate. The present system is not simple and is attended in practice with all the difficulties and complexities (and most of the costs) of a full Income Tax, combined with its own defects of comparative ineffectiveness and inequity.[6]

ANSWERING 'THE CLARKE QUESTION'

Cowperthwaite then went on to cast doubts on the benefits of supporting particular nascent industries. He doubted that inducements of cheap land, or lower taxes, were the driving force in attracting companies to a new location, but rather he suspected that it was the promise of a protected domestic market that was the key draw. And that inducement was not practical in the context of Hong Kong's free-trade policy.

He was, in any case, rather doubtful about the long-term benefits of providing protection to growing industries, arguing that 'an infant industry, if coddled, tends to remain an infant industry and never grows up or expands'.[6]

Cowperthwaite was at his most expansive as he responded to the idea that there could be a greater level of industrial planning in Hong Kong. Where Clarke had posed the question in his 1960 budget speech about the wisdom of relying on a laissez-faire policy, Cowperthwaite wanted to be clear about his views on central planning:

> I now come to the more general and far-reaching suggestion made by Mr Barton and Mr Knowles, that is, the need to plan our economic future and in particular, the desirability of a five-year plan. I would like to say a few words about some of the principles involved in the question of planning the overall economic development of the Colony.
>
> I must, I am afraid, begin by expressing my deep-seated dislike and distrust of anything of this sort in Hong Kong. Official opposition to overall economic planning and planning controls has been characterized in a recent editorial as 'Papa knows best'. But it is precisely because Papa does not know best that I believe that Government should not presume to tell any businessman or industrialist what he should or should not do, far less what he may or not do; and no matter how it may be dressed up that is what planning is.

Cowperthwaite, aware of the trends towards bigger government that prevailed around the world, and in particular the increased government involvement in the UK economy, explained why he felt that Hong Kong particularly needed to retain its laissez-faire stance:

> Economic planning is fashionable in countries which need some artificial stimulus to development of their natural resources, and in countries which, for doctrinaire reasons or because they are rich enough to afford the luxury, are more concerned with easing social and economic transitions and with the distribution of wealth than with its maximization. But we must be careful to understand that practically all economic theory for the last fifty years with a bearing on this has had as its basic assumption the existence of a closed economy. We are the extreme case of an open economy; we are, as a mathematician would say, at the limit where factors vital elsewhere are negligible, and where factors relatively negligible elsewhere are vital. Our case is not in the modern text books.
>
> An economy can be planned, I will not say how effectively, when there are unused resources and a finite, captive, domestic market, that is, when there is a possibility of control of both production and consumption, of both supply and demand. These are not our circumstances; control of these factors lies outside our borders. For us a

> multiplicity of individual decisions by businessmen and industrialists will still, I am convinced, produce a better and wiser result than a single decision by a Government or by a board with its inevitably limited knowledge of the myriad factors involved, and its inflexibility.

He concluded, as he had before and as he would again, by echoing the words of Adam Smith in defence of a market-based approach:

> Over a wide field of our economy it is still the better course to rely on the nineteenth century's 'hidden hand' than to thrust clumsy bureaucratic fingers into its sensitive mechanism. In particular, we cannot afford to damage its mainspring, freedom of competitive enterprise.

THE ADMINISTRATION CLOSES RANKS

To reinforce the message that the colony did not intend to go down the path of planning, the colonial secretary, Claude Burgess, in closing the Budget debate, described why the government did not see a five-year plan as the way forward.[6] He started with the problems of trying to predict the future:

> In the final analysis the plan is worth no more than the result it achieves. To achieve any result at all it must be based on assumptions that are at least relatively stable and relatively sure. There are I suggest remarkably few assumptions that could be made about our economic future that would fulfil these requirements. We have a free economy that changed freely and without official direction from a mainly entrepôt character to a largely industrial character. That free economy has served us very well.

While agreeing that increasing export restrictions on textiles created a need to find new industries, he doubted whether a government plan was the best method to achieve this. He went further and questioned how a plan to diversify the industrial base might work. Acknowledging that there were many approaches, the one he had heard mentioned most was to limit growth in specific industries, thereby forcing businesses to diversify. This could be combined with a favourable stance towards chosen sectors. He thought that the government's ability to decide when to limit growth in an industry was limited:

> My honourable Friend, the financial secretary, tells me that it was in about 1947 that he was first told that our textile industry was too big and that further expansion should be stopped. We have certainly been told the same story over the intervening

> years. It is perhaps fortunate that Government did not yield to those arguments; for whatever the troubles its success has brought, the textile industry is the foundation of our present fortunes. And we still have less than 10% of existing international trade.

Burgess then emphasized that his opposition to a planned economy was the practical one that it would not work. Perhaps making a friendly dig at Cowperthwaite, he accepted that there were also those who were opposed on issues of principle:

> There may be some honourable Members who feel that it would be morally wrong to impose restrictions of this kind; and there may be others who feel that it would be economically revolutionary – and suicidal; but I will content myself with saying that the practical difficulties of any such scheme would be virtually insuperable. Who would be the fortunate industrialists to be so protected? At what stage of output would the line be drawn? To what types of industry would the privilege be restricted? And who is to say that the new man, if he can succeed in establishing himself, is not going to do better, in prices and quality and markets, than his long-established competitor?

His argument was not that government had no role but rather that it had a limited role as an enabler, with overseas representation, and with a business-friendly environment. But the heavy lifting would need to be done in the private sector.

Burgess's wrapping up showed that Cowperthwaite had succeeded in uniting the administration around the value of free markets and of the private sector having primacy in resource allocation. The government had answered the question posed by Clarke in his last budget. Laissez-faire – or rather the pragmatic, Hong Kong version of it – would continue. The idea of a planned economy had been rejected.

COWPERTHWAITE'S MANIFESTO

That Cowperthwaite should have orchestrated such a response is not a surprise. He accepted the key tenets that underpinned the economic policy of the Hong Kong administration. Not only did he accept them, he believed them. He had helped shape them and he was one of their most thoughtful and lucid proponents. He believed that Hong Kong needed to be a free port, with free trade at its core. He believed that the market was best at allocating resources and determining what was produced and how. He saw government's role as creating the legal framework in which property rights could be upheld and contracts relied upon. Beyond that, government should mostly step aside unless there was very clear evidence that the market would not work. He believed in the government balancing its books and not running up debts. Given his beliefs that capital must necessarily be free to move from Hong Kong and the desirability of allowing that to happen, he understood that there were real limits to the ability to tax the productive base of the economy. Logically, if the government should balance its books, and there was a limit on tax raising, then government spending must be carefully managed to stay within the boundaries that these rules set.

His belief was not only that many of these tenets were right and necessary, but also that following them would lead to a virtuous circle of success. Free trade and free enterprise could allocate labour and capital to the activities that would provide the best return. With good returns, and low taxes, businesses would reinvest, creating further growth. Increased productivity and higher levels of capital would raise earnings and living standards. A larger, more profitable economy, with higher levels of earnings, would increase government revenues and therefore in turn facilitate higher levels of government spending. Now that he oversaw economic policy, he could entrench these beliefs even more vigorously in Hong Kong.

CHAPTER 13

FISCAL FUNDAMENTALS

After a hectic start to the job, Cowperthwaite had the chance to firmly establish his fiscal policy over his next three budgets in 1963, 1964 and 1965. These allowed him to detail his broader economic policies as he focused on domestic economic issues. He would explain his thinking on how public services should evolve and the relationship between public spending, taxation and economic growth.

THE BLACK PHILOSOPHY

Governor Sir Robert Black introduced the 1963 and 1964 budgets. In 1963, he characterized the previous year as one in which a number of potential threats had not come to pass, especially after Britain's application to join the EEC had 'come to a curious ending for the time being'.[1] The following year, in his seventh and final pre-budget address,[2] he celebrated the growth in exports. In both addresses the governor fêted the success of social policy while acknowledging that Hong Kong was very much a developing rather than a developed economy.

Primary and secondary school numbers had hit new highs, although provision was still patchy beyond the normal school leaving age of twelve. In 1964 he celebrated the establishment of a Chinese University. Public health provision was improving, particularly in regard to vaccinations, as cholera, tuberculosis and polio remained prevalent and a cause of many deaths. Housing provision and resettlement continued to be a priority, particularly in the light of very high immigration levels. Water provision was a major challenge requiring significant investment given population growth and increased consumption. The 1963 drought had led to water often only being available from standpipes.

The governor could reflect that the previous six years had seen a remarkable expansion:

> Although, as yet, we have no national income statistics, everything points to the economy expanding at between 10% and 15% a year compound during at least the last four or five years of this period. It is also apparent that individual incomes have increased very significantly. The population has increased by about 37%. Total exports have increased by 60%, re-exports of Hong Kong products by about 90%. The number of registered factories has increased by 30%, but their average size is much larger as employment in them has risen by 135%. Industrial wages have increased by about 60%, while the retail price index, which in 1958 stood at an average of 117, now stands at 124. Electricity consumption has grown by about 100%. Recurrent revenue, with only minor tax changes, has more than doubled, and capital revenue has increased six-fold as a consequence of the boom in land values. Bank deposits have risen by 300%, and bank advances to commerce and industry by rather more. Surely this is an astonishing picture of sustained growth?[2]

The governor put this success down to 'the quality of our people, their thrift, industriousness and quickness to react to economic stimuli – all old-fashioned virtues'. These virtues had:

> been given full scope by the economic environment we have maintained in Hong Kong: a stable currency, low direct taxation, freedom of enterprise, and absence of governmental control or interference with the free interplay of the forces of the market. These have been and remain the preconditions of our ability to overcome the handicaps that nature and geography have imposed upon us.

Black ended his 1964 address with a broader articulation of his philosophy, emphasizing how economic progress improved people's lives but stressing that social progress must follow economic progress rather than the reverse:

> Economic progress, of course, is not an end in itself. Its raison d'être is to enhance the well-being of the whole community. Our basic aim is to raise the standard of living of our people.
>
> The best guarantee of social progress in Hong Kong is full employment in an efficient and expanding economy which not only permits but also promotes a process of levelling up rather than levelling down.
>
> We must, therefore, always carry through extension in the field of social legislation with a close eye to its effect on economic expansion.[2]

In both years, after setting the scene Black gave the floor to Cowperthwaite to deliver the budget.

THE 1963 BUDGET

In the 1963 budget Cowperthwaite acknowledged that the favourable environment had boosted government revenues. As usual, expenditures were below the budgeted levels. The net effect was to turn a forecast deficit for 1962/63 of $164 million into a surplus Cowperthwaite believed would exceed $100 million. He again pointed out that he was not unduly concerned by the swings in the forecasts:

> In recent years we have not generally allowed estimated deficits or realized surpluses in any one year to influence unduly either our plans for development or our levels of taxation.
>
> Critics of mis-estimates in the annual Budget, underestimate the difficulties of predicting even one year ahead (and they always speak from hind sight and also overestimate the real margin of error), are wrong in implying that these mis-estimates significantly affect policy; and even more wrong to suppose that they are deliberately induced to justify policy.[1]

Turning to the year ahead, Cowperthwaite underlined his conservative approach to budgeting, noting that:

> It would not, I think, be sound public finance to forecast on the basis of a continuation of our exceptionally rapid economic growth, although I, for one, will be by no means surprised if we in fact achieve it.

Cowperthwaite also drew attention to the balance between recurrent spending and capital expenditure. He considered the relationship between recurrent revenues and recurrent expenditure as being an important sign of the health of public finances. He viewed recurrent spending as a commitment that it was only possible to change with some difficulty. Capital spending, on the other hand, could be dialled up or down, at least to some extent, as revenues expanded or contracted. For him, the fact that recurrent spending was well covered by recurrent revenues was of great comfort.

Having explained his budgeting philosophy, Cowperthwaite turned to his proposed changes for the year. True to his laissez-faire approach, and contrary to any pressure to be seen to be doing something, his proposal was complete inaction:

> In the light of these figures what are my proposals for changes in taxation? Virtually none.
>
> Modern orthodoxy might suggest that, in our present period of relative prosperity and influx of capital, and their inflationary side-effects, I should increase taxation to damp down this inflation now and at the same time create a surplus from which our rate of spending, and so the economy, can be maintained in the event of a depression. I do not think this appropriate at this stage, partly because we have a reasonable nest-egg laid on already, partly because, as I said last year, I am old fashioned enough to believe that money should be allowed, so far as possible, to 'fructify in the pockets of the tax payer'. Furthermore, I will not be surprised if, once again, the estimated deficit turns into a surplus or at least a smaller deficit, even if financial caution must temper my budgeting.
>
> It has alternatively been suggested to me that I might consider some reduction in taxation. Equally I do not think that that is appropriate. Our present tax structure is clearly not inhibiting our economic growth.

Cowperthwaite's belief in reasonable tax rates was illustrated at the most micro level by a change he had made the previous year to duties on Chinese prepared tobacco. He noted that his 'experiment' in reducing the duty had increased the yield from $110,000 to $1,200,000. When the Unofficials replied to the budget, Lee would underline the benefits of low tax rates:

> The reduction in the rate of duty has resulted in a ten-fold increase in revenue. This gratifying result amply proves that a reasonable rate of duty rather than a high one ultimately brings in the revenue. It is sound policy to lay down a rate at which people could be induced to obey the law rather than to break it.[3]

ISSUES FOR THE FUTURE

Turning to the longer term, Cowperthwaite had repeated the five-year forecasting exercise while acknowledging its imprecision. But he felt that 'a glimmer of light is probably better than no light at all'. He noted that recurrent expenditure would be covered by recurrent revenues but that over the following five years capital expenditure was forecast to total $2,900 million. This would produce a deficit over the planning period of $570 million: slightly more than the equivalent forecast the previous year. He viewed the forecasts as being manageable and thought that they represented an appropriate level of growth in public spending over the years. He favoured a steady path:

> I would suggest that, when looking at annual surpluses (or deficits for that matter) one should not take the view that Government expenditure should fluctuate closely with the ups and downs, or, as I hope it will rather be, with the irregular, but continuous, upward movement of our economy. Recurrent expenditure is adjustable only within fairly narrow limits; while capital expenditure cannot be generated, or brought to a standstill, overnight.
>
> Our aim must be a steady forward progress, which is as rapid as efficiency and economy allow, makes adequate allowance for possible down-turns in the economy, and, very important, gets the priorities right.

He was also concerned that the capital expenditure programme should be fairly stable, rather than being overly sensitive to the state of government finances:

> Capital construction is already taking a very high proportion of our national product. I have already spoken of the danger that attempts to go too fast will merely raise costs without producing any more. It is, of course, possible that, as in recent years, our construction industry will be able to continue to expand its capacity very rapidly without inflating costs, but here another apprehension arises. It would be disastrous if, having induced an expansion of the construction industry, Government then had to apply a sudden brake on public works because of shortage of funds. Quite apart from the effect on the particular industry directly concerned, it is undesirable from a general economic point of view that an economic depression should coincide with a brake on Government activity.

He then addressed the issue of how the forecast deficit of $570 million might be met. His intention was to balance the books with an equal contribution from extra taxes and from extra borrowing in the open market. However, there was one route that he wanted to be clear that he would not countenance:

> I will not be proposing a course which has been under some public discussion recently – deficit financing. It is wholly inappropriate to our economic situation. In its least extreme form it is based on the theory that additional money generated by a Government deficit (and given currency, as necessary, by use of the printing press) will stimulate consumption and thereby production, in time to match the excess money with goods before real inflationary harm is done. Unfortunately we don't, and can't, produce more than a small fraction of what we consume, and increased consumption would merely mean increased imports without matching exports; and a severe balance of payment crisis, which would destroy Hong Kong's credit and confidence in the Hong Kong dollar; and which we could not cure without coming close to ruining

> ourselves. Keynes was not writing with our situation in mind. In this hard world we have to earn before we spend.

THE UNOFFICIAL RESPONSE

The unofficial members of Legislative Council welcomed the 'unexciting' budget and hoped future budgets would be equally unexciting.[3] The Unofficials' speeches were filled with the normal mix of topics close to their own interests, ranging across education, health, housing and other areas where they felt government should be doing more. When Cowperthwaite replied to the comments made at the next Legislative Council,[4] he rather ungraciously observed:

> I had hoped that the routine nature of this year's Budget would reduce the number of shots fired at me in the debate and that to-day I would have little to do. Instead I find myself somewhat more heavily engaged than last year, although perhaps the shot has been of rather smaller gauge.

Perhaps the most important issue that the Unofficials were united on was their dislike of inheritance tax. They disliked it in principle and also argued that it was having a detrimental effect on Chinese businesses, where the head of household nominally controlled the family assets despite real ownership being distributed among family members. This created problems when the family head died, and all the family assets were taxed. Cowperthwaite did not argue that the tax itself was right but rather that it was effective and better than placing that tax burden elsewhere, such as on profits.

To a suggestion that the whole forecast future deficit be financed by loans, Cowperthwaite responded:

> I am also, I must confess, a little sceptical of the theory that we have a right, if we could, to pass on our capital burden to future generations. I remarked last year in this context that our predecessors had not passed any significant part of their burden on to us.

And to a proposal to restrict capital flows, Cowperthwaite reiterated his belief in the benefit of free capital flows:

> We enjoy a considerable net inflow of capital and I am sure that a condition of its coming, and staying, is that it is free to flow out again. It is also important for Hong Kong's status as a financial centre that there should be a maximum freedom of capital movement both in and out.

UPDATING LONDON

Alongside his 1963 budget Cowperthwaite wrote several times to Donald Kirkness at the Colonial Office to provide an update.[5] In early March Kirkness enquired about progress on tackling the 'ramshackle' tax structure.[6] Cowperthwaite replied that progress on introducing a full income tax had 'slipped a bit into the background'. He could not see how that agenda could be advanced until 'we manage a deficit or two'.

Kirkness also wondered whether there 'might be advantage in having something like a development plan for the future which could be coherently implemented rather than paying for as much of current departmental forecasts as the money ran to'. This earned a rebuke from Cowperthwaite:

> As regards a development plan I fear it is not in our philosophy. But it is a little hard, I think, to describe our present policy as 'incoherent'.[7]

After presenting the 1963 budget, and with everything looking under control, Cowperthwaite took four months' leave between 19 June and 17 October 1963.

THE EXCHANGE FUND

On his return to work Cowperthwaite introduced the Exchange Fund Amendment Bill. Until 1935 the Hong Kong dollar had been backed by silver. After that it was backed by sterling and the silver was converted to a sterling exchange fund, which backed the dollar notes issued. In order to be allowed to issue dollar banknotes, private note-issuing banks deposited sterling assets into the exchange fund. The fund invested these deposits in sterling securities and the income accrued to, and was held by, the government. Over time a very healthy surplus had been built up within the fund and it continued to grow each year.

But no mechanism had been created to transfer the surpluses in the fund to allow it to be used elsewhere in government. This bill remedied that by permitting any excess of assets over 105 per cent of the liabilities (i.e. the value of notes in issue) to be transferable as directed by the government and the Secretary of State. Having 105 per cent backing level was extremely conservative, but Cowperthwaite argued that:

> It is important for the international standing of the Hong Kong dollar, and therefore for our economic prosperity, that a high level of external cover should be maintained. It is our intention to maintain the full 105% cover in sterling.[8]

With this decision, Cowperthwaite effectively created a position where the note issue was in Hong Kong dollars but backed by sterling assets. This mismatch would cause significant issues in the future.

For now, even at the 105 per cent level the available surplus was over $380 million and was growing at $40 million each year. However, Cowperthwaite was keen to avoid any belief that this represented an opportunity to raise spending:

> I should add that, while we are only now proceeding to introduce [a] mechanism for releasing these funds, I have taken them fully into account in the last two years' Budgets, when assessing our future financial prospects. They are not a new and unbudgeted windfall.

THE 1964 BUDGET

Cowperthwaite's 1964 started with being appointed a Companion of the Most Distinguished Order of Saint Michael and Saint George on 1 January.[9]

The budget season started with the normal upward revision of previous estimates.[2] For the year ahead he forecast modest increases in revenues and a slightly faster growth in expenditures, driven by public works, particularly in improving water supplies, producing a forecast deficit of $118 million.

Cowperthwaite was conscious of how his forecast deficit might be viewed and acknowledged that he expected the actual results to be better than his current forecasts. As before, he described his approach to budgeting, explaining that the main function of the expenditure forecast was:

> the control, in some, but not excessive, detail, of expenditure of public funds on agreed programmes and objectives within the practical limits of efficient and economical expansion. The annual estimates are intended to determine as far as possible the pattern of Government spending for the year and each head and subhead of expenditure must be provided with an adequate sum to carry out its intended purpose.

Given the need to allow for expenditure that might occur through the year, it was natural that the departments would overestimate likely spending. If they were too cautious, and later needed funds, it would mean making cuts or returning to the Legislative Council for supplementary provisions.

Equally, revenue forecasts were designed to paint a broad picture of likely available funds:

> Revenue estimates are intended to show whether or not, on a reasonable view of the future, present taxes are likely to be adequate – or excessive, taking into account

reserves and the possibility of borrowing if appropriate, to meet the calls upon the public purse.

Cowperthwaite pointed out that the deficit or surplus was merely the mathematical result of reconciling two broad estimates. Given the way that strong economic growth would affect revenues, he explained why there would tend to be upward revisions when the economy was strong:

> For these reasons we have never in recent years used our estimated deficits as a justification for substantially increased taxation, nor, conversely, to reduce the rate of expansion of the public service.

He saw the surplus or deficit as an output, rather than as a potential policy tool. As in the past he showed his belief in classical economic policy, leaving the private sector to invest surplus cash:

> Economists of the modern school will no doubt protest that I have said nothing of the use of budget deficits or surpluses for the control of the economy in general. I doubt if such techniques would ever be appropriate in Hong Kong's exposed economic position; and I think they are certainly not appropriate at present, when in strict orthodoxy they would suggest the need to plan for a very substantial surplus 'to take the heat out of the economy'. Although we have in fact run substantial surpluses in recent years we have not done so with deflationary effect because we have not removed them from the economy but have left them inside the Colony's banking system to continue to work for the economy.

Given this philosophy and his doubts as to whether the forecast deficit would actually occur, he announced that he had no intention of increasing taxation generally.

He was quite aware that the booming economy and the resulting increase in government revenues could lead to demands for spending that were likely to be unsustainable in the longer term, whereas in downturns spending was likely to be examined very carefully. For this reason, he concluded that 'a Financial Secretary's life is paradoxically easier when money is scarce than when it is plentiful; he is riding with a tighter rein'.

SURPLUSES, TAXATION AND PUBLIC SERVICES

Cowperthwaite ended his speech by addressing the 'apparent paradox' of having annual surpluses, low taxation and inadequate public services. He argued that there were limits on how much the government could invest efficiently over the short term.

Increasing spending rapidly would, he believed, potentially lead to inflating costs, and it ran the risk that any surge in spending would be poorly controlled and delivered. In the longer term, he saw the task as balancing the likely long-term resources available to the government and the expected long-term needs. He had three main concerns: first, that public services, once introduced, were affordable on a sustainable basis; second, that recurrent spending did not crowd out more useful longer-term investments; and third, that services could be more widely provided as take up increased, and as population changes occurred.

To illustrate the issue, he pointed to a recent report on educational provision. The report had estimated that universal free education at primary and secondary level would cost $190 million per year. He doubted that the government could practically grow the education service quickly enough to provide this, and even if it could, the costs would be equivalent to a tax rate on earnings and profits of 17 per cent: a rate he did not believe was achievable without affecting long-term growth. Building the associated schools would require deep cuts in other capital investments. He stressed that his issue was one of timing and balance:

> I do not say that we will not be able to meet costs of this relative order over the whole field of public service at some future date while keeping taxation within bounds; but there is no evidence at present that we will be able to. What evidence we have is that we must either reduce costs or continue to provide a limited public service – or fail to keep taxation within bounds.

He then explained how he saw low rates of tax as central to economic growth, and in turn how economic growth was the engine of social progress and public services:

> Revenue has increased in no small measure, I am convinced, due to our low tax policy which has helped to generate an economic expansion in the face of unfavourable circumstances. Recurrent revenue has more than doubled in the five years since the year 1958/59 with no significant change in taxation. High taxation could not itself have produced this increased yield.
>
> Economic expansion remains the door to social progress and I am convinced that in our circumstances low taxation can in general produce a greater growth in revenue than can tax increases. I am not saying, however, that there is no scope for tax increases too; there clearly is.

Lastly, Cowperthwaite drew out some reasons as to why the financing of public services in Hong Kong would differ from the approach taken in Britain and most other developed economies. He offered two approaches that he considered fair. The first was progressive taxation and free services for all. The second was charging fees for services but with remission for those who cannot afford them. Both met the objective of making public services available to all. He argued that rich, developed countries would tend to progressive taxation and free services, because they believed they could apply progressive taxes without hurting the economy and they were willing to accept the waste inherent in universal free services. He saw Hong Kong as being more like poorer countries, where progressive taxation was difficult and where waste would be unacceptable.

However, he accepted that Hong Kong's approach had a number of contradictions:

> We do not consistently follow either course. Our system of taxation can barely be called progressive but many of the well-to-do enjoy quite heavily subsidised social services.
>
> We come closer to the category of society where fees should be charged to cover costs with remission for those who cannot afford them. I do not think that we could take progressive direct taxation very far at present without adverse economic effects, although I do not say that when the time comes we shall not be able to take it rather further than we do at present.
>
> But even if we can look forward to a sufficiency of social services one day, free of charge where appropriate, we can hardly accept it as equitable if, as is likely, the extent of subsidies enjoyed by the well-to-do must retard significantly, in the intermediate period, the extension of subsidised or free services to the poor. I have seen it claimed that the well-to-do have a right now to fully subsidised services because they pay for them in taxes. This is palpably not so in our present tax situation with its relatively low rate of direct taxation. If these taxes are to be regarded as payment for social services, then our poorer fellow-citizens are paying more than their fair share of other public expenditure.

The budget was well received and there was little disagreement with the analysis and the decisions that had been made. The press and the Unofficials had little to criticize. Cowperthwaite would do some tidying up of the Inland Revenue rules later in the year, but other than that he could afford to be sanguine about fiscal policy.[10]

In April 1964 Sir David Trench* became governor when Sir Robert Black retired after six years in office. Cowperthwaite worked with Trench during his first six

---

* David Trench was born in British India in 1915 and attended Jesus College, Cambridge. He joined the Colonial Office as a Cadet in the British Solomon Islands before serving in the army during the war. In 1950 came to Hong Kong working in defence, and became deputy financial secretary in 1956 and then deputy colonial secretary. Between 1961 and 1964 he was High Commissioner for the British Western Pacific Territories before returning to be governor in Hong Kong. He died in 1988.

months and then took leave in the autumn, between 12 September and 9 November, to go travelling, including visiting his sister Janet in Jamaica, calling on the governor-general while he was there.[11]

AN EFFECTIVE MODUS OPERANDI

Cowperthwaite had many pulls on his time but would involve himself in any policy area that had an economic dimension. As he engaged with an issue he took considerable time to understand it in detail. He wanted to understand how the economics worked. How did costs behave? What determined revenues? What levels of capital and labour were needed? What role did competition play? How did regulation affect the issue? What determined people's interests? He came to these questions with some existing frameworks, based on classical economics, which helped him shine his searchlight in the right areas. The resultant deep understanding made him a formidable advocate, and adversary. His arguments were based on expert knowledge combined with intellect, and on an ability to generalize and bring a coherent economic paradigm to bear. When he worked like this he usually got his way.

As he would discover over the next few years there were areas, such as banking, where his knowledge was not at the same level; and there were areas where he had little control over the outcome, such as UK macroeconomic policy. Alongside his natural abilities, the economic success of Hong Kong in the early 1960s, combined with his career to date, provided him with political and economic capital that would help him weather the challenges ahead.

THE LULL BEFORE THE STORM: THE 1965 BUDGET

Sir David Trench, the new governor, made his inaugural pre-budget statement at the Legislative Council on 25 February 1965.[12] An emerging banking crisis was only just beginning to unfold, and therefore, while it preoccupied some, it had little effect on the proceedings. Cowperthwaite did not see the nascent crisis as something that might affect fiscal policy unduly:

> The estimates had been virtually completed and this speech drafted before the recent banking difficulties came on us. Such events inevitably leave some scars and, although I am confident that they will heal quickly and Government will do all it can to assist, they could meanwhile have some effect on next year's revenue. There would in any case be no question of altering the expenditure estimates.

Trench spoke about the progress made across a wide range of public activities. He highlighted successes in providing better water supply and in completing the reservoir at Shek Pik, with a capacity of 24 million cubic metres. More than ninety resettlement blocks had been built, housing 109,000 people. The low-cost housing programme, the housing authority and the Housing Society had all been active, such that 'the total number of people housed directly or indirectly with the aid of public funds is now of the general order of 1,000,000 persons'. A social welfare programme had been launched, and Trench was keen to legitimize the role of social services:

> In all cases the aim of the social services is the same; namely, to work actively to restore those in need of help to the maximum degree of self-sufficiency and self-respect, and to develop the best that is in them in the interests of human dignity; and, as a lesser but still important aim, to limit their dependence upon the community. It is proper that everyone, be so approached, and never regarded as recipients of charity as of right or as mere vessels for the exercise of good works.

In education, primary school enrolment now exceeded 500,000, secondary schools had expanded, and the Chinese University was up and running. Medical facilities, particularly in radiology, were expanding and public health measures were improving.

The governor only briefly referred to the favourable economic environment that existed through 1964, with exports up by more than 15 per cent. Trench was clearly content to let Cowperthwaite talk to the economic brief while he dedicated his time to the many other areas of progress in the colony. This did not indicate any differences in philosophy between the two men: both believed in the primary need to get the economy to work, and then to use that success to create social and public progress.

TRADITIONAL START

Cowperthwaite's fourth budget speech began, as usual, by upgrading previous forecasts. The final outcome for 1963/64 was a surplus of over $100 million, against the estimate of a year earlier of $39 million and the original forecast a year before that of a deficit of $163 million.

For the current year, 1964/65, revenues were now estimated at $1,497 million versus the original forecast of $1,382 million. Expenditure was just below the original forecast, resulting in the forecast deficit of $114 million now becoming an estimated surplus of $8 million. Cowperthwaite believed the actual surplus would be even higher, although he did point out that the surplus was somewhat smaller than in previous years.

For 1965/66, the year ahead, he forecast revenues up 9 per cent to $1,626 million and expenditures up 15 per cent to $1,709 million. The resultant forecast deficit of $83 million was lower than for recent years but Cowperthwaite thought that his more aggressive revenue projections meant that there was less chance of the actual out-turn being a surplus. For once his caution would prove well founded.

Given the forecast he did not intend to increase taxes. He did, however, want to increase charges for two commodities supplied by government on a semi-commercial basis: sand and water. Sand prices were raised to cover direct costs. For the more complex issue of water charges, it was clear that Cowperthwaite had spent a considerable amount of time understanding the economics behind the water industry, and this is reviewed in the following chapter.

THE ROLE OF THE FINANCIAL SECRETARY

Cowperthwaite had noted a growing belief that he had an over-powerful voice in the shaping of policy, and that that voice was usually used to limit government. He used his budget speech as an opportunity to expand on his view of the role of the financial secretary in the budget process. Given his very active involvement in a very wide range of decisions throughout government, his views should probably be taken with a pinch of salt:

> I should like to try to dispel some misconceptions which seem to be prevalent about the powers and purposes of a Financial Secretary in the making of our budgets. It appears that many people are under the impression that he sits at his desk and with dictatorial ruthlessness slashes away at requests by Departments for the funds they consider necessary for the carrying out of their policies and purposes, and so, fashions the shape of the year's public services to his own conservative view of the prudent extent of public expenditure. It does not happen at all like that. I doubt if I can influence the amount of the year's estimate of expenditure by more than a very few million dollars. The estimates, year by year, flow, not from my arbitrary judgement, but from a multiplicity of decisions continuously being taken by Government as a whole on the desirable, and possible, rate of priorities of expansion of our public services, mostly in the shape of long-term programmes or objectives. I do not say that I am not without influence—for good or ill—on these decisions but mine is only one voice among many; and not always, I like to think, on the illiberal side.

Slightly at odds with this perspective he then pointed out that he was particularly concerned about decision makers who were themselves used to a higher level of services saddling the economy with a set of policies that were in reality unaffordable. In past years he had used the five-year plan to have that debate, but rather embarrassingly he had to admit that the five-year plan had not been completed this year due to uncertainty about plans and prospects. No doubt dealing with the financial sector had put him under some time pressure. But there can be little doubt that while Cowperthwaite might have found it difficult to significantly alter ongoing spending commitments, his was a powerful voice in determining the shape and level of government fiscal policy.

The *Far East Economic Review* suggested that Cowperthwaite was being somewhat disingenuous. They thought it would be 'surprising and somewhat disturbing' if the financial secretary only had minimal influence on spending levels.[13] And in any case they thought the criticisms that were levelled at Cowperthwaite were not about his budgetary function but rather that he had:

> imposed a stranglehold on local administration – partly because our system of government is archaic (requiring most drafts and proposals to be channeled through the Secretariat for its approval, thus effectively crushing initiative in other Government departments), partly because he combines both financial and economic functions and partly because of the strong personality and the considerable mental powers possessed by the present incumbent. Mr Cowperthwaite in fact has established such an excellent grasp of his job and can so ably marshall his arguments in defence of his decision, that very few of his colleagues can apparently hope to take on his Department with much hope of success. Mr Cowperthwaite is in fact too good at his job.

What everyone could agree on was that Cowperthwaite had used these early years of his term of office to establish a well-defined set of fiscal policies for the colony. They built on the work of his predecessors, but they embedded an economic policy that was very much driven by Cowperthwaite himself. Future challenges would test his commitment to this approach.

CHAPTER 14

THE BOUNDARIES OF THE STATE

Cowperthwaite wrestled with how far the state should be involved in the provision of services in the colony. He was of course only one voice in that debate, but a very important one. He believed it was vital for the state to uphold the rule of law and property rights and to protect its citizens. This 'night-watchman' state requires spending on a government executive, defence forces, police and a judiciary.* Cowperthwaite and the broader administration saw these as the basic obligations of government in creating a civilized society.

How far to go beyond these basic functions was the issue. There were questions about where to intervene: public utilities, health care, education, housing, welfare, working conditions, and so on. There were questions as to who should be eligible to receive government services: only those in greatest need, or a broader part of society. And there were questions about how to intervene: persuasion, regulation, state funding, state ownership, and so on. In his early years as financial secretary, Cowperthwaite had to decide where to draw the boundaries of government involvement in a number of areas, ranging from car parking to water provision, to education and housing. As might be expected, he threw himself into understanding each area in terms of the need, the economics, the second-order effects and its affordability versus other needs.

* The term 'Nachtwachterstaat' was first used by Ferdinand Lassalle, a German socialist, in 1862, but the idea of a minimal state was common in classical economics, and has more recently been championed by economists and philosophers such as Friedrich Hayek, Ludwig von Mises and Robert Nozick.

THE STATE'S ROLE IN CAR PARKING

In the 1963 budget Cowperthwaite applied the full force of his economic logic to the mundane issue of car parking. The increasing number of cars in Hong Kong had created a demand for parking spaces and he had been lobbied to provide these on government land. Cowperthwaite did not think this was a good use of a scarce government resource and he was opposed to any tacit subsidies for car owners.

Cowperthwaite claimed that the direct cost of building a car parking space was around $5,000 (noting this was about the same cost as a housing authority apartment for five adults). And this did not include the cost of the land. He had been informed that the cost per car space in a city-centre multistorey car park would be $65,000, of which $60,000 would be the cost of the land. He could see no reason why those that were using these car parks should not bear the full costs as did other users, such as private housing schemes or even public utilities.

Moreover, he was concerned that providing government car parking spaces at below their full cost would stifle the construction of private parking. Indeed, he was worried that that was already happening, and he wondered if it was preventing private capital from meeting the needs of the growing car-owning public, noting that 'one trouble is ... when Government gets into a business it tends to make it uneconomic for anyone else'.

On this relatively minor issue Cowperthwaite combined a fairly detailed knowledge of the economics of car parking with some insights into the effect of government involvement. He had no problem applying his broader framework to specific issues. For him it was clear that the government did not need to involve itself in car parking, and if it did because of its ownership of land, then a full market price should be charged.

WATER PROVISION

Obtaining water supplies was a critical issue for Hong Kong since it did not have sufficient natural supply. There was a need to construct major reservoirs and, in drought years, to import water. In 1963 Hong Kong spent around $66 million on emergency water supplies, and in the 1964 budget Cowperthwaite drew on his classical education, citing a Greek poet, Pindar, who had said:

> The best thing is water; although gold like burning fire shines through the night above all other proud wealth.*

* Pindar's *Olympian Odes*. Pindar was born in Thebes around 518 BCE.

Figure 14.1. Long queues caused by 1963 water shortages.

He observed that Hong Kong had been converting gold into water at an alarming rate. Cowperthwaite had launched an economic study to determine the best way to invest in further water provision, be that desalination or more reservoirs. This exploration had raised a question in his mind about how much the government should spend to insure against shortages. To be completely sure that shortages would never occur would require massive investment, reducing spending elsewhere. Taking some risk on provision would significantly lower the already substantial resources needed. Cowperthwaite lamented that even considering options had generated opposition:

> I find myself considered inhumane or unprogressive or sometimes merely odd, by some of my colleagues as well as members of the public, when I suggest that it is not axiomatic that a twenty-four hour supply in all circumstances must be our immediate aim. I cannot myself see any grounds for the belief that a twenty-four hour domestic water supply is an inalienable right of civilized man. It may be, if he can afford it and is prepared to pay the price.

Cowperthwaite had no problem if, in a free market, people chose to pay the true cost of a guaranteed twenty-four-hour supply. But that would mean the cost of water would be very high:

> Clearly charges at this level would be a hardship for those who are contented with less at lower prices; and I think there must be, in the case of a public utility like water, an overriding principle that the rate should be low enough for everyone to pay for enough to meet his reasonable needs.

And he objected very strongly to subsidizing the costs of investing in the infrastructure needed to create a superior level of provision:

> What cannot in my view be justified is investment of very large amounts of public capital (for which there are so many competing demands) for the provision of a supply for maximum consumption on the basis of normal Government pricing at non-commercial interest rates.

He returned to the issue in his 1965 budget, arguing that there were two revenue sources from the supply of water: the first, accounting for about a third of revenue, came from a charge on the rateable value of properties and was designed to pay for investments such as dams over a fifty-year period at a modest assumed rate of interest; and the second revenue source was a charge for actual water consumed, which stood at $1 per thousand litres.

The unit cost of water had been rising and now stood at around $1.50. It had been possible to keep charges at $1 because the rateable values of properties had been rising so quickly, providing a cushion. But now water demand was rising, and the droughts had limited supplies, creating the need for expensive imports. Large losses were now forecast.

Cowperthwaite accepted that estimating future revenues and costs was hard. Rainfall was uncertain, capital charges were dependent on volumes, costs were higher if imports were needed, or desalination used, and so on. His modelling, however, calculated that by 1970 costs would be around $2.80 per thousand litres. Rates would bring in around 67¢ of this, leaving $2.13 in remaining costs. He felt that if provided privately, with commercial interest rates and the need to produce competitive returns, costs would be near $5.

Given his analysis, Cowperthwaite concluded that a basic rate of $2 should be charged, double the existing level: a level that generated much opposition.

Cowperthwaite was clear that the government should have a role in the vital area of water supply. The infrastructure costs were huge, and the projects were long term, and building a water network was effectively a public monopoly. The challenge was whether to provide a lower service level at a more affordable cost or a higher service level at a higher cost. What he tried to avoid was extravagant subsidies displacing spending on other vital projects.

A DIVE INTO THE TELEPHONE INDUSTRY

In 1964 Cowperthwaite introduced the Telephone Ordinance to allow the Telephone Company to raise its charges to customers, which were set by government.[1] It was a delicate issue because many were very critical of the performance of the company, and yet Cowperthwaite had become convinced that it needed to raise very substantial capital.

The company already had a $200 million capital programme designed to increase the number of telephones in operation from 145,000 at the beginning of 1963 to 260,000 by the end of 1967. The British Post Office had advised on an even greater expansion, adding five new exchanges and an additional 170,000 lines between 1966 and 1969. Such expansion would cost an extra $125 million up to 1967, in addition to the existing capital plan, and then a further $50 million–$60 million a year until 1980.

Given this, Cowperthwaite set out the case to increase charges to enable the company to fund the investment:

> Deprived of adequate finance no utility can be efficient or keep up with rapidly increasing demands; and in the case of a private enterprise utility this means that the regulatory authority must allow it to levy charges adequate to provide a return which can attract sufficient long-term private risk capital into the enterprise, in competition with other uses for money.[1]

He disagreed with those who argued that the company's poor performance made it inappropriate to raise charges. If charges were not increased, the company would be unable to attract capital, and:

> All that would be achieved by that would be to perpetuate, and very seriously aggravate, present deficiencies.

Cowperthwaite pointed out that the alternative to allowing adequate funding for a private telephone operator was nationalization.

As usual, Cowperthwaite had developed a quite detailed view on the economics of telephone operations, and had come to the opinion that the capital-intensive nature of the business, and dis-economies of scale, meant that costs could grow faster than subscribers:

> In most businesses, economies of scale normally occur when the business expands. But the business of providing telephone services is unusual because, as the system expands, it is necessary to install expensive exchange equipment to enable new subscribers to be connected without delay to a growing number of other subscribers. Because of this, requirements for exchange equipment tend to grow more rapidly than the number of

> subscribers and, consequently, the unit cost of facilities increases as more subscribers are added to the system. In mathematical language, there is a substantial element of costs which grows with expansion in geometrical rather than arithmetical ratio.

Cowperthwaite showed that he was very aware of the need to look at returns to capital as he explained that capital and operating costs had risen since prices were last agreed, and that profits were now too low to finance expansion or attract capital:

> The return on capital employed in the undertaking, a common criterion for public utilities, has declined from 14.3% in 1956, the first full year in which the last changes in the terms of the company's franchise were effective, to 6.9% in 1963.
>
> It is true of course that the absolute amount of the Company's profit has increased very substantially between 1956 and 1963, from about $6¼ million to $14½ million, an increase of 130%. The public is often misled by looking at such profit figures by themselves into believing that the Company and its shareholders are doing more than twice as well as they were in 1956. But this is, of course, not so. Profits must be related to the capital which is invested in the business in order to make these profits. During the period 1956 to 1963, when profits were increased by 130%, the capital which had to be invested increased by almost 300%. The rate of return on this additional capital is therefore very low indeed.

Given that, Cowperthwaite proposed and supported an increase in charges from $300 per business line to $350, and from $225 per residential line to $235. Having benchmarked returns elsewhere, these were designed to give a 9 per cent return on total capital employed, and given debt, around a 12 per cent return on shareholders' funds.

To ensure that the Telephone Company met its promises and targets, Cowperthwaite proposed setting up an advisory committee to monitor and report to the governor on progress. Although many had reservations, these were mitigated by the new controls, and the way in which Cowperthwaite had made the case, and the new charges were agreed.

In this regulated, private sector monopoly, Cowperthwaite had once again used his examination of the business's economics to shape the role that government played: in this case, determining pricing, and therefore returns and consequently capital spending in the colony's telephone provision.

EVEN EDUCATION MUST PASS COWPERTHWAITE'S SCRUTINY

In the middle of 1965 there was a major review of education provision.[2] This had been an area of investment and focus for the government for many years and the subsequent white paper called for a further extension of provision. Given Cowperthwaite's background it is not surprising that he was a great believer in the value of education. But this did not stop him applying his economic philosophy to assess the costs and benefits of investing in it. He neatly summarized his view as follows:

> I regard education as a good thing. But we must still ask what a good thing costs, how much of it we can afford and who is going to pay for it.[3]

Cowperthwaite believed that Hong Kong's historical approach of using expensive expatriate teachers to educate a small elite was only affordable if there was limited access to subsidized schooling: it became unaffordable if broad subsidized access was the goal. He highlighted teacher salaries as a particular problem:

> Although our wealth per head is considerably less than a third of Britain's, the salaries of non-graduate teachers in Government and aided schools are about three quarters of those in Britain; graduate teachers are relatively even more expensive; they start on salaries substantially higher than in Britain and, particularly in Government schools, go very much higher.

He was not against the long-term goal of providing greater access to education, but he worried that the full costs of greater provision would only be felt over a period of some years, and therefore were being underestimated.

Cowperthwaite was very annoyed that several proponents of broadening education provision had implied that the cost would fall on the government, rather than on the people of Hong Kong:

> Now comes the question who is to pay. I notice that most people, including a number of my honourable Friends during this debate, speak of the cost to Government; the cost does not fall on the Government, but on the community; it is the community that must pay, more specifically the taxpayer.
>
> I have pointed out in the past that a community can pay for public services either in the form of fees for actual services received or in the form of taxes – or in some combination of the two. I have frequently expressed the view that, with our economic and social structure, a full fee structure with remissions for those who cannot afford the fees is preferable in many cases to heavily subsidized or free services and high taxes.
>
> It is true that, unlike most other public services, it is commonly held that a free education is the birthright of every child – but, I would suggest that it is not the birthright of every parent, irrespective of his wealth.

Cowperthwaite developed his argument that there were problems of equity in subsidizing the well off and middle-income groups given the existing tax system. It was a theme that Cowperthwaite would reinforce over the years, but one which he would never quite find a solution for:

> We have here a tax system which is certainly not progressive in its incidence – I have sometimes wondered if it is not regressive – and also an expensive education system relatively to our wealth; it is also an education system where the most expensive parts of it, the secondary schools, have admitted and still admit the well-to-do in disproportionate numbers. If we are to have a system of universal primary education and substantial secondary education, then we must either have an adequate fee structure with remissions only in relation to need; or we must introduce a progressive form of direct personal tax so that means are taken into account in the assessment of tax, even if they cannot be taken into account in the assessment of fees. One way or another there must be a proper relationship between the parent's means and what he is called upon to pay in fees or tax.

He illustrated his concerns with an example:

> A man earning, say, $3,000 a month (which puts him very high up in our income scale), if he has one child at an aided secondary school and one at an aided primary school, pays less direct tax at present than he receives in educational subsidies. This is grossly inequitable.

Cowperthwaite knew his ability to solve the problem was limited. On the one hand the chances of introducing a progressive income tax policy were effectively nonexistent, and on the other he knew he could not prevent (nor did he necessarily want to prevent) the extension of education. His compromise was to sound a warning, and to hope that that warning encouraged a frugal approach as service provision was widened.

THE DIFFICULTY WITH HOUSING

Rather surprisingly, the government had developed a very major role in the construction and provision of public housing.

Once again Cowperthwaite was alert to second-order effects and unintended consequences. In the 1963 budget he emphasized the need not to oversimplify the world into blocks of people or to de-emphasize the needs of the worse off:

> I should like to begin with a philosophical comment. I do not think that when one is speaking of hardships or benefits one can reasonably speak in terms of classes or

social groups but only in terms of individuals; and in the context of housing one must compare the position of an individual in the lowest income group who does not yet enjoy subsidized housing with that of an individual in the middle income group in the same circumstances. I make this distinction largely in order to make the point that whatever we do for the middle income groups must not be such as to prejudice, by diversion of resources or energy, the continuation of our maximum housing effort at the lower end of the scale. It is normal in richer countries that Government moves into the field of state-aided housing for the middle classes, only where demand lower down the income scale is nearing satisfaction.[4]

Figure 14.2. The need for housing.

In the 1965 budget he returned to housing in more detail. He traced the history of the role of government in housing provision dating back to the Shek Kip Mei disaster and the resultant Housing Ordinance of 1954. Since that time the government had housed close to 1 million people, and it planned to resettle or rehouse 1.4 million more over the next six years. Private enterprise had housed a further 800,000 over the previous nine years. He contended that the situation had changed materially but that there was a risk that the government agencies involved in housing had taken on an institutional life of their own, divorced from the changing reality:

There appears to be a tendency to take the view that their aim should be to build as much housing as they physically can, irrespective of what may be happening in the private field; and that priority must be given to the provision of public funds for this purpose. I do not think I can subscribe to this view myself.[5]

Figure 14.3. Newly constructed high-rise government housing.

He was also concerned that the three government agencies involved in construction had different design parameters, particularly about occupational density. Cowperthwaite could not see any logic for this:

> There should be one standard of construction for public housing, rather than several standards related to distinctions of class or wealth. There is generally one and the same basic standard of housing at any given time; to which a man, in certain circumstances, has a claim. We have three, if not more, standards.

His second concern was to ensure that some limit should be put on the extent of the push by government into subsidized public housing:

> It is unrealistic to think in terms of mass public housing at subsidized rents. We must continue to rely very substantially on new private housing, both because we are most unlikely to have the resources to do otherwise, and because we must not create a situation where a large part of the population has the privilege of having its housing subsidized from public revenue to which the less fortunate minority also contribute.
>
> An adequate field must therefore be left open to private enterprise housing; and government subsidized housing must not be allowed to depress rents below the level to which, with supply and demand in reasonable equilibrium, commercial rents might fall without inhibiting further private development.

Cowperthwaite was particularly concerned that the momentum of the public sector initiative should not swamp the role of the private sector. If the government agencies were to mistakenly see their role as building the maximum number of units possible, then this could crowd out commercial construction. Rather, he felt that the role was to build enough to bring commercial rents down and to be indifferent as to who actually built the apartment blocks.

While expressing these concerns, Cowperthwaite wanted to underline his approval of the role that the various agencies had played in providing leadership that could then be spread more widely. It once more reinforces his view that government's role should be more to shape and underpin rather than necessarily to produce output itself:

> I do not suggest, however, that physical production of houses is the only role of the Authority and the Society. They have a valuable part to play, and have been playing it with success, in experimenting in new forms of housing and in propagating better management practices. I am second to none in my admiration for what has been achieved in these fields.

Despite these views, Cowperthwaite reassured the Legislative Council that he would be making further funds available for housing and that while he recognized that housing policy was not directly under his remit, he was keen to raise these longer-term issues.

THE CROSS-HARBOUR TUNNEL

In the early 1950s there were calls to build a tunnel linking Hong Kong Island and Kowloon. There were, of course, many different opinions as to what should be built and how it should be financed. In February 1955 a firm of consulting engineers conducted a feasibility study and concluded that it was practical and they recommended that two single-lane tunnels be constructed.[6] The estimated cost was around $161 million.[7] Later that year, Cowperthwaite was asked to chair an interdepartmental committee to examine the financial, commercial and economic elements of the proposal.

The idea of a tunnel had first surfaced in the early 1900s and it had a number of vocal supporters, both within the civil service and with members of the Legislative Council. Cowperthwaite pushed back against the idea that the funds should come from government, since the benefit would go only to users of the tunnel. After a period of illness had delayed the report, Cowperthwaite completed it in 1956.[8] He concluded that:

> If the premises and arguments are accepted, the conclusions are definitive. The major conclusion is that a tunnel would be unlikely to pay for itself in the foreseeable future.

> A tunnel constructed by Government would therefore mean a diversion of Government's real resources from other spheres of development. The Working Party does not rate the economic and social benefits of a tunnel very highly, and we are left in little doubt that housing, water, education, sites for industry, hospitals and resettlement should all have priority in claims upon Government's limited resources.

Cowperthwaite made clear that he was not against private investment funding a tunnel:

> Commercial interests should be permitted to undertake its construction if they are prepared to do so and the land required can be made available.

Over the following years various commercial parties did float plans for a bridge or tunnel but it would take nearly a decade for a scheme to get approval. In July 1965 the Legislative Council approved a tunnel in principle, based on a structure that Cowperthwaite had negotiated.[9] The Cross-Harbour Tunnel Company would construct, own and operate a new tunnel, but as a franchisee. They would invest the estimated $280 million cost and make a $12 million contribution to the government for the cost of building associated roads. At Cowperthwaite's insistence, it would be two lanes in each direction rather than the proposed single lane, and the government would receive a royalty of 12.5 per cent of revenues. Furthermore, after thirty years the tunnel would revert to government ownership, at no cost.

While many critics argued that Cowperthwaite had slowed the building of critical infrastructure, others were relieved that the government had not decided to use limited public funds on a project that had mixed support, and would benefit only those who chose to drive rather than take the regular and efficient ferries. In June 1969 the final plan was approved by the Legislative Council,[10] with the government agreeing to loan $27.5 million on a commercial basis to make further fundraising easier. The tunnel opened in August 1972, and the traffic levels soon proved that Cowperthwaite had been correct in pushing for the extra lanes. In 1999 the tunnel became the property of the government and it now provides a significant revenue-generating asset for the government, at no cost to the taxpayer.

THE BOUNDARIES OF THE STATE

Over his years in office, Cowperthwaite frequently questioned what role the state should play in providing goods and services to individuals. He approached each situation from first principles, combining a top-down set of beliefs with a bottom-up analysis of the sector in question.

He started from the view that one needed a strong case to intervene in the free market, where people could exchange goods and services for themselves, making all the complex trade-offs that they do. He was very aware that government spending necessitated government taxing, and that that involved a simple shift in money out of the pockets of citizens to be spent by civil servants:

> Perhaps I am over-conscious of the fact that every dollar Government takes from the taxpayer is a dollar he might otherwise have spent to meet a need or enjoy a pleasure or might have invested with profit. No-one who has proposed an increase in expenditure has felt under any obligation to propose a compensating increase in taxation.[11]

While Cowperthwaite clearly had a preference for markets to set prices and investment, and for the cost to fall on those who wanted the product or service, he was not naive about markets' limitations, particularly in a small developing country. David Wong (2015) worked for Cowperthwaite and later noted:

> Sir John enjoyed a worldwide reputation for being a free marketeer. Yet it would be a disservice to him if he were known only by that label. He was in fact much less of a doctrinaire free marketeer as certain quarters would like people to believe. They ignored, for instance, the fact that virtually all the public utilities like gas, electricity, buses, trams, ferries and telephone services operated as monopolies under franchises from the government, with profit limitation clauses.

He seems to work through a list of implicit questions. Was this an area that the government should have any involvement in at all? Why was the market unable to work? If intervention was needed, what form should it take? Could it be imposing regulations or providing funding, or was it necessary for the government to be the supplier of the service? Who would benefit from this provision? Would it be the minimum number of people necessary or was an implicit unneeded subsidy also occurring? For those that benefited, how should they pay? Should the service be priced to produce market returns, or should there be a subsidy, or should it be free for users and paid for by general taxation? In each of the practical examples he addressed, one can observe his calculations and the way he tried to draw boundaries to ensure that the shape of the state was optimized as far as possible to provide public services in a way that least inhibited economic growth.

CHAPTER 15

A BIGGER BANKING CRISIS

AT THE BEGINNING OF 1965 Cowperthwaite's reputation was flying high. He had successfully managed various trade negotiations, allowing Hong Kong's exports to flourish, and he had kept taxes low, expanded public services and shaped policy over telephones, water, housing, and more. The economy was performing well and the population's standard of living was rising rapidly. His decision to reject the calls to abandon laissez-faire seemed vindicated.

His early budgets had created an economic framework that was stable, rational and, most importantly, successful. There was little to signal that the next three years would be among the most challenging of Cowperthwaite's career.

His new 1964 Banking Ordinance that had just come into effect would fail to prevent a major banking crisis. The devaluation of sterling would further challenge Cowperthwaite's reputation for competence as millions were wiped off the value of Hong Kong's reserves, and China would also attempt to destabilize the colony as it launched its Cultural Revolution. But Cowperthwaite stuck to his underlying philosophy through these tribulations, and with the benefit of hindsight it is clear that they were merely bumps along the road to higher levels of prosperity. At the time, though, each problem threatened to blow Hong Kong and its financial secretary off course.

THE 1965 BANKING CRISIS

While Cowperthwaite downplayed the scale of the 1965 banking crisis in his February budget speech, Jao (1974) argues that the 1965 banking crisis was comparable to the 1866 crisis that led to more than half of Hong Kong's banks folding:

> The 1965 crisis had no less shaken the banking system to its very foundation. Thousands of depositors lost their savings, and hundreds of firms went bankrupt in the wake of the liquidity scramble. More importantly the crisis mercilessly exposed the serious deficiencies of the banking system.

The crisis resulted from a combination of factors that had been well, if unhurriedly, debated in creating the 1964 Banking Ordinance following the failure of Liu Chong Hing Bank in 1961. Regulation was still weak and allowed banks to take significant risks in their loan portfolios. The booming real estate sector once more played the role of the sirens, providing enchanting prospects for the banks. But property cycles turn. Taking the most volatile asset, construction land, prices in Central District fell from $1,000–$1,200 per square foot in 1964 to $200–$300 per square foot in 1967 (Jao 1974). Combined with this, the lack of depositor protection made it entirely rational for savers to grab their cash as soon as there was the slightest chance of default. Indeed, it was rational to start queuing for no other reason than that others were.

Cowperthwaite would need to learn that banking was not the same as other industrial sectors. The second-order effects of a textile factory closing were limited to a small range of suppliers, employees and suppliers. The second-order effects of bank failures were more pervasive, and more difficult to contain. In addition, balance sheet banking crises can feed off themselves. As property values fall, loans and banks fail, reducing credit and swamping the market with property assets, which in turn makes property prices fall and the cycle starts again. Furthermore, textile factory owners have little incentive to take risks that might lead to their firm failing. The risk–reward profiles for bankers using depositors' money to earn high speculative returns in real estate were obviously somewhat different. While the debtors' prisons and unlimited personal liability of Adam Smith's time helped concentrate the minds of bankers, the trade-offs had shifted in the intervening centuries.

Cowperthwaite had invested much personal capital over the years in arguing for limited intervention in the banking sector, despite calls from many, including major banks, for much tighter regulation. Others were more adroit in understanding that mass deposits and weak regulation were a dangerous mix. The Banking

Commissioner Leonidas Cole, appointed under the 1964 Banking Ordinances, took the opportunity in the middle of the crisis to suggest that 'the policy of laissez-faire and banking do not mix; supervision and direction are essential'.[1]

It would take the crises of 1965 to get Cowperthwaite to move some way towards the same conclusion.

THE UNFOLDING CRISIS

In January 1965 a small unincorporated bank, the Ming Tak Bank, was rumoured to be in difficulty, and on 27 January queues of depositors formed to extract their savings: a scene reminiscent of the 1961 crisis. The Banking Commissioner quickly took control of the bank and discovered that it was insolvent, with a very illiquid real estate loan portfolio.

On 6 February a run started on the more substantial Canton Trust and Commercial Bank. The run was temporarily stopped when Hongkong Bank appeared to pledge their support for the bank, only to 'clarify' the following day that their support was limited (Jao 1974). The run resumed, and the Banking Commissioner took control.

Rather late in the day, Cowperthwaite tried to reassure the public about the strength of the banking sector, but this did little to help, and on 8 February queues started to form outside the Hang Seng Bank, Kwong On Bank, Dao Heng Bank and Wing Lung Bank. Soon the police were needed, and as evening fell the queues settled in to be ready for the banks reopening the following morning. Overnight, Hongkong Bank pledged unlimited support for Hang Seng Bank and more general support for other banks. Chartered Bank pledged unlimited support for Dao Heng and Kwong On banks.

However, on 9 February rumours now spread to include Far East Bank, and the runs showed no signs of abating. Later that day the government limited cash withdrawals to $100 from each account. In addition, because of people hoarding currency, sterling was declared legal tender and a shipment of pounds was flown in from London. A few days later, on 16 February, the restriction on cash withdrawals was lifted.

Early in the crisis there were some who felt that the government was in part to blame. In their 18 February edition, the *Far Eastern Economic Review* argued:

> It is impossible to avoid the conclusion that the Government could have acted with greater skill and dispatch. As long as 'non-interference' is the Government's financial and economic watchword any regulations or controls which Government is prepared

> to sponsor are likely to fall short of the requirements of a modern economic unit. Hong Kong, in fact, has just seen its philosophy of laissez-faire run riot – and it was not a pretty sight. Perhaps it is time for our financial authorities to update their economic theories.[2]

Cowperthwaite convened a Banking Advisory Committee to advise on what further regulation might be needed. At its first meeting on 18 March, Cowperthwaite rather prematurely attributed the crisis to 'a loss of confidence due to the difficulty of two banks and not from any shortcomings of the provisions of the Banking Ordinance as has been widely stated'.[3]

However, the crisis had not ended yet, and in mid March rumours started about the Hang Seng Bank. Depositors started to withdraw their funds: slowly at first, but by 9 April large queues had again formed outside branches. The Hang Seng was in fact reasonably solvent and a relatively conservatively financed bank, but over 90 per cent of its loans were to the property sector and these were very illiquid (Schenk 2001). The run on the bank only ended when Hongkong Bank took a majority stake in it the following day, although it would take them many years to change what Hongkong Bank's chief accountant called their 'unacceptable banking practice of borrowing short and lending long', described by him as the Chinese banking practice.[4]

The crisis rumbled on through the whole year. Fortunately, Cowperthwaite had few major pieces of legislation to manage in 1965, and he was able to attend the Commonwealth Finance Ministers Meeting in Jamaica in September 1965,[5] and take leave between 19 October and 3 December 1965. But his leave was interrupted when, in November 1965, Far East Bank needed extensive support and the government organized a rescue. In 1966 Yau Yue Commercial Bank became insolvent and Cowperthwaite agreed to Hongkong Bank taking control and for all depositors to be protected.

REGULATION LAISSEZ-FAIRE

It had required an uncomfortable journey for Cowperthwaite to understand how to adapt his laissez-faire approach to banking. He still believed in the private sector providing banking, but he was dragged by events to see the need for a different level of regulation and supervision than was needed for, say, a textile manufacturer.

Cowperthwaite, working with the Banking Advisory Committee, recommended that there be an improvement in auditing, improved bank inspections, and that the government have the power to withhold banking licences and to control branch openings.[3] The Banking Ordinances would, in fact, need to be strengthened again in 1967: doubling the amount of capital required, excluding interbank assets from liquidity calculations, increasing the provisioning for bad debts, greatly increasing reporting and transparency, and strengthening the powers of the Banking Commissioner to intervene in the market.

Why was Cowperthwaite blind to the risk of a banking crisis? In part it was undoubtedly down to his long-standing belief in the power of markets to correct themselves. Equally, he was very cautious about getting the government involved in areas that it did not understand, and he had a relatively weak understanding of banking. He no doubt thought about businesses as essentially owner-run, and did not at first fully grasp the disjointed incentives that can exist in banking. And he was very sensitive to the longer-term risks of moral hazard if the government bailed out failing banks.

ALLOCATING BLAME

Beyond these failings, he was clearly surprised by the widespread effects of the 1965 crisis. For some commentators, it made the whole colonial administration vulnerable, and as tensions with China rose in 1967 some saw the banking crisis as a strategic blunder, raising questions about the government's basic economic competence. Unsurprisingly, Cowperthwaite did his best to deflect blame, in particular pointing the finger at bad bankers and poorly managed banks. While this was no doubt true, his narrative rather left out the role played by government in encouraging and celebrating the real estate boom and, through lax regulation, letting the banks take on far too much risk. He would not be the last finance minister to resort to this line.

When Cowperthwaite recapped the causes of the crisis in his February 1966 budget speech, in a story that will be familiar to today's readers, he saw the failures as part of a global problem as much as a local one, although he did acknowledge that credit had grown very rapidly in Hong Kong:

> Our local events were part of a pattern observable in much of the developed world (and frequently in much more serious form than here), a pattern of over-rapid expansion of credit and consequent strains in and pressures on economies; over-investment in real estate development and over speculation in stocks and shares; and, of course, the political situation in South-East Asia, sterling difficulties and the British import surcharge had brought a degree of economic unease in late 1964 and early 1965.[6]

For good measure, the bankers were blamed for excess credit creation:

> In recent years credit has been rather too easy in Hong Kong for good banking and commercial discipline in some sectors of the economy. The banking system brought into use substantial facilities previously unused and did so to an excessive degree. For example, in 1958 bank loans and advances amounted to only 58% of deposits but this had grown to 71% by the end of 1964; this in itself causing some additional expansion through the credit-creating processes of bank lending.

The fact that investors could earn a good return on borrowed funds had created a credit bubble:

> An unreal situation, where many people assumed that once credit was accorded it would never be recalled; and where some banks themselves assumed that their deposits would continue to grow as rapidly as ever and were accordingly over-generous both with their immediate advances and with their promises of future loans. This led to an unhealthy state in some sectors of the economy where the inefficient and incompetent were never called to account.

Cowperthwaite was keen to spread the blame widely. Bankers had been lax. Depositors had been too tempted by high rates. Developers had borrowed too much and tied up funds in illiquid construction projects. And this was a worldwide problem and was not restricted to Hong Kong anyway. The only group he did not publicly censure was government.

EX POST RATIONALIZATION

Cowperthwaite even found a silver lining in the banking crisis. The market had corrected. The parts of the economy 'on which our living standards basically depend, industry, commerce and tourism, have gone ahead with a vigour which is remarkable in the circumstances'. Furthermore, Cowperthwaite expressed the view that a certain amount of creative destruction was to be welcomed:

> An economy with virtually no liquidations or bankruptcies is not really in an healthy state.

With the correction, and the policies that had been adopted, Cowperthwaite argued that

> we are emerging from our recent troubles in a much healthier state, with some of the diseased parts of our economy excised and some of its strains and stresses alleviated; and can look forward with confidence to renewed, and more solid, growth.

SOME DOUBTERS

Not everyone was as quick to pass over the government's role in the crisis. In the 1966 budget debates, Mr Kan Yuet-keung, for example, asked some difficult questions about how far the government may have contributed to the problem:

> My honourable Friend the Financial Secretary has traced the causes of this financial upheaval to 'bad banking practices' of certain banks and to 'over-rapid expansion of credit, over-investment in real estate development and over-speculation in stocks and shares". I have too great a respect for him to suggest that he speaks from hindsight; consequently, the following points come to my mind. How long before the storm finally broke had this state of affairs existed to Government's knowledge? Could not some effective steps have been taken to remedy the situation before it got out of hand?[7]

Cowperthwaite came out fighting against the idea that the government could have intervened to prevent the credit and real estate bubble from bursting:

> I find it a little extraordinary now, after so many years of being told that civil servants should not interfere in commercial matters because they are not qualified to do so, to hear it suggested by my honourable Friend that Government should have known what businessmen all too clearly did not know and should have imposed measures which businessmen would have fiercely resisted.[8]

He rather tetchily complained that government could not win:

> I suppose it is inevitable that Government should be regarded as wrong if it interferes when in public eyes all is apparently well (particularly as, after the event, it can never prove that its intervention made things better); and equally wrong if it does not interfere and later things go bad.

More usefully, Cowperthwaite reiterated his strong belief that even if there were economic ups and downs, it did not mean that government intervention would be of help:

> In any case, I largely agree with those that hold that Government should not in general interfere with the course of the economy merely on the strength of its own commercial judgment. If we cannot rely on the judgment of individual businessmen, taking their own risks, we have no future anyway.

> I still believe that, in the long run, the aggregate of the decisions of individual businessmen, exercising individual judgment in a free economy, even if often mistaken, is likely to do less harm than the centralized decisions of a Government; and certainly the harm is likely to be counteracted faster. Our economic medicine may be painful but it is fast and powerful because it can act freely.

BUOYANT STERLING RESERVES

One consequence of the 1965 banking crisis was that it would emphasize for Cowperthwaite the importance of having significant reserves to support the banking sector should another crisis emerge and to ward off the dangers of credit deflation (Goodstadt 2007). It would reinforce Cowperthwaite's existing desire to be fiscally conservative and to hold significant reserves abroad (in London).

In his 1966 budget speech Cowperthwaite underlined that the banking crisis had not had a negative effect on the sterling assets held by the colony, which were used as backing for the note issue. Indeed, sterling assets had actually risen during 1965, from £235 million to £280 million. This had caused Cowperthwaite to ponder again on the openness of the Hong Kong economy and the implications this had for monetary policy:

> I have often said that we have an un-Keynesian economy in the sense that we cannot spend our way out of depression; to try to do so would merely cause an immediate balance of payments crisis – unless of course we were spending funds obtained from outside Hong Kong rather than merely printing our own money as so many countries do nowadays.[9]

He now believed that this analysis had implications for the nature of official assets. Some had argued that the assets backing the note issue should be held locally rather than in sterling assets in London. Cowperthwaite had been on the fence on this issue, but he now thought it critical that these assets be held offshore:

> During our bank runs and the consequential degree of temporary deflation of credit in February to May last year, it was forcibly borne in on me that the leverage Government can exert in these circumstances towards relieving the economy from the effects of such a deflationary trend as we experienced, is directly proportionate to the liquid foreign assets at the disposal of Government for support of the internal money supply. Resources locked up in unrealizable local assets are of no use whatever for this purpose.

> I am therefore now more than ever convinced that it is essential in our economic interest that the Government's reserves should be substantial and be held to a great extent abroad. This is after all what central banks do with their countries' reserves. This is one of the few elements of modem monetary policy we can safely indulge in, even if it is in the severely orthodox form of saving before we spend. This half of the Keynesian thesis at least we can practise.[9]

Cowperthwaite would find that his emerging conclusion on reserve policy and its ability to soften the cycle would turn out to be built on shaky foundations. Not so much because of the policy logic but because, in practice, all of the colony's reserves were held in one undiversified currency: sterling. When the pound devalued in 1967, Hong Kong's reserves would be devalued proportionally.

CHAPTER 16

THE PRESSURES OF A DOWNTURN

BETWEEN 1965 AND 1968 ECONOMIC progress in Hong Kong seemed to slow. Real GDP per capita stagnated for a few years, and even the population grew at a slower rate. The banking crisis, the property crash, the blocks on exports and the uncertainty and slowdown in key export markets all combined to create a downturn – or to be more precise, a plateauing. This created a call for intervention from many quarters, and it would be the 1966 and 1967 budgets that addressed that call. These were uncertain years for the colony and its administration, and this uncertainty pervaded the budgets delivered in the spring of both years.

A GLOOMY OVERVIEW

Sir David Trench surveyed the difficult environment in his 1966 address.[1] He recalled the banking failures, hoping that the worst was now over, then turned to the issue of tariffs and quotas, hoping the new textile quotas would be satisfactory.

He was on happier ground as he turned to social progress in the colony. Infant mortality was down. Communicable diseases had fallen. New hospitals and health centres had opened. Housing and resettlement had moved further forward. Water supplies had improved. There were more children at school. But he was concerned about how the ever-increasing costs of the public sector would be met:

> If Government is to continue to be urged to expand and improve the services provided for the community, as we would all like to expand and improve them, then the money must come from somewhere; either by increased contributions towards the cost from those who benefit from the services most directly, and can afford to contribute, or from natural expansion of the revenues as our economy grows, or from increased taxation; or, more probably, from all three.

Unusually, Cowperthwaite did not start his budget speech with the financial out-turns of the previous and current years but instead spent a considerable time reviewing the previous year's banking crisis, after which he returned to the traditional structure of the budget speech.

AN UNUSUAL DEFICIT

For once the review of past forecasts provided a surprise. While for 1964/65 the outcome had been a surplus of $77 million (versus an original forecast deficit of $114 million), for the current year, 1965/66, the original forecast had been optimistic. The forecast $60 million deficit was now estimated to have grown to a $190 million deficit. Even excluding various 'abnormalities and distortions' that Cowperthwaite listed, the estimated deficit stood at $122 million.

The main cause of this deterioration was that expenditures were for once higher than originally estimated, by $80 million. After many years of underspending, various departments had chosen an interesting year to exceed their spending estimates. Revenues were $49 million worse: the net of recurrent revenues being $81 million ahead of the original estimate and the capital account being $130 million behind. Almost all of this was due to a collapse in the revenue accruing from land sales by the government, which was in turn due to the property market falling away. Perhaps the one redeeming feature was that this performance vindicated some of the conservatism exhibited by Cowperthwaite and his predecessors.

For the year ahead Cowperthwaite forecast revenues up 6 per cent to $1,602 million and expenditure up 5 per cent to $1,878 million. The departments' spending plans had clearly been subject to closer scrutiny than normal:

> This year, because of expected deficits, I addressed a special plea to Heads of Departments to keep their estimates as modest as they reasonably could in the light of their essential needs or of planned policies of expansion. It seemed to me necessary and desirable to treat next year as a year of consolidation rather than of growth.

This created a forecast deficit of $186 million, or $201 million if the repayment of some loans was included. While Cowperthwaite hoped for a favourable economic wind that would reduce this deficit, he was concerned that if the recommendations of the currently underway Salaries Commission were adopted, that would make the situation even worse. He felt that the Salaries Commission had not adequately considered the affordability of their recommendations, and he was deeply concerned that high pay rates would either slow the broadening of the provision of public services or lead to excessive taxation that would harm the economy.

Cowperthwaite pointed out that the level of reserves, which had been at $1,200 million the year before, would fall to $800 million within two years if the deficits were as forecast and if the Salaries Commission recommendations were accepted. Cowperthwaite concluded that:

> This is an uncomfortably rapid rate at which to run down our reserves. It was once our aim to have a year's expenditure in hand but on these estimates we would have less than half of this by the end of the next financial year.

The five-year forecast, which Cowperthwaite had resurrected for this year, showed an equally bleak picture. The projected deficit over the five years was $1,000 million, or $1,150 million including salary increases. It was a sum that exceeded the total reserves. This was clearly not sustainable. It caused Cowperthwaite to reflect again on the appropriate level of public service provision in a developing country like Hong Kong:

> I do not say that this means that there is no scope for increased public services. There clearly is. My fear is rather, if I may repeat what I have said year after year, that we are developing public services which are too expensive per unit (both in recurrent terms and in capital terms), and of too high a standard, for our means, if we are to extend them as they should be extended.

He again argued that public services should be designed to alleviate basic needs, seeing a risk that

> the decision-takers and policy-makers, both inside and outside Government as I have said before today, being themselves from the better-off (to use a popular euphemism) sectors of our society, not only demand the highest standards of provision of public services to meet what they consider their own essential needs (for example, in public car parks); but also find it difficult to think of provision for the rest of the population in terms of standards relative to our real total resources.

The ominous fiscal situation caused Cowperthwaite to describe more fully than at any time before his own views on how the provision of public services should be set and how it should evolve:

> There is one particular aspect of the situation which causes me considerable apprehension, the tendency to demand that subsidized services be extended, at these high standards, to all citizens irrespective of need. It seems to me that we have three choices; first, public services of high standard and cost but of limited scope, leaving unfilled a substantial part of the present gap, not necessarily benefiting those in real need and benefiting many who are not in need at all (this has been our historical approach); second, public services to meet the requirements of all, with the beneficiaries making a contribution by way of fee according to their means, and with adequate provision for complete remission in suitable cases; or third, universal public services provided for rich and poor alike on terms the poorest can afford; that is, the welfare state where all benefit and the whole cost is met by the taxpayer in general.
>
> I think it is well-known that I am an advocate of the second approach.

He did not think that a welfare state with high levels of provision was appropriate for Hong Kong:

> 'State universalism', as I have heard it called, may be something that a rich country can afford, although I have doubts even about that unless it is very rich.

Indeed he believed that 'universalism' would endanger the survival of Hong Kong in its then present form:

> What 'universalism' would certainly mean in our context is a very high rate of direct taxation and one extending much further down the income scale than at present. This is what the advocates of indiscriminate subsidy of the best may be leading us towards.
>
> I myself remain wholly convinced that Hong Kong's prosperity, and therefore our hopes of adequate public services, cannot survive under such a tax regime because of its economic effects and I remain firm in my convictions; first, that our public services are excessively expensive and growing rapidly more so; second, that those who benefit from them should pay directly, according to their means, for what they get.
>
> If we do not adopt the course I advocate, I believe that, sooner rather than later, we will be faced with the alternative of curtailing our plans for the expansion of public services or of introducing potentially ruinous rates of taxation – which would, in any event, tend themselves to cause just such a curtailment of public services because of their inhibiting effects on our economy.

TAX RISES

Cowperthwaite turned to tax increases, arguing that a $90 million increase in taxation was the minimum that he could propose. He maintained that increases in direct tax would do the least damage to the economy. He noted that at 12.5 per cent, the rate was low by standards elsewhere, and that it had been argued that a rate of up to 20 per cent would be bearable for the economy. In fact, his proposal was for a 15 per cent rate. Combined with increases in tobacco taxes and motor fuel, this would produce the $90 million targeted.

Cowperthwaite had considered introducing a payroll tax, which he believed would raise significant sums, be easy to administer and promote productivity improvements. It would also counter some of the criticisms abroad that Hong Kong had an unfair trade advantage in not having social security taxes. On the other hand, he believed such a tax distorted the optimization of the mix of labour and capital: a favourite topic in classical economics. For now, he had decided to float the idea rather than introduce the tax, and some thought he had only raised the idea in case there was a need for further tax rises the following year.[2] It received little support and was not pursued.

RELUCTANT SUPPORT

Cowperthwaite had seized the right moment in his tenure to increase taxes. The press and the unofficial members of the Legislative Council were broadly supportive. While not welcoming the rise in direct taxation rates, they accepted the need for it and thought that the rise to 15 per cent was not excessive.

But alongside this general support there were challenges. Several Unofficials challenged Cowperthwaite's aversion to borrowing to fund government expenditure. One, Watson, claimed that:

> By insisting on cash in hand, a whole generation may be forced to do without amenities which they would expect to enjoy in other countries, countries which find nothing immoral or unduly risky in raising loans and mortgaging the future in order to allow its people to enjoy benefits within their own lifetime.

He rejected Cowperthwaite's assertion that public service provision should be subordinate to a goal of maximizing economic growth, arguing that government should instead set an ambitious goal for services. Economic constraints should then be considered only after that. This was in some ways a philosophical argument, since both approaches required balancing private sector growth and public spending. But which was the true goal, and which the means to that end, was more than a philosophical debate. It could influence behaviours and decisions.

Cowperthwaite clarified that he was not completely against borrowing, but rather saw significant limitations in its usefulness to cover spending. Given other comments, and his long-standing aversion to borrowing, this refinement of his views was perhaps more theoretical than practical. Later in the debate, in reply to Mr Wong, he would echo Ricardo in equating the risks of higher taxation and higher debt levels:

> My honourable Friend Mr Wong has reminded me that high taxes can discourage foreign investors. I am well aware of that and have no intention of letting the rate of direct taxation go high, so far as that rests with me. But I would suggest to my honourable Friend that the foreign investor is at least as discouraged by high national debt for that, as all example shows, is the surest precursor of high taxation.[3]

But largely he ignored these challenges to his economic orthodoxy, in part because these were the musings of unofficial members rather than a coherent alternative manifesto, and in part because the government held all the levers of power. Rather than any display of humility after a difficult year, Cowperthwaite pushed back against most of the suggestions. To those who had suggested subsidizing schemes that might help growth, he argued:

> Perhaps not so surprising after all; it is natural that Government intervention by way of subsidy should meet less opposition in the business world than intervention by way of regulation or tax.

And to those proposing greater spending he fell back on a favoured argument:

> My honourable Friend reminded me apropos of a certain tax that 'it is our money and not his'. I could retort 'tu quoque',* for it is no more his money than mine and he has no more right to impose his ideas on how it should be spent than I have, while I have very special responsibilities for its proper management. At the same time, I notice he speaks of 'the cost to Government' of some form of spending he advocates. I would suggest that he should better say 'cost to the taxpayer' or 'cost to the public'. My own views on all matters of public revenue and public expenditure are conditioned by an acute appreciation of whose is the sacrifice that produces public revenue and to whom accrues the benefit of public spending.

* 'Tu quoque', or 'you too', refers to an ad hominem fallacy under which a counterargument is rejected because it applies as much to the person objecting as to the proponent.

PAYING FOR THE DEFENCE OF HONG KONG

In the summer of 1966 Cowperthwaite was involved as the UK government tried to increase the contribution that Hong Kong made for the armed forces stationed in the colony. This usually consisted of six battalions, some RAF aircraft and some Royal Navy coastal mine sweepers. The United Kingdom calculated this cost to be more than £10 million, and Hong Kong's contribution was only £1.5 million. The UK government was trying to cut costs and the Chancellor, James Callaghan, had proposed (and the Cabinet had agreed) targeting savings of £100 million across overseas expenditures.[4]

Denis Healey, the Secretary of State for Defence, had visited Hong Kong several times to meet the troops. He had found dining with the governor to be 'pure Edwardian – one sherry only before dinner, then pairing off with the appropriate lady in long white gloves, followed by a meal that would have disgraced a minor prep school' (Healey 1989).

Now he met Cowperthwaite and other Hong Kong officials in London in July 1966.[5] Cowperthwaite presented some facts about the state of the economy, including that GNP was around £550 million, that there was no public support for further tax increases, and that there was much to be done in education, health and other areas. Healey was conducting a Defence Review and knew he had to deliver savings. He proposed that Hong Kong contribute £5.5 million, leaving the United Kingdom to contribute £5 million: the equivalent of around three battalions. Healey argued that a contribution that was around 1 per cent of GNP was not onerous. Cowperthwaite did not try and refute the idea that Hong Kong should eventually contribute more, but argued that it would be easier to phase increases in slowly, with greater local support.

The Cabinet debated the issue over the summer. The Colonial Office, having sounded out the Hong Kong government, pointed out that Hong Kong would be happy with a smaller garrison, and lower costs. In addition, the £11 million cost was being challenged since it included the costs of visiting Royal Navy ships. The prime minister was dragged into the argument as the Cabinet tried to justify what level of expenditure should be covered by Hong Kong. In the end, the Secretary of State for the Colonies visited Hong Kong and thrashed out a deal whereby they would increase the contribution to £5 million and there would be a reduction of about one battalion in the strength of the garrison. This reduction would be postponed because of tensions over Macau in late 1966.[6] In fact, the forces in Hong Kong would be increased in the late 1960s because Hong Kong would no longer be able to draw on forces based in Singapore after their withdrawal in 1971.[7]

However, for now Healey was very happy with the settlement, given that he perceived that the colonial officers in Hong Kong always 'supported the local interests against Whitehall' and, as he noted in his memoirs (Healey 1989):

> I always retired hurt from my encounters with the redoubtable Financial Secretary, John Cowperthwaite.

THE 1967 BUDGET

The 1967 budget would come as a 'pleasant surprise' and Cowperthwaite was in confident form.[8] Trench started proceedings with his annual address, summarizing what he described as 'a year full of incident', ranging from the visit of Princess Margaret to the spring riots in Kowloon, from serious flooding in the middle of the year to increased defence spending. Many new laws had been passed, and the executive council had been restructured to have an Unofficial majority. But most significantly, the economy had started to bounce back. The governor could paint a rosy picture:

> I will only say that the strength and resilience of Hong Kong's finances continue to amaze me, used as I am to these phenomena. But, speaking in more general terms, confidence in 'the banking system' has been restored, and deposits now stand at a record figure. Trade has been buoyant, and in all categories, imports, domestic exports and re-exports, we have registered gains in terms of value.

Trench welcomed progress on managing trade relations with major partners. Agreement had been reached on a five-year deal with the United States on cotton exports and a four-year deal with the United Kingdom. Hong Kong was active in GATT and had established a Trade Development Council, and the Commerce and Industry Department had opened offices in Geneva and Washington. While the government freed up trade barriers, the number of factories increased and industrial employment enjoyed double-digit growth. Textiles and garments continued to grow, but so too did the rapidly growing electronics industry.

Trench then covered the many ways in which the government was trying to 'make Hong Kong a better place to live in'. Progress in housing had been slowed by the financial crisis, but building levels were now back on track. Educational provision was being widened and improved. Health spending and provision were up.

Cowperthwaite prefaced his remarks with a reprimand to those who had been pessimistic about the economy, and its ability to adapt:

> It is apparent that the economy has redeployed itself with speed and with considerable success. We now have a sounder base from which the economy is continuing to expand at a steady and satisfactory rate. Even our gloomier Jeremiahs are beginning to accept, some of them it is true, with reluctance, that we are not in the depths of a depression.

For 1965/66 the final outcome was a deficit of $137 million: better than the $190 million deficit estimated a year before. For 1966/67 the original forecast had been for a $94 million deficit. Profits and salaries taxes were up, and the effect of the salary awards had been less than forecast. But the biggest difference was that capital spending was nearly $100 million below forecast. Cowperthwaite expected that the final results would show a surplus.

The positive out-turns meant that total reserves were much stronger than Cowperthwaite had expected, totaling $1,265 million. Cowperthwaite defended the policy of keeping reserves abroad, predominantly in London. He argued that it was critical that reserves were kept in a liquid form so that they could be drawn on quickly in times of need. Only a small part of the reserves were held in Hong Kong because there were few available assets that were sufficiently liquid and of scale, and because if the funds were deposited at local banks, withdrawing them at a time of need could create a credit squeeze at exactly the wrong moment. For these reasons, reserves were best kept in London:

> It is normal for countries, independent as well as dependent, to keep a part of their reserves in foreign currency and one of the two main reserve currencies is sterling, the form in which we keep ours. This is not because we are a British colony but because we are members of the sterling area and our currency is linked in practice to sterling. Independent countries such as Singapore and Malaysia follow exactly the same policies as we do in this respect.

He reassured members that the reserves were earning a high rate of interest and were readily available. Later he would question his decision to leave large balances in sterling but for now he was happy to celebrate the considerable war chest that had been created.

For the year ahead he forecast a modest rise in revenues, mostly from rates. Recurrent expenditure was forecast to grow more quickly, particularly in education, where provision was increased. Non-recurrent capital spending was expected to fall slightly, with a slowdown in the housing spend and with a number of major projects reaching completion. Overall, Cowperthwaite was forecasting a small deficit.

The five-year forecast was healthier this year than last but still showed a net deficit over the period. Additionally, Cowperthwaite could see substantial unbudgeted investments in the port, public transport and the airport. But for now Cowperthwaite did not want to 'spoil today's not unhappy occasion by mentioning them'.

Given this positive picture, Cowperthwaite confirmed that he would not need to raise taxes, but rather could make some minor cuts in taxes that were 'inequitable or irritating or particularly difficult or expensive to collect'. He had three candidates to propose: broadcasting licences, stamp duty and estate duty, which cost $11 million in total.

In Hong Kong a $20 annual licence was required to listen to radio broadcasts, with the funds subsidizing Radio Hong Kong. As radio ownership boomed with the development of cheap transistor radios, the proportion of radio owners paying the fee had fallen. There was an argument to meet the cost from general taxation and he therefore proposed abolishing the radio licence fee, at a cost of $4¼ million. He had decided to retain a television licence fee, which he saw as a tax on a luxury item.

His second tax change was to reduce stamp duty on low-value properties to encourage home ownership. Properties selling for less than $20,000, which accounted for around 9 per cent of sales, would now be free of duty, and for the 60 per cent of properties that were sold for between $20,000 and $40,000, duty would be halved from 2 per cent to 1 per cent. The cost to revenue would be $5 million.

His third measure was to reduce the rate of estate duty (i.e. inheritance tax) from 40 per cent to 25 per cent. He was not persuaded by those that felt the tax drove investment abroad or was too easy for some to avoid. Indeed, he thought it was an essentially fair tax. But he did agree that the 40 per cent rate was high compared with the 15 per cent rate on salaries and profits. He was keen to clarify that his motives were purely economic:

> This proposal may be criticized as relief for the rich or rather for the heirs of the rich but its real justification is economic, not social, just the opposite in fact of my proposal on Stamp Duty which is made for social rather than economic reasons.

REACTION

The more positive tone was welcomed by the Unofficials as they raised their usual wide-ranging points.[9] Cowperthwaite batted away various proposals on depreciation allowances, mortgage interest tax relief, tax emptions for charitable giving, and so on.[10] Li had revived the idea of a full income tax, and teasingly asked Cowperthwaite why he had descended from his previous 'state of innocence' when he had supported the idea. In reply Cowperthwaite pointed to the benefit of not having an over-powerful tax system:

> I do not propose to make a full confession, but merely to mention one or two factors in my lapse from grace. One of these is an increasing awareness of the benefits to our economy, particularly in terms of investment and enterprise, both local and from overseas, of not having the inquisitorial type of tax system inevitably associated with a full income tax.

He went on to express his surprise at how quickly tax revenues were growing at a low rate of tax:

> Even I, who have always believed in the vigour of our economy under our present tax regime, have been surprised by the growth of revenue generated at our present rates.

Some years later, Arthur Laffer* would posit that there is an optimal tax rate at which tax revenues are maximized, and that pushing rates up beyond this level would lead to total revenues raised falling.

Cowperthwaite again expressed his reservations about deficit financing:

> Deficit financing proper is rather the process whereby a Government spends more money that it withdraws from the economy by taxation, borrowing, running down reserves, etc.; thereby causing in most circumstances, and very acutely in ours, monetary inflation and severe pressure on the balance of payments.

Cowperthwaite reiterated that he was not completely opposed to borrowing for capital projects in principle. His concern was that there were limited cases in which the returns would be high enough to repay the loan and interest, and he was concerned about borrowings where government could have 'recourse to the printing press'.

Cowperthwaite rejected suggestions that there was a credit squeeze occurring, driven by increased banking reserves. In fact, bank loans were up by around 7 per cent. It was true that the liquidity ratio of the banks had risen above the required 25 per cent to a level of over 36 per cent, but Cowperthwaite put this down to deposits rising at a very fast pace and the banks being unable to grow their loan books as rapidly.

---

* Arthur Laffer was an American economist who came to prominence during the Reagan administration. He did not claim to invent the Laffer curve, merely to popularize it after sketching it on a napkin in a meeting with Dick Cheney and Donald Rumsfeld in 1974.

Some concerns had been raised about the very high levels of overseas capital held in Hong Kong, and whether there were measures that could be taken to stop or discourage an exodus of that capital. Cowperthwaite reiterated the importance of the free flow of capital:

> Simply put, money comes here and stays here because it can go if it wants to go. Try to hedge it around with prohibitions, and it would go and we could not stop it; and no more would come.

And he explained that he was not concerned about the consequences for the balance of payments:

> Our balance of payments mechanism is, and must be, self-adjusting. Even if we were unfortunate enough to experience a capital outflow, to try to correct it by restriction or any form of discrimination would merely make matters worse. Our only course is to ensure that the economic and political conditions here are such as to give every inducement to come and to stay; this policy has worked and will, I believe, continue to work.

Cowperthwaite reserved his most scathing comments for Watson, who (among other issues) had raised the problem of car parking provision:

> My honourable Friend Mr Watson has given us another brilliant exhibition of special, indeed specious, pleading on behalf of his favourite cause, the provision of subsidized car-parks at the expense of the whole community. He has once again made our hearts bleed for the wretched lot of that small, indigent and oppressed minority, the car owner, who, unlike the more fortunate 95% majority of our fellow citizens, is apparently denied the facilities of the public transport services.

Watson had also noted that road users paid twice as much in road taxes as the government spent on roads. Cowperthwaite felt that 'the Watson theory of taxation, which lays down that all taxes must be returned to those that pay them in direct benefits related to the activity which bore tax', was not worth countering in detail because 'its fallaciousness seems patently obvious'.

Li had asked whether Hong Kong should diversify its substantial reserves. Cowperthwaite reassured him with some words that would read quite differently later that year:

> [Mr Li] would appear to be suggesting that we should leave the sterling area. I doubt if that would be wise and, while we are members, we must accept the obligations as well as the benefits of membership. Our links with sterling are too strong to be lightly

> broken. In any event, as I am sure my honourable Friend is aware, Her Majesty's Government have repeatedly emphasized their firm resolve to maintain the exchange value of the pound.

With the economic recovery and his confident handling of the 1967 budget, it looked very much as if Cowperthwaite was back in a commanding position in driving the economic policies of Hong Kong. However, later that year he would face a major setback from an unexpected area when Harold Wilson decided to devalue the pound, leaving Hong Kong's foreign exchange policy in tatters and the government nursing major losses on its sterling reserves.

CHAPTER 17

DEVALUATION AND INDECISION

THE DEVALUATION OF STERLING IN 1967 left Cowperthwaite and Trench looking powerless, conflicted and indecisive. Hong Kong's response to the devaluation was not Cowperthwaite's finest hour. Coming so soon after the banking crisis of 1965, and with the troubles stemming from the Cultural Revolution, it risked undermining Cowperthwaite and the government more broadly.

HONG KONG'S STERLING ASSETS

The Hong Kong dollar had been fixed in terms of silver until 1935. After World War II, Hong Kong joined the sterling area, with the exchange rate being tied to sterling, which itself was fixed to the US dollar under the Bretton Woods system. The US dollar was convertible into gold at the rate of $35 per ounce. This created a system where each currency was fixed against others, and against gold via the US dollar. After a major sterling devaluation in 1949, the exchange rate was set with £1 being worth US$2.80 and HK$16.

The sterling area was a vestige of the pre-1914 world in which sterling and the City of London stood at the centre of the world's financial markets. Well over half of all the world's trade was conducted in sterling, and then settled by sterling balances in London. Governments would keep a large part of their official reserves in sterling, alongside their holdings in gold. With sterling being convertible into gold, having pounds was as good as holding gold itself. After World War II the role of reserve currency was taken by the US dollar, but there remained a small part of the old Empire that still settled trades in sterling and held significant sterling reserves. Members included Australia, New Zealand, Malaysia, Singapore, South Africa and many smaller dependencies.

Hong Kong, for unique reasons, held nearly a quarter of all externally held sterling balances (Welsh 1997). The string of government surpluses that had been achieved over the previous twenty years were partly held in sterling, and the issued dollar notes were backed by sterling. Three private 'British' banks – the Hongkong and Shanghai Bank, the Chartered Bank and the Mercantile Bank – issued the clear majority of banknotes, and 105 per cent of the value of issued banknotes was backed by certificates of indebtedness bought by the banks from the government's Exchange Fund with sterling. Thus, the banks held dollar-denominated notes as liabilities and sterling certificates as assets. The government was not permitted to diversify its reserves out of sterling and the banks could not easily hedge against the exchange rate risk. Hong Kong and its banks were rather more entwined with sterling than they perhaps fully realized.

WILSON'S ECONOMIC PLAN

In the early 1960s the pound had been under pressure, and this pressure became intense in the summer of 1966. In March 1966, just seventeen months after he first came to power, the prime minister, Harold Wilson, called and won a snap election. Instead of an insecure majority of four MPs he now had a majority of ninety-six. Wilson had inherited a large trade deficit, and with his newly enlarged parliamentary majority, the markets started guessing that he might address the deficit by devaluing the pound.

The government was conflicted between those wanting an austerity programme to dampen demand and reduce imports and those who wanted to devalue to avoid the unemployment of austerity. Unlike those in charge in Hong Kong, Wilson was a great believer in government-led economic planning. For example, he had created the Department of Economic Affairs to set targets to stimulate investment and growth, and this was the era of the prime minister himself getting involved in individual strikes by inviting union leaders, industrialists and ministers for 'beer and sandwiches at Number Ten'. With their large new majority, the government tried to simultaneously reduce demand and mitigate rising unemployment. Speculators, sensing that this policy contradiction would unravel, increased their bets against the pound.

Wilson was determined not to devalue. Labour had been in power in 1949 when the pound had last been devalued, that time by over 30 per cent, and he did not want Labour to be 'the party of devaluation' (Thorpe 2001). New measures were introduced to prevent tourists from taking more than £50 abroad. In April 1966 the Exchange Control Act banned individuals from buying gold coins. As the government defended the pound, the reserves drained away.

OPERATION PATRIARCH

By the autumn of 1967, however, the government concluded that a devaluation was inevitable. The Bank of England had been preparing plans since 1965 for this eventuality, under the code 'F.U.', for 'forever unmentionable' (Newton 2010). On 1 November the Treasury and the Bank of England started specific and detailed planning in complete secrecy under the code name Operation Patriarch. They moved quickly and covered much ground at speed. There were a great many issues to resolve. Two days into the process the officials realized that they would need to 'give further thought to our responsibilities to the dependent territories in the event of a devaluation'.[1] A week later, this further thinking did identify that Hong Kong was 'the difficult one'.

The officials identified two key issues: would the Hong Kong dollar need to follow the pound and what would happen to the sterling balances held by Hong Kong.

Since they were keen that others did not follow with competitive devaluations, they were quite sanguine about the Hong Kong dollar not following the pound, and instead appreciating against it. They were also aware that a devaluation would raise the price of imports such as rice and that that might cause unrest at a difficult time. However, they did not think it appropriate to do further work on this, or to hint to the Hong Kong government that they should.

On the banks' sterling balances, they were rather parochially concerned about any effect on confidence in sterling. The issue of the very large sterling balances held by the Hong Kong government did not seem to feature heavily in their thinking.

The lack of preparation was avoidable. A year earlier the Bank of England had already raised the question of Hong Kong's position with the Commonwealth Office and had suggested some research on the legal position that was not done.[2] In October 1967 Cowperthwaite, while on a visit to London, had asked David Hubback* at the Treasury some questions about things that were worrying him and Hong Kong's

---

* David Hubback, born 1916, attended King's College, Cambridge. He served in the Army through the war and then became private secretary to the Permanent Secretary to the Treasury. He served as PPS to the Chancellor, Selwyn Lloyd, between 1960 and 1962. He retired as Deputy Secretary of the Department of Trade and Industry in 1976.

governor:[3] namely, whether Hong Kong could diversify her reserves out of sterling and, if not, would Hong Kong be compensated if the pound devalued; and, if the pound was devalued, whether Hong Kong should follow. He did not receive very clear answers on any of these issues, and indeed received some reassurance that it was a remote possibility. As Hubback notes:

> Cowperthwaite left me with the plea that Hong Kong, as a Colony, was totally dependent on the United Kingdom and that they had to look to us to safeguard their interests. I said we fully realized this.

Within a month Cowperthwaite would be left with a quite different perception. His questions were circulated around a small group of senior officials in London who quickly came to the view that the United Kingdom should not provide compensation, and that it was a matter for the Hong Kong government if it wanted to compensate local note-issuing banks.[4]

On Saturday 18 November 1967 the pound was devalued by 14 per cent, to US $2.40. Wilson argued that the devaluation would tackle the root cause of Britain's economic problems by increasing its competitiveness. He made his now-infamous remarks that 'it does not mean that the pound here in Britain, in your pocket or purse or in your bank, has been devalued'.

SHORT NOTICE

There was a very carefully choreographed plan of informing central banks, overseas governments and domestic bodies. The specific time of the devaluation was to be 21.30 GMT on 18 November, and the telegram for Sir David Trench and Cowperthwaite was scheduled for 15.30 GMT on that same day. The telegram confirmed that it was a matter for the Hong Kong government whether to follow sterling in devaluing or to maintain the previous rate, depending on 'where Hong Kong's interests lie'.[5] With the time difference, and the very late notification, Trench and Cowperthwaite had very little time to formulate a response, and they would be extremely bitter about the fact that they had not been trusted with the information earlier.

Eric Haslam,* an advisor to the governor of the Bank of England, flew into Hong Kong on the afternoon of Sunday 19 November to explain the position at a hastily arranged executive council meeting at 6.00 p.m. that evening.[6] Cowperthwaite

* Eric Haslam was born in Wellington, New Zealand in 1912. He went to Balliol College, Oxford in 1935 as a Rhodes scholar. He joined Commonwealth Bank of Australia before joining the Bank of England in 1948.

had met Haslam on his arrival and had immediately asked about compensation arrangements. Haslam had kept to the agreed line and said there were none, and that it was not possible to be simultaneously in the sterling area, have a free currency market, enjoy the right to diversify reserves and have very weak exchange controls.

At the council meeting Jake Saunders,* the chairman of the Hongkong and Shanghai Banking Corporation, emotionally overplayed his hand, asking Haslam

> a question which he put quite brutally but perhaps fortunately for me in a form so extreme as to make it easier for me to answer. He asked what the UK reaction would be to demand to remove all their sterling, and reconstitute their reserves in gold or dollars. My answer was that such a demand would invoke the bald constitutional relationship. For a variety of reasons we could not allow them that right though, I added, in calmer times a choice of that sort might have existed but only at the cost of their being excluded from the sterling area. In the light of political realities this theoretical choice was somewhat unreal.[6]

The Hong Kong government was not at all sure what to do. If they devalued alongside the pound then the sterling balances held by the government and the banks would retain their value in Hong Kong dollars. But a devaluation would push consumer prices up sharply as most foodstuffs and essentials were imported. This would significantly hit the colony's inhabitants. If they did not devalue, then the banks' and the government's sterling assets would take a hit in Hong Kong dollars. To confuse matters further, Singapore and Malaysia, both also in the sterling area, had decided that evening not to follow the pound. Their quick and unexpected decision put further pressure on the government to act.

Unsurprisingly, the banking members of the council argued for devaluing but the Chinese members were more concerned with the prospect of rising import costs. Haslam left the room but reported that only one official member voted against devaluation while all the Chinese members bar one voted to maintain the old rate. The majority, however, was for following the pound down. And so the dollar followed sterling down.

---

* John (Jake) Saunders was born in 1917 in Uxbridge. He joined the Hongkong and Shanghai Banking Corporation in 1937. He joined the Army as a private in 1939 and rose to the rank of major during the war. He was awarded a Military Cross and a Distinguished Service Order in action. After the war he returned to the bank and became chief manager (effectively CEO) in 1962 and also chairman in 1964. He retired and was knighted in 1972.

RETHINK

On the Monday the media attacked the move and Cowperthwaite came under pressure in television and radio interviews. As Haslam noted:

> the issue is banking and trading losses versus the less obvious but widely and regressively spread burden of rising food prices over the community at large.

Cowperthwaite gave a television interview arguing that the devaluation of the Hong Kong dollar represented a choice between two evils.[7] He noted that Hong Kong's own funds and those of banks and individuals were in sterling, so 'if the sterling is devalued and the Hong Kong dollar is not, these banks, firms and individuals all take an immediate loss'. On the other hand, 'most industrialists think that the devaluation is a mistake because of their own anticipation of the increased cost of raw materials'.

By Tuesday morning the government was less sure about its chosen path. Cowperthwaite came to Haslam's hotel for breakfast and asked his advice on whether they could ask the IMF for a revised (higher) exchange rate, and whether the Bank of England could help them sort out possible compensation arrangements for the banks. Haslam, who had been surprised that they had devalued, was further surprised that they should risk being exposed 'to the charge of vacillation', but he agreed to seek advice.[6]

Trench and Cowperthwaite did not wait for that advice and instead decided to revalue the Hong Kong dollar by 10 per cent before hearing back from Haslam.[8] The Hong Kong government sent a telegram to the Commonwealth Office on the Tuesday evening to let them know that the new rate would be announced at 7 a.m. Hong Kong time on Wednesday 23 November. That was only a few hours later: a point unlikely to have been lost on the participants. And given the time difference there was nobody in Hong Kong with whom to debate the plan before the markets opened. William Ryrie[*9] at the Treasury hurriedly contacted the IMF to get their agreement, which he managed to do in the limited time available. He dryly noted:

> For the record, I think we had better explain to Mr Cowperthwaite that changes in parity, even of Hong Kong, required IMF approval and that a little longer notice is

---

* William Ryrie was born in 1928 in Calcutta, where his Scottish father was a missionary. He was educated in Darjeeling and Scotland. He joined the Colonial Office and then the Treasury in 1963 as assistant to Sir Alec Cairncross, and he drew up the contingency plan for the 1967 devaluation. He was later private secretary to three Chancellors: Roy Jenkins, Iain MacLeod and Anthony Barber.

> desirable to say the least. The fact that we gave him short notice of UK devaluation (though a good deal longer than he gave us) is not relevant.[10]

Tempers were still high when Sir David Trench sent a telegram to the Commonwealth Office on 28 November.[11] In unusually undiplomatic language Trench wrote:

> I find it difficult to find words to express my feelings, and those of my Advisers, official and unofficial, on the manner in [which] Britain has now defaulted on its very large net financial obligations to Hong Kong.

The way that the process had been handled had clearly also irritated him intensely:

> I find it very hard to excuse the manner in which responsibility for solving the exceedingly complex problems devaluation presented was thrust upon us without the least prior consultation as to where our interest lay (indeed after several refusals to enter into serious consultations), without advice of any kind, and without the same amount of warning as was given to other independent countries.

Trench asked for urgent discussions on compensation and about how to avoid similar issues should there be a further devaluation of the pound. He suggested that Cowperthwaite fly to London the following week for consultations. The London officials had decided to 'play a long game' and were not keen to rush into negotiations. In London they tried to work out what options were workable. Haslam felt that Trench and Cowperthwaite were exaggerating in claiming they had no idea a devaluation might occur.[12] However, he acknowledged that perhaps they were surprised that they were given a choice, and that they were not well prepared to make it. At one point Cowperthwaite had said to Haslam that he 'would have been personally happier if the rate had been dictated to me'. Haslam felt that the UK government was being blamed for Hong Kong having a choice – albeit a constrained choice – between either having domestic prices rise or taking a hit to the reserves. In a rare note of frustration, he commented that 'one has the feeling that with these people one cannot really win'.

REVALUATION WELCOMED

The revaluation was broadly welcomed in Hong Kong. It reduced the likely price increases that basic imported goods would otherwise have suffered, and the impact on banks' balance sheets was of limited concern to most people. Cowperthwaite gave a very full explanation in the press about the process, and about the issues that the government had considered. The press covered the story extensively and on the day of the revaluation he was quizzed by more than sixty journalists at a hectic press conference.[13] He gave a very detailed account of how Hong Kong had been kept in the dark and about the issues that had led to the first decision to devalue, and then to revalue. Despite his focus on devaluation, when asked about whether the government would police importers who had already raised prices, he maintained his traditional philosophy, replying: 'No, no. We are relying on market forces to bring prices down.'

Figure 17.1. Cowperthwaite revaluation press conference (HKSAR Government).

But the press increasingly focused on the issue of Hong Kong's sterling reserves. Asked to disclose the extent of these, Cowperthwaite 'hesitated, then said he thought that, although this was normally a confidential matter, in the present circumstances it would do some good to reveal the numbers'. He disclosed that the reserves held in London stood at £350 million. The pressure on Cowperthwaite to resolve this increased when the Legislative Council discussed the devaluation in an adjournment debate on 29 November.[14]

THE SEARCH FOR A SOLUTION

Sir Arthur Galsworthy* of the Commonwealth Office was in Hong Kong on 14 December to continue the discussion with Trench. As he passed through Manila

* Sir Arthur Galsworthy (1916–86) was appointed as High Commissioner to New Zealand in 1970 as Ambassador to the Republic of Ireland in 1973.

he was briefed by telegram by the Foreign Office,[15] which wanted to answer the issues raised by Trench in his emotional telegram of 28 November. Galsworthy was asked to argue that Hong Kong had suffered no worse than other sterling holders and that compensation was not possible. He was to say that the British government had left it up to Hong Kong as to whether to devalue, and he was to push back on the suggestion that Hong Kong had been given inadequate notice, although the telegram noted that it was true that some independent countries had been given somewhat earlier notice.

More helpfully, he was allowed to mention that Britain would likely be willing to contribute £3¼ million to the new airport scheme and to offer Hong Kong the right to limited future diversification of their reserves.[16] It also hoped that the resignation of James Callaghan as Chancellor, because he had broken his pledge to maintain the parity of the pound, would assuage some anger.

On 15 December Galsworthy met with the unofficial members, many of whom he had known for years and some of whom he considered personal friends. He quickly sensed that 'feelings ran strong indeed, much stronger than over any previous issue [he] had had to take up with them'. They reiterated the two main issues: the inadequate notice, and here anger had intensified markedly when they had heard from other sources that Malaysia and Singapore had been told before Hong Kong; and the demand to diversify the reserves beyond sterling.

Galsworthy deftly pointed out that while it was in Britain's interests to work with Hong Kong as the second largest holder of sterling, it was also in Hong Kong's interests not to weaken Britain's ability to defend Hong Kong. As he put it:

> If Hong Kong expected one-ness in defence, without which Hong Kong could not survive, they could not necessarily expect separateness in these currency questions. Basically Hong Kong and Britain were in the same boat: if Hong Kong holed it, they would sink with Britain.

On 20 December Galsworthy met again with the Unofficials, including Jake Saunders of the Hongkong and Shanghai Bank, who suggested the idea of a paid-for guarantee. Hong Kong would retain its reserves in sterling but Britain would guarantee, say, 60 per cent of the reserves in return for an appropriate premium, which Saunders estimated might be £1.5 million per annum. While Galsworthy tried to play down any particular solution in case it gain too much traction, he was very aware of the need to act.

He reported back that he was in no doubt as to the strength of feeling in the colony or about the benefits that the devaluation controversy gave to the communist provocateurs. He also warned that if a solution was not found, then he believed that several of the unofficial members would resign, creating enormous political problems for the government. Galsworthy pinned his colours to the mast by concluding:

> I believe the position can be very largely restored if we now deal sympathetically with the request to diversify which Mr Cowperthwaite is coming to London to discuss this week. To my mind it would be unthinkable that we should refuse this request.

Before leaving Hong Kong Galsworthy asked Cowperthwaite to give him a brief note on the problems that the devaluation had caused for the Hong Kong dollar. Cowperthwaite hurriedly dictated his thoughts and Galsworthy later circulated them within the Commonwealth Office, but not to the Treasury or the Bank of England.[17] Cowperthwaite argued that it was critical that the Hong Kong dollar be directly linked to a stable outside standard of value, and that the currency be fully backed since the government had no drawing rights at the IMF and so could not support the currency by intervention. He also believed that it was critical that there was an automatic link between the balance of payments and the money supply, since Hong Kong was entirely reliant on trade.

Cowperthwaite emphasized the need for stability:

> The rate of exchange between the Hong Kong dollar and its reserve currency (or currencies) is of no importance, so long as it is stable. The economy automatically tends to equilibrium; that is, other things being equal, exchange rates determine costs and prices. If exchange rates change (as a consequence, for example, of a decision to devalue sterling in order to correct its over-valuation), the Hong Kong dollar becomes at once under-valued and a process of restoration of equilibrium begins. During this period there is considerable dislocation and earning power is lost because of the change in terms of trade. Change of exchange rates cannot be beneficial in any circumstances.[18]

The 1949 devaluation of sterling had not caused a problem because the colony had negligible sterling assets and because the free-market Hong Kong–US dollar rates were already close to the rates that were adopted. The current problem had arisen because Hong Kong 'had no sterling debt but, in the case of both banks and the Exchange Fund, rapidly increasing sterling assets against Hong Kong dollar liabilities'.

Hong Kong had not been permitted to resolve this mismatch by diversifying their reserves, or by buying forward cover. Indeed, the government had given the note-issuing banks an informal guarantee in 1966 that if they suffered an exchange loss because of their function as residual holders of sterling, then the Exchange Fund would cover this.

Cowperthwaite once more expressed his indignation at only getting 'four hours notice', before attempting to quantify the problem:

> The act of devaluation imposed a very large immediate loss on Hong Kong (between £50–£70 million probably) and the problem was basically to distribute this loss while causing the minimum of dislocation, hardship and further loss. To follow the pound, while protecting the banks and the majority of merchants against exchange losses, would have both lowered the living standards of the people and caused a loss of foreign exchange earnings due to the worsening terms of trade.
>
> If, on the other hand, the Hong Kong dollar's previous gold parity were maintained, there were prospects of serious consequences on industry and trade by reason of their sterling commitments, leading possibly to bankruptcies, factory closures and unemployment.

Cowperthwaite also alluded to a concern that public confidence in the banking sector, shaken by the 1965 bank runs and the 1967 disturbances, was fragile and that the government had wanted to be sure that none of the unauthorized banks would be at risk of bankruptcy if the government did not follow the pound down. He argued that this was in part behind the rather messy process by which Hong Kong devalued by 14 per cent only to revalue three days later. The resultant net 5.7 per cent devaluation against sterling was the result of balancing the various pressures.

Looking to the future Cowperthwaite observed that the colony would have lower reserves for fiscal shocks that might occur, and that banks and others would question sterling's role as a reserve currency. Having laid out the economic argument, Cowperthwaite concluded by appealing to a sense of fairness:

> It seems clear that, in equity, means must be devised of giving Hong Kong, as a dependent territory, the same degree of protection for its exchange assets and its exchange parity as is made possible for independent members of the Commonwealth and sterling area.

PAYING OFF THE BANKERS

The Hong Kong government continued to discuss compensation for the local banks directly with them. Trench estimated that the banks had lost something of the order of £12 million, and on 21 December he let London know that he intended to compensate them for that part of the loss that it was not possible for banks to cover – a sum he estimated at around £10 million.[19] The remaining losses could in theory have been met by a forward contract or by fixing rates in sterling contracts. Neither of these methods was widely used and Trench therefore expected that the banks would shy away from sterling. He was prepared to guarantee future compensation if there was a further devaluation but not without a counter-guarantee from London. Once more Trench gave London a very limited window of time, insisting that any deal needed to be completed by the next day. Cowperthwaite sent the same message to the Treasury and the Bank of England. As before they did not receive a promise of a future guarantee.

INCONCLUSIVE NEGOTIATIONS

Cowperthwaite met with all the key officials on 8 January 1968 in the Commonwealth Office in London.[20] Among other officials, Sir Arthur Snelling and Sir Arthur Galsworthy represented the Commonwealth Office, David Hubback and William Ryrie the Treasury, and Eric Haslam the Bank of England. Cowperthwaite explained that the partial revaluation was to create 'the most even balance possible' between the public losses from higher prices and the bank losses from devaluing their sterling reserves. He argued that the banks would be unable to continue to take the risk of holding sterling balances and Hong Kong dollar liabilities, and that this would hurt the economy. Therefore, the Hong Kong government had been obliged to use their Exchange Fund to compensate the banks for their resultant losses. But this was simply a one-time remedy.

Cowperthwaite offered two potential long-term solutions: either a diversification of the reserves, primarily into US dollars and gold; or some form of guarantee from the UK government to make good any losses from future devaluations. Lengthy discussions followed about solutions, the impact on sterling of such measures, the need to reassure the Hong Kong public, and the benefits that Hong Kong enjoyed by being a British colony. The meeting ended with Cowperthwaite being asked to draft a paper 'setting out exactly what diversification the Government of Hong Kong sought, the time scale of it, and the extent to which it would be concealed or overt'.

The same group met again two days later at the Commonwealth Office on 10 January.[21] Cowperthwaite announced that he would shortly return to Hong Kong but was available for a follow-up meeting later that month or in early March. Galsworthy asked Cowperthwaite if he could 'hold the position in Hong Kong until April', and Cowperthwaite replied that he could try, using the imminent budget as an excuse for delay. They agreed that he would let the Legislative Council know that a guarantee was unrealistic but that some form of diversification was probably negotiable.

Cowperthwaite wrote a memorandum, circulated on 8 February, outlining his ideas on the protection that Hong Kong wanted. He proposed that over time, 50 per cent of the reserves should be diversified away from sterling, with roughly 10 per cent of reserves being moved out of sterling each year until that target was met. Until then, the undiversified portion should be guaranteed by the United Kingdom against gold rather than backed solely by sterling.

Christopher Fogarty of the Treasury visited Hong Kong at the end of February for an extensive round of discussions.[22] Fogarty and Cowperthwaite spoke frequently over his visit, not just about the devaluation but about the British and Hong Kong economies more generally:

> As usual there was a good deal of conversation about Hong Kong's economic affairs and outlook (generally prosperous at the moment) and the decadence of Britain (countered to the best of my ability).

On the issue of protecting Hong Kong against future sterling devaluations, Fogarty discussed a solution with Trench and Cowperthwaite whereby Hong Kong paid a fee for a guarantee.

THE BUDGET IMPLICATIONS

During his budget speech on 28 February 1968, Cowperthwaite addressed the issue of the devaluation and how it had affected government reserves.[23] He started by explaining the cause and size of the loss to the reserves:

> Sterling devaluation has cost the Fund, both by way of additional sterling cover to meet the Fund's Hong Kong dollar obligations to holders of Hong Kong banknotes, and by way of meeting the exchange losses of the authorized exchange banks in view of their role as holders of part of our foreign exchange reserves, about $400 million.

Cowperthwaite pointed out that the cost to official funds was lower because there had been a net devaluation of 5.7 per cent. If the dollar had maintained its old gold parity and not devalued, losses would have been nearer $750 million.

The net result was that the level of reserves going into the next financial year would be of the order of $1,000 million compared with $1,300 million at the same point in the previous year. Cowperthwaite then turned to the issue of what purpose reserves served, and how they could best be used. The reserves backed the notes in issue. They could also be used for future public spending. He had seen this surplus as funds for a rainy day but now he wondered if they were needed instead to back the currency, given his belief that Hong Kong needed unusually strong reserves of foreign exchange.

Cowperthwaite had no simple answer, but for now he had made a working assumption that:

> for the purposes of the Five Year Forecast, we have assumed that the existing surplus of about $150 million will be available for fiscal purposes but that only half of future accretions will be so available. I have hopes that we can do better than that in the event.

A BREACH OF CONFIDENCE?

Reporting on the budget on 28 February, the *Times Business News* wrote an article titled 'Hong Kong may reduce sterling holdings', and the press reported that Cowperthwaite had 'revealed that discussions were being held in London on holding the colony's foreign assets in other currencies besides sterling'.[24] The *Financial Times* picked up the story the following day under the heading 'Hong Kong to cut UK assets', observing that Treasury officials had been visiting Hong Kong and 'it is thought likely that negotiations have been taking place on the extent and the timing of Hong Kong's diversification of her sterling assets'.[25]

Inside the UK Treasury, Ryrie wrote a strongly worded note to Hubback suggesting that Cowperthwaite was responsible for a serious breach of confidence in revealing this. Trench replied to a terse Commonwealth Office enquiry by noting:

> There was in fact no (repeat no) suggestion of intention to reduce sterling holdings. The inference was probably drawn by [the] correspondents because in their capacities as editorial staff of *Far Eastern Economic Review* they have themselves been advocating it.[26]

This did not stop Snelling sending a telex the same day directly to Cowperthwaite arguing that sterling had come under 'heavy pressure' in response to his statements. The Commonwealth Office and the Treasury clearly wanted to pin part of the blame on Cowperthwaite.[27]

On 7 March Cowperthwaite wrote a detailed letter to Snelling.[28] While noting that he was sorry if his budget speech had caused any problems, he had no intention of making an apology. He had gotten hold of the original report filed by the *Times Business News* correspondent and given its differences from the published reports he surmised that the paper had already received information from the Treasury or the Bank of England.

He then pointed out that:

> It was simply not possible for me to conceal the devastating effect of sterling's devaluation on our public funds and on future social development. Equally, having had to confess to a loss of $450 million (at least), it was completely impossible not to go on and give some re-assurance that we were taking steps to try to insure ourselves against similar losses in the future.

Cowperthwaite explained that the situation was still unresolved in Hong Kong, The banks, especially the note-issuing banks, were nervous about the risks they were being asked to take, and many businesses were acting to limit their exposure to sterling. He observed that he had been informed that the British Bank of the Middle East in Kuwait (a subsidiary of the Hongkong and Shanghai Bank) had obtained permission to cover its forward sterling positions and he considered the inequality of treatment to be very unfair. If the Commonwealth Office was expecting some contrition, they would be disappointed. Cowperthwaite's clear anger at the treatment that Hong Kong was receiving was evident in his questioning the moral position of the UK government in using Hong Kong to support sterling:

> Hong Kong has not had a single concession and remains at full and increasing risk, although the risk is relatively greater than any other country's. It is not very difficult to see the reason for this difference of treatment. In our case H.M.G. knows that it can escape the responsibility [of protecting banks' sterling deposits], for it can instruct this colonial government to refrain from taking any step in Hong Kong's interest which it deems to be against its own. Surely it would not be unreasonable to describe this as a clear misuse of Colonial power?

TALKS RESUMED

As London procrastinated, Trench tried to push them to resolve the substantive issues. He was himself under increasing pressure in Hong Kong. On 5 March 1968 he wrote to Galsworthy, enclosing a letter that had been handed to him by the two senior Executive Committee members, Sir Albert Rodrigues and C. Y. Kwan, and signed by Unofficials and representatives of banks and industry. Trench described their intervention as being 'entirely reasonable and responsible' while 'expressing the most serious concern'.[29] He relayed to Galsworthy that Sir Albert had stated that if Trench and Cowperthwaite could not reach agreement in the next round of talks, then the signatories would want to send a delegation to London to 'seek interviews with Ministers and press their cause'.

The letter proposed a solution: that the gold value of Hong Kong's sterling balances be guaranteed, initially for one year, and for a fee.[30] Trench noted acerbically: 'it seems likely too simple an answer to be entirely practical'.

A few days after this exchange, the Commonwealth Office invited Cowperthwaite to resume talks in London in late April, arguing that the British budget would make them unavailable before then.[31] Before this meeting the various parties prepared briefing papers, with the objective of getting close to a solution. Some believe that the Hong Kong banks had threatened to convert other funds into dollars, selling pounds and putting further pressure on sterling.[32] Whatever the reason, the mood had shifted in the United Kingdom from delay to resolution.

Eric Haslam drafted a paper that he then circulated to UK officials in March, building on Cowperthwaite's proposal of some diversification with an element of a guarantee. Haslam thought the best option would be to go back with an offer in those terms, but at a level that would be acceptable to the United Kingdom. Cowperthwaite had suggested a 50 per cent diversification over five years and Haslam suggested instead offering 25 per cent diversification over three years. Because this would offer very limited protection for Hong Kong in the early years, Haslam explored different ways in which some form of guarantee, paid for by Hong Kong, might be offered, covering, say, 40–50 per cent of the Exchange Fund for seven years.

Fogarty agreed to the plan but thought it was not enough.[33] Galsworthy, Ryrie, Haslam and Cowperthwaite met again in London on 29 April and Cowperthwaite pushed for higher levels of guarantees. On 28 May Trench put the plan to the executive council and it was reluctantly accepted. The Unofficials accepted that they had no choice but to support the agreement in public, for fear of creating a political backlash, but they asked that the following message be transmitted to the Commonwealth Office in London:

> This scheme has been offered to Hong Kong without alternatives and we can therefore do no more than advise its acceptance. We do so however without any enthusiasm and indeed under protest. We would like the whole arrangement formally reviewed, if Hong Kong so requests it, at the end of 1969.[34]

In a personal follow up telegram to the Commonwealth Office Trench expanded on how difficult the discussion had been, noting that:

> it has not been easy for Cowperthwaite and me to preserve unofficial members trust in us personally. Some fairly outspoken language was used by both Chinese and Europeans, and I fear confidence in H.M.G.'s good intentions towards Hong Kong may have suffered further.[34]

On 30 May 1968 the Commonwealth Office formalized the agreement between Britain and Hong Kong regarding the partial protection of their reserves.[35] Under the Hong Kong Dollar Bond Scheme, the colony would be able to hold 50 per cent of its official assets in protected bonds, up to a maximum of £150 million. As Cowperthwaite had wanted, official assets comprised the Exchange Fund and official funds held in sterling, including with banks in Hong Kong. The protected bonds would be provided by the UK government and would effectively be repayable (in either pounds or dollars) at the exchange rate prevailing at the time that they were purchased. Cowperthwaite formalized the arrangement into an Exchange Fund Bill that he presented to the Legislative Council in July 1968.[36]

THE BASEL AGREEMENT

When news of Hong Kong's deal leaked to the other members of the sterling area, they unsurprisingly demanded some similar protection against the pound devaluing again. Under the Basel Agreement of September 1968, Britain introduced the Sterling Guarantee Arrangement, which guaranteed the US dollar value of official sterling reserves held by sterling area countries in excess of 10 per cent of their official reserves. The British government agreed that Hong Kong could be covered by the Basel Agreement, initially for a five-year period from September 1968 (Jao 1974). Under a complicated scheme, the bank's sterling deposits could be classed as official reserves and covered by the scheme too.

The Basel Agreement was a much better deal than the first guarantee scheme and was widely welcomed in Hong Kong. In November 1968 Cowperthwaite described the new arrangement to the Legislative Council, as he amended the Exchange Fund Bill that he had introduced in July.[37] He disclosed that the original deal had required Hong Kong to buy seven-year bonds and to accept a rate of interest slightly below the rate on seven-year public borrowing in London to protect 50 per cent of sterling reserves. The new scheme provided a five-year guarantee of 90 per cent of sterling reserves' US dollar value at no cost.

It had been the persistence of Trench and Cowperthwaite that had led to a broad scheme that the British government had not intended to offer. However, without it the sterling area would likely have collapsed even more rapidly than it did. For Britain the cost of a future devaluation had increased materially, shifting the cost–benefit analysis of any future currency depreciation. There was at last some real protection for Hong Kong's hard-earned reserves, and for Cowperthwaite an arrangement that he believed was fair for the people of Hong Kong.

CURRENCY INDEPENDENCE

In August 1971 Richard Nixon suspended the convertibility of the US dollar into gold, and it became another fiat currency. In September 1971 Hong Kong reduced the proportion of sterling in its reserves from 99 per cent to 89 per cent. A few months later, in December, there was a major realignment of exchange rates under the Smithsonian Agreement, with the US dollar depreciating against most currencies and against gold. Britain decided to maintain its gold parity and therefore to allow the pound to appreciate against the US dollar. Hong Kong decided to follow suit in order to temper any inflation in import prices.

On 23 June 1972 Britain decided to let the pound float, rather than be fixed against other currencies. A fortnight later Hong Kong decided to link the Hong Kong dollar to the US dollar at a rate of HK$5.65 = US$1. This again showed a preference to limit any imported price inflation. It also showed how far Hong Kong had moved since 1967 in deciding its own fate in currency markets rather than being tied to the decisions of the British government. Cowperthwaite's difficult passage through the events of 1967 had created a new set of possibilities for his successors.

Hong Kong maintained its independent stance when, on 13 February 1973, the United States devalued the US dollar by a further 10 per cent by raising the gold price from US$38 per ounce to US$42 per ounce. Hong Kong decided to maintain the gold parity for the Hong Kong dollar, effectively revaluing by 10 per cent against the US dollar and by 6.7 per cent against sterling (Jao 1974).

A SILVER LINING

The 1967 devaluation, and the subsequent negotiations to prevent a repeat hit on Hong Kong's reserves, was a very difficult period for Cowperthwaite. He had just been through the 1965 banking crisis and consequently already had some critics. The lack of notice and then the indecision as to how to respond made Cowperthwaite look weak and not on top of his brief. Some questioned his loyalties: was he furthering the interests of the United Kingdom or of Hong Kong? Was he looking out for the bankers rather than the people? Cowperthwaite had been asking the right questions before the devaluation but had not pushed himself to explore all his options. He would have preferred to work within a set of constraints, and indeed acted as if he was even when he did not need to.

However, once the devaluation occurred Cowperthwaite worked to create a level of protection for Hong Kong. He extracted concessions that other sterling area countries had not achieved, despite being a civil servant in a colony. He was dogged in trying to avoid this happening again, and through that started Hong Kong down the road to having an independent exchange rate policy.

CHAPTER 18

FRICTION WITH CHINA

THE CULTURAL REVOLUTION SPILLS OVER

THE RUMBLINGS WITHIN HONG KONG as to alternative approaches to the economy and to society were diverse and disorganized. They never achieved a critical mass or the coherence to challenge the orthodoxy promoted by Cowperthwaite and Trench. The bigger threat to the colony continuing down its established path would come from neighbouring China.

Mao Zedong had led Communist China since its creation in 1949 as chairman of the Communist Party of China. He had established a single-party state with a very high degree of centralized power. Mao launched a number of campaigns, starting with the Hundred Flowers Campaign in 1956, in which he encouraged the expression of different views. Within a year this turned into a crackdown as some used the opportunity to express views about Mao's competence that were different to the ones he held himself.

The Great Leap Forward followed in 1958, aiming to rapidly industrialize China. Peasant populations were collectivized and huge investments made to modernize the agricultural sector. Much of the change was achieved through brute force. Widespread mismanagement and an ideologically driven approach led to output collapsing. An estimated 20–30 million people died from starvation and violence. This doomed campaign ended in 1961, leaving a short gap for China to recover before Mao's next initiative.

The Great Proletarian Cultural Revolution started in May 1966 and would last for a decade, until Mao's death in 1976. Its aim was to cement communism and to remove the remnants of traditional Chinese culture and capitalism. Using a well-worn formula, Mao claimed that there was an enemy within, formed of revisionist bourgeois elements who had infiltrated the state, the party and the country at large. Ten million (mostly young) people created Red Guards units to weed out these counter-revolutionary forces. Millions were persecuted as the Red Guards attacked the 'four olds': old customs, old culture, old habits and old ideas. Many elements of society slowly ground to a halt as individuals tried to avoid being caught in the widening net. Education effectively stopped for many years, and much traditional culture was destroyed. Millions were imprisoned and hundreds of thousands died.

In 1966 in Hong Kong several minor disturbances were associated with the turmoil in China. This became more serious and widespread the following year (Welsh 1997). In April 1967 communist protesters took to the streets in Kowloon and in May there were demonstrations in front of Government House, but they were peacefully dispersed (Bickers and Yep 2009). A number of communist sympathizers also went on strike. On 22 May the protests became violent and a number of arrests were made. Government employees who had gone on strike were dismissed from their jobs.

Tensions rose on 8 July when Chinese soldiers crossed the border and killed five Hong Kong policemen at Sha Tau Kok. The Hong Kong government responded cautiously, keen to avoid the dispute escalating into a broader Sino-British conflict, but eventually sent a detachment of Gurkhas to the area. It slowly became apparent that there were splits in the Chinese government as to how far to push the dispute in Hong Kong.

The hardliners in Beijing gained some traction when in August the Hong Kong government arrested three editors of communist papers in Hong Kong and banned their publications. On 20 August the British chargé d'affaires in Beijing received an ultimatum to reverse the ban, which the British refused to do. Two days later the Red Guard burnt down part of the British Embassy in Beijing. The risks of the protests getting out of control and creating a broader British–Chinese conflict were rising. Alongside these events, local agitators started a bombing campaign in Hong Kong. Over the summer months many bombs were planted through the colony and fifteen people died.

The government, led by the authoritative Trench, faced the violence with calm resolution, but it was an uneasy time for all in Hong Kong as the more radical elements in China sought to spread the disruption. It would turn out that China was too engaged in its internal issues for the senior actors to want to increase tensions with

Hong Kong, but through the early years of the Cultural Revolution no one in Hong Kong could be sure in what direction the waves from China might head.

Figure 18.1. Demonstrators wave their little red books outside Governor Trench's residence in 1966.

THE UNITED KINGDOM UPDATES ITS EVACUATION PLAN

The British government had an outdated contingency plan, called DIGIT, for the evacuation of Hong Kong filed away. They took the threat of disturbances sufficiently seriously to decide that this should be updated. The Cabinet set up a secret subcommittee,[1] and the work was done in London by UK-based civil servants.

The report could see a number of scenarios that would lead to a British evacuation. One could be that Britain voluntarily withdrew because China became much more moderate, or because the people of Hong Kong wanted to rejoin China, perhaps in the context of a major economic depression. Neither of these was considered likely. More likely was China making life untenable, e.g. by preventing food and water from getting into Hong Kong. Direct military takeover was also possible.[1]

The scale of any potential evacuation was substantial. There were 61,000 British citizens or service personnel in the colony, including the Gurkha regiments. A further 15,000 non-Chinese foreign nationals might need repatriating. And of course there was the issue of what would happen to the local population. Around 30,000 were estimated to be 'vulnerable' as they worked for the police, civil service and other such bodies. With their dependants, the total number involved might be 90,000–135,000 people.[1]

While assuming that all physical assets would have to be abandoned, further work had been done on how the sterling balances held in London could be frozen and either used as a bargaining chip or confiscated.[2] It would be one of the few levers available to the United Kingdom.

CALLS FOR A POLITICAL BUDGET

This context meant that the 1968 budget debate, both within the Legislative Council and in the press, was more substantial than in previous years. People were unsettled, and many were not sure that the government was responding sufficiently. Once more there would be calls to change economic direction. Before the budget, the *Far Eastern Economic Review* argued that:

> 1968 is not a year in which the Financial Secretary can simply keep to his old strategy of orderly progress in expanding the Government's various building, medical, education and health programmes. The events of the last 12 months have changed the climate of Hongkong, and it is now a matter of urgent necessity that the community get its priorities right.[3]

For the *Far Eastern Economic Review* this required 'cutting the ground from under the communists by tackling the Colony's most urgent problems', especially infrastructure investment and social and welfare provision. Given Cowperthwaite's aversion to borrowings, the magazine argued that tax rises would be needed. To emphasize the importance that it placed on confronting these issues, its article was headed 'The cost of survival'. However, the editor was not optimistic that Cowperthwaite would listen to this advice:

> His reputation has grown so imposing over the years that even the more senior of his colleagues regard it as an impertinence to proffer advice on what policies the Financial Secretary should adopt. Sadly, the Unofficials and the public are in an even weaker position to influence the mind of the Financial Secretary.

THE 1968 BUDGET

As usual the governor introduced the 1968 budget sessions on 28 February 1968. Trench described the disruption of the previous two years:

> Let it suffice that our way of life was subjected to assault; that the overwhelming majority of the people of Hong Kong made it abundantly clear that they were not willing to submit.[4]

He noted that the size and complexity of the activities in the colony now made it virtually impossible to summarize the previous year and look ahead to the next in an annual speech. The best he could aim for was to touch on some key areas in general terms. He started with the very strong export performance of 1967. Over 800 new factories had opened and industrial employment had risen again. Textiles still accounted for a majority of exports but other industries were growing rapidly, including toys, electronics and wigs. Other areas such as tourism and construction were more subdued.

Trench celebrated the housing of the millionth settler. A new design for apartment blocks would now allow for 35 square feet per adult. There were improvements in education, with the aim still being to provide subsidized primary school places for all children requiring them by 1971. A new hospital was to be built and health care and other services were to be further extended. He also described new programmes to provide services to young people.

Trench concluded with the hope that 1968 would be quieter than the last two years, so that there could be

> real uninterrupted progress with all our manifold plans for improving and raising the standards of living of our people. As a Government, this is and must always be our primary aim.

COWPERTHWAITE SIGNALS A RETURN TO NORMAL

A significant part of Cowperthwaite's budget speech was devoted to the sterling devaluation as previously described, but he started by announcing that he expected revenues for 1967/68 to be pretty much as originally forecast, albeit with a different shape when it came to where taxes were raised. Expenditures were, however, over $100 million below his original forecast, with the bulk of the underspend occurring in capital spend, which he ascribed to lower than expected tenders for works. The original forecast deficit of $37 million had now become an estimated surplus of $74 million. He advised against any celebration, however, given the hit that the devaluation had inflicted on the reserves.

For the coming year Cowperthwaite forecast revenues would be higher, at $1,952 million, and expenditures 9 per cent higher, at $1,965 million. This was after

Cowperthwaite had applied some gentle pressure on department heads to consider postponing or reducing the scope of larger projects:

> I did not, let me make it quite clear, require them to make any cuts. The need for such, shall I say, ruthless action, has fortunately not come. Some Heads of Departments have clearly heeded my request; others, I am afraid, have gone ahead much as usual, some, admittedly, because they were clearly justified in doing so or could not help it; others, I am afraid, because of the general high priority they consider all their departmental schemes and activities deserve to that of others.

Cowperthwaite went through the various line items offering some commentary where he felt he had a point to make. For example, university spending had for the first time been split out as a separate line item, and he noted that spending on universities would be $68 million, representing the sixth largest category of government spending. He noted the increase in the medical budget, with the addition of nearly 500 new beds at Queen Mary Hospital.

No item was too small for a Cowperthwaitian comment. He turned his mighty intellect to the issue of whether an indoor stadium should be built:

> I should add that, while we are convinced that such a stadium is very desirable, we hope that a reasonably simple stadium at reasonable cost will be possible. Over-ambitious or extravagant ideas are apt to kill or at least seriously delay a project of this kind. It must, I suggest, be designed for the use of the people as a whole, not for narrow special interests, and, while uncomplicated, be adaptable to the widest variety of uses. Rather a tall order, perhaps, for the architects.

Given the numbers, Cowperthwaite did not intend to propose any increases in tax, but nor did he intend to repeat the previous year's reductions since he had not been able to identify a tax that was particularly inequitable or hard to collect. His plan was, therefore, to do nothing.

COWPERTHWAITE REJECTS FASTER EXPANSION

As he had in previous years, Cowperthwaite warned against seeing these positive results as a reason for increasing spending. To justify his concern, he pointed to the fact that recurrent spending had grown by more than 10 per cent in the previous year: a year in which they had been trying to make savings. While revenues grew strongly this was not a problem, but Cowperthwaite pointed out that spending tends to rise, and could only be cut with difficulty:

> The point I really want to make is the extent of the built-in increase, and again I stress, increase, in expenditure which we could not, without great waste, suddenly decelerate or reverse if we were to find ourselves beset by financial stringency for any cause. This is a natural phenomenon in any rapidly developing society and one which is often not adequately recognized. Britain itself is experiencing exactly this difficulty at the present time.

He noted that the increase in recurrent spending was in part cushioned by capital spending being well below plan. This was unlikely to be sustainable. Equally, reserves were a smaller percentage of expenditure. He had calculated that reserves were about ten months' expenditure five years previously, but for this budget year they were only six months' expenditure.

He remained as apprehensive as ever about how to manage the growth of public service provision, particularly if this involved universal services or benefits.

NUDGING THE DIRECTION OF THE SUPERTANKER

Cowperthwaite returned to an old theme about his role in the budget process, and the importance of the momentum already in the system:

> The truth is, as I have said more than once before, that there is little scope for influencing significantly the shape or form of any one year's expenditure in the context of that year's Budget. The expenditure estimates flow from a multiplicity of decisions already taken, some during the previous year, some years ago.

Rather, he saw the budget process as a chance to take stock on the direction of travel:

> The object of the annual estimates, apart from the opportunity it gives this Council to carry out its primary duty of controlling public expenditure, is to take stock year by year of the budgetary effects of agreed policies and programmes of action in the public sphere, to look at our probable revenues and make proposals about how the year's spending should be financed, for example, by running down reserves or by imposing additional taxation; and generally to ensure that we are not in danger of living beyond our means or over-stretching the public demand on our resources and that our priorities continue to be about right on a dynamic rather than a static basis.

As government spending grew, and in particular as the government made commitments to recurrent spending, Cowperthwaite felt that many were unaware of the way this created an implicit requirement to fund greater spending:

> When commenting on the fact that most of the $140 million increase in recurrent expenditure estimated for next year was virtually unavoidable without dislocation of public services, I referred to the generally unrecognized scale of magnitude of the inbuilt growth in future expenditure which is implicit in our existing plans of expansion. There is an ever-present danger here that we must not overlook.

In part his solution was to use the budget cycle to ensure that wise decisions were being made, cognizant of the long-term implications of making spending commitments:

> It is with this last point in mind that we also attempt an annual forecast of revenue and expenditure five years ahead, in spite of its very great margins of error, because one year's estimates give inadequate advance warning. This is not a wholly negative approach, for the annual Budget not only fulfils the immediate purpose of regulating authoritatively our taxing and spending for the year ahead but also, in conjunction with the longer-term forecast, helps us to assess what scope there is likely to be, and on what conditions, for further expansion of public services, within our means.

In an important clarification he underlined the need for government to do its own long-term planning to optimize its taxation and spending policies:

> I am known for my opposition to state planning of the economy; but planning, so far as that is practicable, the state's own exercise of its compulsory powers of appropriating and spending the resources of the community is a very different matter.

BACKLASH FROM THOSE WANTING MORE

Those who had wanted a more expansive and political budget had been disappointed. Rather than tackle the emerging political uncertainty with a fiscal olive branch, Cowperthwaite had instead stuck to 'business as usual'. The arguments about the best path forward spilled into the open when Dhun Ruttonjee,* as the senior Unofficial, led the response. In this his final budget response he 'broke decades of precedent'[5] to criticize the budget, the government and the governor himself.

Ruttonjee suggested that it was naive to underestimate the resolve of the communists to undermine the government. The colony had won the first round against

* Dhun Jehangir Ruttonjee was born in Hong Kong in 1903. His family founded Ruttonjee Sanatorium after his sister died of tuberculosis in 1943. He graduated from the University of Hong Kong. He served on the Legislative Council from 1953 until 1968. He died in 1974.

violence and bombs, but Ruttonjee worried that in the next round, of winning hearts and minds, the government was not doing enough. For example, he felt that social and welfare legislation was being unnecessarily delayed. On the budget, he complained that Cowperthwaite had 'made the task of critical comment difficult, if only by the absence of any controversial – or indeed any – proposals'.

But Ruttonjee argued that Cowperthwaite had in fact made a cogent case for raising taxes to fund greater services but then 'appeared to be unable to accept his own arguments'. He believed there was popular support for a higher level of provision coupled with higher levels of taxation. He believed there was a political imperative to move in this direction but that Cowperthwaite was frustrating the government's ability to respond:

> It sometimes seems to me that our future is being sacrificed on an altar of financial orthodoxy. And, in case my honourable Friend should counter this by asking – one can anticipate him after a few Budget Debates – whether I am advocating financial heresy, the answer is I am not; I merely observe that the Financial Secretary cannot and must not compile his Budget and remain indifferent to political realities.

Ruttonjee went further in raising what he saw as the main issue facing the colony. In an unprecedented move he emotionally criticized the governor and the administration:

> There is a vacuum of leadership waiting to be filled, and I urge this Government – and I urge you, Sir – to fill that vacuum before it is too late. Nothing has been said by any senior member of the Government that gives any indication that it is prepared to meet the enormous challenge it faces. Let it do so before it is too late. Sir, I beg of you, let it not be said of you, and of this Government, as it was said of Belshazzar 'you have been weighed in the balances and found wanting'; but rather as Rudyard Kipling had said it: 'Let us admit it fairly as a business people should. We have had no end of a lesson, it will do us no end of good.'

When the official members contributed to the debate a fortnight later they were very conciliatory, led by the colonial secretary, who attempted to reassure the unofficial members that their concerns had been heard and would be considered carefully. Cowperthwaite, however, took a different tack and rebuked those advocating increased taxation, which Cowperthwaite provocatively argued was an agenda shared only by the communists. He reiterated his philosophy of putting growth first:

> I have always regarded the fostering of economic development as one of the most important tasks, if not the most important task, of my office and I would consider it most illogical to discourage it, and the natural growth of revenue it brings, by increasing taxes merely for the sake of setting aside additional reserves. It would be shortsighted in the extreme.

He went on to attack the Ruttonjee approach in robust terms. He clearly viewed it as being a real threat to his own approach:

> The important thing is to ensure that our revenue grows to keep pace with our necessary social development. Additional taxation now would not help to solve that problem and might, by inhibiting economic growth, make it more difficult. There is, I believe, a political as well as an economic trap set for us here, deliberately by our enemies and unconsciously by our friends.

Others had again raised the criticism that Cowperthwaite was stifling necessary infrastructure projects because of his aversion to borrowing. He referred to the lengthy explanation he had made in 1966 about his views on borrowing. But it must have seemed that while Cowperthwaite might claim to be open to borrowing in the abstract, his conditions made it impossible in practice. There was certainly little evidence that he had tried very hard to borrow for a specific project, despite his broader discussions with the World Bank and the like. But equally there would be little point in borrowing while running a surplus and building reserves.

SCORNFUL ABOUT EXPERTS

One major infrastructure investment under consideration was the Mass Transit Proposal. He was concerned that some members had described it as 'absolutely essential', claiming that the colony 'cannot afford not to adopt it'. He disliked the absolutism behind these remarks. Furthermore, he felt no particular need to be impressed by the reports from the experts calling for the investment:

> There is nowadays, I believe, far too much uncritical respect for the technical expert. A report of this kind, no matter how beautifully reproduced, should not be exempt from critical examination. The authors are indeed expert in certain fields and I would have no wish to dispute their views in these fields; but a critical reading of the whole report shows that perhaps 25% of technical expertize has been diluted with 75% of opinion, speculation and crystal ball gazing; and the 75% then tends to be accorded the same degree of authority as the 25%.

> I cannot believe for example that anything useful can be said today about income distribution or car-ownership in 1986. It is true that one must look ahead but one must recognize that such looks ahead are not, and cannot be, scientifically accurate. They are subject to the widest margins of error. It is noteworthy, for example, that the traffic using the Lion Rock Tunnel is running at only about 50% of the forecast figure.

And when it came to the modelling of the financial costs and revenues of the project he was scornful. The consultants had modelled the scheme and projected it would be loss making. They had solved this by assuming 'assistance' from public funds. Cowperthwaite lambasted them for not being clear that this was nothing other than a subsidy.

To those such as Watson who believed it could be financed from future growth, Cowperthwaite suggested he was 'talking fantasy and I suspect he knows it'. While others were excited by the potential investment, Cowperthwaite thought it should be considered objectively:

> I know that I will be accused in some circles of caution, lack of imagination and so on, for these words. But we have got to give the project a cool appraisal in the light of our resources and of our priorities for using them, and in that light I cannot see how we can afford not to reject it as it stands.

HOLDING THE LINE AGAINST GOVERNMENT ACTIVISM

Wong had proposed an economic advisory committee to help steer the economic development of the economy. This would obviously diminish Cowperthwaite's role and he was quite opposed to it:

> It is kind of Mr Wong to wish to relieve me of the burden of my responsibilities, but I am afraid that I cannot abdicate from them; and, of course, we already have access to a great deal of economic and financial advice in various fields.

Unsurprisingly Cowperthwaite objected to the idea of an activist economic policy. Remarkably, given his own reliance on an economic philosophy, he was painting Wong's approach as rather theoretical:

> It seems to me in any case that Mr Wong's suggestion is based on a rather theoretical or academic view of economic matters; it smacks a bit of the textbook. It is a view which is not really relevant to the realities of our own economic situation, which are external rather than internal and so not wholly in our own control. I cannot see, for

> example, what price control on staple foods would achieve for us, except interfere with and distort supplies. Our economic situation has found no place in the textbooks for many years and the scope for experiment with the 'New Economics' is severely limited here.

Dr Chung, meanwhile, had suggested an Industrial Development Council, a proposal that filled Cowperthwaite 'with considerable dismay'. Cowperthwaite argued passionately that this was nothing less than a move to industrial planning, and he linked that with an erosion of freedom:

> It is not so much the idea of such a Council that dismays me but the attitude adverse to freedom of private enterprise which is implicit in its suggested functions. These are 'to establish priorities on development, to provide inducements for new industries and to discourage over-expansion of existing ones' – a complete blueprint for government regulation of industry, negative as well as positive, even if my honourable Friend shies away from the word 'planning'.

His aversion to planning was deep-seated:

> I am afraid that I do not believe that any body of men can have enough knowledge of the past, the present and the future to establish 'development priorities' – which presumably means procuring some developments as being good and prohibiting others as being bad.

Chung had also floated the idea of providing special inducements to 'desirable' new industries, e.g. by way of cheap loans. But Cowperthwaite was extremely sceptical that this would lead to success:

> What mystifies me is how he or any one else can determine what is a desirable type of industry such as should qualify for special assistance of this kind. In my own simple way I should have thought that a desirable industry was, almost by definition, one which could establish itself and thrive without special assistance in ordinary market conditions. Anything else suggests a degree of omniscience which I, at least, am not prepared to credit even the most expert with. I trust the commercial judgment only of those who are themselves taking the risks.

Cowperthwaite reserved his greatest disdain for the idea of limiting specific industries:

> It is the [proposed] Council's third suggested function which dismays me most – discouragement of over-expansion of existing industries. By what standard can one

possibly measure over-expansion? On what basis can one forecast it? On whose judgement can we rely? Who is to decide who is to have the good fortune to reap what I have heard called 'the spoils of economic planning'? Do we no longer put our faith in the judgement of free private enterprise? I can myself recall being told repeatedly, in the early post-war years and at intervals thereafter, that the cotton spinning industry was over-expanding. It has expanded many times since then and still thrives. I recall even more vividly a prominent and influential businessman telling me in 1956 that Government must take early steps to restrict the further growth of the garment industry because it was already too large; since then it has expanded its exports by ten times or $2,000 million a year. I, for one, will not forget that lesson.

In the context of several unofficial members proposing a move away from laissez-faire, Cowperthwaite defended his approach with vigour:

One of the things that most surprises me about my honourable Friend's remarks is that he characterizes his proposal for state intervention in, and control of, industry as 'innovation and a spirit of adventure' and condemns free private enterprise as 'prosaic precedent'. This is a strange paradox. I would put it precisely the other way round. What he advocates is based on the 'prosaic precedent' of many of our rivals who have to resort to wooing industry with artificial aids and have had remarkably little success at it. Recent events have shown that enterprising spirits still prefer our economic freedom to the restrictive swaddling clothes offered elsewhere.

Possibly I am a romantic in this but I, for one, do not believe that our spirit of adventure is in need of artificial stimulation – nor do I believe that we can afford the wasteful application of our scarce resources which they would entail – we are neither desperate enough, nor rich enough, for such expedients to make economic sense. It is, of course, all the fashion today to cry in any commercial difficulty, 'why doesn't the Government do something about it'. But I would rather go back to the old days when even the most modest attempt by Government to intervene in commerce and industry was rudely rebuffed than contemplate the kind of guided and protected economy Dr Chung appears to propose.

Facing demands for intervention, Cowperthwaite reflected on why many were attracted to a planned economy, with high levels of government intervention. In words that could have equally been used by Adam Smith or by James Nisbet, he argued that Wong and Chung were attracted by a mirage:

I believe that [they] are innocently guilty of the twentieth century fallacy that technology can be applied to the conduct of human affairs. They cannot believe that anything can work efficiently unless it has been programmed by a computer and have lost

> faith in the forces of the market and the human actions and reactions that make it up. But no computer has yet been devised which will produce accurate results from a diet of opinion and emotion. We suffer a great deal today from the bogus certainties and precisions of the pseudo-sciences which include all the social sciences including economics. Technology is admirable on the factory floor but largely irrelevant to human affairs.

Cowperthwaite concluded by challenging the suggestion that he had not been innovative enough in the context of the colony's challenges. As usual he attacked those that disagreed with him:

> What gives me concern in so much of the comment is the implication that the people of Hong Kong have to be given a reward, like children, for being good last year, and bribed, like children, into being good next year. I myself repudiate this paternalistic, indeed colonialist, attitude as a gross insult to our people.

No wonder the *Far Eastern Economic Review* concluded that

> Even the best of the Officials' speeches were put in the shadow by the Financial Secretary whose willingness to grasp a few nettles demonstrated that beside his economic acumen he possesses his fair share of the politician's ability to twist his opponents' arguments, steal their clothes and emerge unscathed from public debate, while they retire nursing their wounds.[5]

But the article also hoped that the Unofficials would 'return to the fray' in criticizing the government rather than revert to the old status quo:

> Mr Cowperthwaite's ripostes are a small price to pay for the Unofficials' achievement in forcing the administration to take a fresh look at itself and engage in genuine debate in order to justify its acts and omissions before the public.

On 31 May 1968 Cowperthwaite was knighted as a Knight Commander of the Most Excellent Order of the British Empire (KBE).[6] He would now be Sir John and his wife would be Lady Sheila. Having navigated the political challenge from those wanting to intervene more, he took leave between 2 August and 29 September 1968.

CHAPTER 19

CONSOLIDATION AND CONTINUITY

HAVING WEATHERED THE BANKING CRISIS of 1965, the devaluation disaster of 1967 and the political troubles stemming from the Cultural Revolution, Cowperthwaite was able to spend his last years in office on his preferred ground of facilitating the economic growth of Hong Kong through his liberal economic policies. He would present three more budgets between 1969 and 1971, his eighth, ninth and tenth. Trench would remain as governor through these. Together they were an effective team.

FISCAL GOOD FORTUNE

Between the fiscal years of 1968/69 and 1971/72 government spending rose by nearly 12 per cent annually, to $2.9 billion. This was a very fast rate of growth, and the involvement of government was wider and more substantial than ever. For many who had seen the pared-back post-war state, it must have seemed incredible.

Revenues had risen even more rapidly, at over 14 per cent annually, to reach a total of $3.5 billion. The budget surpluses were therefore very substantial. For Cowperthwaite's first budget in 1961 the Cumulative Official Surplus stood at $493 million; by 1967 it had risen by over a half, to $787 million; but by his last budget in 1971 it had nearly quadrupled to $2,886 million. At this level, the reserves stood at around one year's worth of all government spending.

Over these last few years all the unforecast surplus came from unexpectedly strong revenues, which were around 15 per cent higher than had been forecast. These increased revenues were reasonably broadly based, coming from earnings and profits tax, land sales, stamp duties, post office revenues and other areas. Expenditure outcomes were very close to forecast.

Each budget followed a familiar pattern, with Trench describing broader progress and Cowperthwaite presenting the more financial perspective. With the economy and government revenues doing so well there was little to do as far as Cowperthwaite was concerned. But the calls to do more and to change policy were constant and garnered a suitably grumpy response from Cowperthwaite. The benefit of this, however, was that it forced him to articulate the policies being followed and their benefits. With less requirement to fight fires, Cowperthwaite was at his most eloquent over these years.

THE 1969 BUDGET

Trench started proceedings with the Governor's Annual Review, noting that in future this would take place in the autumn. The plan was to have a broader policy debate in the Legislative Council in the autumn and then focus on the financial and economic agenda in the spring. It would transpire that these debates were rarely easy to separate.

As usual, Trench pointed to the progress being made in the economy and in public service provision. One emerging area he wanted to highlight was social security, which he divided into public assistance to 'help those who have genuinely fallen on hard times' and social insurance. He wanted to push the first but was very concerned about embarking on the latter.[1]

Cowperthwaite welcomed thc upgrades in forecasts.[1] Rather than see this as an error that would have allowed higher expenditure, he argued that it showed that those who had argued for higher taxes the year before had been mistaken. And while he thought revenues would remain strong, he was concerned about how the major proposed works, including investments in the Underground and in reservoirs, would be managed

For the planning year ahead, Cowperthwaite forecast a surplus of $64 million – the first budgeted surplus since World War II.

With a forecast surplus, Cowperthwaite had some room to manoeuvre on taxes, and he decided to abolish stamp duty on property purchases. A tax had been introduced after the war on the increased value of a property being sold but this had become a straight 3 per cent stamp duty in 1948 for administrative reasons. Land and property prices had been falling since 1964, and transactions were now taxed even if the property had fallen in value. Cowperthwaite had looked at various ways of reforming the tax but concluded that the best course was to simply abolish it, at a cost of around $9 million. His second giveaway was to reduce the fees for primary schools from $40 a year to $20 a year.

Figure 19.1. Cowperthwaite giving the 1969 budget address (HKSAR Government).

Cowperthwaite showed a more mellow side as he turned to the increasing need for 'public assistance' or benefits for those in need, alongside the existing programmes in housing, medical and educational provision. He described it as a paradox that the need for such organized assistance emerged as a society became more developed, and he was fully aware that many saw him as being against providing such benefits. He wanted to clarify his position:

> I myself have no doubt in the past tended to appear to many to be more concerned with the creation of wealth than with its distribution. I must confess that there is a degree of truth in this, but to the extent that it is true, it has been because of my conviction that the rapid growth of the economy, and the pressure that comes with it on demand for labour, both produces a rapid and substantial redistribution of income directly of itself and also makes it possible to assist more generously those who are not, from misfortune temporary or permanent, sharing in the general advance. The history of our last fifteen years or so demonstrates this conclusively.

He supported greater spending in this area, subject to two caveats. First, that benefit levels should be set so 'that they do not have any adverse effect on employment and wages', and second, that there was a step-change in the administration's ability to deal with 'abuse and malpractice'.

REACTION TO THE BUDGET

The budget was widely welcomed in the press and by the Unofficials. The *Far Eastern Economic Review* jovially lamented the rejection of hallowed tradition when

> for the first time in living memory, Hongkong's Financial Secretary admitted that it would be safe to assume that the Colony's economy might prosper for one more year at least, and Sir John Cowperthwaite astounded his audience by budgeting for a surplus.[2]

The Unofficials, as usual, raised a wide range of minor points, but in the context of better times these lacked the power of their responses in previous years. Wong suggested a form of quantitative easing whereby the government would use banks' 'idle' deposits to create money.[3] Cowperthwaite was quick to suppress the idea as a 'recipe for violent money inflation, a disease likely to be fatal in our circumstances'.[4] He chastised Watson for seeing the five-year forecast as the government's plan rather than a 'summation of departmental estimates'.

The discussion on forecasts gave Cowperthwaite the opportunity to summarize his two golden rules for fiscal policy:

> One is that the tax structure must be kept as stable as possible to give a stable framework for industry and commerce; the second is that the growth of the public services should proceed at a steady pace whatever the speed of that growth. Given those premises, there is no necessary reason why the growth curve of revenue and of expenditure should exactly coincide every year.

And he reiterated his concern about the momentum of public spending that came from a growing public service, and

> the virtually irreversible momentum of plans for the expansion of the public services. This phenomenon is well known. One only has to look at the serious difficulties Britain has had in reducing the rate of expansion of public spending there. The growth of spending is a much more certain thing than the growth of revenue.

Wong had again argued for an economic advisory committee, in part to provide a broader set of inputs into economic policy to supplement the 'guidance of a prudent and giant financial hand' that had brought the colony to financial maturity.[5]

Cowperthwaite brushed the proposal aside. Kan had complained about 'priorities set by one department or one man', and Cowperthwaite countered:

> Decisions on priorities and programmes of expansion are not taken by one man, not even by me; they are arrived at, so to speak, as a resultant of various forces, various views, knowledge, judgement, etc. That is how society works and I myself believe that in a rapidly developing society and economy, it works better than any attempt at sophisticated planning for which there can never be an adequate factual basis, and which in our changing world leads to undesirable rigidities.

He returned to an old theme in responding to Kan's view that Cowperthwaite was blocking increased spending by prioritizing economic growth:

> My honourable Friend Mr Kan was no doubt aiming at me again, when he remarked that it was time to put the horse before the cart and make our financial decisions subject to the vital needs of the community rather than make decisions on our needs subject to our finances. I cannot really believe that he means this literally, and indeed there is considerable scope for interpretation of the question-begging words 'vital' and 'needs'. But surely he has his metaphor the wrong way round. It is finance, like the horse, which provides the motive power on which progress depends; I have never heard of the cart propelling the horse.

Cowperthwaite concluded the budget response with a positive view for the future. He had predicted a surplus and he was content that the reserves were rising again. He expected the economy to grow and with it government revenues, and therefore public services. He could even see scope for new initiatives, but he wanted the government to be very careful in the commitments that it chose to adopt.

GNP MEASURES

Cowperthwaite's sense of the economy's prospects was based on judgement rather than economic statistics. Throughout his time in government Cowperthwaite refused to compile and distribute official data for economic output. For most of his tenure as financial secretary he simply batted away requests for the data. When Milton Friedman visited Hong Kong in the early 1960s, he asked Cowperthwaite why there was such limited information on national income (Friedman and Friedman 1998):

> Cowperthwaite explained that he had resisted requests from civil servants to provide such data because he was convinced that once the data was published there would be pressure to use them for government intervention in the economy.

Under pressure from the Unofficials, British officials and economists to gather national income data, Cowperthwaite resorted to the ploy of appointing an expert to examine the issue. Roy (E. R.) Chang of Hong Kong University was awarded a government-funded two-year fellowship to understand how and whether to collect and publish national income data. Given Cowperthwaite's views this was an unenviable task.

When, seven years later, in 1969, an unofficial member of Legislative Council asked about progress, Cowperthwaite noted that Chang had not presented his final report, which Cowperthwaite argued showed 'the intractability of the issue'.[6] One can see in the files that Cowperthwaite himself may have had a hand in making the presentation of the 'final' report somewhat onerous, and oddly enough it was published later that year.[7] In an internal file note Cowperthwaite argued not that the data was not available from Chang but that it was not useful to publish it, or to collect it in the future. He wrote:

> Mr Chang, in suggesting uses, starts from a number of false premises and indulges in paradoxes. The correct answer, I am afraid, is that we have virtually no economic uses for national accounts, partly because we cannot be in control of our economy and partly because our economy has a dynamism which outpaces such accounts.[8]

In typical Cowperthwaitian style, he then throws down the practical challenge to anyone believing the opposite:

> I am prepared, of course, to reconsider this view if anyone can suggest practical uses for these accounts which are at least proportionate to the time and effort required to compile them.

In December 1969, another Unofficial, Dr Chung, tried to draw Cowperthwaite out by asking him to comment on an independent estimate by Dr Pick that Hong Kong's per capita national income in 1968 was $3,000.[9] Cowperthwaite replied:

> Sir, national income statistics are, at best, approximations with a fairly wide margin of error. On what evidence is available to us (and in our free economy we have less evidence than more regulated ones), we would put Hong Kong's 1968 per capita gross national product at something of the order of $3,600 rather than $3,000.

In his summing-up speech for the 1970 budget Cowperthwaite returned to his reasons for not collecting national income data:[10]

> Gross National Product figures are very inexact even in the most sophisticated countries. I think they do not have a great deal of meaning, even as a basis of comparison between economies. That other countries make use of them is not, I think, necessarily a good reason to suppose that we need them.
>
> I suspect myself, however, that the need arises in other countries because high taxation and more or less detailed Government intervention in the economy have made it essential to be able to judge (or to hope to be able to judge) the effect of policies, and of changes in policies, on the economy.
>
> But we are in the happy position, happier at least for the Financial Secretary, where the leverage exercised by Government on the economy is so small that it is not necessary, nor even of any particular value, to have these figures available for the formulation of policy. We might indeed be right to be apprehensive lest the availability of such figures might lead, by a reversal of cause and effect, to policies designed to have a direct effect on the economy. I would myself deplore this.
>
> My own conclusion is that the expense and effort needed to produce even very approximate figures in our free economy outweigh the value of having them. The budgetary cost is only a small part of the story; I doubt if our friends in commerce, finance, the professions, etc. would relish the form-filling that would be necessary; for their time also is money. In the meantime we have a rough idea of where we are, certainly enough for any practical purposes.
>
> But I feel myself that, in Hong Kong, GNP and other national accounts are a proper subject for academic rather than official research; as it was indeed in other countries at a time when the relationship of Government to the economy was not dissimilar from ours today.

In an interview later that year, Cowperthwaite asserted that he was 'much more immediately interested in growth of fiscal revenues than in GNP'.[11]

The Guardian, in its obituary for Cowperthwaite, recalled that he was once asked what was the key thing that poor countries should do to improve their growth.[12] His reply was that 'they should abolish the office of national statistics'. It is not hard to see why someone with Cowperthwaite's beliefs held that view. As Coyle (2014) points out in her review of the history of GDP, the measure was first used by Roosevelt to justify the New Deal and was championed by Keynes and his followers as a tool to be used for managing the economy. As Coyle argues:

> The story of GDP since 1940 is also the story of macroeconomics. The availability of national accounts statistics made demand management seem not only feasible but also scientific.

Cowperthwaite's successor, Haddon-Cave, would take a softer and more compliant line after Cowperthwaite's retirement. Official estimates of GNP would be published in the 1973/74 budget estimates, with data backdated to 1967.

THE RETURN OF PROTECTIONISM

During 1969 the United Kingdom and the United States both returned to the issue of attempting to limit their imports of textiles from Hong Kong. The issue had been simmering for years but was mostly managed under voluntary agreements with the United Kingdom and the United States and the agreements under GATT. Since the United Kingdom had agreed to GATT on behalf of Hong Kong, this should have given Hong Kong most-favoured-nation tariff treatment in most developed countries, but that did not stop the pressure to establish 'voluntary' quotas (Rabushka 1973).

The UK Textile Council had conducted a major review of the cotton industry and proposed that the system of quotas applying to Commonwealth countries be replaced with tariffs. The UK government agreed, and in July 1969 it announced that from 1 January 1972 a tariff would be placed on cotton imports from Commonwealth countries. Whereas before, with Imperial Preference and Commonwealth Preference, cotton textiles did not suffer tariffs, yarn would now have a 6.5 per cent tariff, cotton cloth a 15 per cent tariff and garments 17 per cent. This move would hit Hong Kong manufacturers' profits.

The United States was also trying to stem imports again. By 1969 the United States textile industry employed around 2.5 million people. Cotton imports had been limited by agreements but one effect of this was that exporters had moved their focus to other textile products. Nixon had sent Maurice Stans, the US Secretary for Commerce, to Asia to see if he could get similar voluntary agreements to limit imports. Stans met with Cowperthwaite in May 1969 and made the case, arguing that Nixon was a proponent of free trade but needed help (through limiting trade agreements) to contain protectionist forces in the United States and in Congress.[13] Cowperthwaite was not very impressed by the logic of Stans's argument and cross-examined him closely. This caused Stans much irritation, and at one point he angrily asked, 'Are you playing games with me, sir?'[14]

Unsurprisingly they made little progress and the arguments would continue for years to come. In 1974 the Multi-fibres Arrangement would supplement the 1961 Long-Term Cotton Agreement. While the United States could slow the decline of their textile industry, they could do little to reverse it.

HADDON-CAVE ACTS FOR COWPERTHWAITE

Cowperthwaite took leave from 18 June 1969 to 9 August, and Haddon-Cave covered his role as acting financial secretary while he was away. In July Dr Chung challenged Haddon-Cave to how surpluses were to be used,[15] no doubt hoping for a fuller response than Cowperthwaite usually provided, or at least a different one. Haddon-Cave answered that the surplus would be added to the general reserve as a safety net to support the Hong Kong dollar, and to underpin spending in an emergency or a recession.

At the same meeting, Haddon-Cave led a discussion on the importance of tourism to the colony. He was more amenable than Cowperthwaite would have been when asked to assess the impact that tourism had on the economy. He estimated that tourism accounted for around 5½ per cent of national income and that its share was growing. He estimated that manufacturing, by comparison, contributed around 40 per cent of national income. He agreed that the government could assist the industry by supporting a possible extension to the airport runway.

FIRST AUTUMN POLICY DEBATE

Cowperthwaite was back for the newly moved Governor's Address in October.[16] He claimed that he had hoped that he would have little role to play in the policy debate now that it was separated from the financial and economic proposals of the budget, but he concluded that this had been a 'forlorn hope'. Politics and economic policy were inevitably intertwined.

Wong again pushed his interventionist views, this time quoting Plato.[17] This allowed Cowperthwaite to argue that he detected in Wong's remarks 'a leaning towards a certain Platonic totalitarianism'.[18] Cowperthwaite was particularly dismayed by Wong's suggestion that labour be directed into attractive industries and away from trades such as hawking that Wong claimed did 'not contribute to production', to prevent an 'undesirable development in employment structure'. Cowperthwaite argued that Wong was making the same mistake as the Physiocrats in his prejudice against retailing, and was wrong in his belief that labour could be centrally directed:

> Such direction seems to me to be an evil in both political and economic terms. In any case, I, for one, would not be able to identify an 'undesirable development in employment structure'. I suspect that my honourable Friend has in mind the fallacy that retail distribution is not productive in an economic sense. Any shift of labour from hawking to industry must come about, in my view, as a consequence of the ability and willingness of industry to offer sufficiently attractive terms.

Chung once more pushed his belief in the power of 'scientific management' but Cowperthwaite argued that it was a 'fallacy' to think that the tools used to improve an individual firm's performance could be applied to an economy. He was loath to centralize planning:

> Looking back over the last twenty years or so it is remarkable how almost invariably our departures from reliance on market forces have ended in, if not disaster, at least unfortunate or embarrassing situations.

A couple of Unofficials who believed in laissez-faire expressed a concern that the economy might be overheating given its fast rate of growth. This Keynesian language also earned a rebuke. Cowperthwaite did not intend to fine-tune the economy via government fiscal or monetary policy.

Some had commented that rising wage rates would price Hong Kong out of several markets. Again Cowperthwaite would have none of it:

> One phenomenon of our expansion which seems to worry people is one which I am happy to see – the increase in wages – not only because I am happy to see greater rewards going to labour from our prosperity. I do not share the often-expressed concern that increasing wages may price us out of markets and let our rivals in. In our type of economy wages rise in general, no further and no faster than our competitive position allows; they do not rise independently of it. We do not need to achieve greater productivity because wages have risen; rather wages are rising partly because we are achieving greater productivity.

Cowperthwaite had once more defended the laissez-faire approach, both from its critics and from those who broadly supported it but wanted to adjust it at the edges. But whereas in earlier years it had seemed a battle of equals, there was now no doubt who was going to prevail.

THE 1970 BUDGET

Presenting another set of healthy numbers, Cowperthwaite maintained that there was little novel to say about the estimates given 'the need for continuity in expenditure, rather than great leaps'.[19] He also argued that, in holding government policy steady over the economic cycle, government spending could be mildly countercyclical:

> It seems to me, good policy grounds for underspending in the good years with a view to overspending in the not so good. Our normal course tends to the reverse order, with the danger that public sector activities exaggerate both depression and boom. I have always maintained that we had little scope for Keynesian economics but, although we cannot create money to spend our way out of depression, we can at least set aside surpluses in good years for spending to some little of the same effect in bad.

Cowperthwaite spent some time reflecting on the growing surplus. He knew that there were calls for him to use it either to increase spending or to reduce taxes. He was adamant that he would not shift spending up and down simply because revenues rose or fell in a particular year. He was also opposed to cutting taxes for the same reason – stability – believing that 'the important thing for sustained economic growth is not only a low but also a steady tax structure'. He did not believe that the current tax rates were impeding growth and argued that maintaining tax rates would put off the day when 'we have to push taxation higher to levels where the effects on growth and prosperity are less predictable'.

He was therefore inclined to do nothing based on the growing surplus. However, he did propose six minor measures reducing or abolishing taxes for reasons of equity or public policy. These included more generous tax allowance for those looking after dependent relatives, for working women and for the very lowest paid. He also abolished the tax on live entertainment, and the 'public dance halls tax'.

The tax had been introduced in 1947 when the colony had been examining every opportunity to generate revenues. Observing that dance halls were booming and that professional dancers were offering to dance the foxtrot or the rumba with single visitors, the government introduced a 10 cents per dance tax. By 1970, however, revenues were only $2 million and Cowperthwaite thought it a suitable time to bring this unusual tax to an end.[19] It was the demise of this last tax that created the greatest press comment.[20]

Lastly, he proposed reducing estate duty from 25 per cent to 20 per cent. Woo had proposed abolishing estate duty completely, but Cowperthwaite argued that its retention was 'a matter of equitable principle, particularly in the light of our necessarily incomplete form of Income Tax'.

On the other hand, he accepted a proposal to raise the exemption limit on salaries tax from $100,000 to $200,000. Cowperthwaite was torn on this issue. He made these changes despite also arguing that the level of personal allowances was very high relative to many countries: perhaps double those that applied for a family in Britain, and more than three times the level set in Japan. He felt these differences verged on the 'fantastic', especially given the very low rate of tax. He wondered if there were benefits in 'more people becoming payers of direct taxation as a token of their citizenship'. While not fully accepting this, Cowperthwaite believed that with low rates of tax the tax base should not become too narrow. This would be even more important as services expanded and required greater tax revenues.

The Unofficials did not disappoint Cowperthwaite, proposing a variety of schemes to spend the growing surpluses and, of course, calling for a simultaneous reduction in taxes. Cowperthwaite responded to this by trying to dampen the more enthusiastic expectations:

> Many people appear to be reacting to our present prosperity as if we had won first prize in a cash sweep and should be looking around to see what we should splash it on.[21]

Cowperthwaite wanted to underline just how big an increase in expenditure was already built into the budget. He noted that the planned increase was the largest ever budgeted and that it was of a similar magnitude to the whole expenditure for the 1952/53 fiscal year. As he had done before, he reiterated that money was only one element of what was required to deliver a useful expansion in public services. It took time for projects and policies to be delivered, and often even longer to staff them up effectively. He noted:

> A magic stroke of the Director of Education's wand will not produce an 'instant' secondary school and its complement of teachers; nor that of my honourable Friend, the Director of Medical and Health Services, an 'instant' 1,000-bed hospital with staff and equipment.

Cowperthwaite reiterated his view that policy was built continuously and broadly through the years, and the budgets provided a snapshot rather than an opportunity to add commitments:

> There is, indeed, a case for not having annual budgets at all because public spending cannot be readily forced into the artificial framework of a year. This case is reinforced by the continuing inability of many public commentators to understand this. But I

> myself, in spite of this, hold very strongly that the annuality of Budgets is an essential safeguard of the constitutional duty of this Honourable Council to control the public purse; just as annual balance sheets are essential to the proper conduct of a commercial corporation.

He was very keen to emphasize how much of future revenues and expenditures were already a given, even without any policy changes:

> I have become so concerned at these misunderstandings that I think that we might in future adopt the practice of publishing annually a forecast of expenditure arising from existing policies, not only for the next financial year but for the four years following it.
>
> I should like to give the basic figures today because without them it is not easy to understand the full extent of our existing policies of expansion and the growth of expenditure built into them. We estimate that between now and 1973/74 expenditure will rise from $2,100 million this year to $3,200 million in 1973/74, an average increase of $275 million a year.

Cowperthwaite took the chance to clarify his views on countercyclical spending, which he had advanced the year before:

> Although I have said, and some have agreed with me, that underspending in good years and over-spending in the not so good is a sound practice, this does not mean that I believe we should deliberately go out to seek a surplus with this in mind (far less with any Keynesian ideas). But surpluses and deficits are a natural result of a steady growth of expenditure and steady tax rates, in conjunction with fluctuating but generally steep rates of economic growth.

Cowperthwaite took leave between 1 May and 20 June 1970.

THE RETURN OF EUROPE

Britain's first application to join the EEC had been vetoed by de Gaulle in 1963. A second request to join had been tabled in May 1967, and in June Cowperthwaite wrote a file note that he thought it would be some time before the UK government got into actual negotiations, adding 'if they ever do'.[22] Haddon-Cave noted during meetings he had in London in July 1967 that 'Whitehall is as divided as the Government on the wisdom of going into Europe'. Once more the French vetoed the application.

But by 1969 the United Kingdom had once more approached the EEC to ask to join. This time it would be successful, but it would not be finalized until 1 January 1973.

THE 1970 POLICY REVIEW

The Legislative Council held their second autumn policy debate in 1970, in theory to separate policy and finance, and yet Cowperthwaite talked at length on a very wide range of topics.[23]

Inflation had become a key issue around the world. Cowperthwaite wanted to differentiate the nature of inflation in Hong Kong from that elsewhere:

> We do not suffer in Hong Kong from true self-induced inflation in the sense of an excessive creation of spending power chasing too few goods. Our spending power derives almost wholly from what we earn through our external trade; we do not create it internally and artificially.

However, he recognized that external inflation could affect internal prices. Rapid economic growth and prosperity, even if created by export success, could push up wages and the cost of capital. The undesirable form of inflation was accompanied by a declining balance of payments, and this was not the Hong Kong experience. He could see that Germany and Japan were in a similar situation.

Some wanted to stabilize the situation, with the government intervening to soften price increases. Cowperthwaite acknowledged that the government had tried to control rents, for what he considered to be social reasons, but he did not think the government should act more broadly:

> We face, in short, the familiar dilemma between rapid growth and stabilization, although fortunately not in its acutest form, for we have no associated balance of payments problem and we are clearly more than paying our way. I cannot myself believe that anyone in this Chamber, and very few in the community as a whole, would wish to reverse all our previous policies and choose stabilization rather than growth; and it would certainly go contrary to the other views expressed by honourable Members about the need to promote the further growth of trade and industry. Not only would we be fore-going the creation of additional wealth and what this can bring, and has brought, in social advance, but we would also, I believe, permanently damage that climate of economic activity which has taken us so far and so fast.

Moving on, Cowperthwaite once more defended the fact that the market caused industries to ebb and flow:

> I was particularly struck in this context by my honourable Friend, Mr K. S. Lo's concern at the decline in the enamelware industry as an example of the effect of lost

> advantages, as if this decline were a loss rather than a gain to the community. It has declined, I believe, because we have learned to use our resources of enterprise, capital and labour in other more profitable directions. That is progress. We would be in a sorry way if enamelware was still our fourth biggest industry.

He was relaxed that some industries might wane, especially if was due to wage rates rising:

> In a rather similar vein my honourable Friend, Mr Ann takes the wig industry to task for offering inducements to labour. In my view it is best that labour should be employed by the employers who can pay it most, even if it has adverse effects on employers who cannot match their terms. That, too, is the way of progress.
>
> We hear much today about the danger of rising wages as if wages were the price of a commodity or a raw material. I suggest that we should look at rising wages from the point of view of the receiver as well as that of the payer and what it means to him. Furthermore, I myself welcome increasing wages which result by ordinary economic processes from the pressure of economic growth on our resources of labour, because they help to ensure both maximum export prices and the most productive use of our scarce resources; and at the same time redistribute more fairly our growing national income.

Lo and Wong wanted to subsidize the development of small industries, as had been recommended by a recent report, but Cowperthwaite's response was predictable:

> I must confess my distaste for any proposal to use public funds for the support of selected, and thereby, privileged, industrialists, the more particularly if this is to be based on bureaucratic views of what is good and what is bad by way of industrial development, but I have been studying the report referred to with some interest.

This was, of course, an area Cowperthwaite had himself reviewed a decade earlier, and he returned to the key piece of data he had concentrated on then: the committee had found no evidence that industrial development was being hindered by a lack of finance. Given that, he felt that the conclusion that help should be given was obviously false. In any case he was very doubtful that the government was well placed to make lending decisions:

> I find odd the view that a Government institution is better placed to evaluate 'the technical and financial viability' of a project than a commercial bank. It may well be that our banks are deficient in the kind of expertize required for assessing projects but then what we should be doing is encouraging banks to acquire such expertize or to make use of outside, commercial, expertize. I myself tend to mistrust the judgement of anyone not involved in the actual process of risk-taking.

THE 1971 BUDGET

In his last budget, Cowperthwaite celebrated the very strong performance in 1970/71, with revenues around $3 billion and expenditure slightly ahead of forecast at around $2.5 billion. With a substantial surplus the reserves now stood at $2.4 billion. The picture for the year ahead looked equally positive.[24]

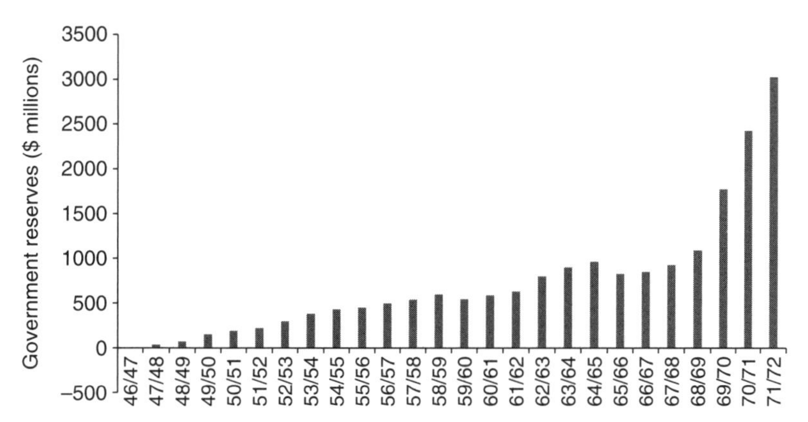

Figure 19.2. Hong Kong fiscal reserves, 1946/47–1971/72. (*Source*: Hong Kong Statistics 1947–67, Hong Kong estimates.)

Given that, Cowperthwaite was keen to caution against taking on too many new commitments given his views that expenditure growth should be smooth and constant, but he did recognize that prosperity had led spending departments to think more expansively. Interestingly, he picked on the proposed provision of primary education (which would cost only $14 million) to warn against universal benefits:

> I cannot say that I myself am particularly happy to make this announcement, which extends free primary education beyond those who cannot afford to pay for it (and are not being asked to do so at present) to very many on whom primary school fees are no burden. There may be very good grounds for universal compulsory primary education but I see none for universal free education, even if that education is compulsory; for there is no principle that I am aware of which lays down that it is proper to levy compulsory taxes but not compulsory fees, so long, that is, as there is adequate provision to avoid hardship for those with low incomes. I hope that we shall be able to do something to limit free primary education, and possibly, for that matter, heavily subsidized primary education, to the schools which do not cater for the affluent. This is generally the situation in other countries with free primary education; our system has been distorted by its historical development.

Figure 19.3. Cowperthwaite arrives for his last budget address (HKSAR Government).

He returned to the ratio of recurrent spending to recurrent revenues as a key metric of the sustainability of spending. Over the previous ten years it had varied between 65 per cent and 75 per cent, and for the year ahead he forecast it would be 74 per cent: very much at the upper end of the range.

Cowperthwaite proposed no tax increases. He abolished the television licence fee because televisions were no longer a luxury and the fee was hard to collect.

A large portion of his speech dealt with plans to bring new water capacity on stream and discussed ways of charging for it. Cowperthwaite proposed material increases in both domestic water charges and those for business users. This created significant objections by those who thought the increases were too substantial.

More broadly, while Unofficials complimented Cowperthwaite's handling of the economy, several were quite negative about his tight rein on spending.[25] Kan had added together the unforecast surpluses over Cowperthwaite's tenure and they totalled $2.3 billion. Chung accused him of a lack of candour. Woo argued for greater social spending. Szeto accused him of 'cautious budgeting, usually by understating revenues', and argued for greater infrastructure spending. Wong argued that more should be spent on social services. In particular, he was exercised about the shortage of public housing. Private landlords were charging more than ten times the cost of publicly funded accommodation, and such differences were vital to poorer families' livelihoods. Li welcomed greater spending on education and asked for an expansion of social welfare.

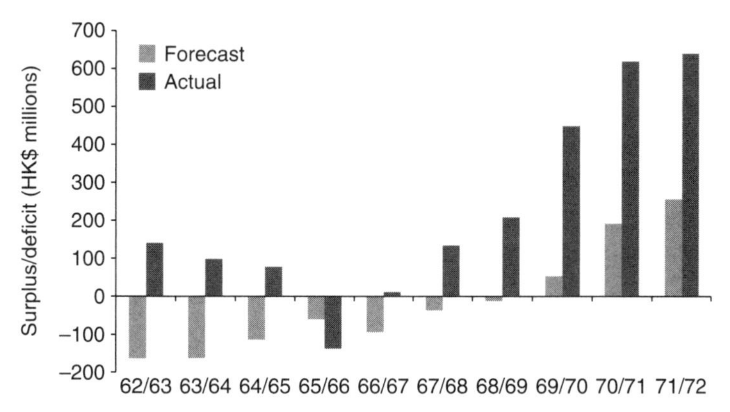

Figure 19.4. Actual versus forecast surplus/deficit, 1962/63–1971/72.

Even though this was his last budget, Cowperthwaite felt the need to counter every criticism and argue every point.[26] Rather than graciously let some slip by, he went through each of the Unofficials' points one by one. This made for a rather bitty and defensive speech, but he was able to reiterate his core beliefs on fiscal policy:

> I hold that two principles are important; first that there should be a steady expansion of public services, not an irregular one related to revenue accruing in any particular year; the second that taxes should be constant over long periods (provided, that is, that they are neither burdensome nor inequitable).

Chung's accusation of a lack of candour had clearly riled him and he defended himself:

> I must make allowances for his own sincere belief in scientific management which leads him to suppose that the estimating of public finances can be done with scientific accuracy (and there are a number of economists who appear to agree with him). Alas, it is not lack of candour but inability to see into the future with a prophet's vision, and to forecast human actions and re-actions, that is the cause of errors in estimating revenue.

The increase in water charges had become the most contentious issue in the press and Cowperthwaite spent a considerable amount of time arguing the case for an economic charge for water, and for it to be treated like other commodities. However, he did offer a concession whereby the first 2,000 gallons used per quarter would be free for domestic customers, with the new rate of charges only being applied for usage beyond that. This would cost $12 million annually but Cowperthwaite welcomed the fact that this would likely mean that the poorest families would end up paying less than they currently did.

MAKING SPEED

After a tumultuous period as financial secretary Cowperthwaite could enjoy the relative calm of his last few years in office. He was master of his department and his brief, and the external challenges seemed very manageable compared with those of earlier years. The economy seemed to grow larger each year, and with that growth government revenues rose. The significant rises in government spending seemed almost effortless, and Cowperthwaite's budgets had few new measures or initiatives. Having set the course so clearly, it must have been gratifying to see the growth that followed.

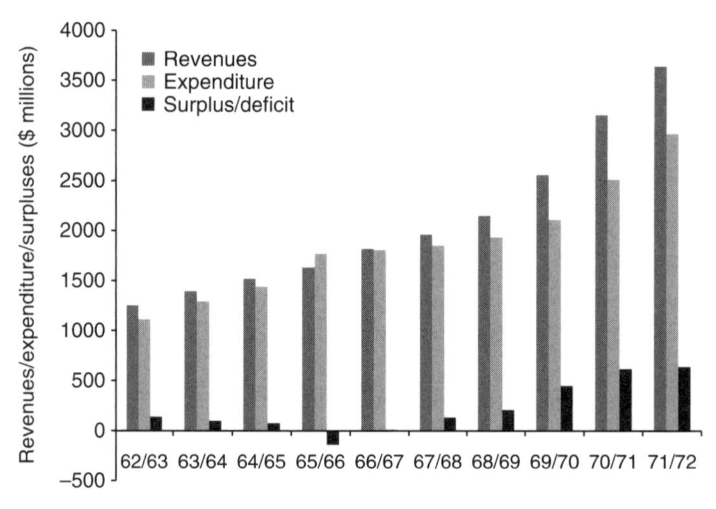

Figure 19.5. Government revenues, expenditures and surpluses under Cowperthwaite, 1962/63–1971/72. (*Source*: Hong Kong Statistics 1947–67, Hong Kong estimates.)

CHAPTER 20

CHANGING GUARD

After thirty years, Cowperthwaite's public service ended in 1971. His association with Hong Kong had started when he was appointed a Cadet in 1941 and, after a short detour to Sierra Leone, he had dedicated his entire professional life to this small colony far from his native Scotland. No one could have had any doubt as to his commitment to creating success for his adopted country. He retired on 30 June 1971.

PRAISE

At his last Legislative Council on 23 June 1971, the acting governor, Sir Hugh Selsby Norman Walker, observed how central Cowperthwaite had been to the colony's economic success:

> He became substantive Financial Secretary, and thus an ex officio member of this Council, more than ten years ago. Since then Hong Kong, despite difficulties and setbacks, has enjoyed a period of almost unparalleled economic development. This is very much more than a mere coincidence.

Walker emphasized Cowperthwaite's role as an enabler of success. Hong Kong's people had created their own prosperity, but within the policy environment created by Cowperthwaite:

> It has been his constant and successful endeavour to create the climate and the framework within which the initiative and ingenuity and resilience of the people of Hong Kong can find their fullest expression; and at the same time to ensure that the Government of the Colony has the means at its disposal to satisfy in the public sector the legitimate aspirations of a rapidly developing society.

Cowperthwaite had influenced almost every area of government, well beyond his theoretical responsibilities. His view seemed to be that if any topic could affect the economic performance of the colony, then it was within his remit. That left very little out:

> Perhaps his most striking attribute is his protean grasp of many of the problems which this Government has faced, is facing and will continue to face – I have yet to find an aspect of Government's responsibilities on which Sir John's knowledge and advice have not been both penetrating and valuable. We shall miss him.

The post of colonial secretary was now held by Mike Clinton, who had worked as deputy to Cowperthwaite for many years. Clinton had been a bomb disposal expert during the war and one bomb he was disarming had blown up, badly injuring his face. He had been awarded the George Medal and Bar but was too modest to ever mention this. Like Cowperthwaite, he was a shy, dedicated man (Wong 2015). They had been a very effective team for many years and Clinton added a personal tribute:

> I know only too well how wise he can be. I also know what a kind heart beats under his severe exterior – though he would never admit it. He has often, in my view, been unfairly criticized but, as Financial Secretary, he has done far more for Hong Kong than most people, and much more than most people realize. The measure of his stature, like Lord Keynes, may only be fully appreciated after the years have rolled by.

It reveals much of the man to observe how Cowperthwaite reacted to this barrage of praise. In the briefest of replies, he dryly noted:

> Sir, may I now thank you for your kind words, and I also thank my honourable Official and Unofficial colleagues, to work with whom has always been an honour and a privilege and nearly always a pleasure.

And with that he left the stage.

LAST EMERGENCY FLIGHT TO LONDON

Cowperthwaite retired on Wednesday the 30th of June, exactly a week after his last Legislative Council meeting. But in his last hours in office a crisis emerged that required his immediate attention. On 28 June, Emma and Bluey had been sent ahead on a BOAC flight to Heathrow, but while being transported to the terminal Bluey had made a run for it and disappeared.[1]

The Cowperthwaites' dogs had been sent ahead to start their quarantine but now one was missing. It transpired that Bluey, a seven-year-old Alsatian, had bitten through his cage during the flight. Cowperthwaite's son, Hamish, travelled to Heathrow to join in the search and did spot the missing dog but was unable to apprehend him.

Cowperthwaite had frequently had to jump on a plane to deal with an emerging crisis and he decided that he must do so again, so on the evening of his retirement he flew on a BOAC flight to London to join the search. Unsurprisingly there was some press interest, and Bluey was found in a nearby village on the Saturday and safely escorted to quarantine. Mission accomplished, Cowperthwaite could catch the Monday flight back.[2]

The speedy resolution of the crisis meant that Sir John and Lady Cowperthwaite could leave on their planned retirement cruise to Australia later that week knowing that their much-loved dogs were safe and sound.

A DIFFERENT SORT OF GOVERNOR

The year 1971 was one of change for the Hong Kong government. Sir Murray MacLehose replaced Sir David Trench as governor and Philip Haddon-Cave replaced Cowperthwaite as financial secretary. MacLehose was more sympathetic to government having a wider role than Trench had been and Haddon-Cave was more orthodox than Cowperthwaite, but the colony's economic and social policy would remain on the same trajectory, although perhaps with a little less rigour and zeal.

MacLehose was a reformer who would become Hong Kong's longest-serving governor, remaining in post for four terms until May 1982. He had helped train Chinese guerillas during the war, had worked at the embassy in Beijing and had been ambassador to Vietnam. He took a more political and less economic view of policy, and his links with the Labour Party would suggest he was inclined to push welfare reform. However, he remained constrained by local business interests and the history of successful laissez-faire economic policy.

Nonetheless, MacLehose oversaw a very significant expansion of the role of the state. Education provision was extended, the housing programme was broadened, social assistance and community facilities were provided, and welfare payments were introduced for the disabled and the unemployed. Regulations in many areas were extended and greater rights were accorded to workers and others.

After MacLehose retired in 1982 there was considerably less stability in the governorship as the colony approached the handover to China. Sir Edward Youde briefly served as governor before dying of a heart attack in Beijing in 1986. He was succeeded by Sir David Wilson, a well-regarded Sinologist who struggled to win the trust of Hong Kong pro-democracy campaigners as he participated in the planning for returning Hong Kong to China. He left after his first term in 1992 and was replaced by Chris Patten, who would be Britain's last governor of Hong Kong.

HADDON-CAVE AS FINANCIAL SECRETARY

Cowperthwaite could have retired in April 1970 when he reached fifty-five years of age but David Trench had persuaded him to extend his service for a year and to see in the 1971 budget.[3] For Trench this had the added advantage that he would see out his posting with someone he knew well. There were two internal candidates to succeed Cowperthwaite and one, Clinton, was unwilling to be considered for the post. That left Haddon-Cave.

Philip Haddon-Cave succeeded Cowperthwaite as financial secretary in 1971 and would hold the post for ten years, as had his two predecessors. Haddon-Cave had been born in Australia in 1925 and educated at the University of Tasmania and King's College, Cambridge. He had joined the British Colonial Service in 1952 and served in Kenya for a decade before being appointed as financial secretary in the Seychelles in 1961. In December 1962 he transferred to Hong Kong, and he had served as deputy economic secretary and deputy financial secretary. He had therefore worked with Cowperthwaite for many years and had acted as financial secretary when Cowperthwaite was away in 1969 and 1970.[4] He was widely seen as a very intelligent man and a very able civil servant.

Several British civil servants were looking forward to the change. When he toured the various departments in London prior to taking over, many noted that there was a chance that he would move away from Cowperthwaite's 'rather idiosyncratic methods'.[5] There were very early indications that he might loosen the purse strings a little, do more to coordinate the management of banking and currency reserves, and be more open to compiling a wider set of economic statistics.

Haddon-Cave's first budget was on 1 March 1972. He could confirm that for Cowperthwaite's last full year, 1970/71, revenues had been over $3,000 million and expenditures $2,452 million. The surplus for the year was $619 million. For 1971/72 he expected the surplus to now exceed $700 million.

He shared Cowperthwaite's view that revenues determined expenditure:

> I am sure honourable Members will have noticed that both Sir John Cowperthwaite and Mr Clarke always dealt with the revenue estimates before the expenditure estimates and for obvious reasons: in our circumstances, there are severe limits to the range of indirect taxes which can be imposed; and there are severe limits also to the marginal rate of direct taxation. By and large, therefore, we must fit public expenditure to available public resources and not extend those resources to fit expenditure.

It was clear that while there would be evolution, the key tenets of Cowperthwaite's economic philosophy would continue. But whereas Cowperthwaite had been inclined to emphasize the dangers of state intervention, Haddon-Cave was more nuanced, and perhaps more politically astute in his development of the idea of positive non-interventionism.

In 1973 he argued that government should sometimes intervene, in particular where there were market imperfections:

> The Government must accept such responsibilities as are necessary to ensure that management decisions are not frustrated by imperfections in the operation of the market mechanism, leading to economic inefficiency or social distress which only the Government can remove.[6]

In December 1980, while addressing the Federation of Hong Kong Industries, he gave perhaps his fullest description of positive non-interventionism:

> I have frequently described the Government's economic policy stance as being one of 'positive non-interventionism'. Not surprisingly, perhaps, some have claimed that this is really just a fancy term for laissez-faire or, less kindly, that it covers up a 'do-nothing' approach. This is simply not so: positive non-interventionism involves taking the view that it is normally futile and damaging to the growth rate of an economy, particularly an open economy, for the Government to attempt to plan the allocation of resources available to the private sector and to frustrate the operation of market forces, no matter how uncomfortable may be their short-term consequences.

He was keen to point out that each decision needed to be considered on its merits. When it could be properly justified, though, he had no difficulties with supporting the involvement of the government:

> I do qualify the term 'non-interventionism' with the adjective 'positive'. What it means is this: that the Government, when faced with an interventionist proposal,

> does not simply respond that such a proposal must, by definition, be incorrect. Quite the contrary.
>
> It is true that, more often than not, we come to the conclusion that the balance of advantage lies in not intervening; and, I must confess, I would be alarmed if we didn't. Yet, in all cases, the decision is made positively, and not by default, and it is not the non-outcome of a do-nothing approach. But, there are many examples of the Government deciding, usually on the advice of its boards and committees, to intervene, in one way or another, in the free play of market forces.[7]

Given the government's role in building infrastructure, such as the airport, tunnels, bridges and the like; its role in health, housing and education; and in regulation, policing and defence, many would have thought this a statement of the obvious. But it was only because Hong Kong's government was less interventionist than many others around the world, and consumed a smaller portion of national output, that such an articulation of government policy made sense.

COWPERTHWAITE JOINS JARDINE FLEMING

As MacLehose and Haddon-Cave took over the running of the colony, Cowperthwaite spent time travelling. It was reported that a number of taipans had been keen to employ him or that he might lecture at St Andrew's.[8] After a long holiday and setting up home in Scotland, Cowperthwaite took up a post as advisor to Jardine Fleming & Co in November 1972.[9]

Jardine Fleming was a Hong Kong-based investment bank, and Cowperthwaite was careful to construct the role in such a way as to ensure there would be no conflict with his previous position. He would be an 'international advisor' and have no day-to-day dealings with the Hong Kong government. He would continue to live in Scotland but would spend two months a year working in Asia, visiting Jardine Fleming's operations outside Hong Kong. But he would be based in Hong Kong, and would add personal holidays around his business activities. This structure gave Cowperthwaite the opportunity to stay in touch with an area of the world that he loved while not compromising his integrity. He remained with the firm until his retirement in 1982.

Jardine Fleming was founded in 1970 as a 50/50 joint venture between Jardine Matheson and Robert Fleming & Co, a London merchant bank. The firm was to be Hong Kong's first investment bank, aiming to serve the increasingly sophisticated Asian markets and Hong Kong's emerging high-net-worth population.[10] Jardine could provide access to a wide network of firms and individuals and Fleming could bring financial expertise.

At the end of 1972 Cowperthwaite also took a seat on the board of Pedder Japan Investment Co Ltd, a small investment company focused on Japanese equities. It was part of the Jardine Fleming universe in that they acted as investment managers for the company.

Cowperthwaite was also invited to become a member of the Mont Pelerin Society. Founded in 1947 by Friedrich Hayek, the society was formed to bring together scholars who wanted to discuss and defend the freedoms of classical liberalism against encroachment from ever-larger state involvement (Hartwell 1995). The growth of socialism on the one hand and a Keynesian inspired interventionism on the other worried these scholars. They argued that freedom required that decision making be distributed, and that free markets were key to doing that. In an early version of public economics, they also believed that large state bureaucracies would increasingly be run for their own ends, and this too would suck power away from individuals.

The society had an impressive membership, including seven winners of the Nobel Memorial Prize in Economic Sciences, and for many, Hong Kong was a very good example of the sort of free society that they espoused. Cowperthwaite was instrumental in organizing a meeting of the society in Hong Kong in September 1978, attended by Friedrich Hayek and Milton Friedman and more than 300 delegates. Cowperthwaite persuaded Philip Haddon-Cave to give a speech about financial and public policy.[11]

On his trips to Hong Kong Cowperthwaite kept in touch with old friends and colleagues. He also took the opportunity to continue to play golf regularly at the Royal Hong Kong Golf Club in Fanling.

THE NIXON RAPPROCHEMENT

From his part-time role at Jardine Fleming, Cowperthwaite could follow the dramatic rapprochement between China and the United States. This would create a realigned world, but more parochially it would make the handover of Hong Kong to China in 1997 more likely. As this date approached, politics would adapt to the inevitable change.

Nixon was inaugurated as president in January 1969 and, with his National Security Advisor, Henry Kissinger, started planning how to extract the United States from the Vietnam War and how to normalize relations with Communist China. The United States still recognized the Taiwan government, the Republic of China, as the authorized government of all of China. After twenty years of communist rule on the mainland this required ever-increasing levels of delusion. In addition, Nixon and Kissinger saw a prize in changing policy. It would further divide Moscow and Beijing, and through that fragment the communist bloc; it could also help America extract itself from Vietnam.

As a signal, China invited the US table tennis team to visit in April 1971. Nixon sent Kissinger to meet secretly with Premier Zhou in Beijing to further pave the way, and midway through his second year, on 15 July 1971, Nixon announced that he would visit Beijing the following year. The visit lasted a week (21–28 February 1972) and changed the global balance of power for the next two decades.

On 25 October 1971 the United Nations General Assembly passed Resolution 2758 recognizing the People's Republic of China as the sole representative of the Chinese people. The People's Republic of China would now sit, for the first time, on the Security Council. This United States about turn was elegantly explained by the country accepting a 'One-China policy'. When in Shanghai on 28 February 1972, Nixon released a communiqué (Welsh 1997):

> The United States acknowledges that all Chinese on either side of the Taiwan Strait maintain that there is but one China and that Taiwan is part of China. The United States does not challenge that position.

Since World War II Britain had always known that Hong Kong was indefensible should China choose to invade. Indeed, it was also well known in London that China could effectively ruin the Hong Kong economy by cutting its supply of food or, more importantly, water. America's rapprochement with China effectively ended the 1957 agreement between Macmillan and Eisenhower to view Hong Kong as a joint defence problem. It was not very realistic to expect the United States to engage in a conflict with China to defend a British colony.

In 1972 the British prime minister, Edward Heath, visited Beijing and started the long process of discussions and positioning that would eventually lead to the negotiations that concluded with the colony returning to China in 1997.

A WELL-EARNED RETIREMENT

In 1981 Cowperthwaite, now sixty-five, retired fully and lived with his wife, Sheila, in their home in South Street in St Andrews. They had bought 25 South Street in 1969. It was a classical, elegant three-floor house in the centre of town, a hundred metres or so from the university. They had slowly refurbished the house over the years as they split their lives between St Andrews and Hong Kong. Sheila had developed a great interest in Chinese art over the years in Hong Kong.

Indeed, she had become an active and accomplished painter herself, and she led the decoration of their home.[12]

The Cowperthwaites continued to travel, visiting friends and relatives, sometimes for up to six months of the year. As they had in the past, they would often visit the United States on their way to or from Hong Kong,[13] where several members of John's mother's side of the family lived. They would also visit the many American friends they had made through the US consulate in Hong Kong.[14] These longer trips were supplemented by weekend breaks with the family at Sheila's cottage ten miles to the south of St Andrews, near Ansthruther, where the family and close friends could go bird watching or walking or simply stay home and discuss the news and solve the crossword.[15]

Cowperthwaite continued to read ancient Greek manuscripts and eighteenth-century French literature throughout his retirement, making full use of the university library. Sundays were reserved for collecting their two grandchildren from Merchiston School for Sunday lunch before driving them back in the afternoon.

Cowperthwaite played golf and was an active member of the Royal & Ancient, as he had been of the Royal Hong Kong Golf Club. He had clearly found time to practice in Hong Kong since he won the Bing Crosby Trophy at the Old Course, St Andrews in 1981[16] and for many years he had a five handicap.[17] He retained his interest in horses, watching races on television and placing small bets at his local bookmakers.

It seemed like an ideal retirement, and for more than twenty years it was.

THE 1997 HANDOVER

Cowperthwaite would live to see the handover of the colony to China in 1997. Despite this momentous change he would have been gratified by how much of his philosophy was retained in the handover agreement, and in the budgets of financial secretaries under this new arrangement.

The bulk of the Hong Kong territories were leased from China and that lease was to expire in 1997. Some believed that China would renew the lease in order to retain a successful economic entity on its doorstep, but it was increasingly clear that China put the issue of sovereignty ahead of economics, and in any case did not believe that a return of Hong Kong to China would damage the economy.

The negotiations with China were difficult. While Margaret Thatcher abhorred the idea of relinquishing the colony, she had no useful alternative strategies so she simply huffed and puffed. After winning the 1983 election she became reconciled to the reality and negotiations began in earnest. The foreign secretary, Sir Geoffrey Howe, and key officials worked with China to produce the Sino-British Joint Declaration on the Future of Hong Kong in September 1984. Chinese sovereignty was agreed and, in return, Hong Kong could retain laws and customs that differed from those in China itself: one country, two systems.

In Hong Kong there was acceptance of the inevitable, but in 1989 protests in China, leading up to those in Tiananmen Square, would spill over into the streets of Hong Kong. However, with the passage of time it became clear that the 1997 handover would occur as planned. The legal structure for Hong Kong, the Basic Law, was agreed in 1990. Trade with China continued to grow, and the direction of travel seemed set.

The Basic Law had a number of clauses that protected Hong Kong's economic philosophy for the years ahead. Several articles committed Hong Kong to free trade and to being a business-friendly setting for international trade and finance. Article 107 guaranteed financial prudence and limited the growth of government spending to the overall growth of the economy. Article 108 identified Hong Kong's low-tax policy as the benchmark for future policy decisions.

In April 1992 John Major, the new prime minister, appointed Chris Patten to the governorship. Patten had managed the Conservative general election campaign and pulled off a surprising national victory while simultaneously losing his own seat in parliament. As Major's friend and ally he hoped to bring greater democracy to Hong Kong before the handover to China, but having had little experience of China he struggled as Beijing made its views clear about this last-minute change of policy. Patten's changes planted a flag for democratic processes two years before Britain departed but it will probably be some time before the benefits of that decision can be fully assessed.

When Chris Patten met Cowperthwaite on the eve of the handover he reportedly remarked: 'so, you are the architect of it all'.[18] Even for Cowperthwaite, the wealth and resilience of Hong Kong by 1997 must have seemed remarkable. The Hong Kong he had witnessed in 1945 had become a rich metropolis. And he would see it grow even richer in the subsequent years. Patten (1998) would contrast how 'economic managers in Asia like John Cowperthwaite in Hong Kong and Lee Kuan Yew's team in Singapore looked inspired in comparison with some of their perspiring Western peers'.

THE FAMILIAR STRUCTURE OF THE 1997 BUDGET

The first post-colonial financial secretary presented the 1997 budget shortly before the handover. Donald Tsang Yam-kuen celebrated the philosophy of non-interventionism:

> Hong Kong thrives by deliberately leaving as much room as possible for enterprise and innovation. Our low, simple and predictable tax regime is rightly famous. The level of government regulation of trade and investment is the lowest in the world.[19]

Much of his speech followed a format that would have been familiar to financial secretaries of the past, even if the scale of the numbers would have shocked them. He revised his forecast surplus for the year just past, 1996/97, from $1.6 billion to $15.1 billion. For 1997–98 he forecast revenues of $235 billion and expenditures of $203 billion. This produced a 'huge' forecast surplus of more than $30 billion. As had happened so often before, he argued that this was due to one-offs and special circumstances, and could not be relied upon.

And by the time of Hong Kong's most recent budget, for 2016/17, the numbers had again increased.[20] Revenues were around $460 billion with expenditures a little lower, creating a surplus of around $30 billion. Fiscal reserves were now around $860 billion, around twenty-four months' worth of government spending. But the nature of the debate was quite different from those of the past. There was still the normal list of external challenges that needed to be met, but of much greater concern was a new list of internal issues about the very fundamentals of how society operated. There were doubts as to the rule of law, questions about the government's authority, and outside the chamber there were violent protests. The economic juggernaut continued, but the cracks seemed to be dividing government, society and individuals. Only time will tell if these are another set of bumps along the way or if they are issues of a different nature than those of the past.

TRAGEDY IN THE PHILIPPINES

Sir John's son John James 'Hamish' had been born in Sierra Leone in 1944 and had grown up in Hong Kong. After studying architecture at Cambridge, also at Christ's College, he had become a professional architect and had a practice in Hong Kong. In May 2004 he travelled to the Philippines to meet with Manfred Schoeni, a Hong Kong art dealer who also owned the Ashanti wine estates in South Africa and a restaurant in Beijing, and Anton Faustenhauser, a German property developer, to view a resort that they were considering buying. All three of them and a Filipina maid were found stabbed to death at Faustenhauser's beach villa on Boracay Island, south of Manila.[21]

The police identified a prime suspect but he slipped out of the country in early 2005,[22] ending up in Germany. There was no extradition treaty between Germany and the Philippines but there was a law allowing a German citizen to be prosecuted for killing another German national even if the crime occurred abroad. However, the prosecutor's office decided that there was insufficient evidence to proceed, while the police and prosecutors in the Philippines maintained the charge.[23] Hamish's funeral took place at St John's Cathedral in Hong Kong on 14 May 2004.

Cowperthwaite had two grandchildren by his son: Nathan and Adam. Both attended Merchiston Castle School like their grandfather, and then went on to university and careers in the financial sector. Cowperthwaite had the pleasure of seeing the birth of great grandchildren before he died.

COWPERTHWAITE'S DEATH

Sir John James Cowperthwaite died on 21 January 2006, aged ninety, at Ninewells Hospital in Dundee. A few days after his funeral Sheila travelled to London but was taken ill. She was admitted first to the Clementine Churchill Hospital in Harrow and then to the Cromwell Hospital, where she died on 13 February 2006.[24] Her funeral was held at Dundee Crematorium on Monday 6 March 2006.[15] John's brother, David, died later that same year, in October.

It was a sad ending. Cowperthwaite, his only son, his wife and his brother all died over a short two-year period. Fate bestowed no favours on a man who had improved the lot of millions.

Cowperthwaite was remembered in lengthy obituaries in the major papers. *The Guardian* argued that he was the 'Free-market thinking civil servant behind Hong Kong's success'.[25] *The Times* ran with the headline: 'Civil servant whose laissez-faire approach to business created Hong Kong's dynamic economy from the 1960s onwards'.[26]

The Times recalled a *Sunday Times* article from 1996 in which Peter Clark had written that

> it was one of those glorious accidents that a man unversed in the 20th century's fad for socialism could apply his 18th-century ideas in a territory unencumbered with democracy. Governors came and went, but Cowperthwaite kept balancing budgets, lowering taxes and keeping markets open, including the market in immigrants.

The Times also noted the very substantial increase in wages, and the fall in the numbers in poverty. They wondered, however, whether there would have been less unrest if Cowperthwaite had spent more on social programmes.

The Telegraph wrote a fulsome tribute, arguing that

> his extreme laissez-faire economic policies created conditions for very rapid growth, laying the foundations of the colony's prosperity as an international business centre.

> Cowperthwaite was a classical free-trader in the tradition which stretched from Adam Smith to John Stuart Mill and Gladstone, rather than a modern monetarist. He was also a seasoned colonial administrator, with a strong streak of common sense.

The *South China Morning Post* had the headline 'Hong Kong can thank the man who did very little'.[27] In its obituary, Sir David Akers-Jones, who had worked with Cowperthwaite, called him a towering figure and described him as

> a mixture of friendliness and austerity, a wonderful mixture. He was quite a hard taskmaster and always asked very penetrating questions. He did not like shoddy work. He also had many friends in the community. I think he laid the foundation for the prosperity Hong Kong has today.

David Wong (2015), who worked for Cowperthwaite for many years, believed that Cowperthwaite was the critical government figure in facilitating Hong Kong's post-war economic success:

> He, more than any other official, laid down the economic and financial foundations for the city and charted out the path to its present prosperity and financial health. In my humble opinion, his contribution to Hong Kong has probably been greater than that of any of its long string of colonial Governors before him or afterwards.

Wong had huge respect for Cowperthwaite's willingness to fight for the interests of Hong Kong even when that was in conflict with the interests of London. He also admired Cowperthwaite's desire to connect with the Chinese community:

> Unlike most of his expatriate colleagues, he paid close attention to what the Chinese population was up to and made friends with many of them. He noted that they were self-reliant, usually with strong family ties, and ever anxious to re-establish their own social and business relationships without waiting for help or handouts from officialdom.

This was an environment that fitted well with Cowperthwaite's belief in Adam Smith's philosophy. Wong and others who worked with Cowperthwaite have been at pains to point out that Cowperthwaite was not a cold or unkind person, and that his policies derived from a desire to help ordinary people, not from a desire to impose on them a system that would exploit them. Wong argues:

> He was in my book one of the kindest, most humane and possibly the least understood colleagues I have ever had the privilege to work for in the government.

> Intellectually, I would say he stood about three cuts above most of his contemporaries, a veritable Mount Everest towering over a litter of those who merely strove to reach the base camps. He never failed to argue his principles throughout the aberrant and sometimes politically jangled times over which he presided. Nor did he ever lose his nerve when the going got tough.

Cowperthwaite is still remembered in Hong Kong and is occasionally mentioned in the press, or by government officials, who ask what he would have thought of a particular policy or decision. And his record in Hong Kong emerges occasionally in commentaries on contemporary economics, and on the search for economic growth. Such moments are, though, rather infrequent given the magnitude of his achievements.

CHAPTER 21

HISTORY LESSONS?

JOHN COWPERTHWAITE DEVOTED THE BULK of his professional life to building the foundations of one of the world's most successful economies. To understand the magnitude of his achievement we must evaluate how successful it was. Given Cowperthwaite's aversion to collecting national income statistics this is more difficult than it might be. From his speeches and actions we can draw out the policy elements that Cowperthwaite believed were central to that success, and we can attempt to identify what lessons can be drawn from his exceptional experience, perhaps even speculating on how he might view the issues of today.

HOW SUCCESSFUL WAS HONG KONG?

There are many measures of economic progress. Jao (1974) has summarized some of the financial and non-financial indicators of growth over the period when Cowperthwaite was serving in Hong Kong. Across a broad range of development measures real progress was substantial. Hong Kong enjoyed a rapidly rising population, a large part of which was from immigration. Fortunately, employment grew in equal measure, particularly in the industrial sector. Exports and imports grew at over 8 per cent annually. The annual growth in government revenues and expenditure was even more dramatic at 13.6 per cent and 12.5 per cent, respectively.

Indicator	*Period*	*Real growth rate (% p.a.)*
Population	1946–72	3.7
Total employment	1947–71	3.5
Industrial employment	1947–72	10.4
Registered factories	1947–72	13.1
Output of fabrics	1955–72	9.8
Electricity production	1947–72	17.7
Total exports	1947–72	8.8
Total imports	1947–72	8.8
Government revenue	1947–72	13.6
Government expenditure	1947–72	12.5
GDP	1948–72	7.8
GDP per capita	1948–72	4.3

Figure 21.1. Measures of economic development 1946–72 (Jao 1974).

ESTIMATING GDP PER CAPITA

Hong Kong's GDP per capita has surged over the period since World War II. Given Cowperthwaite's hostility to collecting GDP data it requires some detective work to estimate the rate of growth. In the 1970s the government estimated GDP per capita as far back as 1960, and several academics (notably Chou and Szczepanik) made estimates for the earlier years back to 1948. Using this government data, and the average percentage changes estimated for earlier years from various economists, we can estimate real GDP per capita from 1948 to today. This shows tremendous growth: from around $19,000 per person to around $340,000. This is an eighteen-fold increase in real incomes.

Over the post-war period Hong Kong's GDP per capita has grown annually at around 4.3 per cent. The rate of growth was somewhat higher before 1997 than it has been since. Hong Kong's real annual per capita GDP grew at 5 per cent between 1948 and 1997 and by 2.6 per cent between 1997 and 2016. Most countries would be happy with either figure but the level of growth in the early period is clearly exceptional.

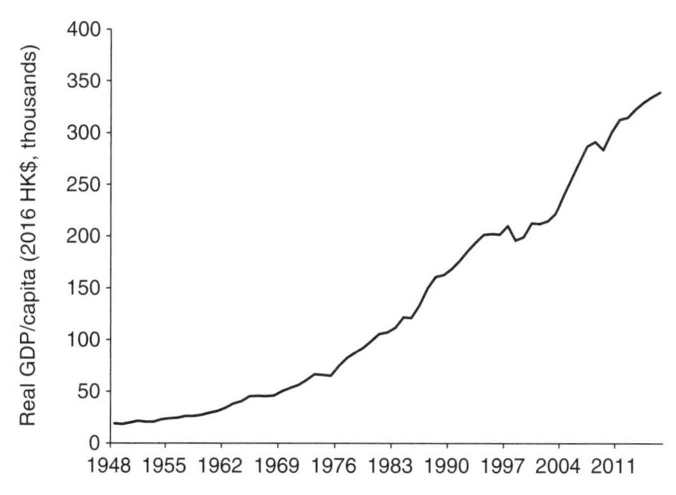

Figure 21.2. Hong Kong's real GDP per capita.

Cowperthwaite would often argue that a higher, but more variable, growth rate was preferable to a lower, more stable, one. The fast growth in GDP per capita certainly came with a fair amount of annual volatility. Cowperthwaite would have felt that any attempt to dampen this would be unlikely to succeed and might indeed be counterproductive to the delivery of faster growth.

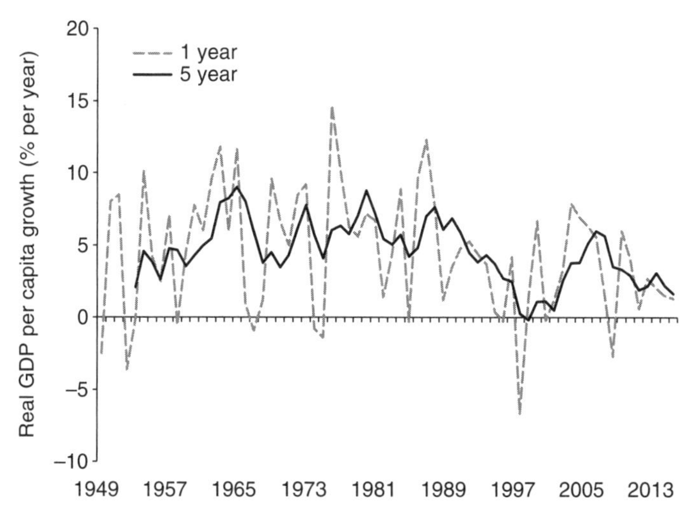

Figure 21.3. Annual rate of growth in real GDP per capita over one- and five-year periods.

NON-ECONOMIC MEASURES OF PROGRESS

Some worry that a focus on economic growth comes at the expense of other non-economic measures, but there is little sign of that in Hong Kong. Life expectancy in Hong Kong has risen from 63 years in 1950, to 79 in 1997, and by 2015 was the highest in the world at 84 years.[1] In Britain, life expectancy hovered at just below 40 years for the three centuries up until the late 1800s. At that point, with rising incomes, improved sanitation and improved health care, life expectancy started to take off. It was similar in the United States. In 1950 an American or a Brit could expect to live five to six years longer than someone from Hong Kong. By 1997, though, it was the Hong Kong person who lived two years longer. By 2015 this had extended to three years longer than a Brit and five years longer than the average American. As Cowperthwaite would have predicted, it is not obvious that laissez-faire is bad for your health.

Despite having built the education system more recently than other countries, the educational achievement of fifteen-year-olds, as measured by PISA in 2015, placed Hong Kong second in the world in maths and reading and ninth in science. The United Kingdom by comparison was twenty-seventh, twenty-second and fifteenth, respectively, in those rankings.[2]

Since Cowperthwaite believed that economic progress was the driver for broader social progress, these improvements would not have surprised him.

One thing that would probably have bothered him is the distribution of income in Hong Kong, which is even more skewed than it is for the United Kingdom or the United States. The highest-earning 10 per cent of the population earn nearly eighteen times the amount earned by the lowest-earning 10 per cent. This is similar to Singapore, slightly higher than the US ratio of sixteen, and ahead of the United Kingdom's ratio of fourteen. Cowperthwaite accepted wide income inequality in his day because he could see the growth in average earnings and general wage rates. Despite the greater inequality in Hong Kong, given the higher level of average income versus the United Kingdom, the median and bottom quartile family in Hong Kong is still better off than the equivalent family in the United Kingdom. But Cowperthwaite would certainly have wanted to target government programmes on the poorer sections of society.

RELATIVE WEALTH

With these very fast rates of economic growth, Hong Kong has become one of the most prosperous nations in the world. To compare relative wealth we can calculate

GDP per capita in inflation and purchasing power adjusted dollars, called international dollars (Int$), or Geary–Khamis dollars, which have the same purchasing power as a current US dollar. The International Monetary Fund[3] and the World Bank[4] both create such numbers.

Using this methodology, the current-day US dollar GDP per capita for Hong Kong stood at around Int$3,600 in 1948, which is around the level of Bangladesh or Zambia today (Maddison Project 2013). By the time of Cowperthwaite's retirement from office in 1971 this figure was around Int$10,000, about as wealthy as the former Yugoslavia is today. By 1997 it was over Int$36,000: equivalent to New Zealand or South Korea today. And today it stands at around Int$57,000, comparable to the United States and Switzerland.

In two generations Hong Kong moved from being one of the poorer nations of the world to being one of its richest. After the war Hong Kong's real GDP per capita was 30 per cent of that in the United Kingdom and 18 per cent of that in the United States. Today Hong Kong matches the United States and has an income per head that is 40 per cent higher than in the United Kingdom.

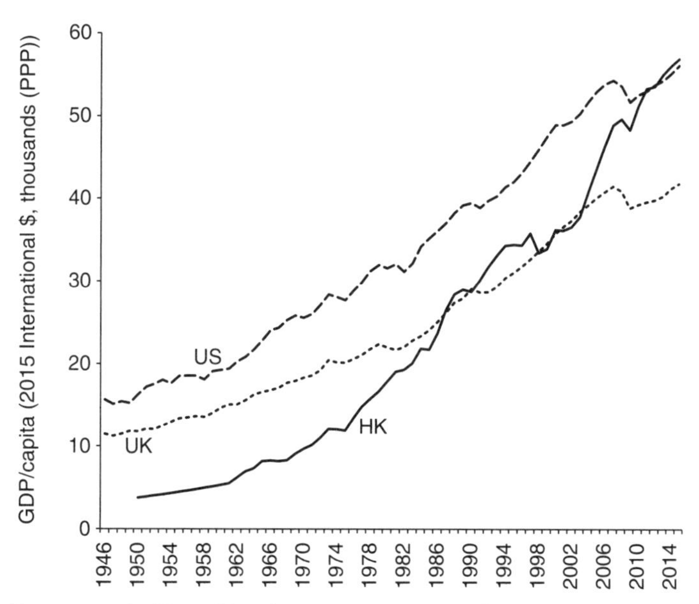

Figure 21.4. Hong Kong's comparative growth in GDP per capita.

World GDP per capita has grown at a little over 2 per cent per year since 1950. Hong Kong's growth rate has been more than double that: a performance shared by only seven of the world's 200 or so countries: namely, China, Japan, South Korea, Thailand, Singapore, Oman and Botswana. The difference between growing GDP per capita at 4 per cent annually and growing it at 2 per cent is dramatic given the effects of compounding. Over a thirty-five-year working career, incomes will double at a 2 per cent growth rate, and they will quadruple at a 4 per cent growth rate. Over a seventy-year lifetime, incomes will quadruple at a 2 per cent growth rate, whereas at 4 per cent, they will increase fifteen-fold. A high growth rate of GDP per capita sustained for several decades is the key to rapid economic growth.

HISTORICAL COMPARISONS

When Cowperthwaite became deputy financial secretary in the early 1950s, Hong Kong had a GDP per capita of around Int$4,000 in real, purchasing power parity dollars. By his retirement it was around Int$10,000. It took Hong Kong twenty years to deliver this growth in living standards.

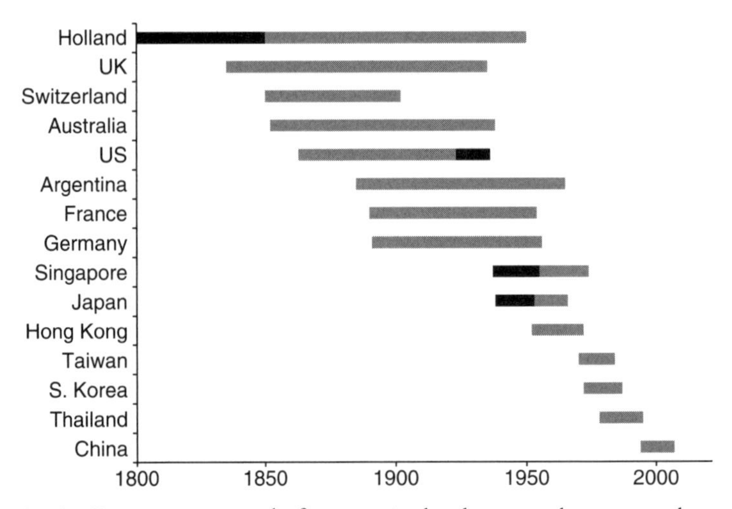

Figure 21.5. Comparative speed of economic development: bar starts when a GDP per capita of Int$4,000 is achieved and ends when it reaches Int$10,000 (darker shade indicates when incomes fall back so the threshold is crossed twice).

Britain by contrast attained a GDP per capita of Int$4,000 in 1835. It would take the United Kingdom 100 years to raise that to Int$10,000, achieving that milestone in 1935, driven by the Industrial Revolution, trade and providing services to the Empire and beyond. In fact, it was not Britain but Holland that had been the first nation to have a GDP per head of Int$4,000. Holland won that prize two centuries earlier, in 1600. But incomes fell and stagnated after that, and by 1850 Dutch incomes were no higher than they had been 250 years earlier. It would take Holland until 1950 to reach the level of Int$10,000, so they took between 100 years and 350 years to deliver the growth in incomes that Hong Kong delivered in two decades.

A string of countries followed the United Kingdom in the late nineteenth century. Switzerland took only fifty-two years to cover the ground, on its way to becoming the economic powerhouse it is today. The United States passed the Int$4,000 mark in 1863 and took only sixty years to reach Int$10,000, in 1923. But the Great Depression meant that incomes fell back and only reached the Int$10,000 again thirteen years later. France and Germany took around sixty-five years.

Singapore and Japan both crossed the Int$4,000 barrier pre-war only to have incomes fall back, so they both crossed it again in the 1950s. After Hong Kong's twenty-year sprint, Taiwan and South Korea raised the bar to fourteen/fifteen years and China to thirteen years.

The potential speed of economic development is clearly dependent on the technologies, opportunities and environment that exist elsewhere, and how much headroom already exists in other countries. What is perhaps surprising is how many countries have not been able to leverage that for their own benefit. There are fewer Hong Kongs, Singapores and Thailands than there should be.

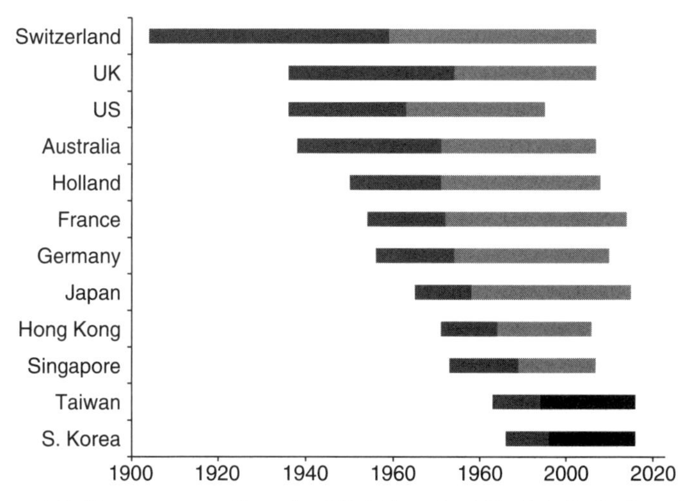

Figure 21.6. Years to move from Int$10,000 to Int$20,000 (darker), and from Int$20,000 to Int$40,000 (lighter). (Black indicates Int$40,000 not yet achieved).

The success of the Hong Kong model is further reinforced by looking at subsequent stages of economic development. Hong Kong moved rapidly to the Int$10,000 GDP per capita level, but as we know, it did not stop there. In only thirteen years Hong Kong doubled GDP per capita to Int$20,000, and only twenty-two years after that, it hit Int$40,000. This speed of development is remarkable.

By any standards Hong Kong is a phenomenal economic success story. It is one of no more than a handful of countries that have achieved a world-class standard of living and experienced very rapid economic growth. It has transformed the lives of its people. Given these remarkable results, Hong Kong is clearly worthy of study.

WHAT WERE THE ECONOMIC POLICIES OF HONG KONG DURING THIS PERIOD OF SUCCESS?

Studying Hong Kong should be valuable to economists both because of its progress and because of the way in which it achieved its success. As early as 1974, Jao wrote: 'The Hong Kong economy is one of the very few surviving instances of largely unfettered laissez-faire, and this fact alone provides a fascinating object for study.' Friedman claimed that 'if you want to see capitalism in action, go to Hong Kong'.

As a leading researcher into Hong Kong's economy and policies, Rabushka, wrote in 1973:

> There is another cogent reason for serious study of Hong Kong. Its government and economy, more than any other country in the world, approximate the classical economic notion of laissez-faire that postulates a limited role for government: law and order, contract enforcement, a definition of property rights, and perhaps defense against foreign enemies. This approximation to the textbook model is, of course, made possible by the absence of an electorate.

Hong Kong had a very consistent set of economic policies in the post-war period. These could be broadly labelled as laissez-faire, or classical economics, or capitalism, or as positive non-interventionism. But of course, no label can quite define the unique set of policies that the Hong Kong government created. A great deal of the policy stance built on classical economic beliefs, but there were divergences from this, e.g. in housing, and there were areas where the government probably wished it had diverged further than it did, e.g. in banking regulation. But there is no doubt that the policies adopted were distinct, both relative to almost every other country at that time and relative to our experience today.

Cowperthwaite's central economic beliefs were mostly built on classical economics but supplemented with a view of human psychology and of philosophy. And as Cowperthwaite's career evolved, a large dose of experience and pragmatism was added too. In addition, Hong Kong's situation, being small, dependent on trade and with few natural resources, also played a major role in limiting the available policy options.

From his speeches and actions, there are perhaps a dozen key elements that were central to Cowperthwaite's beliefs.

1. Free markets, creating a competitive market price, provide the best signal to consumers on the costs of producing something, and to producers as to the value of making it.
2. Government has a critical role in enabling free markets to function, including establishing the rule of law, the enforceability of contracts and property rights.
3. Equally, governments should intervene if markets are not working, be that to create competition, set regulations, overcome tariffs and quotas, or at times where the market fails to function.
4. Private enterprises, risking their own capital, are best placed to decide where investment should optimally be allocated.
5. Therefore, government planning, subsidies and industrial strategies are likely to misallocate resources, lead to an inferior allocation of capital, and result in retarding economic growth.
6. The capitalist process is dynamic, with ever-changing sources of growth, requiring that firms adapt, that new firms and industries are born, and, just as importantly, that some firms and industries decline and die.
7. Free trade will allow firms (and therefore countries) to specialize where they have the best relative advantage, and this promotes growth over the longer term. There is usually no value in imposing tariffs even on those who use tariffs against you, unless it is a bargaining chip designed to lower all tariffs.
8. Allowing capital to flow freely into and out of a country will best attract capital in the long term.
9. Tax rates should be low to attract and retain capital, and to provide surplus profits that will be reinvested to provide compounding growth.
10. Long-term government spending should be below long-term government revenues to ensure that expenditure grows steadily and smoothly and because there is a strong momentum to spending programmes.
11. Governments should be conservative and should aim to run a surplus rather than borrow. Borrowing from future generations is unfair, and it is also ineffective because borrowing will be seen as a future tax liability and therefore have little beneficial effect. Government debts can also lead to volatile government spending.

12. Governments can improve a society by investing in public goods and services and by providing for the least well off in society. This is best done by providing products and services at market costs but with complete remission of charges or fees for those most in need.

COMMON SENSE, IF NOT COMMON PRACTICE

To modern ears, much of this policy mix sounds like common sense even if it is not always common practice. Cowperthwaite's beliefs about the limits of government have won much of the intellectual argument, but they have not always been adopted or implemented with the same degree of rigour as was the case in Hong Kong after the war. Since the 1960s there has been a backlash against government planning. And yet, in most countries, the size of the state is bigger than ever.

While almost all politicians and government agencies might claim they believe in the principles of minimum involvement, or positive non-interventionism, there must clearly be very different interpretations of this given the divergent levels of government spending and the vast differences in bureaucracy and regulation that exist across countries.

Free trade was in the ascendancy before 1914 but then fell back in the inter-war period. Since 1945 there has been, until recently, a consensus that free trade is beneficial, and GATT, the emergence of trading blocks and bilateral deals mean that we have freer trade than has existed for a century. Cowperthwaite supported all of these moves to remove blocks to freer trade. But protectionist sentiments are rising up the agenda again as governments try and balance the perceived benefits of lower-cost imports with the effect this has on domestic industries and unemployment. Cowperthwaite took the view that trade barriers were detrimental, even when others might impose tariffs or quotas on your exports. He would be a proponent of an open economy as a way to raise living standards and to best focus export efforts.

There are perhaps four areas of Cowperthwaite's philosophy that seem very alien to us today: his belief in markets; his aversion to borrowing and deficit financing; his thoughts on the size of the state; and, more implicitly, his thoughts on the difference between economic freedom and democracy.

A BELIEF IN MARKETS

Cowperthwaite would often refer to how he believed the market was better at allocating resources and setting prices than any centrally driven plan could be. But he went further than most in believing that a competitive market could often be left to sort things out without needing heavy regulation or government involvement. He would be very surprised at how much government regulation, involvement and basic interference occur today in almost every market. His bias was to let the market drive companies to make the right trade-offs and decisions.

His belief in markets should not be seen as a belief in companies. He viewed businesses as being driven by self-interest. And where a monopoly existed, Cowperthwaite had no hesitation in regulating prices and even investment plans. His was a belief in markets not in private enterprise per se. Without the controlling influence of a market, he, like Adam Smith, was suspicious of the behaviour of companies. So while he would be surprised at how far many governments interfere in competitive markets today, he would be equally surprised at how slow many governments have been to control obvious monopolies and oligopolies.

One area that clearly perplexed Cowperthwaite throughout his tenure was the financial sector. At first he viewed it as another market, which from the outside appeared competitive. But he would learn, as many other finance ministers have had to since, that the financial sector is different. Failure has too many second-order effects, and the sector is riddled with perverse incentives. A key part of Cowperthwaite's belief in companies allocating resources was that the owners of the companies would bear the risk involved and therefore be extremely careful about where to put their money. This is not the case in much of the financial sector, where the decision makers get the rewards but pass the risks to others.

His approach was always to go back to the detail and to first principles in deciding the best role for government in any particular case. If there was a competitive market, he would usually argue that the government had almost no role to play. If a monopoly, he would replace the power of the market with the power of regulation but with day-to-day management in the hands of the private sector. If a true public good, he would allow direct government involvement. This structured approach contrasts with the rather random involvement that many governments have in different sectors today.

DEFICIT FINANCING

While many professional economists believe it is not a problem to run a deficit or to use quantitative easing to stimulate growth, by and large the public do not believe them. Given the difficulty of reducing government spending, which was frequently highlighted by Cowperthwaite, it is informative that many electorates and governments support cutbacks and balancing the books. There are some countries running surpluses – notably Norway, Singapore, Germany, Switzerland and New Zealand – but most countries are running government deficits. And very few have had the continuity of surpluses over the years that has led to Hong Kong's huge build-up of reserves, apart from countries that have had great natural resource finds.

Hong Kong started its post-war journey with no net reserves. By the time Cowperthwaite became financial secretary in 1961, reserves were just over $0.5 billion. By the time he stepped down in 1971 they were $2.4 billion. By 1997 the reserves, at $330 billion, were described by the then governor, Chris Patten, as 'the greatest dowry since Cleopatra'.[5] Today they stand at $860 billion.

Cowperthwaite had three main arguments against running deficits. First, he objected to passing debts on to future generations to pay. His very-long-term view, and perhaps the lack of a need for him to win elections, meant that he could view the taxpayer of tomorrow as being equal in worth to the taxpayer of today. He found the idea of transferring wealth from the latter to the former morally dubious. Second, he often alluded to the idea of Ricardian equivalence. This argument, advanced by Ricardo, is that debt is a delayed form of taxation because it must at some point be repaid. Given that, markets and individuals will react to an increase in debt as they would to a rise in taxation, thereby cancelling any positive effects. Third, he believed in the benefits of smooth growth in public expenditure, and was concerned that not having a substantial reserve, and a string of surpluses, would lead to inefficient and unnecessarily volatile public spending.

THE SIZE OF THE STATE

Perhaps the most dramatic disconnect between Cowperthwaite's beliefs and the practice of today concerns the optimal level of government spending. Cowperthwaite's model was one based on classical economics, and the idea of productive and non-productive activities. The language is perhaps unnecessarily divisive: non-productive does not mean not worthwhile, rather it describes investment in an activity that will not produce a future surplus that can be reinvested.

For classical economists, much of state spending was unproductive, and would therefore reduce a country's growth rate. Add in Cowperthwaite's belief in a balanced budget and low taxes must then also imply equally low spending. For Cowperthwaite, lower taxes led to higher savings and investment, and those investments produced future earnings, thus growing the tax base. Conversely, higher taxes slowed investment and therefore reduced the growth rate of the economy. This has been an area of considerable academic and policy debate, over decades if not centuries, but what is reasonably clear is that governments across the world spend a very large part of most country's GDP. There are of course many different measures of government spending, but the OECD (2017), for example, estimates that the governments of countries such as France, Belgium and Austria spend over 50 per cent of GDP; those in Sweden and Italy around 50 per cent; and Germany, Holland, Spain and the United Kingdom around 45 per cent. The United States and Japan are a step lower, and Switzerland's government spends around 35 per cent of its country's GDP. These are all very high compared with Hong Kong and Singapore at less than 20 per cent.

Government spending has tended to rise persistently over time. For example, in the United States, government spending was only $20 billion in 1900, or 7 per cent of GDP. By 2012 this had become $15,547 billion – 150 times higher after adjusting for inflation – and just under 40 per cent of GDP. Government spending in 1900 was around $500 per head (in today's money) but stands at around $19,000 per head today.

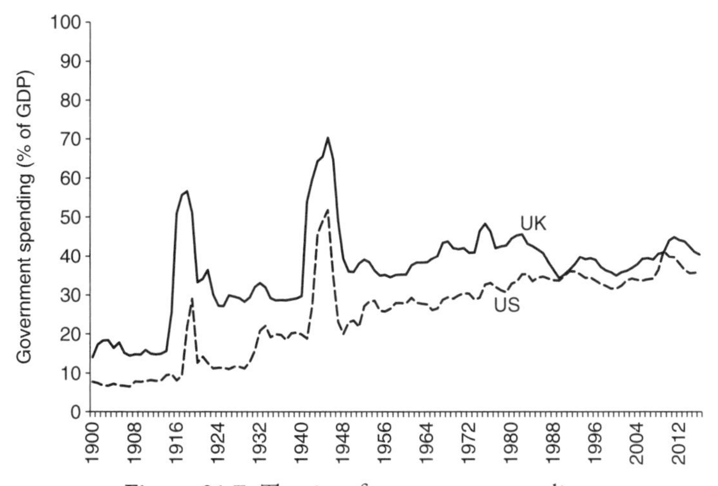

Figure 21.7. The rise of government spending.

Growth in government spending followed a similar path in the United Kingdom. Government spending in 1900 accounted for a slightly larger share of GDP than in the United States. The biggest difference was that Britain was spending more on defence, which accounted for over a quarter of the total spend. The costs of keeping an Empire, and the wars that doing so entailed, meant that government spending was around £700 per head in 1900 (in today's money; about $900). Today that number is over £11,000 per person.

Hong Kong has taken a very different path. Government spending was around 10–15 per cent of GDP up until 1997. Looking back, we can see that countries often had low taxes during the period in which they raised incomes from around the Int$4,000 level to the Int$20,000 level. For Britain and the United States this was mostly before World War I, when the state was much smaller. South Korea has government spending today in the region of 35 per cent of GDP, but it was below 20 per cent during its period of faster growth. What is unusual about Hong Kong (and also Singapore) is that they have maintained low taxes and spending as they have become wealthier.

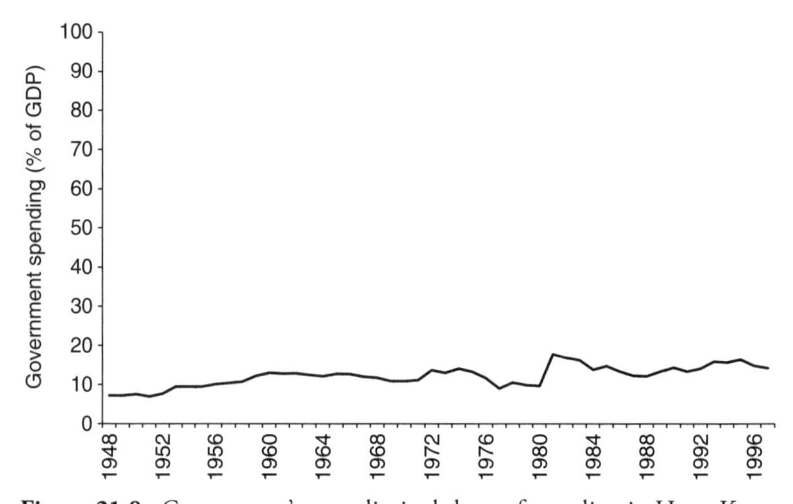

Figure 21.8. Government's more limited share of spending in Hong Kong.

In the post-war period there have been a very wide range of views on the optimal size of the state, ranging from those promoting complete state ownership of the means of production, through those wanting the state to own the commanding heights, to proponents of a mixed economy, through believers in privatization, to supporters of private enterprise and champions of a night-watchman state. Much of Cowperthwaite's time was spent explaining why he believed in a smaller state, with lower levels of government spending. This he believed was the route to faster economic growth and greater prosperity.

GOAL HIERARCHY, TIME PREFERENCE AND TRADE-OFFS

Cowperthwaite is often portrayed as being against growth of the state. This presents something of a paradox given how government spending per person grew from around $1,300 (in 2016 Hong Kong dollar terms) in 1948 to over $6,000 per person in 1971. By 1997 it reached $30,000 per person, and today it stands at over $60,000.

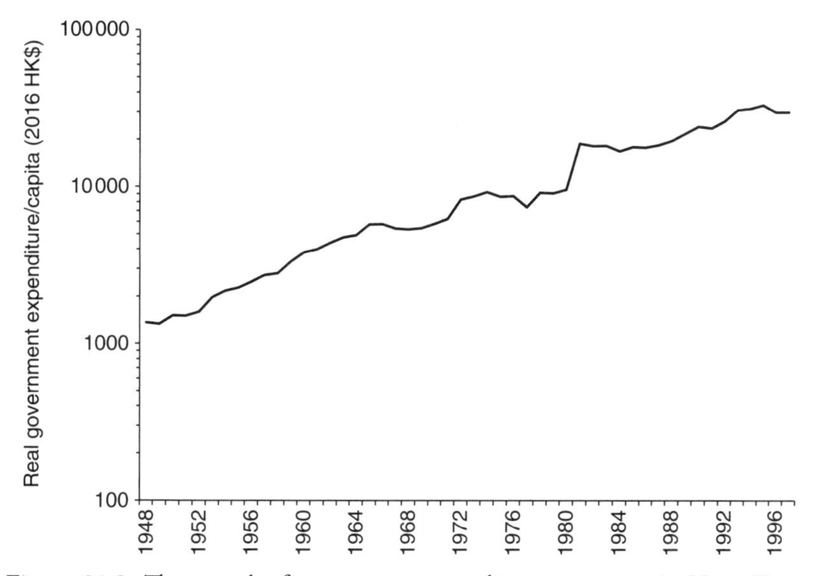

Figure 21.9. The growth of government expenditure per person in Hong Kong.

How do we reconcile this conundrum of rapidly growing spending and his frequent assertions about wanting to expand services with his desire for low taxation? His words and actions suggest that he had a sincere goal of helping to raise the living standards of the people of Hong Kong. But, more specifically, for him this goal was to do that over the very long term. Not needing to be elected, he could afford to weigh the welfare of future citizens, even those who had not yet been born, nearly as highly as that of living adults.

We can combine this point with some trade-offs that he frequently pointed to. First, he believed that a dollar left for private enterprise to invest would turn into a multiple of that in future tax revenues. Therefore, there was a trade-off between adding a dollar of public spending now and materially less spending in the future. Second, he believed that many government interventions were popular but were in fact inefficient, and that state involvement was often wasteful and sometimes even counterproductive.

Given these beliefs in these trade-offs, for him the risk of additional government activity becomes clear. Such initiatives might not be very efficient and would also reduce future growth, reducing the living standards of future citizens and the ability of the state to provide services for them. Such a logic borders on issues of morality. To provide a wasteful service to today's voters at the expense of the welfare of future generations could be viewed as indecent, especially if that provision involved getting some benefit oneself.

This becomes even more stark if one considers the idea of compounding: an idea that Einstein dubbed 'the eighth wonder of the world'. Say you could choose between one society that spent 20 per cent of its income on government support and grew at 5 per cent annually and another society that provided double that level of support to its citizens but only grew at 2 per cent. The attraction of offering and receiving that support today is clear. But after twenty-four years the two models are spending the same in absolute terms in government spending (excluding all the benefits that the faster-growth economy has in the larger non-government sector), and after forty-eight years the small-government society is spending twice as much per person as the large-government society. This is the conundrum that challenges those, such as Cowperthwaite, who believe that greater government spending reduces economic growth.

One important case in the years ahead will be to see how China balances the state and private sectors. It may surprise many in the West to know that communist China has a lower level of state spending, at around a quarter of GDP, than the United Kingdom or the United States. Some argue that China has studied the example of Hong Kong in detail and that its policy of greater economic liberalization combined with centralized political control is an attempt to replicate some of the logic of Cowperthwaite's economic model. What is unclear is whether economic freedom can be separated from other freedoms.

DIFFERENCES IN SPENDING

Despite being a poorer country, Britain's government spends nearly twice as much per head as Hong Kong's. About a fifth of this is because Hong Kong does not have debt-financing costs and has limited defence spending. Add in the fact that Hong Kong spends less per person in the key areas of education and health care and you can explain half of the difference with the United Kingdom.

The other half of the difference comes from welfare, and most notably pension provision. In Hong Kong the payments to older citizens, colloquially called fruit money, have been much more limited than in developed Western countries. In spending terms they are a fraction of the amounts paid to British pensioners. One often-cited argument is that these pensions have been paid for by previous National Insurance contributions, but this is a complete fiction since there is no pot of National

Insurance assets being drawn down by retirees. That generation has spent the same money twice: once in general expenditure and again with their pension claims.

Even excluding these transfers of income, Hong Kong's government spending is low by international comparisons, even today. Monies actually spent by the government directly, rather than transferred, are called government final consumption expenditure.

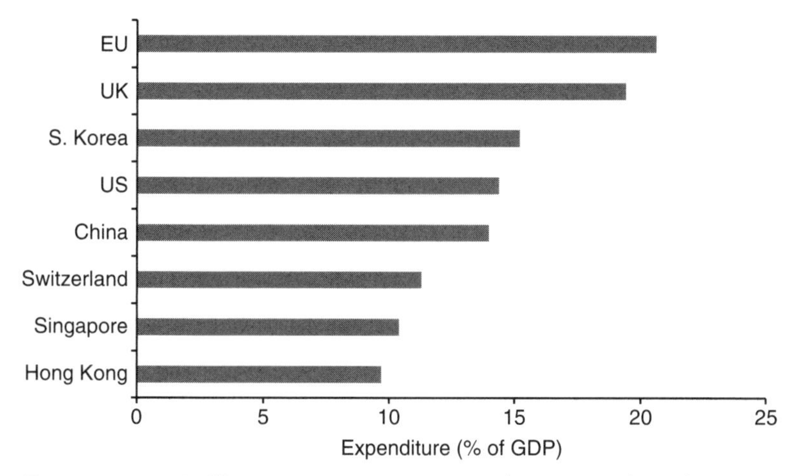

Figure 21.10. Differences in government spending on goods and services.

Even a brief review of the items behind countries having higher government spending than Hong Kong reveals the difficulty of moving from a high-tax/high-spend model to a Cowperthwaite approach. One can see why Cowperthwaite was so careful about taking on new commitments, and why he highlighted the difficulties of reducing spending and controlling the momentum of government spending.

UNDEMOCRATIC BUT ECONOMICALLY FREE

One of the most puzzling elements of this success story, at least to Western ears, is the absence of a democratic system and democratic control over government. Democracy is, of course, not simple to define. While it is technically true that Hong Kong's governors could act against the will of the people, in practice considerable effort was taken to craft policy that was acceptable to the population – or at least when it came to key elements of policy. A good example is the history of taxation in Hong Kong, where the UK government and indeed many local officials were unable to implement their preferred approach.

Despite the democratic deficit, Hong Kong has been consistently rated as one of the most economically free countries in the word. The Heritage Foundation and the *Wall Street Journal* have placed Hong Kong in first position every year since they founded their Index of Economic Freedom in 1995.[6] The index looks at property rights, freedom from corruption, fiscal and monetary freedom, business and labour freedom, and trade, investment and financial freedom. The Cato Institute's Human Freedom Index includes some non-economic freedoms (such as religious freedom) and again has ranked Hong Kong as the freest society in the world for many years.[7]

This may well be changing. China ranks well down the lists for economic and human freedom: typically around 140th in the world. It is in stark contrast to Hong Kong and tensions are clear between Beijing's desire to control elements of Hong Kong and their commitments under the Basic Laws. It is too early to know how this will evolve, but between the end of World War II and the 1997 handover we can see the fascinating contrast of a very free, undemocratic country.

One reason that this worked was undoubtedly the values held by the key public servants such as Cowperthwaite. They were essentially decent people trying to do their best for their adopted land, and Cowperthwaite was fortunate to spend the bulk of his career operating in an environment where his ideas were aligned with those of his fellow administrators, and with those of society at large.

One of the most interesting parts of the Hong Kong story is how a fairly broad cadre of British civil servants determined a policy to better Hong Kong and its people that was so completely at odds with the polices being deployed in the United Kingdom at that time. Asked how to improve the lot of the people of Hong Kong, they strongly pushed for a laissez-faire approach with limited state involvement and spending. Meanwhile, their colleagues in Britain were busy implementing policies that were considered disastrous in Hong Kong.

CRITICISMS OF COWPERTHWAITE'S APPROACH

Despite the remarkable economic performance of Hong Kong, and the key role that Cowperthwaite played in enabling that, he was widely criticized during his tenure in office, as we have seen, and also subsequently from a wide array of perspectives. Obviously, those who disagreed in principle with small government, or a laissez-fair approach, found little to like in his policies, or indeed in their obvious success.

Others such as Jonathan Dimbleby, working on a book about Patten's governorship, present a confused interpretation (Dimbleby 1997). At first, he acknowledges that:

> Under the direction of Financial Secretary Sir John Cowperthwaite, a laissez-faire economist, the British colony acquired all the characteristics of a free-trade port. Cowperthwaite imposed a regime of minimum public spending and minimal restraint on the maximization of profits. Between 1960 and 1970, wages rose on average by 50 per cent and the number of people living in acute poverty fell from over 50 per cent of the population to under 16 per cent.

But then Dimbleby disputes the claims that Hong Kong was increasingly comparable with developed countries as

> an exaggeration: an ideological hostility towards the concept of the welfare state, combined with the Financial Secretary's refusal to countenance public borrowing, left Hong Kong's basic services woefully underfunded.

One can only assume that this is a plea to both have lower taxes and spend more. It perhaps reveals a misunderstanding that Cowperthwaite did not have an objective to have the smallest state possible: rather, he wanted to have the highest level of state spending that would not inhibit rapid growth.

From the other end of the spectrum, some argue that Cowperthwaite was not truly laissez-faire. The government played a major role in housing and transport, and even in providing subsidized land to enterprise. Government spending increased each year, rather than restricting itself to the constant roles of the night-watchman state.

Some economists point out that Cowperthwaite's model of stable growth in government spending was modestly countercyclical, even Keynesian, with spending growth being maintained in economic downturns. Cowperthwaite himself acknowledged this point but his reason for doing it was a practical one: to spend government funds efficiently rather than to smooth demand.

Lastly, some point out that there are other successful countries that have delivered strong economic growth with a different policy mix. In particular, Japan, South Korea, Taiwan and Singapore are cited as countries that had much higher levels of government planning and intervention. That is obviously a huge topic for another book, but there are perhaps more similarities than differences between these examples. While there may have been an articulation of industrial strategies, they shared a great deal with Hong Kong: the desire to have clear property rights, the rule of law, the use of markets both domestically and for exports, a high level of economic freedom, low levels of taxation, and very little government involvement in the actual management and operations of business. How much the 'industrial strategies' were driven by government or by the underlying businesses is a fascinating debate.

In particular, there have been several in-depth comparisons between Hong Kong and Singapore, because at face value their successes look very similar (Young 1995). Both have relied heavily on capital investment to propel growth, as much economic theory would predict. However, Hong Kong relied a little less on that than its rival and instead had much higher productivity growth. This is important, because while the rate of investment is at some point limited, growth through productivity can continue independently.

Cowperthwaite always argued that his strategy was developed specifically for Hong Kong: a small, open economy with few resources and limited government. He would also add that the commercial skills of the Hong Kong people far exceeded those of the Hong Kong government. If he had crafted the policies for another country it is hard to see that he would have journeyed far away from his classical approach, although he would have undoubtedly examined the data and considered alternatives carefully.

Such wide-ranging criticisms did not overly worry Cowperthwaite during office or after. His belief in his policies came from first principles, not from whether they were popular or not. And he could, of course, increasingly point to the facts and the data on the ground, as Hong Kong became one of the most successful economies in the world.

LESSONS FROM THE PAST

If Cowperthwaite were alive today, he would no doubt be very reluctant to offer his advice or opinions on the issues that we currently face. But maybe, in private, he might pose us some questions. Are we sure that we are right to have moved so far away from the teachings of the classical economists? Is our government intervening too much in things that they cannot do as well as others could? Is our high level of government spending, at nearly half of GDP, inhibiting economic growth? And if it is, how can we justify depressing the standard of living of future generations? Do we think that deficits and borrowing have helped raise our standards of living? And perhaps most difficult of all, if one believed, as he did, that a low-tax, market-based, small-state model would best raise living standards, how would one get support for such a programme in a modern democracy?

And no doubt, while leaving us to ponder all that, he would head off for a round of golf.

ENDNOTES

Introduction: Architect of Prosperity

1. 'The real lesson of Hong Kong', speech by Milton Friedman at Mandel Hall, University of Chicago, 14 May 1997.
2. Alex Singleton, *The Guardian*, Obituary of John James Cowperthwaite, 8 February 2006.
3. Hansard, 25 March 1966.
4. Speech by Sir Philip Haddon-Cave to the Federation of Hong Kong Industries, December 1980.

Chapter 1
An Unlikely Start

1. Lord Palmerston, 21 April 1843.
2. Letter written by Churchill to General Hastings Ismay, 7 January 1941, quoted in Welsh (1997).
3. World Economic Outlook Database, International Monetary Fund, 2016.

Chapter 2
A Classical Education

1. Birth certificate, John James Cowperthwaite, District of Morningside, Edinburgh, Register of Births in Scotland, 1915.
2. Marriage certificate, John James Cowperthwaite to Jessie Wemyss Barron Jarvis, Parish of Ferry-Port-on-Craig, Register of Marriages in Scotland, 1913.

3. Birth certificate, John James Cowperthwaite (father), Parish of Ferry-Port-on-Craig, Fife, Register of Births in Scotland, 1882.
4. Birth certificate, David Jarvis Cowperthwaite, District of Morningside, Edinburgh, Register of Births in Scotland, 1921.
5. Valuation Rolls for Edinburgh, Scotland's People VR100/493/85, 1925.
6. Marriage certificate, St Giles, Edinburgh, 685/04, 1555.
7. UK outward passenger lists, Board of Trade, National Archives for SS Scythia departing Liverpool on 6 January 1940.
8. *The Daily Gleaner*, Jamaica, 6 February 1940.
9. *The Daily Gleaner*, Jamaica, 23 June 1948.
10. *The Daily Gleaner*, Jamaica, 24 November 1952.
11. Montego Bay High School website.
12. *Who's Who Jamaica 1960.*
13. *The Daily Gleaner*, Jamaica, 21 October 1991.
14. *London Gazette Supplement*, 17 July 1942.
15. Letter from Williams to D. J. Cowperthwaite, PRO CO 554/126/3, 16 July 1942.
16. *Who's Who 2004* (A & C Black, 2004).
17. Andrews Newspaper Index Cards.
18. Birth certificate, Ann Elizabeth Cowperthwaite, District of Edinburgh, Register of Births in Scotland, 1952.
19. Death Certificate, David Jarvis Cowperthwaite, District of Edinburgh, Register of Deaths in Scotland, 2006.
20. Merchiston Castle School website.
21. *Dundee Courier*, 5 July 1934.
22. *Fife Today*, 3 March 2006.
23. Briefing note for EEC negotiating delegation on Cowperthwaite's background, National Archives, PRO CO 852 2073.
24. *Fife Today*, 2 February 2006.
25. Obituary, *Alumnus Chronicle,* Volume 65 (University of St Andrews, 1974).
26. 'Professor James Wilkie Nisbet: an appreciation', Alan Peacock, *Alumnus Chronicle*, Volume 61 (University of St Andrews, 1970).
27. Marriage certificate, John James Cowperthwaite and Sheila Mary Thompson, District of Perth, Register of Marriages in Scotland, 1941.
28. *Aberdeen Weekly Journal,* 18 September 1941.
29. *The Scotsman*, 30 January 2006.
30. Report to Officer Commanding 11th Bn. The Cameronians, 11 May 1941, National Archives, WO 199/3288A.
31. Edinburgh telephone directory, 1939, 1940, 1941.

Chapter 3
Cadet Cowperthwaite

1. Briefing note for EEC negotiating delegation on Cowperthwaite's background, National Archives, PRO CO 852 2073.
2. Dispatch from Chamberlain to Blake on 13 February 1903 in response to a complaint by Cadets that they were being over looked for promotions, PRO CO 129/313.
3. 'Sketch of a scheme for the establishment of Hong Kong cadetships', PRO CO 129/80, 1861.
4. Letter from Rogers to Hamilton, PRO CO 129/80, 7 July 1861.
5. 'Aspects on Crown Service', Ian MacPherson, in *Hong Kong, British Crown Colony Revisited*, edited by Elizabeth Sinn (Centre for Asian Studies, University of Hong Kong, 2001); quoted in Tsang (2007).
6. Letter from Peel to Ellis discussing Hong Kong and Malay Cadets serving in each other's territories, PRO CO 825/10/4.
7. Letter from N. L. Smith to W. G. A Ormsby-Gore, PRO CO 865/13, 14 June 1937.
8. Letter from N. L. Smith to W. G. A Ormsby-Gore, PRO CO 865/13, 29 July 1937.
9. *Sierra Leone Royal Gazette*, PRO CO 271/50, 16 April 1942.
10. *Sierra Leone Royal Gazette*, PRO CO 271/51, 21 October 1943.
11. UK outward passenger lists, Board of Trade, PRO.
12. *Sierra Leone Royal Gazette*, PRO CO 271/52, 23 March 1944.
13. 'Using RPI', Lawrence H. Officer and Samuel H. Williamson, in *Five Ways to Compute the Relative Value of a UK Pound Amount, 1270 to Present* (Measuring Worth, 2014).
14. *Sierra Leone Royal Gazette*, PRO CO 271/53, 14 June 1945.
15. Note from Sedgwick to Miss Ruston, PRO CO 129/591/10, 9 March 1945.
16. Staff list, Hong Kong government, HKRS 06-11-2013, 1970.
17. Speech by Sir Hugh Selsby Norman Walker at HK LegCo, 23 June 1971.
18. Papers, PRO CO 129/591/11.
19. Extract minutes of the Cabinet, PRO CO 129/591/16 26, 10 August 1945.
20. Telegram from Sterndale Bennet, PRO FO 371/46252, 14 August 1945.
21. Telegram from President Truman to the Prime Minister, PRO CO 129/591/16, 18 August 1945.
22. Telegram from Foreign Office to Chungking, PRO CO 129/591/16, 11 August 1945.

23. Naval Cypher from First Sea Lord to Admiral Harcourt etc for Brigadier MacDougall, en route Hong Kong ex UK via Colombo, PRO CO 129/592/12, 31 August 1945.
24. Interview with David MacDougall conducted by Steve Tsang (1987), Bodleian Library Archives, Manuscripts, Indian Ocean, s. 344.
25. *The Times*, 9 January 1942.
26. *The Times*, Obituary of Sir Edward Gent, 5 July 1948.

Chapter 4
A Focus on Industry

1. 'The British Military Administration, Hong Kong, August 1945 to August 1946', PRO CO 129/595/9, April 1946.
2. Note from Military Secretary, War Office to HQ Civil Affairs on 15 August 1945, National Archives CO 129/591/10.
3. Staff list, Hong Kong government, HK Government Archives HKRS 06-11-2013, 1970.
4. Interview with Cowperthwaite by Steve Tsang in St Andrews on 4 April 1983, noted in Tsang (2007).
5. *Hong Kong (British Military Administration) Gazette*, PRO CO 132/89, 1 December 1945.
6. From War Office to C-in-C Hong Kong, List of arrivals, PRO CO 129/591/10.
7. Letter from MacDougall to Gent, PRO CO 129/591/20, 7 November 1945.
8. 'Government departments in Hong Kong 1841–1969', G. C. Hamilton and S. Young (1969).
9. Report number 1 to London from the DST&I, HKRS 170-1-551-1, 10 October 1945.
10. Report at the end of the first quarter of re-occupation, DST&I, PRO CO 129/595/9, 27 November 1945.
11. Trade and Industry proposal, HKRS 170-1-696, 18 October 1945.
12. *Hong Kong (British Military Administration) Gazette*, National Archives CO 132/89, 30 March 1946 (appointment with effect from 1 January 1946).
13. Report number 4 to London from the DST&I, HKRS 170-1-551-1, 16 April 1946.
14. Report number 5 to London from the DST&I, HKRS 170-1-551-1, 16 March 1946.
15. *Hong Kong Gazette*, PRO CO 132/90, 21 June 1946 and 23 August 1946.
16. *Hong Kong Gazette*, PRO CO 132/90, 23 August 1946 (appointment with effect from 21 August 1946).
17. *Hong Kong Gazette*, PRO CO 132/90, 11 October 1946.

18. Memorandum from director of the DST&I to the financial secretary, PRO CO 129/619/4, dated 21 June 1946.
19. Annual departmental report (1946/47), DST&I, corrected by Cowperthwaite, HKRS 41-1-2180, 11 March 1948.
20. Monthly Report, DST&I, HKRS 170-1-551-1, September 1946.
21. Monthly Report, DST&I, HKRS 170-1-551-1, October 1946.
22. Monthly Report, DST&I, HKRS 170-1-551-1, December 1946.
23. Monthly Report, DST&I, HKRS 170-1-551-1, March 1947.
24. Monthly Report, DST&I, HKRS 170-1-551-1, June 1947.
25. Monthly Report, DST&I, HKRS 170-1-551-1, November 1946–February 1947.
26. Monthly Report, DST&I, HKRS 170-1-551-1, November 1946.
27. Monthly Report, DST&I, HKRS 170-1-551-1, May 1947.
28. *South China Morning Post*, 15 June 1947.
29. *Hong Kong Gazette*, PRO CO 132/91, 13 June 1947.
30. *Hong Kong Gazette*, PRO CO 132/91, 20 June 1947.
31. Report of the DST&I, Hong Kong Archives, 1947/48.
32. UK outward passenger lists, National Archives, Kew, 16 January 1948.
33. Hong Kong annual report of the DST&I for the period 1 April 1948 to 31 March 1949, signed by J. J. Cowperthwaite, 12 May 1949.
34. Monthly report, DST&I, HKRS 170-1-551-1, April 1948.
35. Letter from the governor to the colonial secretary, PRO CO 129/619/4 and HKRS 41-1-2741, 19 March 1949.
36. Letter from the Secretary of State, Colonial Office to the governor of Hong Kong, signed by Listowel, PRO CO 129/619/4 and HKRS 41-1-2741, 27 September 1949.
37. UK inward passenger lists, National Archives, Kew.
38. *Hong Kong Gazette*, PRO CO 132/96, 18 November 1949.
39. *Hong Kong Gazette*, PRO CO 132/97, 18 August 1950.
40. Statement of accounts, Department of Supplies & Distribution, by Lowe, Bingham & Matthews, HKRS 41-1-2741, 12 September 1950.
41. Statement of accounts, Department of Supplies & Distribution, by Lowe, Bingham & Matthews, HKRS 41-1-2741, 16 January 1951.

Chapter 5
The Follows Foundation

1. Hong Kong staff list 1950/51.
2. Interview with David MacDougall conducted by Tsang (1987), Bodleian Library Archives, Manuscripts, Indian Ocean, s. 344.
3. Hansard, 19 July 1946.

4. *South China Morning Post,* 13 October 1939.
5. Hansard, 9 November 1939.
6. War Revenue Ordinance, 1941.
7. Details from an account posted by Ray Chidell, nephew of Paul Chidell, who was one of the examiners. Original notes from Edgar Mathias, also an examiner: 'War taxation – Hong Kong 1940–41', 24 November 2012 (www.claritaxbooks.com).
8. 'Direct taxation in Hong Kong', HKRS 163-1-448.
9. Quoted in Littlewood (2010), sourced from minute to David MacDougall, HKRS 211-2-20, 1, 8 May 1945.
10. Hansard, 25 July 1946.
11. Hansard, 5 September 1946.
12. Draft report of the Taxation Committee, PRO CO 129/595/3, December 1946.
13. Report of the Taxation Committee, PRO CO 129/595/3, 1946.
14. Young telegrams to Creech Jones, PRO CO 129/595/3, 9 September 1946 and 12 December 1946.
15. *South China Morning Post,* 29 July 1950.
16. Pudney note to Follows, HKRS 41-1-2769-1 (7).
17. Eric Pudney memo, PRO CO 129/595/3, 8 January 1947 (also Follows minute to Sir Mark Young, HKRS 41-12769-1).
18. Hansard, 13 March 1947.
19. Hansard, 27 March 1947.
20. Hansard, 24 April 1947.
21. Reuters report sent to London, National Archives CO 129/615/2.
22. Dispatch Sir Mark Young to Arthur Creech Jones, PRO CO 129/595/3, 16 May 1947.
23. Letter from D. R. Serpell (Treasury Chambers) to Palmer (Colonial Office), PRO CO 129/615/2, 9 September 1947.
24. HM Treasury, answer to freedom of information request 11/392, 27 May 2011.
25. Quoted in Endacott (1964).
26. Hansard, 31 July 1947.
27. Hansard, 27 April 1949.
28. Hansard, 17 and 29 December 1947.
29. Hansard, 19 March 1948.
30. Telegram (number 611) from Grantham to Colonial Office, PRO CO 129/157/2, 1 June 1948.
31. Letter from Grantham to Colonial Office, PRO CO 1030/392, 24 September 1948.

Chapter 6
The Decline of the Entrepôt Trade

1. Hansard, 8 March 1950.
2. Hansard, 19 March 1948.
3. Speech by Clement Attlee to the Labour Party Conference, Bournemouth, 11 June 1946.
4. Hansard, 13 December 1950.
5. Hansard, 7 March 1951.
6. Hansard, 21 March 1951.
7. Hansard, 28 March 1951.

Chapter 7
Deputy Financial Secretary

1. Hong Kong Gazette, PRO CO 132/103, 10 April 1952 (Cowperthwaite appointed acting deputy financial secretary with effect from 7 April 1952).
2. Hong Kong staff list 1961.
3. Vacancy form for financial secretary, HKRS 163-1-2504, 1951.
4. Hong Kong staff list 1952.
5. Hansard, 5 March 1952.
6. Hansard, 19 March 1952.
7. Hansard, 27 March 1952.
8. Hansard, 31 December 1952.
9. Hansard, 4 March 1953.
10. Hansard, 18 March 1953.
11. Hansard, 26 March 1953.
12. Hong Kong staff list 1961.
13. Hansard, 29 April 1953.
14. Hansard, 20 May 1953.
15. Hansard, 26 August 1953.
16. *The Cornell Daily Sun*, 27 September 1954.
17. Telegram from the British Embassy in Washington, PRO FO 371 110350, 11 October 1954.
18. Hansard, 3 March 1954.
19. Hansard, 17 March 1954.
20. Hansard, 7 April 1954.
21. Hansard, 14 April 1954.
22. Hansard, 2 March 1955.
23. Report from governor of Hong Kong to Secretary of State for the Colonies, 'Hong Kong: local industry', PRO PREM 11/868, 2 July 1955.

24. Letter to L. Petch, PRO PREM 11/868, 10 August 1955.
25. Hansard, 12 October 1955.
26. Hansard, 26 October 1955.

Chapter 8
Winner's Doubts

1. Hansard, 29 February 1956.
2. Hansard, 27 February 1957.
3. Hansard, 6 March 1958.
4. Hong Kong staff lists.
5. *South China Morning Post,* 1 March 1956.
6. Hong Kong staff list 1961.
7. Reports, PRO CO 132/125.
8. Hansard, 18 December 1957.
9. *South China Morning Post,* 30 December 1957.
10. Hong Kong staff list 1970.
11. Hansard, 25 February 1959.
12. *South China Morning Post,* 26 February 1959.
13. Report of the Industrial Bank Committee, HKRS 163-1-2299, 11 June 1960.
14. Letter from the Chinese Manufacturers' Association, HKRS 163-1-2299, 2 April 1959.
15. *The London Gazette*, 29 December 1959.
16. Hansard, 24 February 1960.
17. Hansard, 16 March 1960.
18. Hansard, 1 March 1961.
19. Hansard, 22 March 1961.
20. Hansard, 29 March 1961.

Chapter 9
Financial Secretary and Chief Trade Negotiator

1. Letter from the governor to the Secretary of State for the Colonies, HKRS 163-1-2504 , 2 February 1961.
2. Vacancy form for financial secretary, HKRS 163-1-2504.
3. *Far Eastern Economic Review Yearbook*, 1961.
4. *Far Eastern Economic Review*, 1 June 1961.
5. Memorandum for the Trade and Industry Advisory Board, HKRS 163-1-2129, 3 February 1960.
6. *Far Eastern Economic Review*, 6 July 1961.
7. *Far Eastern Economic Review*, 24 August 1961.
8. *Far Eastern Economic Review*, 23 November 1961.

9. *The Economist*, 5 May 1962.
10. *Far Eastern Economic Review*, 6 September 1962.
11. *Far Eastern Economic Review*, 17 October 1963, quoting annual departmental reports from the Commissioner of Labour.
12. *Far Eastern Economic Review*, 20 September 1962.
13. Telegram from the governor of Hong Kong to the Secretary of State for the Colonies, 'Transistor radio exports to the United Kingdom', HKRS 163-1-2855, 4 June 1964.
14. Memo from director of Commerce & Industry to financial secretary, 'Transistor radios exported to the United Kingdom', HKRS 163-1-2855, 11 April 1964.
15. *Fife Today*, 3 March 2006.
16. *Fife Today*, 2 February 2006.
17. *South China Sunday Post–Herald,* 11 February 1968.

Chapter 10
The Threat of Brentry

1. Note of conversation between Gorell Barnes and Cowperthwaite, Hong Kong financial secretary, on 26 October 1961, PRO CO 852/2071.
2. Confidential letter from Cowperthwaite to Trafford Smith, PRO CO 852 2071, 4 November 1961.
3. Letter from Gorell Barnes to Cowperthwaite, PRO CO 852 2071, 3 January 1962.
4. 'British membership of the European Common Market and its effects on Hong Kong's Trade', Economist Intelligence Unit, PRO CO 852 2071, October 1961.
5. File note from Vernon to Trafford Smith, Gorell Barnes and others, PRO CO 852 2072, 12 February 1962.
6. File note from Vernon to Trafford Smith and others, PRO CO 852 2072, 1 March 1962.
7. Notes of meeting between Cowperthwaite and Gorell Barnes and others, Hong Kong Government Office, London, PRO CO 852 2073, 4 June 1962.
8. Telegram to Sir R. Black, PRO CO 852 2073, 14 June 1962.
9. Telegram from Cowperthwaite to Vernon, PRO CO 852 2075, 30 October 1962.
10. Note from Trafford Smith to Cowperthwaite, PRO CO 852 2075 , 8 November 1962.
11. Note from Trafford Smith to Sir William Gorell Barnes, PRO CO 852 2076, 27 November 1962.
12. File note by Gorell Barnes, PRO CO 852 2076, 23 November 1962.
13. Note from Gorell Barnes to R. W. Jackling, PRO CO 852 207617, 31 December 1962.
14. Hansard, 18 March 1963.

Chapter 11
A Banking Crisis

1. Referencing correspondence between P. Mardulyn, the manager of Banque Belge, and Cowperthwaite, HKRS 163-1-625, 1960.
2. Hansard, 19 June 1963.
3. Letter from Hallows to Haslam, BE OV14/21, 3 June 1960.
4. *Far Eastern Economic Review*, 27 June 1963.
5. Supplementary notes on draft Hong Kong Banking Ordinance, BE OV14/22, 1 April 1962.
6. Hansard, 19 June 1963.

Chapter 12
Cowperthwaite's First Budget

1. Hansard, 17 January 1962.
2. *Far Eastern Economic Review Yearbook*, 1961.
3. Hansard, 28 February 1962.
4. *Far Eastern Economic Review*, 8 March 1962.
5. Hansard, 19 March 1962.
6. Hansard, 30 March 1962.

Chapter 13
Fiscal Fundamentals

1. Hansard, 27 February 1963.
2. Hansard, 26 February 1964.
3. Hansard, 18 March 1963.
4. Hansard, 29 March 1963.
5. Letters from Cowperthwaite to Kirkness, HKRS 163-1-2210, 30 January, 4 February and 28 February 1963.
6. Letter from Kirkness to Cowperthwaite, HKRS 163-1-2210, 8 March 1963.
7. Letter from Cowperthwaite to Kirkness, HKRS 163-1-2210, 20 March 1963.
8. Hansard, 18 December 1963.
9. *London Gazette*, 31 December 1963.
10. Hansard, 17 June 1964.
11. *The Sunday Gleaner*, Jamaica, 8 November 1964.
12. Hansard, 25 February 1965.
13. *Far Eastern Economic Review*, 4 March 1965.

Chapter 14
The Boundaries of the State

1. Hansard, 5 August 1964.
2. Hansard, 23 June 1965 (and subsequent meetings).
3. Hansard, 30 June 1965.
4. Hansard, 29 March 1963.
5. Hansard, 25 February 1965.
6. Proposed Tunnel between Hong Kong and Kowloon, Engineers' Report, Mott, Hay & Anderson, 1955.
7. *South China Morning Post,* 6 May 1956.
8. Inter-Departmental Working Party on the Proposed Cross-Harbour Tunnel, Government Press, Hong Kong, 1956.
9. Hansard, 28 July 1965.
10. Hansard, 18 June 1969.
11. Hansard, 25 March 1965.

Chapter 15
A Bigger Banking Crisis

1. Interview with Leonidas Cole in *South China Morning Post,* 12 June 1965.
2. *Far Eastern Economic Review,* 18 February 1965.
3. Minutes of the Banking Advisory Committee, Hong Kong PRO 163-1-3185, 18 March 1965.
4. Note from P. E. Hudson of Hong Kong Bank (15 July 1965) quoted in Schenk (2011).
5. *The Daily Gleaner,* Jamaica, 24 September 1965.
6. Hansard, 24 February 1966.
7. Hansard, 10 March 1966.
8. Hansard, 24 March 1966.
9. Hansard, 24 February 1966.

Chapter 16
The Pressures of a Downturn

1. Hansard, 24 February 1966.
2. *Far Eastern Economic Review,* 3 March 1966.
3. Hansard, 24 March 1966.
4. Report, PRO PREM 13-2153.
5. Note of a discussion between the Secretary of State for Defence and officials of the Hong Kong government, PRO PREM 13-2153, 13 July 1966.

6. Note to the prime minister, PRO PREM 13-2153, 16 December 1966.
7. Note to the prime minister, PRO PREM 13-2153, 28 May 1968.
8. Hansard, 1 March 1967.
9. Hansard, 15 March 1967.
10. Hansard, 30 March 1967.

Chapter 17
Devaluation and Indecision

1. Note from W. Ryrie to Hubback, Bank of England Archives, OV 44/139, 9 November 1967.
2. Note from Haslam to Galsworthy, BE OV 44/258, 12 October 1966.
3. Note from Hubback to Goldman, BE OV 44/258 , 27 October 1967.
4. Note from Haslam to Hubback, BE OV 44/258 , 2 November 1967.
5. Telegram from government informing colonies, FU War Book, BE OV 44/144.
6. Telegram 831 from Haslam to Commonwealth Office, BE OV 44/258, 22 November 1967.
7. *South China Morning Post,* 21 November 1967.
8. Letter from Haslam to Goldman (Treasury), BE OV 44/258, 7 December 1967.
9. *The Telegraph,* Obituary, 22 July 2012.
10. Note from W. Ryrie, BE OV 44/258, 23 November 1967.
11. Telegram 1777 from Sir David Trench to the Commonwealth Office, BE OV 44/258, 28 November 1967.
12. Note from Haslam, BE OV 44/258, 5 December 1967.
13. *South China Morning Post,* 24 November 1967.
14. Hansard, 29 November 1967.
15. Telegram from the Foreign Office to Galsworthy (number 389), PRO FCO 48/78, 11 December 1967.
16. Note from Galsworthy, BE OV 44/258, 2 January 1968.
17. Note to Sir Arthur Snelling from Galsworthy, PRO FCO 48/78, 3 January 1968.
18. Note from Cowperthwaite to Galsworthy, PRO FCO 48/78, 21 December 1967.
19. Telegram 1894 from Sir David Trench to the Commonwealth Office, BE OV 44/258, 21 December 1967.
20. Record of meeting held in the Commonwealth Office, BE OV44/258, 8 January 1968.
21. Record of a meeting held in the Commonwealth Office, BE OV 44/258, 10 January 1968.
22. Note from Fogarty to Hubback, 'Visit to Hong Kong', sent from British High Commission, Kuala Lumpur, BE OV 44/259.
23. Hansard, 28 February 1968.

24. Ryrie note to Hubback, BE OV44/258, 29 February 1968 (quote attributed to *Times Business News;* article at PRO FCO 48/48).
25. *Financial Times,* 29 February 1968.
26. Telegram from Trench to the Commonwealth Office (number 357), PRO FCO 48/78, 1 March 1968.
27. Personal telegram from Snelling to Cowperthwaite (number 374), PRO FCO 48/78, 1 March 1968.
28. Letter from Cowperthwaite to Sir Arthur Snelling, BE OV 44/259, 7 March 1968.
29. Letter from Trench to Galsworthy, PRO FCO 48/78, 5 March 1968.
30. Letter from S. S. Gordon and others to Trench, PRO FCO 48/78 , dated 23 February 1968 but delivered later.
31. Telegram from the Commonwealth Office to Hong Kong (number 470), PRO FCO 48/78, 14 March 1968.
32. Goodstadt (2009) citing personal information from interviews in 1967–70 with officials involved in the negotiations.
33. Note from Fogarty to Haslam, BE OV 44/259, 4 April 1968.
34. Telegram 680 from Trench to the Commonwealth Office, 28th May 1968, BE OV 44/260.
35. Note FP 9/551/4 from Commonwealth Office to governor of Hong Kong, BE OV44/260, 30 May 1968.
36. Hansard, 10 July 1968.
37. Hansard, 28 November 1968.

Chapter 18
Friction with China

1. Long term study: Hong Kong, Cabinet Office, PRO CAB 165/623, 17 November 1967.
2. 'Action in the event of a decision to block sterling balances in the context of a forced evacuation', Letter from the Treasury (Mackay) to the Cabinet Office (Rogers), 15 August 1967.
3. *Far Eastern Economic Review,* 29 February 1968.
4. Hansard, 28 February 1968.
5. *Far Eastern Economic Review,* 4 April 1968.
6. *London Gazette*, 31 May 1968.

Chapter 19
Consolidation and Continuity

1. Hansard, 26 February 1969.

2. *Far Eastern Economic Review,* 6 March 1969.
3. Hansard, 13 March 1969.
4. Hansard, 26 March 1969.
5. *Far Eastern Economic Review,* 20 March 1969.
6. Question from Mr Wong, Hansard, 21 January 1969.
7. 'Report on the National Income Survey of Hong Kong', E. R. Chang, Hong Kong Government Printer, 1969.
8. File note by Cowperthwaite, HKRS 163-9-281, 28 August 1969.
9. Question from Dr Chung, Hansard, 3 December 1969.
10. Hansard, 25 March 1970.
11. *The Banker*, July 1970.
12. *The Guardian*, Alex Singleton, Obituary, 8 February 2006.
13. Note of meeting between Mr Stans, US Secretary for Commerce, and officials of Hong Kong department on 17 May 1969, HKRS 163-1-3679.
14. Confidential letter from Whitehead to Sir A. Snelling, 'Visit to Hong Kong: meeting with Mr Stans on 17 May 1969', HKRS 163-1-3679, 22 May 1969.
15. Hansard, 30 July 1969.
16. Hansard, 1 October 1969.
17. Hansard, 2 October 1969.
18. Hansard, 8 October 1969.
19. Hansard, 25 February 1970.
20. *South China Morning Post,* 26 February 1970 and 2 March 1994.
21. Hansard, 25 March 1970.
22. File note, HKRS 163-1-2002, 19 June 1967.
23. Hansard, 9 October 1970.
24. Hansard, 24 February 1971.
25. Hansard, 10 March 1971.
26. Hansard, 24 March 1971.

Chapter 20
Changing Guard

1. *South China Morning Post,* 5 July 1971.
2. *South China Morning Post,* 7 July 1971.
3. Letter from Trench to Sir Leslie Monson, FCO, HKRS 189-1-125, 27 January 1970.
4. Haddon-Cave CV, HKRS 189-1-125, 29 September 1970.
5. Letter from Haslam to the Treasury, HKRS 189-1-125, 6 November 1970.
6. Speech at 'The Conference on Managers in a Changing Hong Kong Environment, November 1973', reported by Joseph Yam, chief executive of the Hong Kong Monetary Authority, in *South China Morning Post,* 24 August 1998.

7. As reported by Joseph Yam, chief executive of the Hong Kong Monetary Authority, *South China Morning Post,* 24 August 1998.
8. *Sunday Post–Herald*, 17 September 1972.
9. *South China Morning Post,* 15 November 1972.
10. 'Jardines – 175 years of looking to the future, Jardine Matheson, 2007.
11. *South China Morning Post,* 5 September 1978.
12. 'Remarkable St Andrean dies', *Fife Today*, 3 March 2006.
13. *The Guardian*, Alex Singleton, Obituary, 8 February 2006.
14. *Fife Today*, 2 February 2006.
15. *Fife Today*, 3 March 2006.
16. *Fife Herald News*, 26 September 1981.
17. *Fife Today*, 2 February 2006.
18. As recounted to the author by Wai-hong Yeung.
19. Hansard, 12 March 1997.
20. Hansard, 24 February 2016.
21. *Independent (South Africa)*, Jo-Anne Smetheram, 5 May 2004.
22. *South China Morning Post*, Raissa Robles, 8 May 2005.
23. *The News Today (The Philippines)*, Nestor Burgos, 3 April 2007.
24. *The Daily Telegraph*, 16 February 2006.
25. *The Guardian*, 8 February 2006.
26. *The Times*, 3 February 2006.
27. *South China Morning Post,* 25 January 2006.

Chapter 21
History Lessons?

1. United Nations World Population Prospects: 2015, United Nations, 2015.
2. Programme for International Student Assessment (PISA) organized by the OECD, 2015 results at www.oecd.org/pisa.
3. World Economic Outlook Database, International Monetary Fund, October 2016.
4. GDP per capita, PPP (current international $), World Development Indicators Database, World Bank, December 2016.
5. *New York Times*, 21 October 1992.
6. www.heritage.org.
7. www.cato.org.

BIBLIOGRAPHY

Bell, D., and Ham, C. 2003. *Confucianism for the Modern World.* Cambridge University Press.

Bickers, R., and Yep, R. (eds). 2009. *May Days in Hong Kong: Riot and Emergency in 1967.* Hong Kong University Press.

Blake, R. 1999. *Jardine Matheson: Traders of the Far East.* London: Weidenfeld & Nicolson.

Bown, C. P., and Irwin, D. A. 2015. The GATT's starting point: tariff levels circa 1947. NBER Working Paper 21782.

Bray, D. 2001. *Hong Kong Metamorphosis.* Hong Kong University Press.

Chang, E. R. 1969. *Report on the National Income Survey of Hong Kong.* Hong Kong: Government Printer.

Chen, A. 2003. Meditation, litigation, and justice. In Bell and Ham (2003).

Cheung, G. 2009. *Hong Kong's Watershed: The 1967 Riots.* Hong Kong University Press.

Chou, K. 1966. *Hong Kong Economy: A Miracle of Growth.* Hong Kong: Academic Publications.

Clark, T., and Dilnot, A. 2002. *Long-Term Trends in British Taxation and Spending.* Institute for Fiscal Studies.

Clarke, P. 2004. *Hope and Glory: Britain 1900–2000,* 2nd edition. London: Penguin.

Collins, C. 1952. *Public Administration in Hong Kong.* London, New York: Royal Institute of International Affairs (published in cooperation with the International Secretariat, Institute of Pacific Relations).

Coyle, D. 2014. *Gdp: A Brief but Affectionate History.* Princeton University Press.

Dimbleby, J. 1997. *The Last Governor: Chris Patten and the Handover of Hong Kong.* Little, Brown.

Donnison, F. 1956. *British Military Administration in the Far East, 1943–46.* London: HMSO.

Dorn, J. 1998. *China in the New Millennium: Market Reforms and Social Development.* Washington, DC: Cato Institute.

Elman, B. 2000. *A Cultural History of Civil Examinations in Late Imperial China.* Berkeley, CA: University of California Press.

Eltis, W. 1984. *The Classical Theory of Economic Growth*. London: Macmillan.

Endacott, G. 1964a. *A History of Hong Kong*. Oxford University Press.

Endacott, G. 1964b. *Government and People in Hong Kong 1841*. Hong Kong University Press.

Ferguson, N. 2003. *Empire: How Britain Made the Modern World*. London: Allen Lane.

Ferguson, N. 2008. *The Ascent of Money: A Financial History of the World*. Penguin.

Friedman, M., and Friedman, R. 1998. *Two Lucky People: Memoirs*. University of Chicago Press.

Gide, C., and Rist, C. 1948. *A History of Economic Doctrines: From the Time of the Physiocrats to the Present Day*. London, Bombay: George G. Harrap & Company Ltd.

Gilbert, M. 1991. *Churchill: A Life*. London: Heinemann.

Goodstadt, L. 2005. *Uneasy Partners: The Conflict between Public Interest and Private Profit in Hong Kong*. Hong Kong University Press.

Goodstadt, L. 2006. Government without statistics: policy-making in Hong Kong 1925–85, with special reference to economic and financial management. HKIMR Working Paper 6/2006.

Goodstadt, L. 2007. *Profits, Politics and Panics: Hong Kong's Banks and the Making of a Miracle Economy, 1935–1985*. Hong Kong University Press.

Goodstadt, L. 2013. *Poverty in the Midst of Affluence: How Hong Kong Mismanaged Its Prosperity*, revised edition. Hong Kong University Press.

Goodstadt, L., and Mao, Z. 1972. *Mao Tse Tung: The Search for Plenty*. London: Longman.

Goulding, J. S. R. 1997. *Ascent to Mona as Illustrated by a Short History of Jamaican Medical Care*. Jamaica: Canoe Press.

Grantham, A. 1965. *Via Ports: From Hong Kong to Hong Kong*. Hong Kong University Press/Oxford University Press.

Hambro, E. 1955. *The Problem of Chinese Refugees in Hong Kong* (report submitted to the United Nations High Commissioner for Refugees). Leyden: A. W. Sijthoff.

Hamilton, G. 1969. *Government Departments in Hong Kong, 1841–1969*. Hong Kong: Government Printer.

Hartwell, R. 1995. *A History of the Mont Pelerin Society*. Indianapolis: Liberty Fund.

Hobsbawm, E. 1987. *The Age of Empire 1875–1914*. London: Weidenfeld and Nicolson.

Hopkins, K. (ed.). 1971. *Hong Kong, the Industrial Colony: A Political, Social and Economic Survey*. Oxford University Press.

Horne, A. 1988. *Macmillan: 1957–1986*. London: Macmillan.

Hughes, R. 1968. *Hong Kong Borrowed Place: Borrowed Time*. London: Andre Deutsch.

Jao, Y. C. 1974. *Banking and Currency in Hong Kong*. London: Macmillan.

Jones, G. 2000. *Merchants to Multinationals: British Trading Companies in the Nineteenth and Twentieth Centuries*. Oxford University Press.

Keynes, J. 1936. *The General Theory of Employment, Interest and Money*. London: Macmillan.

King, F. 1953. *The Monetary System of Hong Kong* (with a chapter on the monetary system of Macao). Hong Kong: K. Weiss.

Kirk-Greene, A. 1999. *On Crown Service: A History of HM Colonial and Overseas Civil Services, 1837–1997*. London: I. B. Tauris.

Lacouture, J. 1991. *De Gaulle: The Ruler 1945–1970*. Harvill.

Lethbridge, H. 1978. *Hong Kong: Stability And Change – A Collection Of Essays*. Oxford University Press.

Li, K. 2012. *Economic Freedom: Lessons of Hong Kong*. World Scientific.

Lindsay, O. 1981. *At the Going Down of the Sun: Hong Kong and South-East Asia 1941–45*. London: Sphere.

Littlewood, M. 2010. *Taxation without Representation: The History of Hong Kong's Troublingly Successful Tax System*. Hong Kong University Press.

Lovell, J. 2012. *The Opium War: Drugs, Dreams and the Making of China*. London: Picador.

Ludlow, N. 1997. *Dealing with Britain: The Six and the First UK Application to the EEC*. Cambridge University Press.

Ma, R., and Szczepanik, E. 1955. *The National Income of Hong Kong, 1947–1950*. Hong Kong University Press.

MacDonald, A., and MacDonald, P. 1989. *Above Edinburgh and South-East Scotland*. Edinburgh: Mainstream.

Maddison Project. 2013. www.ggdc.net/maddison/maddison-project/home.htm.

Malthus, T., and Gilbert, G. 1993. *An Essay on the Principle of Population*. Oxford University Press.

Marshall, A. 1916. *Principles of Economics. An Introductory Volume*, 7th edition. London: Macmillan.

Meyer, D. 2000. *Hong Kong as a Global Metropolis*. Cambridge University Press.

Mill, J. S. 1848. *Principles of Political Economy: With Some of Their Applications to Social Philosophy*. John W. Parker.

Miners, N. 1987. *Hong Kong under Imperial Rule, 1912–1941*. Oxford University Press.

Newton, S. 2010. *The Sterling Devaluation of 1967, the International Economy and Post-War Social Democracy*. English Historical Review. Oxford University Press.

Nisbet, J. W. 1929. *A Case for Laissez-faire*. London: P. S. King & Son.

OECD. 2017. General government spending (indicator). National Accounts (accessed on 27 April 2017).

Oyen, M. 2007. Allies, enemies and aliens: migration and US–Chinese Relations 1940–1965. PhD thesis, Georgetown University.

Patten, C. 1998. *East and West: The Last Governor of Hong Kong on Power, Freedom and the Future*. Basingstoke: Macmillan

Rabushka, A. 1973. The changing face of Hong Kong: new departures in public policy. AEI-Hoover Policy Studies. Washington: American Enterprise Institute for Public Policy Research.

Rabushka, A. 1976. *Value for Money: The Hong Kong Budgetary Process*. Hoover Institution Publication 152. Stanford, CA: Hoover Institution Press.

Rabushka, A. 1979. *Hong Kong: A Study in Economic Freedom*. William H. Abbott Lectures in International Business and Economics. University of Chicago, Graduate School of Business.

Ricardo, D. 1817. *On the Principles of Political Economy and Taxation*. London.

Riedel, J. 1974. *The Industrialization of Hong Kong*. Tübingen: J. C. B. Mohr.

Schenk, C. 2001. *Hong Kong as an International Financial Centre: Emergence and Development 1945–1965*. London: Routledge.

Seaman, L. 1967. *Post-Victorian Britain 1902–1951*. London: Methuen.
Smart, A. 2006. *The Shek Kip Mei Myth: Squatters, Fires and Colonial Rule in Hong Kong, 1950–1963*. Hong Kong University Press.
Smith, A. 1776. *An Inquiry into the Nature and Causes of the Wealth of Nations*. London: printed for W. Strahan and T. Cadell.
Smith, H. 1966. *John Stuart Mill's Other Island: A Study of the Economic Development of Hong Kong*. London: Institute of Economic Affairs.
Szczepanik, E. 1958. *The Economic Growth of Hong Kong*. Oxford University Press.
Thorpe, A. 2001. *A History of the British Labour Party*. Palgrave,
Tsang, S. 1988. *Democracy Shelved: Great Britain, China, and Attempts at Constitutional Reform in Hong Kong, 1945–1952*. Oxford University Press.
Tsang, S. 1995. *Government and Politics*. Hong Kong University Press.
Tsang, S. 2004. *A Modern History of Hong Kong*. London: I. B. Tauris.
Tsang, S. 2007. *Governing Hong Kong: Administrative Officers from the Nineteenth Century to the Handover to China, 1862–1997*. London: I. B. Tauris.
Tu, E. 2003. *Colonial Hong Kong in the Eyes of Elsie Tu*. Hong Kong University Press.
Ure, G. 2012. *Governors, Politics, and the Colonial Office: Public Policy in Hong Kong, 1918–58*. Hong Kong University Press.
Welsh, F. 1997. *A History of Hong Kong*. London: HarperCollins.
Wong, D. 2015. *Hong Kong Fiascos: A Struggle for Survival*. Singapore: Epigram.
Young, A. 1995. The tyranny of numbers: confronting the statistical realities of the east Asian growth experience. *Quarterly Journal of Economics* 110(3), 641–680.
Yueh, L. 2013. *China's Growth: The Making of an Economic Superpower*. Oxford University Press.

ARCHIVAL SOURCES

UK Colonial Office, Public Records Office, Kew, London (PRO CO)
UK Foreign Office, Public Records Office, Kew, London (PRO FO)
UK Prime Minister's Office, Public Records Office, Kew, London (PRO PREM)
UK National Archives, Public Records Office, Kew, London (PRO)
Bank of England Archives, London (BE)
Hong Kong Government Record Service, Public Record Office, Hong Kong (HKRS)
Hong Kong Legislative Council Commission, Hansard (Hansard)

PERIODICALS

South China Morning Post
Far Eastern Economic Review
Far Eastern Economic Yearbook
The Times Archive
Hong Kong Annual Report, Colonial Office

Hong Kong Staff List
London Gazette
Hong Kong Gazette
Sierra Leone Royal Gazette
The Scotsman
Fife Today
The Colonial List

IMAGE SOURCES

Figures 1.1, 1.2, 17.1, 19.1 and 19.3 are from The Hong Kong Information Services Department, used with the permission of the HKSAR Government.
Figures 3.1, 3.3, 4.3, 5.1, 9.1, 14.2, 14.3 and 18.1 are from Getty Images and are used with permission.
Figure 3.2 (© IWM ABS781), Figure 3.4 (© IWM HU46465), Figure 4.1 (© IWM A31079, detail) and Figure 4.2 (© IWM A31085, detail) are from The Imperial War Museum and are used with their permission.
Figure 7.1 is used with the permission of The National Archives (ref. PREM11/868).
Figures 2.1, 8.3, 9.2 and 14.1 are taken from public domain sources such as Wikimedia Commons.
The top image on the cover is from the HKSAR Government, the portrait of Cowperthwaite is from the public domain, and the bottom photograph is from Shutterstock.

ACKNOWLEDGEMENTS

THIS BOOK WOULD HAVE BEEN impossible to write without the records preserved in various archives in London and Hong Kong. I am indebted to the helpful staff at the UK Public Records Office in Kew, at the Bank of England archive and at the Bodleian Library. I am particularly grateful to the staff at the Public Records Office in Hong Kong, who handled my extensive requests, while there and while abroad, with good humour and grace. The Hong Kong Information Services Department was very helpful in locating suitable images, for which I am grateful.

I would also like to thank Richard Baggaley and Sam Clark at London Publishing Partnership. As well as publishing it, Richard helped structure and shape the book from the very beginning and Sam has greatly improved the text in a tight time-frame and the book is considerably enhanced from his involvement. I am grateful for thoughts, comments and advice from Diane Coyle, Wai-hong Yeung, Lord Patten, Romesh Vaitilingam, Eamonn Butler and Nathan Cowperthwaite.

It would have been easier for John Cowperthwaite to set a more conventional path for Hong Kong, that would have delivered less. Instead he did what he believed to be right. His was a particular kind of leadership. I am grateful to John Kendall-Carpenter, Anthony Habgood, Barry Jones, Chris Hogg, Art Peck, John Donaldson, Dave Gibbons, Kate Swan, Richard Handover, Steve Clarke, Paul Geddes, Robert Moorhead, Robert Walker, John Barton and Drummond Hall, among others, for providing me with lessons in how leaders lead.

I have also learnt from my time at two exceptional institutions, albeit some time ago. This book has made me revisit what I learnt about economics, politics, business and philosophy. Some teachers were formative influences and I thank Walter Eltis, Norman Crowther-Hunt, Galen Strawson, Andre Perold and Abraham Zaleznik.

My family and friends have been unfailingly supportive as I have worked on this relatively obscure topic. I am very grateful to Laurence, Victoria, Julie and Hugo for their interest in this project over several years, their questions and comments, and for their encouragement to complete the book. I would also like to note my gratitude to my parents and to Andrew and Katherine. I am grateful for the encouragement of Nancy Amer, Liz and John Buckingham, Stefano Quadrio Curzio, Henry Elkington, Andrew Gilchrist, Joanne Horsfall, Mark and Anne-Marie Loveland, Christoph Sander, Nick Viner and David Wood. My trips to Hong Kong were greatly improved by the generous hospitality of Jerome, and of Warren, Kathie and Will Allderige.

My colleagues at ASMC have been very patient as I have worked on this book instead of the book on strategy I am supposed to be writing. I thank Stephen Bungay, Anthony Freeling, Jo Whitehead, Felix Barber, Mike Goold, Rebecca Homkes, Andrew Campbell and Marcus Alexander for their collegiality and their challenge.

INDEX

G

H

I

J

K

L

REVIEWS AND ENDORSEMENTS OF *ARCHITECT OF PROSPERITY*

"During the 1960s, governments were responding to political unrest and economic challenges with nationalisation, centralised planning and public spending (financed by heavy taxes and debt). There was intense pressure for Sir John Cowperthwaite, the financial secretary of Hong Kong, to join the crowd... A new biography of Cowperthwaite by Neil Monnery tells of a man who replied to these demands with a qualified 'no', and in the process became that most unusual of things: a bureaucrat hero to libertarians. His approach would subsequently be labelled 'positive non-interventionism', meaning governance stopping just short of laissez-faire. As that history becomes increasingly remote, a biography of a key architect becomes ever more valuable. There are few other examples."

— *The Economist*

"I have just read a fascinating new book called *Architect of Prosperity* by Neil Monnery. It's about the role of Sir John Cowperthwaite, Financial Secretary of Hong Kong from 1961 to 1971, in setting the colony on the road to prosperity. It is an astonishing story... Its success derived from brilliant economic policymaking that involved reliance on market forces and minimising the role of the state... You might think that, given the economic record, Britain's economic establishment, including the serried ranks of mandarins and their political masters, might feel that they have a good deal to learn. They have. They should read Monnery's book."

— Roger Bootle, Chairman of Capital Economics, in *The Telegraph*

"Not before time we now have a fascinating book on one of those who helped create Hong Kong's thriving economy. Cowperthwaite was a believer in free market economics well before this idea became popular again. Hong Kong should be grateful to him."

— Lord Patten of Barnes, last governor of Hong Kong and author of *East and West* (1999) and *First Confession: A Sort of Memoir* (2017)

"I am very pleased to celebrate the launch of Neil Monnery's latest book. Indeed, Hong Kong's post-war rise from destitution to its universally recognised status as the world's freest economy is a fascinating story to tell. Sir John, during his decade-long steerage of Hong Kong's economy, adopted a 'positive non-intervention' policy, ensuring minimal government interference in the economic affairs of individuals and society. With free market as his prime principle, he worked to maintain a prudent fiscal policy and a simple tax regime buttressed by low tax rates, providing the conditions that would enable individuals and businesses to thrive. My congratulations to Neil Monnery for his remarkable new book."

— The Honourable Paul Chan Mo-po, Financial Secretary, Government of Hong Kong SAR

"Hong Kong went from being a barren rock with no resources to becoming a dynamic economy with living standards higher than many European countries. A key role in this remarkable story was played by Sir John Cowperthwaite as Financial Secretary. He believed that expenditure should be determined by revenues, not the other way round, that private enterprise should decide where investment should be allocated, tax rates should be low to attract capital and create surplus profits to be re-invested to create compounding growth. He was against deficits because he viewed the taxpayer of tomorrow just as worthy as the taxpayer of today. The results were spectacular and made Hong Kong into the economic miracle it is today. This book charts his wonderful, inspiring and remarkable story and his philosophy is brilliantly expressed. The wonder is that other governments in Europe don't follow this example."

— Lord Lamont of Lerwick, former Chancellor of the Exchequer, author of *In Office* (1999)

"There are figures in history who deserve to be far better known and Sir John Cowperthwaite is one of those. Neil Monnery's account of the way he shaped Hong Kong into a dynamic and successful economy now far more prosperous than its colonial ruler, Britain, is all the more fascinating in the light of the current debate about what drives economic development. Policy makers today can learn a lot from the focus and the willingness to ignore the conventional wisdom of the time demonstrated by Cowperthwaite and his colleagues."

— Diane Coyle, professor of economics at the University of Manchester and author of *The Economics of Enough* (2011) and *GDP: A Brief but Affectionate History* (2014)

"To this day, people have little idea of Sir John's achievements, which deserve a wider audience. This book fills a glaring void. I hope it will have the wide readership that it most certainly deserves."

— Yeung Wai-hong, Honorary Publisher of *Next Magazine*, Hong Kong

"This fascinating account of the rise of Hong Kong as a global economic powerhouse is well written and, as such, easy to read and understand. I'm happy to recommend it wholeheartedly to *CapX*'s discerning readership. [Neil Monnery's] work has immortalised a man to whom so many owe so much. *Architect of Prosperity* is an economic and intellectual history. Above all, it is a tribute to a principled, self-effacing, consequential and deeply moral man. Monnery deserves our gratitude for writing it."

— Marian L. Tupy, senior policy analyst at the Centre for Global Liberty and Prosperity, writing on *CapX*

"There's a book just out which everyone in the Conservative party ought to read: *Architect of Prosperity* by Neil Monnery. It's the biography of one of the 20th century's greatest unsung heroes, Sir John Cowperthwaite, the financial secretary in the British colonial administration whose determinedly low-tax, regulation-light, fiscally austere regime put Hong Kong on its path to prosperity."

— James Delingpole in *The Spectator*

"This is a fascinating story of a remarkable but quiet man, and the astonishing economic results of his benign policy. Sir John Cowperthwaite and a small cadre of civil servants fixed on the objective of making Hong Kong economically prosperous. To achieve this they did exactly the opposite of what the home country was doing – with its nationalisations, controls, economic planning, high taxes, trade barriers, deficit spending, and all the rest. Instead Cowperthwaite largely left the people to their own devices. He concentrated on balancing the government's books; and keeping taxes low to encourage private investment and to expand the long-term tax base. This book demonstrates just how hard it is for any government body to prevent itself from interfering in an economy – with the inevitably counterproductive results. Sir John fought off many such attempts. This story provides a lesson for us in the UK, as we drift on doing so many of the wrong things that have made us 40% poorer than Hong Kong."

— Dr Eamonn Butler, The Adam Smith Institute

"Anyone seeking to understand the true nature of inequality must read Neil Monnery's excellent book. In Hong Kong Sir John Cowperthwaite created a society of great wealth inequality but of great freedom and opportunity. Refugees fled to Hong Kong from the imposed equality of the People's Republic of China in pursuit of the greater equality of opportunity in the British Colony. This book raises fundamental questions about the nature of the equality we seek to pursue."

— Russell Napier, market historian and author of *Anatomy of the Bear* (2016)

"This book tells the story of Hong Kong's success, focusing on the career of Sir John Cowperthwaite, who played key roles in the colony's administration from 1945 to 1971... Monnery tells the story with verve and accuracy, providing one of the best compact economic histories of Hong Kong in the second half of the twentieth century."

— Professor Jack A. Goldstone in *Economic Affairs*

"Sir John Cowperthwaite, who arrived in Hong Kong in 1945 and topped off his career there as financial secretary from 1961 to 1971, was not one to blow his own trumpet and never cultivated a coterie of followers to do it for him. Thankfully, however, Neil Monnery has now published the first biography of Cowperthwaite. Cowperthwaite, a Scotsman by birth, was at the heart of economic policymaking in Hong Kong throughout this period and the colony's success was largely attributable to his particular brand of free-market economics. For those interested in economic management, it is a remarkable tale, and one that Monnery tells with relish."

— Richard Cockett in *The Literary Review*